DEVELOPMENT 1989 SUPPLEMENT

THE MOLECULAR BASIS OF POSITIONAL SIGNALLING

EDITED BY

ROB KAY AND JIM SMITH

Papers presented at a meeting of the
British Society for Developmental Biology
at the University of St Andrews
April 1989

THE COMPANY OF BIOLOGISTS LIMITED

CAMBRIDGE

Typeset, Printed and Published by
The Company of Biologists Limited
Department of Zoology, University of Cambridge, Downing Street,
Cambridge CB2 3EJ

Cover photograph

A *Drosophila* embryo stained with an antibody against *bicoid* protein. The staining intensity is transformed into the stripes of the French flag using an image analysis system and appropriate thresholds. See articles by Wolpert and St Johnston *et al.* in this volume. Photograph kindly supplied by Dr Wolfgang Driever.

Contents

Volume 107 Supplement   1989

Development 1989 Supplement, 1–2
Printed in Great Britain © The Company of Biologists Limited 1989

The molecular basis of positional signalling: introduction

R. R. KAY[1] and J. C. SMITH[2]

[1]MRC Laboratory of Molecular Biology, Hills Road, Cambridge CB2 2QH, UK
[2]Laboratory of Embryogenesis, National Institute for Medical Research, The Ridgeway, Mill Hill, London NW7 1AA, UK

The importance of cell–cell interactions in embryonic development was first described by Driesch (1891), who showed that any of the blastomeres of the 2-cell or 4-cell sea-urchin embryo is capable of forming a complete embryo if cultured in isolation; this implied that in normal development each blastomere is aware of the other and will only form a half- or quarter-embryo, as appropriate. And it was only ten years later that Spemann (1901) discovered the phenomenon of embryonic induction, recently reviewed by Gurdon (1987) and defined as an interaction in which the differentiation of one group of cells is affected by a signal from an adjacent group. Thus the significance of cell signalling during development has been appreciated for almost a century, but, as has frequently been remarked, progress in the molecular analysis of the phenomenon has been slow compared with that in the younger disciplines of, for example, immunology and molecular biology. This slow progress no doubt discouraged younger workers from entering the field, so that by the late 1960s only a few stalwart research groups continued the struggle.

In retrospect, one can see that the reason progress was so slow is simply that the problem of cell signalling in development is so difficult; indeed, as we see in this volume, techniques derived from immunology and molecular biology are required for its solution. But it was not the emergence of these new techniques that was responsible for the revival of interest in cell–cell interactions that occurred in the 1970s and which has led to the current state of optimism. Instead, one spur was the concept of positional information, introduced by Wolpert (1969), and also discussed by Stumpf, Lawrence and Crick. Positional information suggested new ways to design and interpret experiments on organisms as diverse as hydra, slime-moulds, chicks, insects and amphibia – all of which species are discussed in this book. Another spur was provided by genetic studies on *Drosophila* and, more recently, on *Caenorhabditis elegans*. This work identified 'fields' in which positional information might be established and, latterly, has identified genes required for various steps in cell signalling processes. Examples of these genetic studies are also included in this volume.

Although the work of the 1970s identified few signalling molecules (one of the exceptions is discussed in this volume by Schaller), it did predict what such molecules had to do, where they should be, and when they should act. This in turn guided the design of biological assays to detect signalling molecules and in the last five years several candidate morphogens have been identified.

Because mechanisms of pattern formation in different organisms could all be described by the same formal language of gradients and positional information, it was once thought that there might be only one, or just a few, biochemical mechanisms of positional signalling. We now know enough to see that this view was wrong, although we do not know how wrong. One loose way of classifying positional signalling processes, that we have used in arranging this book, is according to the range and location of the signal. The different classifications might imply different mechanisms of signal transmission and localization, and they include: interactions within a single cell (as in the early *Drosophila* embryo, where interaction with cytoskeletal elements might be important for localizing the signal), short-range interactions (as in the *Drosophila* eye, where the signals might be cell-bound) and finally long-range interactions (as in the *Dictyostelium* aggregate or the chick limb) where diffusible signals are involved. Another distinction that might be drawn concerns the type of information passed between and within cells and the way this is interpreted. On the one hand, a signal may consist of the instruction to differentiate as a particular cell type (as occurs in the *sevenless* system,) or even to continue mitotic, rather than meiotic, cell divisions (as in the *Glp-1* system). Although the intracellular machinery required to interpret this information is undoubtedly complicated, it is unlikely to be as complicated as when different concentrations of factors cause different outcomes, as occurs, for example, in the chick limb. In this case, cells may require several thresholds, and the signalling system might be viewed in terms of positional information, with cells first having their position defined with a coordinate system and then using their positional values to decide how to differentiate.

At present the best-understood example of a multi-threshold system is in the anteroposterior axis of the *Drosophila* egg, where the genes *X* and *hunchback* respond to different concentrations of *bicoid* protein. However, this interaction occurs within a single cell, and the *bicoid* protein probably acts directly on the *X* and *Hb* promoters. The situation is different in multicellular systems, where it is not even clear whether single cells have many thresholds or whether thresholds represent a cell population effect. As Gurdon (1987) has pointed out, the answer to this question will depend on being able to analyze single cells, in the absence of cell division. This may require improvements in our cell culture techniques, as well as the development of early markers of response to cell signalling. Such culture systems and markers are now available in the slime mould *Dictyostelum discoideum*.

It is clear that much remains to be done if we are to understand how cell–cell signalling establishes the correct spatial pattern of cellular differentiation in even the simplest organisms. However, the identification of signalling molecules, the essential first step, is now being achieved. This book describes this work and points the way towards analyzing how the factors might act.

As organizers, we should like to thank everyone involved in making the St Andrews meeting such a success. We are particularly grateful to John Tucker, the local organizer, and to the Company of Biologists and American Airlines for financial support.

References

DRIESCH, H. (1891). Entwicklungsmechnische Studien. I. Der Werth der beiden ersten Furchungszellen in der Echinodermenentwicklung. Experimentelle Erzeugung von Theilund Doppelbildungen. *Z. wiss. Zool.* **53**, 160–178, 183–184.

GURDON, J. B. (1987). Embryonic induction: molecular prospects. *Development* **99**, 285–306.

SPEMANN, H. (1901). Uber Korrelationen in der Entwicklung des Auges. *Verh. Anat. Ges., 15 Vers. Bonn (Anat. Anz.* **15**), 61–79.

WOLPERT, L. (1969). Positional information and the spatial pattern of cellular differentiation. *J. theor. Biol.* **25**, 1–47.

Development 1989 Supplement, 3–12
Printed in Great Britain © The Company of Biologists Limited 1989

Positional information revisited

LEWIS WOLPERT

Department of Anatomy and Developmental Biology, University College and Middlesex School of Medicine, London W1P 6DB

Summary

Positional information has been suggested to play a central role in pattern formation during development. The strong version of positional information states that there is a cell parameter, positional value, which is related to position as in a coordinate system and which determines cell differentiation. A weaker version merely emphasises position as a key determinant in cell development and differentiation. There is evidence for boundaries and orthogonal axes playing an important role in positional systems. A positional signal is distinguished from an inductive interaction because the former specifies multiple states, confers polarity, and can act over a long range. A gradient in a diffusible morphogen is just one way of specifying position. There is now good evidence in several systems for substances which may be the morphogen for positional signalling. The product of the *bicoid* gene in early *Drosophila* development is the best prospect. Retinoic acid is unique in its ability to alter positional value and may also be a morphogen. The best evidence for positional value, a concept fundamental to positional information, remains a biological assay based on grafting. The idea of positional value uncouples differentiation and position, and allows considerable freedom for patterning. It is not clear whether positional value or differentiation involves a combinatorial mechanism.

Interpretation of positional information remains a central problem. There is good evidence that cells can respond differentially to less than a two-fold change in concentration of a chemical signal. It may be that interpretation involves listing the sites at which a particular class of cell differentiation will occur. The problem is made less severe when blocks of cells are specified together as in mechanisms based on an isomorphic prepattern. Isomorphic prepatterns could establish repeated structures which are equivalent and which are then made non-equivalent by positional information. This would enable local differences to develop. The combination of these two mechanisms may be widespread.

There is evidence that positional signals within a single animal and in related animals are conserved. It is not clear just how wide this conservation is, but it is at phylotypic stages, rather than in eggs, that similarity might be expected. It is nevertheless impressive that the polar coordinate model can be applied to regulation in systems as diverse as insects, vertebrates and protozoa. The molecular basis of positional signalling is just becoming accessible; the molecular basis of positional value is still awaited.

A brief personal history of positional information is provided in an appendix.

Key words: positional information, pattern formation, inductive interaction, retinoic acid, polar coordinate model.

Introduction

Pattern formation is a central problem in development (Wolpert, 1969). Positional information provides both a conceptual framework for thinking about pattern formation and also suggests possible mechanisms. The basic idea of positional information is that there is a cell parameter, positional value, which is related to a cell's position in the developing system. It is as if there is a coordinate system with respect to which the cells have their position specified. The cells then interpret their positional value by differentiating in a particular way. This differentiation may involve developing as a particular cell type or state, or it might involve changes in growth or motility (Wolpert, 1969, 1971, 1981, 1989a). (For a personal history, see Appendix).

Among the attractive features of positional information is that it provides a unifying concept for understanding the development and regulation of a variety of patterns. The only cell-to-cell interactions that are, in principle, required, are those necessary to specify position. Again, in principle, the same signals and positional values may be used to specify different patterns, the differences arising both from developmental history and from genetic constitution. Regeneration and regulation could be viewed in terms of changes in positional value and the specifying of new boundary regions: morphallaxis and epimorphosis could now be clearly distinguished. Perhaps the least attractive feature of positional information, if the basic idea is correct, is that it places a great burden on the process of interpretation.

The essential features of a coordinate system that is used to establish positional information are: boundaries with respect to which position is specified; a scalar, which gives a measure of distance from the boundary; and polarity, which specifies the direction in which position is measured from the boundary. Using such a framework forces one to construct specific and concrete models. For a one-dimensional system, all the necessary features can be provided by a monotonic decrease in the concentration of a chemical – a morphogen – which could be set up with a localized source or by reaction–diffusion. The concentration of morphogen at any point then provides a scalar measure of distance from the boundary, and the slope of the concentration gradient effectively provides the polarity.

Some confusion has arisen from assuming that a system of the kind just described can only be achieved by the diffusion of a chemical morphogen from a source (e.g. Davidson, 1989). That is not the case. A gradient in a chemical morphogen can be generated by quite other mechanisms, only some of which involve diffusion. Such mechanisms could, for example, be provided by a progress zone model in which the gradient is generated as a group of cells grow (Summerbell et al. 1973), or by cell-to-cell interactions (Babloyantz, 1979). Furthermore, the gradient of a chemical concentration is, itself, only a special case of the yet more general case. Position need not be recorded by the changes in concentration on a chemical. Positional value could be represented by a set of genes – additional genes being activated with increase in distance in a simple additive manner, such as 1, 12, 123...

This last example forces one to ask what would *not* be regarded as a positional system. There is a weak sense in which the idea of positional information is used to refer to differences between cells in developing system. If each cell in a developing system has a unique specification this does not necessarily mean that they all have positional information in the sense of a coordinate system. Thus in the development of the nematode most cells have a unique specification and position by virtue of their lineage; but there are no boundaries and no scalars. In insects and vertebrates the dominant mechanism of pattern formation involves cell interactions rather than lineage (Wolpert, 1989a) but not all interactions involve positional information in the strong sense. For example, the development of the ommatidea in the *Drosophila* eye depends on cells' positions with respect to their neighbours (Tomlinson, 1988). However, this relationship is rather like the specification of position in folk-dancing or a rugby scrum rather than in a coordinate system. Positional information is about graded properties and it is in this strong sense, with its implications for a coordinate system, that it is considered here.

A surprising feature is that all positional fields are small, none being longer than about 1 mm in maximum linear dimension or about 50 cell diameters (Wolpert, 1969). In fact most are much smaller. The other characteristic feature is that the times required to specify position appear to be of the order of hours. It was these two features that lead Crick (1970) to propose a diffusible morphogen for setting up positional fields.

Axes and boundaries

The Cartesian nature of many developing systems is very striking in the sense that many systems seem to develop in relation to orthogonal axes. (One always has, however, to be careful to distinguish between our perception and description of the embryo, and the mechanisms used by the embryo).

In *Drosophila* the anteroposterior axis and the dorsoventral axis are at right angles and are controlled by quite different sets of genes; in Hydra regeneration the specification of a head along the main body axis is at right angles to the specification of the ring of tentacles; in sea urchins and many other embryos with radial cleavage, the first two cleavages are parallel with the animal–vegetal axis and the third at right angles to them; again in sea urchins, the development of the animal–vegetal and dorsoventral axes are at right angles as are the skeletal rods; in the developing vertebrate limb there seem to be different mechanisms for specification of the anteroposterior and proximodistal axes; the main body axis in vertebrates is specified by a mechanism different to that of the dorsoventral axis. Embryos like right angles.

Meinhardt (1984) has considered mechanisms whereby orthogonality of the axes may be specified and also how new boundary regions might develop within a primary positional field. In insects he invokes interactions at compartment boundaries.

In any coordinate system, the boundaries are fundamental and act as reference regions. They must provide both the polarity of the system and be linked to position. Some boundary regions are listed in Table 1. The key operational criterion for a boundary region is that other regions are specified in relation to it. Thus the polarising region of the chick limb bud can specify new structures in relation to it when it is grafted to different positions along the anteroposterior axis of the chick limb bud (Tickle et al. 1975). There is good evidence in the insect egg for two boundary regions with long-range influences on pattern: one anterior and one posterior. Sander (see 1984 review) demonstrated an activity that specifies both polarity and pattern at the posterior end of the *Euscelis* egg, and inferred the existence of an anterior activity. In *Drosophila*, both anterior and posterior organising centres have been demonstrated by cytoplasmic injections (Nüsslein-Volhard et al. 1987); cytoplasm from both regions can specify pattern and polarity when transplanted to ectopic sites, and, in addition, their effects are long range. Of particular importance for later development is the specification of a single line of cells at the end of each parasegment, which may act as a boundary region for the later development of the segments (Lawrence, 1981, 1987; Lawrence et al. 1987).

In regenerating or regulatory systems, the behaviour of the boundaries is of key importance (Wolpert, 1971).

In morphallaxis, new boundaries may be formed and new positional values specified in relation to it without necessarily any growth. By contrast, with epimorphosis, new positional values are generated by growth and the boundary values may play much less of a role.

Polarity

There is an intimate relationship between the gradient of positional information and polarity, the polarity being determined by the slope of the gradient (Lawrence, 1970). In terms of positional information, polarity determines the direction in which position is measured with respect to a boundary region. Polarity in other non-positional systems may have other meanings. Nevertheless the close relation between gradients and polarity is satisfying. In the chick limb bud, for example, the polarity of the hand can be reversed in relation to the polarizing region and the gradient it sets up (Tickle *et al.* 1975). In insects there is a direct marker of polarity provided by the direction in which epidermal structures, like hairs, point. This correlates well with the postulated gradients (Lawrence, 1973). Again, in regeneration in Hydra, polarity is tightly linked to gradients (Bode and Bode, 1984).

Positional signalling and induction

By far the clearest demonstration of a positional signal in a developing system – clear in the sense that it can be directly visualised rather than being inferred from other properties – is in the insect egg. The gradient is in the protein coded for by the *bicoid* gene, which is a key gene in patterning along the anteroposterior axis (Driever and Nüsslein-Volhard, 1988a). Its discovery is particularly gratifying not only because of its importance, but because it has just the anticipated distribution of a morphogen which is made at a source and both diffuses and breaks down. There is also a ventral to dorsal gradient in the protein of the *dorsal* gene, but in this case its mRNA is uniformly distributed and the generation of the gradient requires a different mechanism (Steward *et al.* 1988).

Another example of a positional signal is the polarizing region in the chick limb for which there is good evidence for a graded signal – possibly retinoic acid –

although the signal itself has not yet been unequivocally identified (Tickle *et al.* 1985).

The distance over which a positional signal has been shown to act seems to have decreased over the last two decades. As already pointed out, positional fields are small – usually only 20 to 30 cell diameters or less than 1 mm in maximum linear dimension. For intercalary regeneration it has been argued that the distances over which signals act is no more than a few cell diameters (Bryant *et al.* 1981) and this type of local interaction is said to characterise inductive interactions (Davidson, 1989).

The evidence that positional signals can act over greater distances, while limited, is persuasive. In Hydra there is very good evidence that an inhibitory signal can affect tissues about 1 mm distant (Bode and Bode, 1984). The polarizing region in the wing bud can propagate its signal across leg tissue about 100 µm thick (Honig, 1981) and the local application of retinoic acid can cause apical ridge extension about 100–200 µm away (Lee and Tickle, 1985). In amphibians the graft of an organiser seems to affect tissues several hundred microns away (Smith and Slack, 1983). Injections of cytoplasm into insect eggs seem to exert effects over distances of several hundred microns (Nüsslein-Volhard *et al.* 1987).

It would be a pity if one conflated all cell-to-cell interactions involving cell signalling. A positional signal and induction have distinct and different, and more important, useful meanings. Use of 'positional signal' should be confined to situations where the position of a group of cells is being specified, preferably where positional information is involved. A positional signal should be distinguished from induction in a number of ways (Table 2). Induction is defined as an interaction between two different tissues, one inducing, the other responding (Gurdon, 1987). This at once makes it different from positional signalling, for which two different tissues need not be involved. There are other differences. In general, induction specifies just one cell state such as muscle or neural tissue or cartilage, whereas a positional signal, which need not involve only one substance, specifies, by definition, multiple cell states. Related to this a positional signal is graded whereas induction is basically all-or–none. Along the same lines, induction is short range whereas a positional signal is usually specifying cell states over a greater distance. Again, a positional signal has 'polarity'

Table 1. *Boundary/reference regions*

Hydra	Head Foot	Bode & Bode (1984).
Sea urchin	Micromeres	Hörstadius (1973).
Insect	Egg ends Parasegment boundary	Nüsslein-Volhard *et al.* (1987). Lawrence *et al.* (1987).
Chick	Hensen's node Polarizing region limb	Hornburch, Summerbell & Wolpert (1979). Tickle, Summerbell & Wolpert (1975).
Amphibian	Organiser	Smith & Slack (1983).
Lepidopteran	Wing foci	Nijhout (1980).

Table 2.

Positional signal	Induction
Multiple states	Single state
Graded	All-or-none
Polarity	No polarity
Long range	Short range
Boundary region	Diffuse
Same tissue	Different tissue
Instructive	Instructive or permissive

whereas induction is not related to the polarity of either tissue. A positional signal is provided by, or linked to, a boundary region and as such is localised; inductive signals need not be. Finally, a positional signal is always instructive whereas an inductive signal may be either permissive or instructive. The distinctions made here are somewhat exaggerated to emphasise the differences.

It is thus far from clear to what extent the patterning of muscle in early amphibian development involves primarily induction or whether positional signalling is involved (Smith, 1989).

There is at least one situation where the distinction between induction and positional signal may be blurred; in those cases where induction might be thought of as transferring a set of positional values from one tissue to another (Wolpert, 1981). The classic example where this might be occurring is in primary embryonic induction, where it is claimed that if small pieces of gastrula ectoderm are placed at different positions along the axis of the endomesoderm of an exogastrula they differentiate neural structures according to their position. A similar explanation could explain homoiogenetic induction: induced tissues can themselves induce similar structures. It is thus of great interest that in *Xenopus laevis* the homeobox gene X1H box 1 is expressed at the same level in a narrow band of both neural and mesodermal tissues. This correlation is best explained by homeogenetic transfer of positional information (de Robertis *et al.* 1989).

Morphogen

The word morphogen was coined by Turing (1952). Its original meaning was in relation to pattern formation; the distribution of the morphogen reflected the resulting overt pattern as in the isomorphous prepattern mechanism described above. The essential features of this meaning should be retained but extended to include a concentration gradient that specifies position. An inductive signal is not a morphogen as it does not specify pattern.

What then are the criteria for identifying a morphogen? (Some aspects are considered by Slack and Isaacs (1989) but they include induction). The substance must be distributed in a pattern that generates a pattern; changing the distribution must alter the pattern in the expected manner; blocking the interaction of the putative morphogen with the cells should prevent pattern formation. At present no morphogen meets all these

requirements. The most promising candidates are the *bicoid* protein in early insect development; retinoic acid in limb development (Thaller and Eichele, 1987); and possibly the peptide involved in Hydra regeneration (Schaller and Bodenmuller, 1981) and DIF in the slime mould (Williams, 1988). Of all these the *bicoid* protein is the most impressive since it can be measured directly, and altering its concentration profile alters early patterns. While it is unwise to be too enthusiastic about a particular morphogen, as the history of embryology is littered with false trails, retinoic acid is unique, so far, in its ability to alter positional value, both in development and regeneration (Brockes, 1989).

Positional value

One of the most important concepts related to positional information is that positional value is a cell parameter. The most direct evidence for the existence of a cell parameter that correlates with position comes from experiments of the kind initially carried out by Bohn. He showed that intercalary regeneration in the cockroach leg could be interpreted in terms of a graded set of positional values and the intercalation of intermediate values when non-contiguous regions were placed next to each other. This type of model has been formalised to account for a very wide range of experiments by the polar coordinate model (French *et al.* 1976; Bryant *et al.* 1981). The importance of the model – the details need not concern us here – is that cells have a biological property, positional value, that determines their regulative and regenerative behaviour when grafted to different positions. There are two key features to this behaviour. First, when cells with disparate positional values are juxtaposed, intercalation occurs to smooth out those disparities (cf. Winfree, 1984). Second, and more important, the positional values of the cells are independent of the structures that they form. This second point is essential, for it dissociates position from differentiation. In principle, any structure – bristle, sex comb and so on – could be formed at any position. This uncoupling is fundamental to the concept of positional information and is particularly clearly seen in genetic mosaics in insects (Bryant, 1974). These mosaics not only illustrate uncoupling but also show the identity of positional values in different organs in the same animal.

Molecular genetics has enabled the activity of a wide variety of genes to be mapped during early insect development (Ingham, 1988). The question is whether any of these can be regarded as providing the cells with a positional value. In general the answer seems to be in the negative, though genes like *hunchback* might loosely be thought of as providing blocks of positional value along the main axis. It is not clear to what extent the expression of the homeotic genes can be thought of in terms of positional value.

It is also far from clear whether the specification of cell state or cell differentiation is combinatorial or not. In a combinatorial system the number of signals required, or genes activated, to specify a cell would be small in relation to the total number of specified states. For *Drosophila* at least, while more than one gene is used to specify cell states in early development, the number of genes seems to be similar to the number of states. On this criterion specification would not involve a combinatorial mechanism. Further support for this view comes from the ability of single genes, such as *myo-D*, to cause transfected cells to differentiate into muscle (Davis *et al.* 1987).

While the molecular basis of positional value remains unknown, the report of a position–specific antigen in the developing chick limb is of great interest. This antigen does not correspond to any particular structure but is confined to a position along the anteroposterior axis of the limb (Ohsugi *et al.* 1988).

Non-equivalence

Closely related to positional value is the concept of non-equivalence. Non-equivalence is the property possessed by cells of the same differentiation class that makes them different from one another (Lewis and Wolpert, 1976). It is fundamental to evolution for it enables structures that contain the same overt differentiated cell types, like digits, to develop differently. Non-equivalence is a natural consequence of positional information because even cells that differentiate in the same way have an intrinsic difference related to their positional value. The epidermal cells of insects are clearly non-equivalent as is shown by the intercalation experiments. While positional information demands non-equivalence, the presence of non-equivalence does not, however, imply positional information.

It is worth first noting that in vertebrates, at least some cells are equivalent and others non-equivalent. Thus the connective tissue cells of limbs are non-equivalent but it seems that both for limbs and the head, muscle cells are equivalent. There is also evidence, in the head at least, that endothelial cells, initially at least, are equivalent (Wolpert, 1988*a*).

Previously, much of the evidence for non-equivalence has relied on biological experiments such as grafting. Homeobox genes have now opened up a new approach, and, in the mouse for example, there are striking differences in expression from presomite stages onwards along the anteroposterior axis that do not correspond to any obvious morphological boundaries (Holland and Hogan, 1988). As Holland and Hogan point out these patterns of expression are consistent with, but of course do not in any way prove, a role for homeobox genes in establishing domains of positional value in the mammalian embryo. It is thus of great interest that Ruiz i. Altaba and Melton (1989) have found that a *Xenopus* homeobox (Xhox 3) gene is expressed in a graded manner along the anteroposterior axis of the embryo and that different fates along this axis correspond with the level of the homeobox gene.

Interpretation

The weakness of a positional model has always been the process of interpretation. There are two main problems. First it has always seemed very difficult to imagine how, for example, a monotonic concentration gradient in a single morphogen could specify the necessary number of positional values. Cells, it is thought, would not be able to distinguish reliably between small changes in concentration of a chemical. The second problem is that even if cells acquired a discrete set of positional values, it is far from clear how these would be used to specify a particular pattern, particularly if two-, rather than one-, dimensional patterns are considered (Wolpert, 1985).

If each cell has a discrete and remembered positional value then the specification of that positional value is partly a problem of thresholds. This is not necessarily so if there is an isomorphism between positional information and the way it is expressed – that is, if the continuous gradient in positional information is expressed directly as a continuous gradient in some cellular property such as the number of adhesive sites or the rate of a particular chemical reaction (Wolpert and Stein, 1984). In this case, the responses could be continuous and graded as in adhesive properties (Zackson and Steinberg, 1988) or enzyme distribution (Sweetser *et al.* 1988). However, the problem of thresholds does occur if these properties are retained even when the signal is withdrawn, and some mechanism is then required to maintain the state of the cell, particularly through cell multiplication.

There are several models for the interpretation, or at least the transformation, of a continuous change in chemical concentration into a set of discrete states. One class of model relies on a threshold property arising from a positive feed-back loop (Lewis *et al.* 1977; Meinhardt, 1982). Another could be due to the phosphorylation of a protein (Goldbeter and Wolpert, unpublished). Both give sharp transitions under the influence of an increasing concentration of a morphogen.

How small a change in concentration can cells detect? Studies on chemotaxis (McRobbie, 1986) suggest that in that in some situations cells can detect changes in concentration of about 1 % this might involve temporal rather than spatial differences. More direct evidence comes from the effect of putative morphogens on development and from gene dosage studies (Table 3). Consider first retinoic acid. Local application of retinoic acid to chick wing buds can specify the development of a digit **2**, **3** or **4**, the corresponding concentration being 0.9 nM, 2.5 nM and 25 nM (Tickle *et al.* 1985). Again, local application of retinoic acid to regenerating amphibian limbs cut at the wrist can cause an extra radius and ulna to develop with a concentration of 2–4 mg/limb, an extra part of the humerus with 4–8 mg/limb while 16 mg/limb gives a complete extra limb (Maden *et al.* 1985). These cells are able to respond in rather a dramatic way with changes in concentration as low as a two-fold difference. A similar conclusion might be drawn from studies on the role of lin-14 in the development of the nematode, where mutations that eliminate or elevate the activity of the gene change cell fate

Table 3. *Concentration and interpretation*

System	Character	Concentration change
Insect	Head/thorax boundary	*bicoid* protein × 1.1 (Driever & Nüsslein-Volhard, 1988*b*).
Chick limb	Digit character	Retinoic acid × 2 (Tickle, Lee & Eichele, 1985)
Amphibian limb regeneration	Level of duplication	Retinoic acid × 2 (Maden, Keeble & Cox, 1985).
Amphibian mesoderm	Cell differentiation	MIF × 2 (Smith, Yaqoob & Symes, 1988)
Nematode	Cell fate	Lin-12 × 2 (?) (Ambros & Horvitz, 1987).

(Ambros and Horvitz, 1987). Again there is evidence that the anchor cell produces a graded signal that can stimulate adjacent cells to differentiate into two different types depending on their distance from the anchor cell. In addition the cell nearest the anchor cell appears to inhibit its neighbours (Sternberg, 1988). This means that cells can detect differences in concentration that vary over one cell diameter. A final, and crucial, example comes from changing the concentration of the protein of the *bicoid* gene in early *Drosophila* development. A 10 % change in concentration alters the position of the head/thorax boundary 15 % (Driever and Nüsslein-Volhard, 1988*b*). Taken together these results suggest that quite modest changes in concentration can lead to different cell behaviours. The problem remains but seems somewhat less formidable.

The second problem is that even with a positional field in which each cell is uniquely specified, it is necessary to interpret positional values so as to generate a pattern. A formal solution is that each cell contains a complete specification of the behaviour of every cell in every position. There must be a complete list of all the cells that will differentiate as type A, and another list of those that form type B and so on. For systems like the vertebrate skeleton it seems unlikely that there is a positional specification for every cell that develops into, for example, cartilage. This could partly be resolved if contiguous cartilage cells were specified as a group, and a prepattern mechanism (see below) can provide just such a mechanism. Even so positional fields are small and what seems inelegant or unlikely to us might look quite different to the cell. Moreover there is some evidence that there may be a listing of the type postulated for sensory bristles in *Drosophila*. There are 11 sensory bristles on the thorax of the fly which can be removed, often in pairs, by a series of mutations in the *achaete–scute* complex (Ghysen and Dambly-Chaudiere, 1988). Molecular analysis has shown that the phenotype of most scute alleles can be correlated with their location on the chromosome. These different sites on the chromosome might be thought of as being activated at appropriate positional values. The sites would correspond to sites that were specifically activated in those cells at particular positional values and the sites would then correspond to the list of positions at which interpretation of the bristle phenotype occurred.

There is evidence, in addition, for lateral inhibition increasing the precision of the bristle patterning.

The assumption in the previous example – indeed in the very concept of differentiation *via* interpretation – is that states of cell differentiation are, as it were, specified as a single event. While it is not an absolute requirement, the implication is of a single switch and is in strong contrast to any combinatorial mechanism of specification. It is far from clear whether or not the specification of cell differentiation is combinatorial (see above).

Spacing patterns and prepatterns

A weakness of the original positional information model was, perhaps, that it tried to do too much. It was recognised, quite early, that repeated or metameric patterns like somites or stripes might be generated by a different mechanism (Wolpert, 1971). While the actual mechanism for segment formation or stripe generation is not known, it is not unreasonable to consider that in some cases, at least, they could be generated by an isomorphic prepattern (MacWilliams, 1978).

An isomorphic prepattern, unlike positional information, provides a pattern of cell activities which reflects the overt pattern that will develop. For example, the digits in the hand could result from a wave-like distribution in a chemical morphogen with the peaks and troughs specifying the digits. A number of models, mainly based on Turing's (1952) original ideas of a reaction–diffusion mechanism, have shown how such prepatterns could be generated (Nagorcka, 1989). All these mechanisms generate wave-like patterns that could generate repeated structures. A crucial feature of all these is that the peaks and troughs are all the same. One could not alter one structure without affecting all and this greatly limits the classes of patterns to which they can give rise. But, by combining them with positional information, which will make the waves non-equivalent, a very large variety of patterns can be generated (Fig. 1).

The idea of wave-like prepatterns is more attractive than the evidence in its favour. The evidence is, as yet, just not there. A key case is the segmental pattern in early *Drosophila* development for which wave-like patterns could provide the mechanism, but the basis of segmentation with its beautiful stripes remains, so far, unknown. It is of great interest that the early periodic expression of a pair-rule gene is established by different regulatory elements that do not respond to periodic spatial cues (Goto *et al.* 1989).

In one case, at least, there is good evidence that positional information alone is not sufficient to specify the pattern, and that is the chick limb (Wolpert and Stein, 1984). While models based on positional information can account for a wide variety of experimental results, there are at least two telling experiments that show its inadequacy. The positional information model suggests that, for pattern along the anteroposterior axis of the developing limb, position is specified by a signal – possibly a gradient in a morphogen like retinoic acid – produced at the posterior margin by the polarising region. However, if the mesoderm of the limb bud is disaggregated into simple cells, reaggregated, and enclosed in normal limb ectoderm, limb-like structures, including digits, can develop (Patou, 1973). This strongly suggests that some sort of self-organising prepattern mechanism exists.

The second result comes from a consideration of the specification of the humerus. The predictions of the positional model concerning the development of the humerus when a polarising region is placed at different positions along the anteroposterior axis do not hold. The expected duplication and eliminations do not occur. The results might be better explained if the humerus were specified by a wave-like prepattern. For example, it would only be possible to get an additional humerus if there were substantial widening of the limb to allow the development of another peak (Wolpert and Hornbruch, 1987).

In more general terms the suggestion is that the solution to the French Flag problem (Wolpert, 1969) may involve first specifying three regions by a prepattern and then making them different with a positional signal. A possible interaction between specification of a repeated structure and positional information is in relation to size regulation in somite formation (Cooke, 1988).

There is a further reason for wishing to invoke a prepattern mechanism for repeated patterns. From an evolutionary point of view it is easy to see how such patterns could arise with a reaction–diffusion mechanism and a single threshold, whereas a positional model requires multiple thresholds which would be almost impossible to provide *ab initio*.

The combination of a spacing pattern with positional information could provide the basis for a variety of different patterns. The pattern of vertebrae might be thought of in these terms. Similarly feather patterning in birds may involve a spacing pattern to place the feathers in a regular pattern and positional information to specify both the nature of the individual feathers and whether feathers will form. Mammalian teeth may represent yet another system with a repeated pattern whose individual members then diverge. It may even turn out that all segmental structures where the segments are different are generated by a combination of the two mechanisms.

Morphogenesis

Change in form during development is brought about by cellular forces such as localised contractions and changes in adhesion. Recent studies have placed great emphasis on the pattern of expression of cell adhesion molecules (Edelman, 1986). The view adopted here is that all such changes are an expression of a prior patterning process. Changes in form occur as a result of an earlier patterning event. Many of the changes may be thought of in terms of interpretation of positional information. This is by no means exclusive and other patterning mechanisms and induction itself could be responsible.

This view should be contrasted with the idea that mechanical forces could, themselves, generate spatial patterns as in the case of cartilage condensation in limb

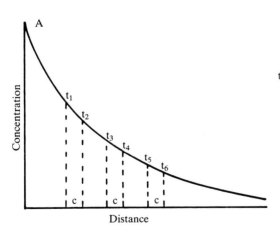
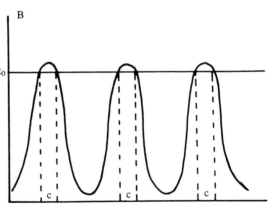

Fig. 1. Diagrams to illustrate a positional information mechanism (A) and a prepattern mechanism (B) to specify three regions of, say, cartilage. The positional information mechanism requires six thresholds, t_1–t_6, whereas the prepattern mechanism just one, t_1. The positional information mechanism could be combined with the prepattern to make the three regions non-equivalent.

development or the development of feather follicles (Oster *et al.* 1985). For the limb, at least, this model has severe defects (Wolpert, 1989*b*).

Universality

One of the attractive features of positional information was that it offered the possibility of universality. That is, in principle, the same coordinate system and the same signals could be used again and again. This ambitious expectation has not been quite fulfilled. There is, however, good evidence that within the same animal – the imaginal discs of insects, the forelimb and hindlimb of vertebrates – the same signals are used. In addition, developing and regenerating amphibian limbs use similar signals (Muneoka and Bryant, 1982) and so do the limbs of amniotes (Tickle *et al.* 1976; Fallon and Crosby, 1977). Nevertheless there is only limited evidence for the conservation of positional signals across phyla. However, the discovery of the homeobox has revealed a highly conserved region of many genes in different phyla possibly involved in patterning. Also there are an increasing number of reports in which similar proteins, such as EGF-like molecules and receptors seem to be involved in patterning. This is very encouraging. Perhaps we will find that there is a common language, just different dialects.

In looking for universal mechanisms and signals, it is likely that the systems in which they are least likely to be found are eggs and very early development. Yolky eggs, for example, provide highly specialized systems compared to the phylotypic stages of development, such as the germ band stage in insect development and the head process/somite stage in vertebrates (Wolpert, 1989*b*).

A further feature of universality is that many of the features of regulation and regeneration described by the polar coordinate model apply to organisms as diverse as insects and amphibia (Bryant *et al.* 1981) and even to protozoa (Frankel, 1984).

Conclusions

Patterning by positional information provides a relatively simple mechanism for making a wide variety of patterns. Alas, compared to 21 years ago, that simplicity now seems more like simple-mindedness. Things seem, at this stage, much more complicated, particularly since molecular genetics has transformed our understanding of early insect development (Ingham, 1989). While there is evidence for some aspects of a positional information mechanism, there are also other interactions. Boundaries, positional signals, positional value and interpretation are still useful concepts that perhaps have to be considered in relation to more complex systems that may involve prepatterns and induction and other cell-to-cell interactions. Nevertheless, for some processes, such as those involved in regeneration, the polar coordinate model still provides

a powerful framework for systems as diverse as protozoa, insects and vertebrate limbs. It would be a great pity at this stage to conflate positional signals, positional values, induction and morphogens. Each still has a useful meaning. Morphogens are only just beginning to be identified and we may have to be even more patient for a molecular understanding of positional value.

References

AMBROS, V. & HORVITZ, R. H. (1987). The lin-14 locus of *Caenorhabditis elegans* controls the time of expression of specific postembryonic developmental events. *Genes and Develop.* **1**, 398–414.

BABLOYANTZ, A. (1977). *J. theoret. Biol.* **68**, 551–562.

BODE, P. M. & BODE, H. R. (1984). Patterning in Hydra. In *Pattern Formation* (ed. G. Malacinski), pp. 213–243. MacMillan, London.

BROCKES, J. P. (1989). Retinoids, homeobox genes and limb morphogenesis. *Neuron* **2**, 1280–1294.

BRYANT, P. J. (1974). Pattern formation, growth control, and cell interactions in *Drosophila* imaginal discs. In *The Clonal Basis of Development.* (eds. S. Subtelny & I.M. Sussex) pp. 63–82. Academic Press, New York.

BRYANT, S. V., FRENCH, V. & BRYANT, P. J. (1981). Distal regeneration and symmetry. *Science* **212**, 993–1002.

COOKE, J. (1988). A note on segmentation and the scale of pattern formation in insects and vertebrates. *Development* **104 Supplement** 245–248.

CRICK, F. H. C. (1970). Diffusion in embryogenesis. *Nature, Lond.* **225**, 420–422.

DAVIDSON, E. H. (1989). Lineage-specific gene expression and the regulative capacities of the sea urchin embryo: a proposed mechanism. *Development* **105**, 421–446.

DAVIS, R. K., WEINTRAUB, H. & LASSAR, A. B. (1987). Expression of a single transfected cDNA converting fibroblasts to myoblasts. *Cell* **51**, 987–1000.

DE ROBERTIS, E. M., OLIVER, G. & WRIGHT, C. V. E. (1989). Determination of axial polarity in the vertebrate embryo: homeodomain protein and homeogenetic induction. *Cell* **57** (in press).

DRIEVER, W. & NÜSSLEIN-VOLHARD, C. (1988*a*). A gradient of *bicoid* protein in *Drosophila* embryos. *Cell* **54**, 83–93.

DRIEVER, W. & NÜSSLEIN-VOLHARD, C. (1988*b*). The *bicoid* protein determines position in the *Drosophila* embryo in a concentration dependent manner. *Cell* **54**, 95–104.

EDELMAN, C. M. (1986). Cell adhesion molecules in the regulation of animal form and tissue pattern. *A. Rev. Cell Biol.* **2**, 81–116.

FALLON, J. F. & CROSBY, G. M. (1977). Polarizing zone activity in limb buds of amniotes. In *Vertebrate Limb and Somite Morphogenesis.* (ed. D.S. Ede, J.R. Hinchliffe & M. Balls). Cambridge University Press, Cambridge.

FRANKEL, J. (1984). Pattern formation in ciliated protozoa. In *Pattern Formation.* (ed. G.M. Malacinski & S.V. Bryant) pp. 163–196. MacMillan, New York.

FRENCH, V., BRYANT, P. J. & BRYANT, S. V. (1976). Pattern regulation in epimorphic fields. *Science* **183**, 969–981.

GHYSEN, A. & DAMBLY-CHAUDIERE, C. (1988). From DNA to form: the achaete-scute complex. *Genes and Devel.* **2**, 495–501.

GOTO, T., MACDONALD, P. & MANIATIS, T. (1989). Early and late periodic patterns of *even-skipped* expression are controlled by distinct regulatory elements that respond to different spatial cues. *Cell* **57**, 413–422.

GURDON, J. B. (1987). Embryonic induction – molecular prospects. *Development* **99**, 285–306.

HOLLAND, P. W. H. & HOGAN, B. L. M. (1988). Expression of homeobox genes during mouse development: a review. *Genes & Devel.* **2**, 773–782.

HONIG, L. S. (1981). Positional signal transmission in the developing chick limb. *Nature* **291**, 72–73.

HORNBRUCH, A., SUMMERBELL, D. & WOLPERT, L. (1979). Somite formation in the early chick embryo following grafts of Hensen's mode. *J. Embryol. exp. Morph.* **51**, 51–62.

HÖRSTADIUS, S. (1973). *Experimental Embryology of Echinoderms.* Clarendon, Oxford.

INGHAM, P. W. (1988). The molecular genetics of embryonic pattern formation in *Drosophila. Nature* **335**, 25–34.

LAWRENCE, P. A. (1970). Polarity and patterns in the postembryonic development of insects. *Adv. Insect Physiol.* **1**, 197–266.

LAWRENCE, P. A. (1973). The development of spatial patterns in the integument of insects. In *Developmental Systems: Insects.* vol. 2, eds. S. J. Counce & C. H. Waddington, pp. 109–157. Academic Press, London.

LAWRENCE, P. A. (1981). The cellular basis of segmentation in insects. *Cell* **26**, 3–10.

LAWRENCE, P. A. (1987). Pair-rule genes: do they paint stripes or draw lines? *Cell* **51**, 879–880.

LAWRENCE, P. A., JOHNSTON, P., MACDONALD, P. & STRUHL, G. (1987). Borders of parasegments in *Drosophila* embryos are delimited by the *fushi tarazu* and *even-skipped* genes. *Nature* **328**, 440–442.

LEE, J. & TICKLE, C. (1985). Retinoic acid and pattern formation in the developing chick wing: SEM and quantitative studies of early effects on the apical ectodermal ridge and bud outgrowth. *J. Embryol. exp. Morph.* **90**, 139–169.

LEWIS, J. H., SLACK, J. M. W. & WOLPERT, L. (1977). Thresholds in development. *J. Theor. Biol.* **65**, 579–590.

LEWIS, J. H. & WOLPERT, L. (1976). The principle of non-equivalence in development. *J. theor. Biol.* **62**, 479–490.

MCROBBIE, B. (1986). Chemotaxis and cell motility in the cellular slime mould. *CRC Crit. Rev. in Microbiology* **13**, 333–375.

MACWILLIAMS, H. K. (1978). A model of gradient interpretation based on morphogen binding. *J. theoret. Biol.* **72**, 341–385.

MADEN, M., KEEBLE, S. & COX, R. A. (1985). The characteristics of local application of retinoic acid to the regenerating axolotl limb. *Willhelm Roux Arch. EntwMech. Org.* **194**, 228–235.

MEINHARDT, H. (1982). *Models for Biological Pattern Formation.* Academic Press, London.

MEINHARDT, H. (1984). Models for pattern formation during development of higher organisms. In *Pattern Formation* (ed. G. M. Malacinski), pp. 47–72. Macmillan, New York.

MUNEOKA, K. & BRYANT, S. V. (1982). Evidence that patterning mechanisms in developing and regenerating limbs are the same. *Nature* **298**, 369–371.

NAGORCKA, B. N. (1989). Wavelike isomorphic prepatterns in development. *J. theoret. Biol.* **137**, 127–162.

NIJHOUT, H. F. (1980). Pattern formation on lepidopteran wings: determination of an eyespot. *Devl Biol.* **80**, 267–274.

NÜSSLEIN-VOLHARD, C., FROHNHOFER, H. G. & LEHMAN, R. (1987). Determination of antero-posterior polarity in *Drosophila. Science* **238**, 1675–1681.

OHSUGI, K., IDE, H. & MOMOI, T. (1988). Temporal and spatial expression of a position specific antigen AV-1 in chick limb buds. *Devl Biol.* **130**, 454–463.

OSTER, G. F., MURRARY, J. D. & MAINI, P. K. (1985). A model for chondrogenic condensations in the developing limb: the role of extracellular matrix and cell tractions. *J. Embryol. exp. Morph.* **89**, 93–112.

PATOU, M. P. (1973). Analyse de la morphogenese due pied des Oiseax a l'aide de melange cellulaires interspecifiques. I. Etude morphologie. *J. Embryol. exp. Morph.* **29**, 175–196.

RUIZ I ALTABA, A. & MELTON, D. (1989). Bimodal and graded expression of the *Xenopus* homeobox gene *X hox 3* during embryonic development. *Development* **106**, 176–183.

SANDER, K. (1984). Embryonic pattern formation in insects: basic concepts and their experimental foundations. In *Pattern Formation.* (ed. C.M. Malacinski), pp. 245–268. MacMillan, New York.

SCHALLER, H. C. & BODENMULLER, H. (1981). Isolation and amino acid sequence of a morphogenetic peptide from Hydra. *Proc. natn. Acad. Sci. U.S.A.* **78**, 7000–7004.

SLACK, J. M. W. & ISAACS, H. V. (1989). Presence of basic fibroblast growth factor in the early *Xenopus* embryo. *Development* **105**, 147–153.

SMITH, J. C. (1989). Mesoderm induction and mesoderm-inducing factors in early amphibian development. *Development* **105**, 665–677.

SMITH, J. C. & SLACK, J. M. W. (1983). Dorsalization and neural induction: properties of the organizer in *Xenopus laevis. J. Embryol. exp. Morph.* **78**, 299–317.

SMITH, J. C., YAQOOB, M. & SYMES, K. (1988). Purification, partial characterization and biological effects of the XTC mesoderm-inducing factor. *Development* **103**, 591–600.

STERNBERG, P. W. (1988). Lateral Inhibition during vulval induction in *Caenorhabditis elegans. Nature* **335**, 551–554.

STEWARD, R., ZUSMAN, S. B., HUANG, L. H. & SCHEDL, P. (1988). The dorsal protein is distributed in a gradient in early *Drosophila* embryos. *Cell* **55**, 487–495.

SWEETSER, D. A., BIRKENMEIER, E. H., HOPPER, P. C., MCKEEL, D. W. & GORDON, J. I. (1988). Mechanisms underlying generation of gradients within the intestine: an analysis using transgenic mice containing fatty acid binding protein-human growth hormone fusion genes. *Genes & Devel.* **2**, 1318–1332.

SUMMERBELL, D., LEWIS, J. H. & WOLPERT, L. (1973). Positional information in chick limb morphogenesis. *Nature* **244**, 492–496.

THALLER, C. & EICHELE, G. (1987). Identification and spatial distribution of retinoids in the developing chick limb bud. *Nature, Lond.* **327**, 625–628.

TICKLE, C., LEE, J. & EICHELE, G. (1985). A quantitative analysis of the effect of all-*trans*-retinoic acid on the pattern of limb development. *Devl Biol.* **109**, 82–95.

TICKLE, C., SHELLSWELL, G., CRAWLEY, A. & WOLPERT, L. (1976). Positional signalling by mouse limb polarizing region in the chick wing bud. *Nature* **259**, 396–397.

TICKLE, C., SUMMERBELL, D. & WOLPERT, L. (1975). Positional signalling and specification of digits in chick limb morphogenesis. *Nature* **254**, 199.

TOMLINSON, A. (1988). Cellular interactions in the developing *Drosophila* eye. *Development* **104**, 183–193.

TURING, A. (1952). The chemical basis of morphogenesis. *Phil. Trans. Roy. Soc.* B **64**, 37–72.

WILLIAMS, J. G. (1988). The role of diffusible molecules in regulating the cellular differentiation of *Dictyostelium. Development* **103**, 1–16.

WINFREE, A. T. (1984). A continuity principle for regeneration. In *Pattern Formation* (ed. G. M. Malacinski) pp. 103–123. MacMillan, New York.

WOLPERT, L. (1969). Positional information and the spatial pattern of cellular differentiation. *J. theoret. Biol.* **25**, 1–47.

WOLPERT, L. (1971). Positional information and pattern formation. In *Current Topics in Dev. Biol.* **6**, 183.

WOLPERT, L. (1981). Positional information and pattern formation. *Phil. Trans. Roy. Soc.* B **295**, 441–450.

WOLPERT, L. (1985). Positional information and pattern formation. In *Molecular Determinants of Animal Form* (ed. G. M. Edelman) pp. 423–433. Alan Liss, New York.

WOLPERT, L. (1988a). Craniofacial development: summing up. *Development* **103 Supplement** 249–289.

WOLPERT, L. (1988b). Stem cells: a problem in asymmetry. In *Stem Cells.* (ed. B. I. Lord & T. M. Dexter). *J. Cell Sci.* Suppl. **10**, pp. 1–9.

WOLPERT, L. (1989a). Positional information and prepattern in the development of pattern. In *Theoretical Models for Cell-to-Cell Signalling* (ed. A. Goldbeter). Academic Press, London. (in press).

WOLPERT, L. (1989b). Evolution of development. *Biol. J. Linneaen Soc.* (in press).

WOLPERT, L. & HORNBRUCH, A. (1987). Positional signalling and the development of the humerus in the chick limb bud. *Development* **100**, 333–338.

WOLPERT, L. & STEIN, W. D. (1984). Positional information and pattern formation. In *Pattern Formation* (ed. G. M. Malacinski & S. V. Bryant) pp. 2–21. MacMillan, New York.

ZACKSON, S. L. & STEINBERG, M. S. (1988). A molecular marker for cell guidance information in the axolotl embryo. *Devl Biol.* **127**, 435–442.

Appendix

The idea of positional information came to me in early 1968. It was a very exciting few days when everything became clear and obvious. Naturally it has not remained so. But at that time all the problems we had been struggling with could at once be explained if cells had their position specified as in a coordinate system and then used this information to determine how they would differentiate.

The origin of the idea came from several sources. The most important was the recognition that the problem of pattern formation and regulation was being grossly neglected. Pattern formation was not part of the embryologist's conceptual equipment at the time, though some workers like Waddington and Rose did recognise its importance. My work on sea-urchin morphogenesis with Trygve Gustafson had introduced me not only to development, but to the founders of the Swedish gradient theory, both Runnstrom and Hörstadius. From the beginning I had great difficulty with gradient theory and how it could explain patterning and size regulation. Gradients at that time were, in the tradition of Child (1941), meant to reflect metabolic rates and I could not understand how they worked or gave rise to pattern. Rate advantage did not make much sense. When marriage ended trips to Sweden I chose Hydra as a simple regulating system to work on pattern formation.

I like to think that I invented the term 'pattern formation'. I had great difficulty finding a suitable name and even consulted a classicist to see if another word would do. For pattern, as normally used in English, is not quite the right word, the essential connotation being template. Pattern formation does, now, seem to have just the right meaning.

With Hydra came the French Flag Problem (Wolpert, 1968). This focused in a very simple way on a basic patterning system that required a solution. Both the sea urchin and Hydra were like a French flag, and with Gerry Webster, Michael Apter and Mary Williams we developed all sorts of quite simple and ingenious models. Michael Apter's solution – he was a psychologist with an interest in computers – was to number the cells in a line from both ends. It was then easy to specify the red, white and blue regions. I initially thought it completely artificial and unrealistic, and dismissed it.

Another motivation was a desire for universality and how to get from the genes to pattern. I was convinced that there had to be universal mechanisms – so many of the phenomena seemed so similar. Also I needed a mechanism which could make use of the fact that all cells had the same genetic information. Positional information thus came from the French flag via Apter's numbering and universality. I think Stern's genetic mosaic studies on insects was important for it suggested a simple interpretation.

I first presented the idea at one of Waddington's 'Theoretical Biology' meetings at the Villa Serbelloni. I travelled from Milan in a taxi with Brian Goodwin who was excited by the idea and, with Cohen, soon developed the phase-shift model (Goodwin and Cohen, 1969). Waddington, by contrast, was unenthusiastic, since he recognised that interpretation carried too large a burden.

In the summer of that year I was at Woods Hole. I presented the new ideas at a Friday evening discourse, which had a very large audience. The reception was very hostile. They did not like being told that for the limb, for example, they had completely missed the problem: it was not in epithelial mesenchymal interactions, but in patterning of cartilage and muscle that the real problem lay. Only Sydney Brenner was encouraging though Howard Schneiderman was at least interested.

Several aspects were not new. Driesch had spoken of position and coordinate systems at the end of the last century, but thought it was impossible. More important, Stumpf in a lovely experiment, had said very much the same thing and Peter Lawrence's ideas on gradients were along very similar lines (Wolpert, 1986).

Gradients had become very unfashionable, and Crick's (1970) support and interest were, I think, crucial to making positional information more or less respectable.

References

CRICK, F. H. C. (1970). Diffusion in embryogenesis. *Nature (London)* **225**, 420–422.

CHILD, C. M. (1941). *Patterns and Problems of Development.* University of Chicago Press, Chicago.

GOODWIN, B. C. & COHEN, M. (1969). A phase-shift model for the spatial and temporal organization or developing systems. *J. theoret. Biol.* **49**, 26–59.

WOLPERT, L. (1968). The French Flag Problem: a contribution to the discussion on pattern development and regulation. In *Towards a Theoretical Biology* (Ed. C. H. Waddington) pp. 125–33. Edinburgh University Press, Edinburgh.

WOLPERT, L. (1986). Gradients, position and pattern: a history. In *A History of Embryology.* (Eds. T. J. Horder, J. A. Witkowski and C. C. Wyle) pp. 347–361. Cambridge University Press, Cambridge.

Development 1989 Supplement, 13–19
Printed in Great Britain © The Company of Biologists Limited 1989

Multiple steps in the localization of *bicoid* RNA to the anterior pole of the *Drosophila* oocyte

DANIEL ST. JOHNSTON, WOLFGANG DRIEVER, THOMAS BERLETH, SIBYLL RICHSTEIN and
CHRISTIANE NÜSSLEIN-VOLHARD

Max Planck Institut für Entwicklungsbiologie, Abteilung Genetik, Spemannstrasse 35, 7400 Tübingen, FRG

Summary

The anterior region of the *Drosophila* embryonic pattern is determined by a gradient of the bicoid (bcd) protein. The correct formation of this gradient requires the localization of *bcd* RNA to the anterior pole of the egg. Here we use a wholemount *in situ* technique to examine the process of *bcd* RNA localization during oogenesis and embryogenesis. While bcd protein becomes distributed in a gradient that extends throughout the anterior two thirds of the early embryo, *bcd* RNA remains restricted to a much smaller region at the anterior pole. The difference between these distributions indicates that the shape of the protein gradient must depend to some extent on the posterior movement of the protein after it has been synthesized.

Four distinct phases of *bcd* RNA localization can be distinguished during oogenesis. Between stages 6 and 9 of oogenesis, the RNA accumulates in a ring at the anterior end of the oocyte. During the second phase, in stage 9–10a follicles, the RNA also localizes to the apical regions of the nurse cells, demonstrating that the nurse cells possess an intrinsic polarity. As the nurse cells contract during stages 10b–11, all of the *bcd* RNA becomes localized to the cortex at the anterior end of the oocyte. During a final phase that must occur between stage 12 of oogenesis and egg deposition, the RNA becomes localized to a spherical region that occupies a slightly dorsal position at the anterior pole.

Mutations in the maternal-effect genes, *exuperantia* (*exu*) and *swallow* (*sww*), lead to an almost uniform distribution of *bcd* RNA in the early embryo, while *staufen* (*stau*) mutations produce a gradient of RNA at the anterior pole. *exu* mutations disrupt the second stage of *bcd* RNA localization during oogenesis, *sww* mutations disrupt the third, and *stau* mutations affect the fourth phase.

Key words: *Drosophila*, *bicoid*, RNA localization, oogenesis, *exuperantia*, *swallow*, *staufen*, gradient formation.

Introduction

The anterior–posterior pattern of the *Drosophila* embryo is determined in response to maternal factors that are deposited in the egg during oogenesis. Three groups of maternal genes are required to specify distinct regions of this pattern; the head and thorax (the anterior group), the abdomen (the posterior group) and the acron and telson (the terminal group) (reviewed in Nüsslein-Volhard and Roth, 1989; Nüsslein-Volhard *et al.* 1987). The anterior portion of the body plan depends on the product of the *bicoid* (*bcd*) gene (Frohnhöfer and Nüsslein-Volhard, 1986). In *bicoid*⁻ embryos, the head and thorax are absent, and the abdominal fate map expands anteriorly. In addition, a duplicated telson forms at the anterior end of the embryo. Transplantation experiments have shown that *bcd*⁺ activity is localized to the anterior pole of the egg, and when transplanted to more posterior positions, can induce the formation of anterior structures at ectopic sites (Frohn-

höfer and Nüsslein-Volhard, 1986; Frohnhöfer *et al.* 1986).

In agreement with the results of the transplantation experiments, *bcd* RNA is localized to the anterior pole of the egg (Frigerio *et al.* 1986; Berleth *et al.* 1988). The protein that is translated from this RNA forms a concentration gradient which extends throughout the anterior two thirds of the embryo (Driever and Nüsslein-Volhard, 1988*a*). This protein gradient appears to determine anterior positional values in a concentration-dependent manner, since changes in the maternal *bcd*⁺ gene dosage produce complementary shifts in both the protein gradient and the fate map (Driever and Nüsslein-Volhard, 1988*b*). Further support for the role of bcd protein as the anterior morphogen comes from the results of experiments in which *bcd* RNA synthesized *in vitro* is injected into early embryos. When the RNA is injected into the middle of a recipient embryo, it can induce the development of ectopic head and thoracic structures (Driever, Siegel and Nüsslein-Volhard, in preparation). The most anterior pattern elements form closest to the site of injection, with more posterior (thoracic) structures developing on either side. This result indicates not only that the bcd protein determines the anterior quality of the structures that develop, but also that the slope of the protein gradient specifies the polarity of the pattern. In addition, the ability of *bcd* RNA to organize anterior pattern in the middle of the embryo shows that no other anteriorly localized molecules are required for this process.

The bicoid protein contains a homeodomain, suggesting that *bicoid* encodes a DNA-binding protein (Frigerio *et al.* 1986). This makes it attractive to suppose that bcd protein specifies anterior positional values by activating or repressing zygotic target genes in a concentration-dependent manner. Genetic and molecular evidence indicates that *bcd* regulates the anterior zygotic expression of the gap gene, *hunchback* (Lehmann and Nüsslein-Volhard, 1987; Schröder *et al.* 1988; Tautz, 1988). bcd protein binds to several sites in the *hunchback* promoter, and acts as a transcriptional activator of *hunchback* (Driever and Nüsslein-Volhard, 1989). Driever *et al.* (in press) have made constructs containing synthetic-bcd-binding sites fused to the hsp70 promoter and a reporter gene. When transformed into flies, the bcd-binding sites drive the anterior expression of the reporter gene in the embryo. The size of this anterior domain of expression is reduced when binding sites with lower affinities for the bcd protein are used. The observation that promoters with low-affinity bcd-binding sites are only activated at high protein concentrations suggests a model for how the bcd protein gradient could activate several zygotic target genes in distinct anterior domains, and thereby determine several levels of anterior development.

The formation of the wild-type protein gradient, and thus the determination of a normal anterior pattern, depends upon the localization of *bcd* RNA to the anterior pole. Mutations in the maternal genes *exuperantia* (*exu*) and *swallow* (*sww*) disrupt this localization during oogenesis, and lead to an almost uniform distribution of *bcd* RNA in the early embryo (Berleth *et al.* 1988; Stephenson *et al.* 1988). Both of these mutations result in phenotypes in which anterior structures of the head are deleted, and the thoracic region is expanded (Frohnhöfer and Nüsslein-Volhard, 1987). Embryos derived from females mutant for the posterior group gene *staufen* show similar but weaker head defects, in addition to the abdominal deletions characteristic of all mutations in this class (Schüpbach and Wieschaus, 1986; Nüsslein-Volhard *et al.* 1987; Lehmann, 1988). These embryos also show an anterior shift in the fate map, which can be seen in a shift in the position of the cephalic furrow and the first *fushi tarazu* stripe (Schüpbach and Wieschaus, 1986; Carroll *et al.* 1986; Lehmann, 1988). The observation that the bcd protein gradient is shallower in the mutant embryos suggests that *staufen* mutations may also alter the distribution of *bcd* RNA (Driever and Nüsslein-Volhard, 1988b).

In this report, we use a non-radioactive, enzyme-linked *in situ* technique developed by Tautz and Pfeifle

(1989) to examine the process of *bcd* RNA localization during oogenesis and early embryogenesis. This technique has the advantage that one can perform hybridizations on wholemount preparations. We have used these wholemount stainings to make direct comparisons between the *bcd* RNA distribution and the protein distribution, as revealed by antibody stainings.

Results

bcd *RNA localization in wild-type embryos*

The localization of *bcd* RNA in wild-type embryos has previously been described by Frigerio *et al.* (1986) and Berleth *et al.* (1988). We have repeated these investigations in order to gain a clearer understanding of the three-dimensional distribution of *bcd* RNA during the first stages of embryogenesis. In very early (stage 1) embryos, *bcd* RNA staining resembles a flattened ball which is closely apposed to the anterior pole, and which frequently occupies a slightly dorsal position (Fig. 1A). The RNA does not seem to be specifically bound to the cortex of the egg, since much of it is in the interior. As development proceeds through pole cell formation (Fig. 1B) to syncytial blastoderm (Fig. 1C), most of the RNA becomes localized to the periphery, in the clear cytoplasm that surrounds each nucleus. This movement to the cortex sometimes results in a slight posterior-wards shift in the RNA distribution. By early nuclear cycle 14, *bcd* RNA begins to disappear (Fig. 1D) and midway through cellularization the signal is no longer detectable (Fig. 1E).

Fig. 1. The distribution of *bcd* RNA in wild-type embryos. The embryos were fixed, and hybridized with a random-primed probe synthesized from a *bicoid* cDNA clone, following the procedure of Tautz and Pfeifle (1989). In all figures, anterior is to the left and dorsal is uppermost. (A) Early cleavage stage. (B) Late cleavage stage, after pole cell formation. (C) Syncytial blastoderm. (D) Late syncytial blastoderm, after the 13th nuclear division. (E) Early cellularization. These embryos have been overstained in order to clearly show the posterior extent of the *bcd* RNA distribution. This overstaining partially obscures the cortical localization of the RNA in syncytial blastoderm embryos (C), which can be clearly seen in understained embryos or in later embryos as the RNA starts to disappear (D).

Fig. 2. The distributions of *bicoid* RNA, bicoid protein and *hunchback* RNA in syncytial blastoderm embryos. (A) *bcd* RNA (B) bcd protein. The embryos were stained with a polyclonal anti-bicoid antibody, as described by Driever and Nüsslein-Volhard (1988a). (C) *hunchback* RNA (Tautz *et al.* 1987).

Fig. 4. The *bcd* RNA distribution in mutant embryos. (A) Wild-type cleavage stage. (B) Cleavage-stage embryo derived from an *exu*^{PJ}/*exu*^{PJ} mother, showing a uniform distribution of *bcd* RNA. (C) Syncytial blastoderm embryo derived from an *exu*^{PJ}/*exu*^{PJ} mother. By this stage a shallow anterior–posterior gradient of RNA has formed. (D) Cleavage-stage embryo derived from a *sww*^{14}/*sww*^{14} mother, showing the early weak RNA gradient. (E) Cleavage-stage embryo derived from a *stau*^{D3}/*Df(2R) PC4* mother. The RNA is distributed in a steep gradient at the anterior end of the embryo.

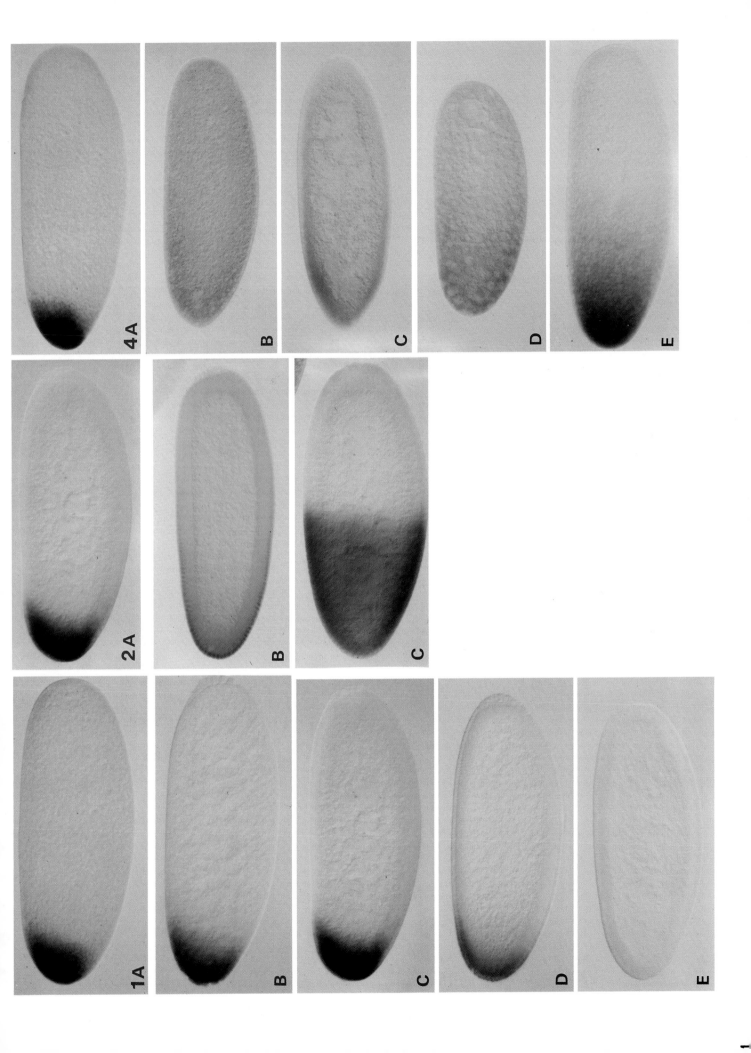

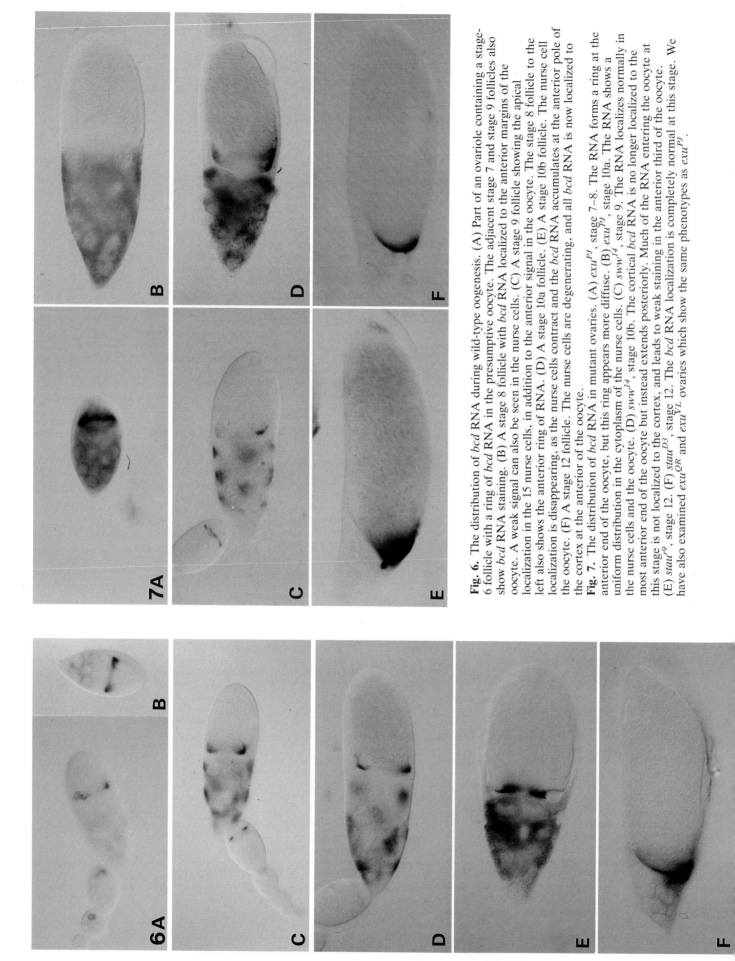

Fig. 6. The distribution of *bcd* RNA during wild-type oogenesis. (A) Part of an ovariole containing a stage-6 follicle with a ring of *bcd* RNA in the presumptive oocyte. The adjacent stage 7 and stage 9 follicles also show *bcd* RNA staining. (B) A stage 8 follicle with *bcd* RNA localized to the anterior margins of the oocyte. A weak signal can also be seen in the nurse cells. (C) A stage 9 follicle showing the apical localization in the 15 nurse cells, in addition to the anterior signal in the oocyte. The stage 8 follicle to the left also shows the anterior ring of RNA. (D) A stage 10a follicle. (E) A stage 10b follicle. The nurse cell localization is disappearing, as the nurse cells contract and the *bcd* RNA accumulates at the anterior pole of the oocyte. (F) A stage 12 follicle. The nurse cells are degenerating, and all *bcd* RNA is now localized to the cortex at the anterior of the oocyte.

Fig. 7. The distribution of *bcd* RNA in mutant ovaries. (A) *exu^{PJ}*, stage 7–8. The RNA forms a ring at the anterior end of the oocyte, but this ring appears more diffuse. (B) *exu^{PJ}*, stage 10a. The RNA shows a uniform distribution in the cytoplasm of the nurse cells. (C) *sww^{14}*, stage 9. The RNA localizes normally in the nurse cells and the oocyte. (D) *sww^{14}*, stage 10b. The cortical *bcd* RNA is no longer localized to the most anterior end of the oocyte but instead extends posteriorly. Much of the RNA entering the oocyte at this stage is not localized to the cortex, and leads to weak staining in the anterior third of the oocyte. (E) *stau^{r9}*, stage 12. (F) *stau^{D3}*, stage 12. The *bcd* RNA localization is completely normal at this stage. We have also examined *exu^{QR}* and *exu^{VL}* ovaries which show the same phenotypes as *exu^{PJ}*.

Fig. 2 compares the distributions of *bcd* RNA and protein at the syncytial blastoderm stage. The levels of RNA and protein were quantified using the procedure described by Driever and Nüsslein-Volhard (1988*a*), and these results are presented graphically in Fig. 3. These measurements clearly demonstrate that the RNA is more tightly localized to the anterior end of the embryo, than is the protein. *bcd* RNA forms a steep gradient at the anterior end of the embryo, in which 90 % of the RNA is restricted to the region anterior to 82 % egg length (0 % EL is the posterior pole). In contrast, bcd protein is distributed in a much shallower gradient, in which only 57 % of the protein falls within this anterior region. The protein must therefore move posteriorly after it has been synthesized. One of the functions of bcd protein is to activate the anterior zygotic expression of hunchback (Schröder *et al.* 1988; Tautz, 1988; Driever and Nüsslein-Volhard, 1989). This anterior hunchback domain is shown in Fig. 2C, and illustrates that the bcd protein gradient must extend to at least 55 % egg length, a position at which *bcd* RNA is not detectable above background.

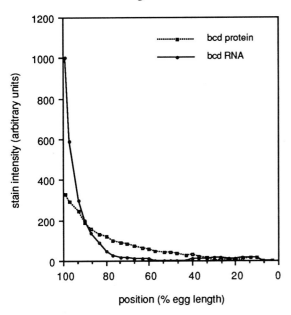

Fig. 3. The distribution of *bcd* mRNA (solid line) and bcd protein (dotted line) in the embryo. Whole wild-type embryos were stained for bcd protein, using an immunohistochemical method (Driever and Nüsslein-Volhard, 1988*a*), or for *bcd* mRNA, using the enzyme linked *in situ* detection technique. Video images of whole-mount embryos were taken and a background image subtracted. The distribution of the stain intensities along the anterior posterior midline was recorded for five embryos (nuclear cycle 13) and the average values at 30 equidistant positions calculated. Signal linearity of the *in situ* detection method was tested by performing the enzymatic colour reaction for 3 and a half or 16 minutes, respectively. Values in the anteriormost 15 % of the embryos appear to be nonlinear in the 16 min reaction and were corrected accordingly. The areas under the RNA and protein curves have been made equal in order to allow a comparison of the two distribution profiles. Anterior is to the left.

bcd *RNA localization in mutant embryos*

In early (stage 1) embryos derived from *exu* homozygous mothers, *bcd* RNA is uniformly distributed throughout the egg cytoplasm (Fig. 4B). However, by syncytial blastoderm a shallow anterior–posterior gradient has formed (Fig. 4C). Berleth *et al.* (1987) have found that *bcd* RNA remains uniformly distributed in eggs laid by mothers which are mutant for both *exu* and the posterior group gene *vasa*. This suggests that the late *bcd* RNA gradient is created by the degradation of the RNA in the posterior region of the embryo, due to the activity of the posterior organizing centre (Nüsslein-Volhard *et al.* 1987).

Embryos laid by *sww* homozygotes have a more variable distribution of *bcd* RNA. While some embryos show no localization, most contain a weak anterior-to-posterior gradient (Fig. 4D). As is the case for *exu* mutant embryos, the gradient becomes more pronounced as development proceeds, due to the posterior degradation of the RNA. The variability of the *bcd* RNA distribution in *sww* mutant embryos is reflected in the variability in the final cuticular phenotype (Frohnhöfer and Nüsslein-Volhard, 1986).

In embryos derived from *staufen* mutant mothers, *bcd* RNA forms a gradient in the anterior region of the embryo (Fig. 4E). This phenotype is clearly distinct from that produced by *exu* or *sww* mutations, and cannot depend upon the posterior degradation of the RNA, since there is no localized posterior activity in *stau* mutant embryos (Nüsslein-Volhard *et al.* 1987; Lehmann and Nüsslein-Volhard, unpublished results). This partial mislocalization of *bcd* RNA leads to a shallower protein gradient (Driever and Nüsslein-Volhard, 1988*b*). The *bcd* RNA distributions in *exu*, *sww*, and *stau* mutant embryos are compared to the wild-type distribution in Fig. 5. Since these comparisons were performed using syncytial blastoderm embryos, *exu* and *sww* both show a shallow anterior-to-posterior RNA gradient.

The process of bcd *RNA localization during wild-type oogenesis*

bcd RNA can first be detected in late previtellogenic follicles (stages 5–6 of King (1970)) accumulating in a single, posteriorly located cell of the germ cell cluster (Fig. 6A). As oogenesis proceeds and the oocyte grows larger than the fifteen nurse cells, it becomes clear that this cell is the oocyte. At these stages, very little RNA can be seen in the nurse cells, and the RNA forms a ring around the anterior margin of the developing oocyte (Fig. 6B). This ring increases in size as the follicle grows. During stages 9–10a, large amounts of *bcd* RNA accumulate in the nurse cells (Fig. 6C,D). Unlike other maternal RNAs, *bcd* RNA is not uniformly distributed within the nurse cell cytoplasm, but is concentrated in a peripheral region adjacent to each nurse cell nucleus. During stages 10b and 11, the localization within the nurse cells gradually disappears, as the nurse cells contract and transfer their cytoplasm to the oocyte (Fig. 6E). Upon entering the oocyte, the *bcd* RNA becomes localized to the cortex of the anterior pole. At

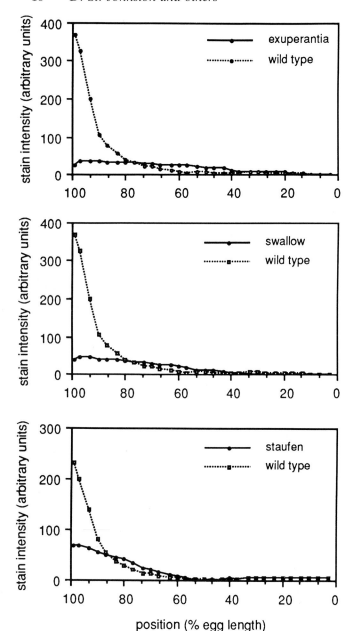

Fig. 5. Distribution of *bcd* mRNA in wild-type embryos and in embryos from females mutant for *exu, sww* and *stau*. The distribution of *bcd* mRNA in early nuclear cycle 13 embryos was visualized and measured as described in the legend to Fig. 3. The RNA distribution profiles of embryos derived from mutant females (solid lines; (A) *exu^PJ/exu^PJ*; (B) *sww^14/sww^14*; (C) *stau^D3/Df(2R) PC4*) were plotted together with those of wild-type embryos (dotted lines; (A and B) wild-type controls stained in parallel to the mutant embryos; (C) wild-type embryos stained in the same batch as the *stau* mutant embryos, which were identified by the lack of polecells).

this stage, the RNA is no longer restricted to a ring around the anterior pole, and instead covers most of the anterior end of the oocyte. By stage 12, when the nurse cells are degenerating, *bcd* RNA is localized in a cap at the anterior end of the egg, with more of the RNA being found ventrally than dorsally (Fig. 6F). During

the final few hours of oogenesis, stages 13 and 14, the follicle cells that surround the oocyte secrete the chorion (King, 1970). We have been unable to analyze *bcd* RNA localization during these stages because the vitelline membrane and chorion prevent the entry of the probe into the oocyte. However, the distribution of the RNA in stage 12 oocytes is different from that observed in very young eggs. In the oocytes, the RNA is localized to the cortex and is more concentrated ventrally, whereas in the early embryo, the RNA is found in a spherical region that extends into the interior of the egg and which is often located slightly dorsally. These differences suggest that there is a redistribution of *bcd* RNA, either during stages 13 and 14 of oogenesis, or immediately after fertilization.

bcd *RNA localization in mutant ovaries*

In order to understand how the mutations that alter the *bcd* RNA distribution in the embryo affect the four phases of RNA localization during oogenesis, we have performed *in situ* hybridizations on *exu, sww* and *stau* mutant ovaries. The earliest differences from wild-type *bcd* RNA localization are observed in *exu* mutant ovaries. The initial accumulation of *bcd* RNA during stages 5–7 occurs normally. As the oocyte increases in size, the RNA still forms a ring at the anterior end, but this ring often appears more diffuse (Fig. 7A). The first major deviation from normal oogenesis becomes apparent during stage 10a, when *bcd* RNA is not localized to the apical regions of the nurse cells, and instead shows a uniform distribution in the nurse cell cytoplasm (Fig. 7B). When this RNA enters the oocyte, it is not retained at the anterior pole, and from stage 10 onwards no localization within the oocyte is visible.

In the ovaries of *sww* homozygous females, the process of *bcd* RNA localization appears entirely normal up to stage 10a. The ring of RNA forms at the anterior end of the oocyte, and RNA accumulates in the apical regions of the nurse cells (Fig. 7C). During stages 10b and 11, the anterior ring of RNA seems to slip posteriorly and become more diffuse (Fig. 7D). In addition, much of the RNA that enters the oocyte during this time is not localized to the cortex. By stage 12, all *bcd* RNA appears to have been released from the cortex and forms a shallow anterior-to-posterior gradient.

In homozygous *stau* ovaries, the process of *bcd* RNA localization appears completely normal up until stage 12 (Fig. 7E,F), the latest stage that we have examined. Since the RNA is distributed in a gradient in early embryos, it must be released from the anterior pole after stage 12 of oogenesis.

Discussion

The experiments presented in this report use a whole-mount *in situ* technique to provide a detailed picture of the process of *bcd* RNA localization during oogenesis and embryogenesis. These results confirm and extend the previous analyses of *bcd* RNA localization, which

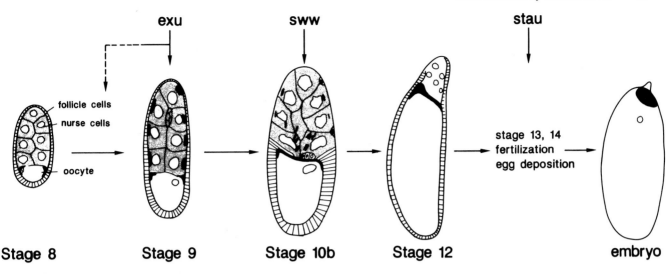

Fig. 8. A drawing showing the four phases of *bcd* RNA localization during oogenesis and the points at which *exu*, *sww*, and *stau* are required. The drawings are based on King (1972).

were performed using radioactive probes on sectioned material (Frigerio *et al.* 1986; Berleth *et al.* 1987; Stephenson *et al.* 1988). The wholemount procedure allows direct comparisons between the *bcd* RNA and protein distributions. As shown in Figs 2 and 3, the two distributions are quite different. Given that no RNA can be detected posterior to 60 % egg length even in overstained embryos, whereas the protein gradient extends at least to 30 % EL, the shape of the protein gradient must depend to some extent on the movement of protein molecules towards the posterior after they have been translated. Simple diffusion of the protein can account for this distribution (Driever and Nüsslein-Volhard, 1988*a*).

The *in situ* hybridizations to embryos derived from *staufen* mutant females reveal that, like *exuperantia* and *swallow*, *staufen* is required for the correct localization of *bcd* RNA to the anterior pole. However, *staufen* mutations only cause a partial mislocalization of *bcd* RNA. The anterior RNA gradient produced by these mutations results in a shallower bcd protein distribution, in which the anterior levels of bcd protein are strongly reduced compared to wild-type, and more posterior levels are slightly increased (Driever and Nüsslein-Volhard, 1988*b*). The anterior reduction in bcd protein concentration accounts for the loss of anterior head structures observed in *staufen* embryos (Schüpbach and Wieschaus, 1986). In addition to the head defects, *staufen* mutations produce a typical posterior group phenotype in which the abdomen is deleted and pole cells do not form. The phenotypes produced in double mutant combinations between *staufen* and other maternal effect mutations strongly suggest that the posterior effects of *staufen* are due to a failure to transport pole plasm constituents to the posterior pole (R. Lehmann, personal communication). Thus the *staufen* gene product is implicated in the localization of maternal factors to both the anterior and posterior poles of the egg.

Based on the geometry of the follicle, Frohnhöfer

and Nüsslein-Volhard (1987) have proposed a simple model for *bcd* RNA localization, in which RNA entering at the anterior end of the oocyte is trapped and attached to the cytoskeleton by factors that are uniformly distributed in the egg. The present data suggest that the process of localization is likely to be more complex. The *in situ* hybridizations to wild-type ovaries reveal at least four phases of *bcd* RNA localization. In the first phase, which extends from stage 6 to early stage 9 of oogenesis, *bcd* RNA is found in a ring at the anterior end of the oocyte. During stages 9–10a, RNA is still found in this ring but *bcd* RNA also accumulates to high levels in the apical regions of the nurse cells. Stephenson *et al.* (1988) have also noticed the nonuniform distribution of *bcd* RNA in the nurse cells of sectioned ovaries. The apical localization of *bcd* RNA within the nurse cells is unusual since all other maternal RNAs that have been examined show a uniform distribution in the nurse cell cytoplasm, and no specialized cytological structures have been observed in these regions (for example Kobayashi *et al.* 1988; Sprenger *et al.* 1989). In the third phase, during stages 10b–12, the nurse cell localization disappears and all *bcd* RNA becomes localized to the cortex at the anterior pole of the egg. A final phase of RNA redistribution must occur after stage 12, to produce the spherical pattern of *bcd* staining seen in early embryos. The *bcd* RNA distributions during these four phases are presented schematically in Fig. 8. The second and fourth phases of *bcd* RNA localization cannot be explained by the simple model, since, during the second phase, the RNA is localized in the nurse cells before it enters the egg, and, in the fourth phase, the RNA is redistributed within the egg.

Since *exu* mutations lead to a uniform distribution of *bcd* RNA in the nurse cell cytoplasm as well as in the oocyte, it seems likely that in wild-type ovaries both localizations occur by similar mechanisms. The apical region of a nurse cell can be considered to be the anterior end of the cell, since it lies on the opposite side of the cell from the ring canals which connect to the other nurse cells and the oocyte. Thus *bcd* RNA may be transiently localized to the anterior ends of the nurse cells in a similar fashion to its localization within the oocyte, suggesting that the nurse cells also possess an intrinsic anterior–posterior polarity. The molecules that are required for *bcd* RNA localization in the oocyte are most probably synthesized in the nurse cells. These molecules could therefore mediate the transient RNA localization within the nurse cells, before they themselves are transported into the oocyte. Since *bcd* RNA is synthesized within the nurse cells, this localization cannot depend upon the polar entry of the RNA into one side of the cell. Thus the localization mechanism can function, at least within the nurse cells, in the absence of an asymmetric source of the RNA. If the process of localization within the egg is similar to that in nurse cells, the anterior accumulation of *bcd* RNA within the oocyte may involve a more active mechanism than the simple trapping of the RNA as it enters at the anterior pole.

None of the mutations examined in this study completely disrupts all phases of *bcd* RNA localization. The earliest phenotypes are seen in *exu* mutant ovaries, in which the RNA does not become restricted to the apical regions of the nurse cells during stages 9–10a. *exu* mutations also seem to have a weak effect on the first phase of *bcd* RNA localization, since the anterior ring often appears more diffuse. Although we have used three different strong *exu* alleles, which all produce the same phenotype, it is possible that none of these is an amorphic mutation. In an *exu* null genotype, even the earliest phase of *bcd* RNA localization might be abolished. Berleth *et al.* (1988) have proposed that the *exu* gene product binds directly to *bcd* RNA, and mediates its attachment to the cytoskeleton. Since *exu* mutations abolish the localization in nurse cells, if *exu* does bind the RNA, it must first do so within the nurse cells. This raises the possibility that *bcd* RNA enters the oocyte as part of a ribonucleoprotein complex that also contains *exu* protein. If this is the case, one might expect *exu* protein to colocalize with *bcd* RNA at the anterior pole of the embryo.

In *sww* mutant ovaries, the third phase of *bcd* RNA localization is disrupted. As Berleth *et al.* (1988) and Stephenson *et al.* (1988) have previously noted, the RNA is gradually released from the cortex of the oocyte during stages 10b–11 of oogenesis. Since *sww* mutations also cause defects in nuclear migration and cellularization during embryogenesis, Frohnhöfer and Nüsslein-Volhard (1987) and Stephenson *et al.* (1988) have suggested that the *swallow* protein is a component of the cytoskeleton. In *sww* mutants, the lack of this protein would cause a destabilization of the cytoskeletal elements that anchor *bcd* RNA to the cortex of the oocyte and lead to a gradual release of the RNA. Our observation that *sww* mutations have no effect on the apical localization of the RNA in nurse cells provide support for the idea that *swallow* encodes an oocyte-specific component of the cytoskeleton.

In *staufen* homozygotes, the process of *bcd* RNA localization appears completely normal up until stage 12 of oogenesis, yet the RNA is not correctly localized in early embryos. The difference between these distributions indicates that the RNA must be released from the anterior pole sometime between stage 12 and egg deposition. This suggests that the *staufen* gene product may be required for the movement of *bcd* RNA from the anterior/ventral cortex to the more dorsally located spherical region observed in early embryos, and provides further evidence for a fourth phase of *bcd* RNA localization. The anterior gradient of RNA observed in *staufen* mutant embryos most probably results from the diffusion of the RNA during a short period of time between its release from the anterior pole and the start of embryogenesis. In general, there is a correlation between the stage at which a mutation affects *bcd* RNA during oogenesis and the distribution of the RNA in embryos. *exu* mutations show the earliest phenotype (stage 9) and result in a uniform distribution in the embryo, *sww* mutations disrupt localization during stages 10–11 and lead to a very shallow embryonic RNA gradient, while *staufen* alleles seem to cause a release of the RNA after stage 12, producing a much steeper gradient at the anterior pole.

This study has identified four phases of *bcd* RNA localization during oogenesis, and has demonstrated that *exu*, *sww*, and *stau* mutations each affect a different stage of this process. At present, we still lack any information on how this localization is achieved at a biochemical or cell biological level. Macdonald and Struhl (1988) have identified a 3' untranslated region of of the *bcd* RNA that is sufficient for localization to the anterior half of the embryo. As the molecular analysis of the *trans*-acting factors involved in this process advances, we may discover how this region of the *bcd* RNA is recognized, and what components of the cytoarchitecture of the oocyte participate in each phase of the localization of *bcd* RNA to the anterior pole.

We thank Maria Leptin, Leslie Stevens, Frank Sprenger and Dominique Ferrandon for their constructive criticisms of the manuscript, and Roswitha Grömke-Lutz and Doris Eder for help with the Figures. This work was supported by an EMBO fellowship to D. St. J, and by the Leibniz program of the Deutsche Forschungsgemeinschaft.

References

BERLETH, T., BURRI, M., THOMA, G., BOPP, D., RICHSTEIN, S., FRIGERIO, G., NOLL, M. AND NÜSSLEIN-VOLHARD, C. (1988). The role of *bicoid* RNA in organizing the anterior pattern of the *Drosophila* embryo. *EMBO J.* **7**, 1749–1756.

CARROLL, S. B., WINSLOW, G. M., SCHÜPBACH, T. AND SCOTT, M. P. (1986). Maternal control of *Drosophila* segmentation gene expression. *Nature, Lond.* **323**, 278–280.

DRIEVER, W. AND NÜSSLEIN-VOLHARD, C. (1988*a*). A gradient of *bicoid* protein in Drosophila embryos. *Cell* **54**, 83–93.

DRIEVER, W. AND NÜSSLEIN-VOLHARD, C. (1988*b*). The *bicoid* protein determines position in the Drosophila embryo in a concentration-dependent manner. *Cell* **54**, 95–104.

DRIEVER, W. AND NÜSSLEIN-VOLHARD, C. (1989). The bicoid protein is a positive regulator of *hunchback* transcription in the early *Drosophila* embryo. *Nature, Lond.* **337**, 138–143.

FRIGERIO, G., BURRI, M., BOPP, D., BAUMGARTNER, S. AND NOLL,

M. (1986). Structure of the segmentation gene *paired* and the Drosophila PRD gene set as part of a gene network. *Cell* **47**, 735–746.

Frohnhöfer, H.-G., Lehmann, R. and Nüsslein-Volhard, C. (1986). Manipulating the anteroposterior pattern of the *Drosophila* embryo. *J. Embryol. exp. Morph.* **97 Supplement** 169–179.

Frohnhöfer, H.-G. & Nüsslein-Volhard, C. (1986). Organization of anterior pattern in the *Drosophila* embryo by the maternal gene *bicoid*. *Nature, Lond.* **324**, 120–125.

Frohnhöfer, H.-G. and Nüsslein-Volhard, C. (1987). Maternal genes required for the anterior localization of *bicoid* activity in the embryo of *Drosophila*. *Genes and Development* **1**, 880–890.

King, R. C. (1970). *Ovarian Development in* Drosophila melanogaster. New York: Academic Press.

Kobayashi, S., Mizuno, H. and Okada, M. (1988). Accumulation and spatial distribution of poly(A)$^+$ RNA in oocytes and early embryos of *Drosophila melanogaster*. *Develop. Growth & Differ.* **30**, 251–260.

Lehmann, R. (1988). Maternal and zygotic control of *Drosophila* segmentation. *Development* **104 Supplement**, 17–27.

Lehmann, R. and Nüsslein-Volhard, C. (1987). *hunchback*, a gene required for segmentation of an anterior and posterior region of the *Drosophila* embryo. *Devl Biol.* **119**, 402–417.

Macdonald, P. M. and Struhl, G. (1988). Cis-acting sequences responsible for anterior localization of *bicoid* mRNA in *Drosophila* embryos. *Nature, Lond.* **336**, 595–598.

Nüsslein-Volhard, C., Frohnhöfer, H.-G. and Lehmann, R. (1987). Determination of anteroposterior polarity in *Drosophila*. *Science* **238**, 1675–1681.

Nüsslein-Volhard, C. and Roth, S. (1989). Axis determination in insect embryos. In *Cellular Basis of Morphogenesis (Ciba Foundation Symposium 144)*, pp. 37–64. Chichester: Wiley.

Schröder, C., Tautz, D., Seifert, E. and Jäckle, H. (1988). Differential regulation of the two transcripts from the *Drosophila* gap segmentation gene *hunchback*. *EMBO J.* **7**, 2881–2887.

Schüpbach, T. and Wieschaus, E. (1986). Maternal-effect mutations altering the anterior-posterior pattern of the *Drosophila* embryo. *Roux's Arch devl Biol.* **195**, 302–317.

Sprenger, F., Stevens, L. M. and Nüsslein-Volhard, C. (1989). The *Drosophila* gene *torso* encodes a putative receptor tyrosine kinase. *Nature, Lond.* **338**, 478–483.

Stephenson, E. C., Chao, Y. and Fackenthal, J. D. (1988). Molecular analysis of the *swallow* gene of *Drosophila melanogaster*. *Genes and Development* **2**, 1655–1665.

Tautz, D. (1988). Regulation of the *Drosophila* segmentation gene *hunchback* by two maternal morphogenetic centres. *Nature, Lond.* **332**, 281–284.

Tautz, D., Lehmann, R., Schnürch, H., Schuh, R., Seifert, E., Kienlin, A., Jones, K. and Jäckle, H. (1987). Finger protein of novel structure encoded by *hunchback*, a second member of the gap class of *Drosophila* segmentation genes. *Nature, Lond.* **327**, 383–389.

Tautz, D. and Pfeifle, C. (1989). A non-radioactive in situ hybridization method for the localization of specific RNAs in *Drosophila* embryos reveals translational control of the segmentation gene *hunchback*. *Chromosoma* **98**, 81–85.

Development 1989 Supplement, 21–29
Printed in Great Britain © The Company of Biologists Limited 1989

Segmental polarity and identity in the abdomen of *Drosophila* is controlled by the relative position of gap gene expression

RUTH LEHMANN* and HANS GEORG FROHNHÖFER†

Max Planck Institut für Entwicklungsbiologie, Tübingen, West Germany

* Present address: Whitehead Institute for Biomedical Research, Nine Cambridge Center, Cambridge, MA 02142, USA
† Department of Genetics, University of Cambridge, Downing Street, Cambridge, CB2 3EH, UK

Summary

The establishment of the segmental pattern in the *Drosophila* embryo is directed by three sets of maternal genes: the anterior, the terminal and the posterior group of genes. Embryos derived from females mutant for one of the posterior group genes lack abdominal segmentation. This phenotype can be rescued by transplantation of posterior pole plasm into the abdominal region of mutant embryos. We transplanted posterior pole plasm into the middle of embryos mutant either for the posterior, the anterior and posterior, or all three maternal systems and monitored the segmentation pattern as well as the expression of the zygotic gap gene *Krüppel* in control and injected embryos. We conclude that polarity and identity of the abdominal segments do not depend on the relative concentration of posterior activity but rather on the position of gap gene expression. By changing the pattern of gap gene expression, the orientation of the abdomen can be reversed. These experiments suggest that maternal gene products act in a strictly hierarchical manner. The function of the maternal gene products becomes dispensable once the position of the zygotically expressed gap genes is determined. Subsequently the gap genes will control the pattern of the pair-rule and segment polarity genes.

Key words: *Drosophila* embryo, segmental pattern, zygotic genes, maternal genes.

Introduction

The anterior–posterior pattern in the *Drosophila* egg is initially evident both in specialized structures of the egg cell covers and within the cytoplasm. Characteristic specializations of the chorion include the dorsal appendages and micropyle at the anterior end and the aeropyle at the posterior end of the egg. Within the egg cytoplasm at the posterior pole are the polar granules which are determinants of the germ line fate (Mahowald, 1962). As development proceeds, additional pattern is established as segments of the embryo become arranged into functional units such as the head, thorax and abdomen. Each segment subsequently acquires a polarized pattern as rows of denticles appear at the anterior margin of each segment followed by a region of naked cuticle. The anterior and posterior ends of the embryo do not develop segmental characteristics, but rather specialized structures referred to as the acron and telson at each end respectively.

The establishment and maintenance of the polar pattern in the embryo is directed by a genetic pathway whose principles can be summarized as follows (for review see Akam, 1987; Ingham, 1988; Nüsslein-Volhard *et al.* 1987): the basic information for the embry-onic pattern is provided by maternal genes. Mutations in these genes affect the development of specific regions of the embryo. By and large, these mutations interfere only with the embryonic pattern without disturbing the pattern of the extra-embryonic egg covers. On the basis of their phenotype the maternal genes can be grouped into three sets: the anterior group that affects the development of the head and thorax; the posterior group that affects the development of the abdomen; and the terminal group that affects the most anterior (acron) and most posterior (telson) structures. Maternal gene products provided by the mother and stored in the egg cell are required for the spatial regulation of transcription of the first genes expressed by the embryo, the gap genes.

The gap genes are expressed in nonrepetitive domains and the products of neighboring gap genes are thought to overlap at the borders (U. Gaul *et al.* in preparation). Several different types of experiments indicate that gap gene expression is controlled both by the products of the maternal genes described above and by the products of the gap genes themselves. First, the phenotype of mutations in gap genes resembles the phenotype of mutations in the maternal genes (for review see Lehmann, 1988). Second, mutations in one gap gene affect expression of other gap genes (Jäckle *et al.* 1986). Accordingly, the maternal anterior system controls the zygotic expression of the gap gene *hunchback* (*hb*) in the anterior half of the embryo (Tautz, 1988), the maternal posterior system affects expression of *knirps* (*kni*) in the prospective abdominal region (Nauber *et al.* 1988), and the maternal terminal system regulates the activity of the gap gene *tailless* (*tll*) at the termini (Klingler *et al.* 1988). Later in development, the polar arrangement of individual segments is established by the patterned expression of pair-rule and segment polarity genes (for review see Ingham, 1988; Ingham and Gergen, 1988).

What are the mechanisms that establish the polarity described above? Do the maternal gene products directly control the expression of gap genes, pair-rule genes and segment polarity genes, or are the maternal gene products at the top of a hierarchy in which the only genes they control directly are the gap genes? Presently, most of our information comes from studies of the gene, *bicoid (bcd)*, involved in development of the anterior pattern. *Bicoid* encodes an RNA that is highly concentrated at the anterior end of the egg (Berleth *et al.* 1988). The product of this RNA is a homeo-domain containing protein that is distributed in an anterior–posterior gradient (Driever and Nüsslein-Volhard, 1988). The *bcd* protein activates transcription by binding to the promoter of the gap gene *hb* (Driever and Nüsslein-Volhard, 1989). Activation of hb is dependent on the concentration of the *bicoid* protein and consequently the *hb* gene is activated only in the anterior half of wild-type embryos (Struhl *et al.* 1989; Driever *et al.* 1989). These experiments show that the anterior system controls gap gene expression directly by transcriptional activation. However, these experiments do not resolve whether the anterior system operates as a hierarchical system or whether the maternal genes also directly control the expression of pair-rule and segment polarity genes.

A key gene within the posterior group of genes is *nanos* (*nos*) (Nüsslein-Volhard *et al.* 1987; Nüsslein-Volhard and Lehmann in preparation). Genetic experiments argue that transcriptional activation of the gap gene *kni* by *nos* involves *hb* (Hülskamp *et al.* 1989; Irish *et al.* 1989; Struhl, 1989). In addition to the zygotic *hb* expression which is under the transcriptional control of *bcd*, *hb* is also expressed maternally. The distribution of the maternal *hb* product is controlled by the posterior system. *nos* does not affect the transcription of the maternal product but seems to interfere with the stability and/or translation of the maternal *hb* product such that *hb* is absent from the posterior region of the embryo. Loss of *nos* function results in uniform, rather than anterior, distribution of maternal *hb* RNA and protein (Tautz, 1988). The abnormally high *hb* concentration within the posterior half of the embryo is correlated with the suppression of transcription of *kni* (Nauber *et al.* 1988). Finally embryos that are derived from a germ line deficient for the *nos* and *hb* products can develop a normal segmental pattern suggesting a normal pattern of *kni* expression. This leaves us with

the question of how, in the absence of posterior maternal information, a normal abdominal segmentation pattern develops. One hypothesis is that the distribution of gap gene expression plays a critical role in the establishment of the segmental pattern independently of maternal information. According to this hypothesis, maternal genes would act in a strict hierarchical manner and maternal information would become dispensable, once the gap gene expression pattern is established. This hypothesis was tested by transplanting posterior pole plasm into embryos of different genetic backgrounds. We show that the polarity and identity of the posterior segments can be determined by the autonomous action of gap genes.

Polarity and identity of posterior pattern does not depend on the relative concentration of posterior activity

Embryos derived from females homozygous for any one of the posterior group genes lack all abdominal segmentation, while the head, thorax and telson develop normally (Boswell and Mahowald, 1985; Schüpbach and Wieschaus, 1986, 1989; Lehmann and Nüsslein-Volhard, 1986, 1987). The abdominal phenotype of posterior group mutants can be completely rescued by injection of wild-type cytoplasm into mutant embryos (Lehmann and Nüsslein-Volhard, 1986, 1987, and in preparation). Only posterior pole plasm is active and best rescue is achieved when posterior pole plasm is transplanted into the prospective abdominal region. The site of localization, the posterior pole, is separated from the prospective abdominal region by the telson, whose development is under the control of the terminal genes. After transplantation of posterior pole plasm into the middle of the embryo, a normal anteroposterior pattern of abdominal segmentation is restored (Fig. 1B,C). Since at the site of injection the normal orientation of abdominal segments is retained, we conclude that posterior activity can not control the abdominal pattern in a concentration-dependent manner. It is more likely that a certain threshold of posterior activity is required for segmentation to occur, but that the orientation of segments within the segmented region is established independently. In the case of *bcd*, on the other hand, a direct quantitative relationship between pattern and concentration has been shown (Frohnhöfer and Nüsslein-Volhard, 1986): injection of high amounts of anterior cytoplasm into the anterior pole of embryos derived from *bcd* females leads to the development of head structures, while lower concentrations give rise to thoracic structures.

Polarity of posterior pattern depends on anterior and terminal information

Although normal pattern requires all three maternal systems, some pattern can be generated in the presence of only one or two of the systems. The precise type of pattern that develops, however, depends upon which maternal systems are active. This point is addressed by injection of posterior pole plasm into the middle of *bcd, nos* embryos, which lack both anterior and posterior information, or by injection into *bcd, nos,torsolike (tsl)* mutant embryos, which lack all three systems of maternal information (Fig. 1). *tsl* is a maternal gene and a member of the terminal group (Frohnhöfer, 1987).

If left uninjected, embryos derived from *bcd, nos* females will develop two telsons in mirror image, due to the presence of the terminal system (Fig. 1D, Nüsslein-Volhard *et al.* 1987). Embryos derived from triple mutant *bcd, nos, tsl* females develop no anterior–posterior pattern (Fig. 1G). After injection of posterior pole plasm into the middle of the double or triple mutant embryos, abdominal segments are formed in mirror image. The polarity of the mirror image depends on the maternal genotype. In *bcd, nos* embryos the duplicated sets of segments are formed in a posterior–anterior–posterior (P–A–P) orientation such that the posterior segments (A8) are juxtaposed to the two telsons (Fig. 1E). After injection into *bcd, nos, tsl* embryos, however, the embryos develop the reverse mirror image with abdominal segments oriented toward the middle and the more anterior abdominal segments formed at both ends (A–P–A, Fig. 1H). These findings indicate that, although posterior activity is crucial for the establishment of segmentation within the abdominal region, the anterior–posterior polarity of the segments depends upon additional positional information. Since parts of the normal abdominal pattern can be established in the absence of anterior and terminal maternal systems, it is possible that this additional positional information is encoded by gap genes.

Polarity of the abdomen can be predicted by the pattern of gap gene expression within the embryo

Three gap genes, *hb*, *Kr*, and *kni* have been characterized on the molecular level and the distribution of their RNA and protein patterns have been described. During the early syncytial blastoderm stages, *hb* is found within the anterior 50 % of the embryo (for RNA: Tautz *et al.* 1987, for protein: Tautz, 1988) *Kr* is found between 40 % and 55 % egg length (for RNA: Knipple *et al.* 1985, for protein: Gaul *et al.* 1987), and *kni* is expressed between 30 % and 45 % egg length (for RNA: Nauber, 1988) (0 % = posterior pole). Although the distribution of the *tll* product has not been determined, genetic evidence suggests that *tll* is active at the anterior and posterior ends of the embryo (Strecker *et al.* 1986; Klingler *et al.* 1988). Thus, the following anterior–posterior order of gap gene expression would be predicted: *tailless, hunchback, Krüppel, knirps* and *tailless* (Fig. 3B). (All gap genes analyzed so far have additional domains of expression which have been omitted from this discussion.)

To test the idea that neighboring gap genes may determine the orientation of the abdominal segments in the embryo, we analyzed the pattern of gap gene expression in different mutant backgrounds. These experiments allowed us to interpret changes in the segmentation as a consequence of changes in gap gene juxtaposition. As in the previous experiments, posterior pole plasm was injected into the middle of mutant embryos. We studied changes in *Kr* expression in embryos lacking either the posterior, the anterior and posterior, or all three systems of maternal information. We also examined the pattern of the *Kr* protein after injection of posterior pole plasm into embryos of these different maternal backgrounds. When embryos had reached the appropriate developmental stage, the distribution of *Kr* protein was detected with anti-*Krüppel* antibodies (Fig. 2A,B). The results of this study, and of studies by others (Gaul and Jäckle, 1987), indicate that all maternal systems act negatively on the expression of *Kr*. In uninjected *nos* mutant embryos *Kr* protein extends further posteriorly than in wildtype (Fig. 2C). In the double mutant *bcd, nos* embryos, the *Kr* domain is expanded anteriorly as well as posteriorly (Fig. 2E). Finally in the triple mutant, *Kr* is expressed homogeneously throughout the embryo (Fig. 2G). Injection of posterior pole plasm into mutant embryos leads to the suppression of *Kr* at the site of injection. After injection into a *nos* mutant embryo, the *Kr* domain narrows, and resembles the domain of *Kr* expression found in wildtype embryos (Fig. 2D). After injection into the *bcd nos* double mutant, *Kr* is completely suppressed from the middle region in some embryos, while in other embryos weak staining remains (Fig. 2F). After injection of posterior activity into the triple mutants, *Kr* expression is confined to both ends of the embryo (Fig. 2H).

In our injection experiments, we monitored the distribution of *Kr* protein but not the expression pattern of the other gap genes. In order to reconstruct the approximate pattern of different gap genes in injected embryos, we extrapolated the pattern of the other gap genes from previous experiments (Gaul and Jäckle, 1987; Tautz, 1988; Nauber *et al.* 1988). Since injection of posterior pole plasm into the middle of a *nos* mutant embryo (Fig. 3A) can restore the wildtype pattern, it seems likely that the expression pattern of all gap genes in such an embryo resembles that of the wildtype. We therefore infer that the injection of posterior pole plasm will activate *kni* expression at the site of injection. A normal orientation of the segmental pattern would thus require that the *kni* domain be bordered anteriorly by *Kr* and posteriorly by *tll* (Fig. 3B). After injection into the *bcd nos* double mutant, *Kr* is suppressed and *kni* is presumably expressed throughout the central region. Thus the *kni* domain must be flanked by the *tll* domains at either end (Fig. 3D). The juxtaposition of *kni* and *tll* would lead to a P–A–P pattern duplication (cf. Fig. 1E). Finally, after injection into a triple mutant embryo, *Kr* is suppressed in the central region and *kni* is presumably expressed in this region. In contrast to the previous experiment, in these mutant embryos *kni* must be flanked by *Kr* whose expression remains at the ends (Fig. 3F). This order of *kni* and *Kr* expression would lead to an A–P–A pattern (cf. Fig. 1H) in accordance

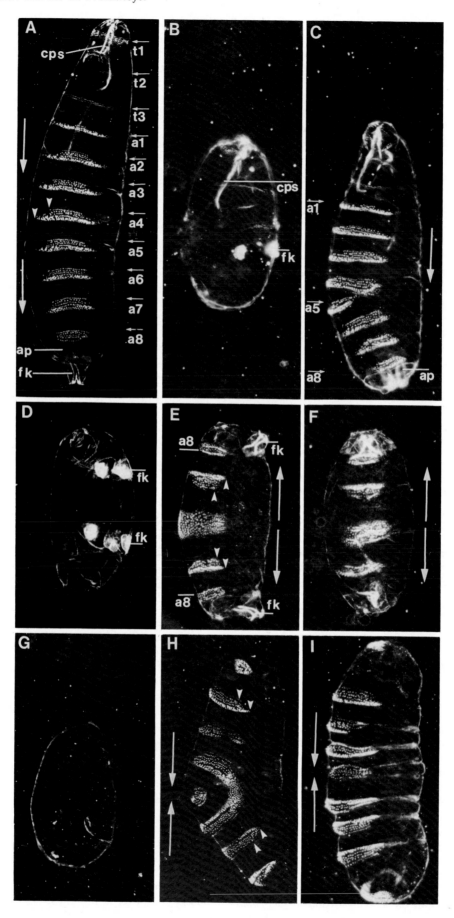

Fig. 1. Cuticle preparations of control and injected embryos. (A) Wildtype embryo. Polarity within each abdominal segment is manifested by the shape of the denticle band located at the anterior margin of each segment. Within each band the more anterior rows of denticles are narrower than the more posterior ones (small arrows, for description of wildtype pattern refer to Lohs-Schardin *et al.* 1979). (B) Control embryo derived from a female homozygous mutant for *nos^L7^*. No abdominal segmentation is formed but head, thorax and telson are normal. (C) Rescued *nos* embryo. After injection this embryo formed an almost complete set of abdominal segments in normal anteroposterior orientation. (D) Control embryo, derived from a female mutant for *bcd^E1^* and *nos^L7^*. This embryo received only maternal information provided by the terminal system. Two telsons in mirror image are formed. (E) *bcd,nos* embryo after injection. Two abdomens in mirror image are formed. The orientation of the denticle bands and the characteristics of the eighth abdominal segment indicate the orientation and character of the segments (see arrows). (F) Injected embryo derived from female homozygous for *bcd, nos* and heterozygous for *tll^L10^*. This embryo resembles that in E. It is phenotypically wildtype for *tll* and thus did develop a normal telson. An uninjected embryo of this genotype shows the same phenotype as the embryo in D. (G) Embryo derived from female homozygous mutant for *bcd^E1^*, *nos^L7^*, *tsl^146^*. This embryo developed a cuticle but no segmental pattern. Some embryos of this maternal genotype form a field of denticles normally found in the abdominal region. The denticles point medially. Dorso-ventral polarity seems unaffected in these embryos since they form a ventral furrow which spans the entire anterior–posterior axis. (H) Injected embryo of the same maternal genotype as embryo in G. Orientation of segments is reverse from that of embryo in E and F. The most anterior abdominal segments are formed toward the ends. In some embryos of the same genotype, the two terminal segments show the characteristics of an A1 abdominal segment. (I) Embryo of the same maternal genotype as embryo in F but homozygous for *tll*. The pattern of this embryo is very similar to the embryo in H. Four and half anterior abdominal segments are formed in mirror image with the most anterior structures towards the ends. Uninjected embryos of this genotype can not be distinguished from embryos lacking all maternal information on the basis of their cuticle phenotype. They differ, however, since *tll* embryos (in contrast to *tsl* embryos) form a labrum and a posterior midgut (Strecker *et al.* 1986). Orientation of embryos: anterior up in A,B,C. The orientation of embryos shown in D–I is arbitrary since the anterior–posterior orientation of the egg cannot be reconstructed after the chorion and vitelline membrane have been removed. Ventral is to the left, except for embryos in A and F where a frontal view on ventral side is shown. Arrows mark the orientation of segments and point in anterior–posterior direction. Arrowheads indicate the polarity of a single band of denticles. ap, anal plate; a1–8, abdominal segments 1–8; cps, cephalo-pharyngeal skeleton; fk, Filzkörper; t1–3, thoracic segments 1–3.

Methods: embryos were injected as previously described (Lehmann and Nüsslein-Volhard, 1986). Injection was carried out with posterior pole plasm from wildtype donors into the middle of mutant recipients. To test whether the presence of anterior or terminal activity in the donor embryos influenced the injection result, we injected *bcd, nos, tsl* and *bcd, nos* embryo with posterior pole plasm from embryos derived from homozygous *bcd, tsl* females. Although injection of high dosage of cytoplasm into the triple mutant embryo can lead to the induction of Filzkörper material (H.G. Frohnhöfer unpubl.), a structure characteristic of the telson, under the conditions used in the experiments described, we could not detect any difference between injections with wildtype or mutant cytoplasm. After injection, embryos were left to develop at 18°C for 48 h and their cuticles were prepared according to van der Meer, 1977.

The cuticle of about 50 embryos was examined for each genotype. In one of the *bcd, nos, tll* experiments we examined 53 cuticles; 42 embryos had developed telson structures and thus were not mutant for *tll*. Of these, 36 developed abdominal segments, 24 embryos showed clear symmetric or asymmetric mirror image duplications as described in the text and shown in Fig. 1. In a few exceptional cases, where only very few abdominal segments (3–4 total) were formed, the opposite orientation of the denticle bands was observed. This suggests that *Kr* expression was not completely suppressed after injection. 11 embryos developed no telson and were thus mutant for *tll*, 10 of these developed abdominal segments and all but one of these showed symmetric or asymmetric duplications of the abdomen. The orientation was always (A–P–A) as described in the text. In summary, of the examined cuticles 20 % were mutant for tll which is slightly less than the expected 25 % and may be due to the fact that not-rescued *bcd, nos, tll* embryos are very fragile and some may have been lost during cuticle preparation.

---

with the more anterior expression of *Kr* in the normal pattern.

The expression of *kni* together with either *tll* or *Kr* seems sufficient to promote the formation of some part of the abdomen. The cooperation of either pair of gap genes determines both the polarity and the identity of the abdominal segments. If *tll* is juxtaposed to *kni*, a posterior–anterior mirror-image duplication of the posterior abdomen (A8–A4/5–A8, c.f. Fig. 1E) is formed. Juxtaposition of *kni* with *Kr* on the other hand results in an anterior–posterior mirror-image duplication of the anterior abdomen (A1/2–A4/5–A1/2, c.f. Fig. 1H). Thus the polarity as well as the identity of each abdominal segment is controlled coordinately by inter-actions among gap genes and their products. This suggests that the relative position of the domains of gap gene expression establishes the pattern of homeotic gene expression, which determines the identity of each segment (White and Lehmann, 1986; Irish *et al.* 1989).

Polarity of the abdomen can be determined without maternal information

To test whether changes in the relative position of the domains of gap gene products do indeed affect polarity independently of maternal information, we injected embryos of identical maternal genotype but which differed in their zygotic genotype. Females homozygous

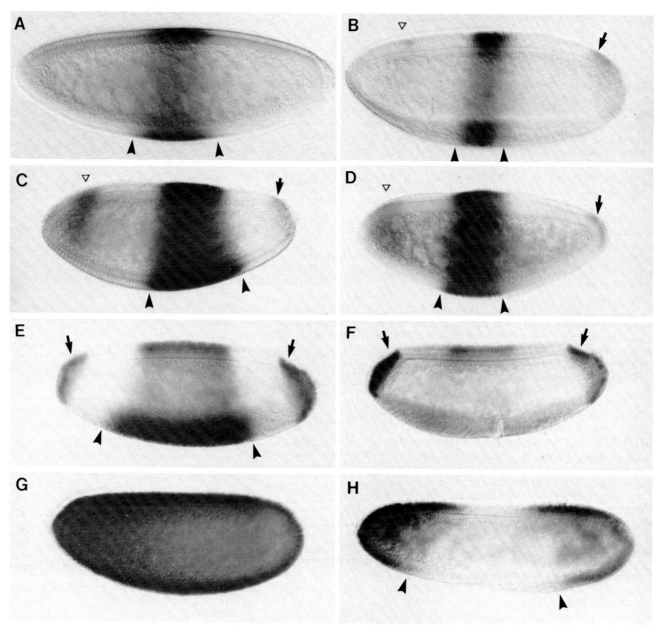

for *bcd* and *nos* and heterozygous for the zygotic lethal gene *tll* were crossed with heterozygous *tll* males. While all of the progeny lacked anterior and posterior maternal information, a quarter of these embryos were homozygous mutant for *tll* and lacked telson structures. Injection into embryos from this cross resulted in two phenotypes. The majority of embryos developed duplications of the posterior abdomen in P–A–P orientation. As described for *bcd nos* embryos (Fig. 1F) this indicates that *kni* is flanked by *tll* and *Kr* expression is suppressed. One quarter of the embryos, the *tll* embryos, developed anterior duplications of abdominal segments in the A–P–A orientation. As described for injected *bcd, nos, tsl* embryos (Fig. 1I) we infer that in these embryos *kni* is flanked by *Kr*. This result indicates that abdominal polarity is established according to the spatial arrangement of gap gene expression. In the

wildtype, however, the different maternal genes ensure the correct positioning of the gap genes and thus ensure normal polarity.

Discussion and Conclusions

A hierarchical system of pattern formation

The activity of the posterior group genes is required for the normal expression pattern of zygotic segmentation genes (Gaul and Jäckle, 1987; Carroll *et al.* 1986; Lehmann, 1988). Cytoplasmic transplantation experiments suggested that posterior activity is distributed in a gradient with its source at the posterior end (Lehmann and Nüsslein-Volhard, 1986). It might have been conceivable that at a given position along the anterior–posterior axis the concentration of posterior activity

Fig. 2. Expression pattern of *Kr* protein in control and injected embryos. (A) Wildtype embryo in late syncytial blastoderm stage (nuclear cycle 14, Foe and Alberts, 1983, stage 4 according to Campos-Ortega and Hartenstein, 1985). *Kr* is expressed in a domain between 55 and 40 % egg length. (0 % egg length=posterior pole). (B) Wildtype embryo at the beginning of gastrulation, stage 6. Central *Kr* domain has narrowed, new *Kr* expression appears in the anterior (open triangles) and at the posterior (arrow). (C) Embryo derived from homozygous *nos* female at nuclear cycle 14, stage 5. The central domain of *Kr* is extended posteriorly (57–27 % egg length). Anterior (open triangles) and posterior domain (arrow) are normal. (D) Injected *nos* embryo of similar age as embryo in C. The central domain of *Kr* is reduced in comparison to uninjected embryo (60–41 %). (E) Control embryo derived from *bcd, nos* female at onset of gastrulation (stage 6). The central *Kr* domain is extended toward anterior and posterior to 68 and 31 % egg length, respectively. At both ends a posterior midgut forms which is marked by the posterior *Kr* domain (arrow). (F) Injected embryo of same maternal genotype and developmental stage as embryo in E. This embryo shows no expression of *Kr* in the central domain ventrally and only slight expression dorsally. In this context it is worth mentioning that injections were carried out by introducing the injection needle into the dorsal side in order to deposit the cytoplasm ventrally. (G) Embryo derived from triple mutant females (*bcd, nos, tsl*) at cellular blastoderm (late nuclear cycle 14, stage 5). Central domain of *Kr* is expressed homogeneously throughout the embryo. (H) Embryo of same maternal genotype and stage as embryo in G. *Kr* is only expressed at the ends. We interpret this expression as remnants of the extended central domain. Similar to the embryo in F, suppression of *Kr* is stronger ventrally than dorsally after injection of posterior activity. Similar results to those shown in E–H were obtained with embryos derived from females homozygous for *bcd,nos* and heterozygous for *tll* crossed to *tll* heterozygous males. Methods: embryos of maternal and zygotic genotypes as described above were injected as described in Fig. 1. When most embryos had reached the late cellular blastoderm–early gastrula stage, embryos were fixed in paraformaldehyde for antibody staining. We chose to stop development at this stage since the posterior domain of *Kr* expression can be used as an internal control for the preparation. Embryos were manually freed from the vitelline membrane and incubated with anti-*Kr* antibody. A biotinylated secondary anti-rabbit antibody was detected histochemically as described by McDonald and Struhl (1986). After dehydration embryos were embedded in Araldite.

would specify the segmental pattern and its orientation. However, this study suggests that the posterior group genes do not control the polarity of the segmental pattern in a concentration-dependent manner. Indeed, we can show that, irrespective of the maternal genotype, the polarity of the abdominal segments depends on the presence or absence of the zygotic gap gene *tll*. Our data do not rule out that the expression of other yet unknown gap genes is important for abdominal segmentation as well. We would predict that in different genetic backgrounds the pattern of expression of such genes would be altered coordinately with *kni* and *Kr*.

Our conclusions may not be limited to the posterior system: double mutants between *exuperantia* which affects the localization of *bicoid* RNA (Berleth *et al.* 1988) and mutants which affect the posterior system result in mirror image duplications of anterior segments (Schüpbach and Wieschaus, 1986). The polarity and identity of the pattern elements formed seem independent of the orientation of the *bicoid* gradient (Struhl *et al.* 1989) and may thus be directed by the relative position of gap gene expression. These findings may suggest that all maternal systems act in a strict hierarchical manner, such that once the domains of gap gene expression have been established, maternal information becomes dispensable.

It is not clear how the pattern of gap gene expression is translated into the repetitive transverse stripes of pair-rule and segment polarity gene expression. It is conceivable from the experiments presented here that a particular combination of two gap genes initiates the expression of a given stripe of a pair-rule gene. In a particular region, however, the relative concentration of a single gap gene product may be critical for the expression of a particular pair-rule gene stripe. Indeed, the medial abdominal segments (A3–A6) are most sensitive to reduction in *kni* activity. According to the fate map, the domain of *kni* expression (between 30 % and 45 % egg length, Nauber, 1988) gives rise to the primordia of segments A3–A5 (Lohs-Schardin *et al.* 1979). Thus a direct correlation can be established between the development of the medial abdominal segments and the domain of *kni* expression.

Pattern formation without maternal information

The activation of *kni* by the posterior group genes is indirect and mediated by the negative effect of posterior activity upon *hb*. In wildtype embryos, the maternal *hb* product is distributed in a shallow anterior–posterior gradient. This gradient depends on posterior activity (Tautz, 1988) and small changes in posterior activity are reflected in changes in the fate map (Lehmann, 1988). In the absence of posterior activity, the maternal *hb* product is evenly distributed in the embryo. This even distribution of maternal *hb* product permits an extension of the *Kr* domain posteriorly while *kni* expression is completely suppressed (Tautz, 1988; Nauber *et al.* 1988). The expression of the gap genes *Kr* and *kni* may thus be very sensitive to changes in the *hb* gradient within the abdominal region. Since the concentration of maternal *hb* product is quite low in comparison to the concentration of the zygotic product, low concentrations of *hb* may have a positive influence on *Kr* expression while high concentrations of *tll* have a negative effect on *Kr* expression (Jäckle *et al.* 1986).

A direct positive influence of *hb* upon *Kr* may also account for the establishment of a normal pattern in the absence of the maternal *hb* product. As we have shown, the proper position of the domain of *Kr* expression is critical for the establishment of normal polarity. Therefore, knowledge of the mechanisms by which the positions of *Kr* and *kni* expression are controlled in these embryos is critical to understand how normal

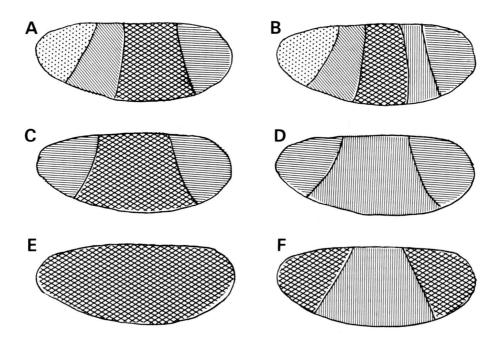

Fig. 3. Schematic presentation of hypothetical expression domains of gap genes in control and injected embryos. This scheme illustrates that the reversal in orientation of the abdominal segments in *bcd*, *nos* and *bcd*, *nos*, *tsl* embryos can be attributed to the pattern of gap gene expression produced after injection (c.f. Figs 3D, 1E and 2F with Figs 3F, 1H and 2H.). (A) Control *nos* mutant embryo. (B) Wild type pattern (expected to be similar to that of rescued embryo). (C) Control *bcd*, *nos* mutant embryo. (D) Injected *bcd*, *nos* mutant embryo. (E) Control *bcd*, *nos*, *tsl* mutant embryo. (F) Injected *bcd*, *nos*, *tsl* embryo. Stipple: in this anterior domain *hb* and *tll* and a hypothetical terminal gap gene (Martin Klingler and Detlef Weigel per. com.) are thought to be active. Diagonal lines: *hb* domain. Cross hatch: *Kr* domain. Vertical lines: *kni* domain. Horizontal lines: domain where *tll* and the hypothetical terminal gap gene are expressed. Note that the actual patterns of expression have so far only been described for *hb*, *kni* and *Kr*. Overlaps between gap gene products and the graded distribution of individual gap gene products have not been considered in this presentation. The domains of the most terminal areas (marked with stipples and with horizontal lines respectively) are based on genetic and developmental evidence and may not represent regions where a single gap gene is expressed or where its product is active.

polarity is established in the absence of maternal *nos* and *hb* products. At present we can only speculate. Perhaps low levels of zygotic *hb* product are sufficient to activate *Kr* and repress *kni* in the anterior abdominal region and thereby set up an asymmetry in the expression of the two gap gene products. Alternatively, it is conceivable that a low concentration of *bcd* activates *Kr* while a high concentration of *bcd* inhibits *Kr*. Although attractive, this model seems unlikely since, in the absence of *bcd*, *Kr* is expressed (Gaul and Jäckle, 1987 and this study). Analysis of this model and other models will require a more detailed understanding of the mechanisms that control *kni* and *hb* expression in the early embryo.

R.L. would like to thank Steve Burden for encouragement and help, Anne Ephrussi, Doug Barker, Francisco Pelegri and Charlotte Wang for criticism on the manuscript and Aji Kron for help with word processing. We are thankful to Ulrike Gaul and Herbert Jäckle for the anti-*Krüppel* antibody. R.L. acknowledges the support received while at the MRC Laboratory of Molecular Biology, Cambridge, UK.

References

Akam, M. (1987). The molecular basis for metameric pattern in the *Drosophila* embryo. *Development* **101**, 1–22.

Berleth, T., Burri, M., Thoma, G., Bopp, D., Richstein, S., Frigerio, G., Noll, M. and Nüsslein-Volhard, C. (1988). The role of localization of *bicoid* RNA in organizing the anterior pattern of the *Drosophila* embryo. *EMBO J.* **7**, 1749–1756.

Boswell, R. E. and Mahowald, A. P. (1985). *tudor*, a gene required for assembly of the germ plasm in *Drosophila melanogaster*. *Cell* **43**, 97–104.

Campos-Ortega, J. A. and Hartenstein, V. (1985). *The Embryonic Development of* Drosophila melanogaster. *Springer-Verlag*, Heidelberg.

Carroll, S., Winslow, G., Schüpbach, T. and Scott, M. (1986). Maternal control of *Drosophila* segmentation gene expression. *Nature, Lond.* **323**, 278–280.

Driever, W. and Nüsslein-Volhard, C. (1988). A gradient of *bicoid* protein in *Drosophila* embryos. *Cell* **54**, 83–93.

Driever, W. and Nüsslein-Volhard, C. (1989). The *bicoid* protein is a positive regulator of *hunchback* transcription in the early *Drosophila* embryo. *Nature, Lond.* **337**, 138–143.

Driever, W., Thoma, G. and Nüsslein-Volhard, C. (1989). Determination of spatial domains of zygotic gene expression in the *Drosophila* embryo by the affinity of binding sites for the *bicoid* morphogen. *Nature, Lond.* **340**, 363–367.

Foe, V. E. and Alberts, B. M. (1983). Studies of nuclear and cytoplasmic behaviour during the five mitotic cycles that precede gastrulation in *Drosophila* embryos. *J. Cell Sci.* **61**, 31–70.

Frohnhöfer, H. G. (1987). Ph.D. Thesis, Universität Tübingen.

Frohnhöfer, H. G. and Nüsslein-Volhard, C. (1986). Organization of anterior pattern in the *Drosophila* embryo by the maternal gene *bicoid*. *Nature, Lond.* **324**, 120–125.

Gaul, U. and Jäckle, H. (1987). Pole region-dependent repression of the *Drosophila* gap gene *Krüppel* by maternal gene products. *Cell* **51**, 549–555.

GAUL, U., SEIFERT, E., SCHUH, R. AND JÄCKLE, H. (1987). Analysis of *Krüppel* protein distribution during early *Drosophila* development reveals posttranscriptional regulation. *Cell* **50**, 639–647.

HÜLSKAMP, M., SCHRÖDER, C., PFEIFLE, C., JÄCKLE, H. AND TAUTZ, D. (1989). Posterior segmentation of the *Drosophila* embryo in the absence of a maternal posterior organizer gene. *Nature, Lond.* **338**, 629–632.

INGHAM, P. AND GERGEN, P. (1988). Interactions between the pair-rule genes *runt, hairy, even-skipped* and *fushi tarazu* and the establishment of periodic pattern in the *Drosophila* embryo. *Development* **104 Supplement**, 51–60.

INGHAM, P. W. (1988). The molecular genetics of embryonic pattern formation in *Drosophila*. *Nature, Lond.* **335**, 25–34.

IRISH, V., LEHMANN, R. AND AKAM, M. (1989). The *Drosophila* posterior-group gene *nanos* functions by repressing *hunchback* activity. *Nature, Lond.* **338**, 646–648.

IRISH, V., MARTINEZ-ARIAS, A. AND AKAM, M. (1989). Spatial regulation of the *Antennapedia* and *Ultrabithorax* homeotic genes during *Drosophila* early development. *EMBO J.* **8**, 1527–1537.

JÄCKLE, H., TAUTZ, D., SCHUH, R., SEIFERT, E. AND LEHMANN, R. (1986). Cross-regulatory interactions among the gap genes of *Drosophila*. *Nature, Lond.* **324**, 668–670.

KLINGLER, M., ERDELYI, M., SZABAD, J. AND NÜSSLEIN-VOLHARD, C. (1988). Function of *torso* in determining the terminal anlagen of the *Drosophila* embryo. *Nature, Lond.* **335**, 275–277.

KNIPPLE, D., SEIFERT, E., ROSENBERG, U., PREISS, A. AND JÄCKLE, H. (1985). Spatial and temporal patterns of *Krüppel* gene expression in early *Drosophila* embryos. *Nature, Lond.* **317**, 40–44.

LEHMANN, R. (1988). Phenotypic comparison between maternal and zygotic genes controlling the segmental pattern of the *Drosophila* embryo. *Development* **104 Supplement**, 17–27.

LEHMANN, R. AND NÜSSLEIN-VOLHARD, C. (1986). Abdominal segmentation, pole cell formation, and embryonic polarity require the localized activity of *oskar*, a maternal gene in *Drosophila*. *Cell* **47**, 141–152.

LEHMANN, R. AND NÜSSLEIN-VOLHARD, C. (1987). Involvement of the *pumilio* gene in the transport of an abdominal signal in the *Drosophila* embryo. *Nature, Lond.* **329**, 167–170.

LOHS-SCHARDIN, M., CREMER, C. AND NÜSSLEIN-VOLHARD, C. (1979). A fatemap for the larval epidermis of *Drosophila melanogaster*: localized cuticle defects following irradiation of the blastoderm with an UV-laser microbeam. *Devl Biol.* **73**, 239–255.

MACDONALD, P. M. AND STRUHL, G. (1986). A molecular gradient in early *Drosophila* embryos and its role in specifying the body pattern. *Nature, Lond.* **324**, 672–675.

MAHOWALD, A. P. (1962). Fine structure of pole cells and polar granules in *Drosophila melanogaster*. *J. exp. Zool.* **151**, 201–215.

NAUBER, U. (1988). Ph.D. Thesis Universität Tübingen.

NAUBER, U., PANKRATZ, M., KIENLIN, A., SEIFERT, E., KLEMM, U. AND JÄCKLE, H. (1988). Abdominal segmentation of the *Drosophila* embryo requires a hormone receptor-like protein encoded by the gap gene *knirps*. *Nature, Lond.* **336**, 489–492.

NÜSSLEIN-VOLHARD, C., FROHNHÖFER, H. G. AND LEHMANN, R. (1987). Determination of anteroposterior polarity in *Drosophila*. *Science* **238**, 1675–1681.

SANDER, K. AND LEHMANN, R. (1988). *Drosophila* nurse cells produce a posterior signal required for embryonic segmentation and polarity. *Nature, Lond.* **335**, 68–70.

SCHÜPBACH, T. AND WIESCHAUS, E. (1986). Maternal-effect mutations altering the anterior-posterior pattern of the *Drosophila* embryo. *Roux's Arch devl Biol.* **195**, 302–317.

SCHÜPBACH, T. AND WIESCHAUS, E. (1989). Female sterile mutations on the second chromosome of *Drosophila melanogaster*. I. Maternal effect mutations. *Genetics* **121**, 101–117.

STRECKER, T., KONGSUWAN, K., LENGYEL, J. AND MERRIAM, J. (1986). The zygotic mutant *tailless* affects the anterior and posterior ectodermal regions of the *Drosophila* embryo. *Devl Biol.* **113**, 64–76.

STRUHL, G. (1989). Differing strategies for organizing anterior and posterior body pattern in *Drosophila* embryos. *Nature, Lond.* **338**, 741–744.

STRUHL, G., STRUHL, K. AND MACDONALD, P. (1989). The gradient morphogen *bicoid* is a concentration-dependent transcriptional activator. *Cell* **57**, 1259–1273.

TAUTZ, D. (1988). Regulation of the *Drosophila* segmentation gene *hunchback* by two maternal morphogenetic centres. *Nature, Lond.* **332**, 281–284.

TAUTZ, D., LEHMANN, R., SCHNURCH, H., SCHUH, R., SEIFERT, E., KIENLIN, A., JONES, K. AND JÄCKLE, H. (1987). Finger protein of novel structure encoded by *hunchback*, a second member of the gap class of *Drosophila* segmentation genes. *Nature, Lond.* **327**, 383–389.

VAN DER MEER, S. (1977). Optical clean and permanent whole mount preparation for phase contrast microscopy of cuticular structures of insect larvae. *Dros. Inf. Service* **52**, 160.

WHITE, R. AND LEHMANN, R. (1986). A gap gene, *hunchback*, regulates the spatial expression of *Ultrabithorax*. *Cell* **47**, 141–152.

Development 1989 Supplement, 31–36 (1989)
Printed in Great Britain © The Company of Biologists Limited 1989

The process of localizing a maternal messenger RNA in *Xenopus* oocytes

JOEL K. YISRAELI, SERGEI SOKOL and D. A. MELTON

Department of Biochemistry and Molecular Biology, Harvard University, Cambridge, MA 02138, USA

Summary

The maternal mRNA Vg1 is localized to the vegetal pole during oogenesis in *Xenopus*. We have cultured oocytes *in vitro* to begin to understand how this localization occurs. Endogenous Vg1 mRNA undergoes localization when oocytes are cultured *in vitro*, and synthetic Vg1 mRNA injected into such oocytes is localized in the same fashion. Vg1 mRNA is associated with a detergent-insoluble fraction from homogenized oocytes, suggesting a possible cytoskeletal association. The use of cytoskeletal inhibitors reveals a two-step process for localizing Vg1 mRNA. Microtubule inhibitors such as nocodazole and colchicine inhibit the localization of Vg1 mRNA in late stage III/early stage IV oocytes, but have no effect on Vg1 mRNA once it is localized. The microfilament inhibitor cytochalasin B, however, has little effect on the translocation of Vg1 mRNA in middle-stage oocytes but causes a release of the message in late-stage oocytes. We propose a model for the localization of Vg1 mRNA in which translocation of the message to the vegetal cortex is achieved via cytoplasmic microtubules and the anchoring of the message at the cortex involves cortical microfilaments.

Key words: Vg1, TGF-β, RNA localization, polarity, microtubules, microfilaments, *Xenopus*.

Introduction

Xenopus oocytes have a clearly defined animal–vegetal (a–v) polarity. In previtellogenic oocytes, the mitochondrial cloud and the chromosomal attachment site in the germinal vesicle (gv) define a polarity that is proposed to be the future a–v axis (Al-Mukhtar and Webb, 1971; Heasman *et al.* 1984). Pigment granules migrate to the animal hemisphere in middle-stage, vitellogenic oocytes (Dumont, 1972), followed by the asymmetric deposition of dense yolk platelets in the vegetal hemisphere (Danilchik and Gerhart, 1987). Around this same time, the germinal vesicle migrates to near the animal pole from its location in the center of the oocyte. After fertilization, the dorsal–ventral axis is generated orthogonally to the a–v axis (Vincent and Gerhart, 1987), and it is along these primary axes that the germ layers become defined.

In addition to these morphological markers, numerous molecular asymmetries exist (see Gerhart, 1979). In particular, a small class of RNAs have been identified which are unevenly distributed in oocytes and eggs (Rebagliati *et al.* 1985; King and Barklis, 1985). The best studied of these RNAs is Vg1, a vegetally localized mRNA whose protein product is a member of the TGF-β family (Weeks and Melton, 1987). Vg1 is initially synthesized in previtellogenic oocytes and is uniformly distributed until the oocyte reaches the end of stage III (Melton, 1987). By the middle of stage IV, Vg1 mRNA is found almost exclusively in a tight shell at the vegetal cortex (Melton, 1987; Yisraeli and Melton, 1988). The

RNA is released from its tight localization after maturation but remains in the vegetal hemisphere, presumably as a result of cellularization, throughout embryogenesis (Weeks and Melton, 1987).

We are interested in understanding how polarity is generated and interpreted in oocytes and eggs. By culturing oocytes *in vitro*, we have been able to analyze and interfere with the localization of Vg1 mRNA. Injected, *in vitro* synthesized Vg1 mRNA can be localized in cultured oocytes in a manner identical to the localization of the endogenous message, suggesting that all the information necessary for proper localization is encoded by the RNA itself. Insoluble pellets of detergent extracts of oocytes, which maintain most of the cytoskeletal elements of the cell, preferentially retain Vg1 mRNA. Using cytoskeletal inhibitors in middle- and late-stage oocytes, we have been able to distinguish two separate steps in the translocation process. The movement of Vg1 RNA to the vegetal hemisphere is inhibited by drugs which depolymerize microtubules, but not by those that affect microfilaments. Anchoring of the Vg1 mRNA, however, can be disrupted by microfilament inhibitors, but not microtubule inhibitors. Thus, at least in the case of Vg1 RNA, the oocyte utilizes common cytoskeletal elements to help generate specific asymmetries in the cell.

Endogenous Vg1 mRNA is localized in cultured oocytes

Large oocytes cultured in the presence of vitellogenin-

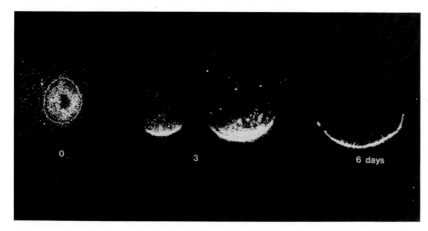

Fig. 1. Localization of endogenous Vg1 mRNA in cultured oocytes. Oocytes were grown in Leibowitz medium supplemented with vitellogenin-containing frog serum as previously described (Yisraeli and Melton, 1988). After the indicated time in culture, the oocytes were fixed and hybridized with a Vg1 probe made to the coding region (Melton, 1987; Yisraeli and Melton, 1988). In these dark-field photographs, silver autoradiographic grains appear white.

containing serum continue to grow and incorporate vitellogenin (Wallace *et al.* 1980). In order to make use of this *in vitro* system for our studies, it was important to show that smaller oocytes retained their ability to localize endogenous Vg1 message in culture. As shown in figure 1, oocytes grown *in vitro* in the presence of frog serum containing vitellogenin localize endogenous Vg1 mRNA in the same pattern as oocytes grown *in vivo*. Oocytes incubated in either saline or medium without serum demonstrate no localization of the endogenous mRNA (data not shown). Only those oocytes grown in the presence of vitellogenin increase in diameter, a result of micropinocytosis of vitellogenin, the precursor for the yolk proteins (Wallace *et al.* 1970). *In situ* hybridization to oocytes of different stages (Melton, 1987; Yisraeli and Melton, 1988; unpublished observations) suggests that localization of Vg1 RNA occurs within a small window of oogenesis between the end of stage III and the middle of stage IV. *In vivo*, this period of growth probably requires several weeks to a month (Keem *et al.* 1979). Oocytes cultured under the conditions described here grow at least three to four times faster. Nevertheless, the progressive accumulation of Vg1 mRNA along the vegetal cortex coupled with the graded loss of the mRNA from the cytoplasm in an animal-to-vegetal direction is identical *in vivo* and *in vitro*.

Localization of exogenous Vg1 mRNA

The endogenous, steady-state level of Vg1 mRNA remains constant from previtellogenesis until after maturation (Melton, 1987). In addition, as mentioned above, localization of Vg1 mRNA occurs in a particular pattern, regardless of whether that movement takes five to six days or three to four weeks. Finally, the accumulation of Vg1 message at the vegetal cortex is accompanied by a graded disappearance of message, first in the animal hemisphere and then throughout the oocyte, as opposed to a general loss of message everywhere. These observations suggested that the localization of Vg1 mRNA is not the result of specific degradation of the message away from the vegetal cortex, but rather the accumulation of Vg1 message at its proper location. In order to explore this possibility

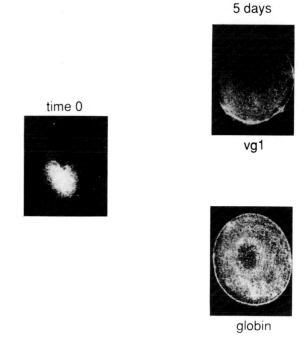

Fig. 2. Localization of exogenous *in vitro* synthesized Vg1 mRNA injected into oocytes. Capped, radioactively labeled Vg1 and globin transcripts were synthesized as described (Krieg and Melton, 1987). Oocytes injected with message were cultured as above for 5 days. *time 0*, the initial site of injection; *5 days*, oocytes injected with the indicated message fixed after 5 days in culture.

further, and to begin to determine how the specificity of localization is achieved, we synthesized Vg1 and globin RNAs in the presence of both radioactively labelled UTP and GpppG (a cap analog whose incorporation at the 5′ end of synthetic RNA transcripts prevents 5′ exonucleolytic degradation). Late stage III oocytes injected with synthetic Vg1 message were capable of localizing the exogenous message when cultured in vitellogenin-containing serum for five days (figure 2). The kinetics and pattern of this localization are virtually identical to those of the endogenous message and the fact that the injected RNA is relatively stable throughout the entire incubation period further argues that localization is not due to degradation or differential stability (Yisraeli and Melton, 1988). Injected globin RNA, however, becomes distributed throughout both the animal and vegetal hemispheres over the course of the culture period. The information necessary for the specific localization of Vg1 mRNA is thus present in the naked Vg1 RNA molecule itself. Studies are now under way to define further the *cis*-acting sequences which are involved in the process. Initial studies using a deleted Vg1 RNA lacking 62 nucleotides from the 5′ end, including the start codon and putative signal sequence, have shown that this region is not necessary for the proper localization of the RNA (Yisraeli and Melton, 1988).

Association of Vg1 mRNA with the detergent-insoluble fraction of oocyte extracts

The striking distribution of Vg1 mRNA at the vegetal cortex suggested that cytoskeletal elements might be involved in its anchoring. A large number of RNAs have been shown to be associated with a detergent-insoluble fraction of extracts from different cells, a fraction that has been shown to contain cytoskeletal elements such as microtubules, microfilaments, and various intermediate filaments (e.g. Lenk *et al.* 1977; Jeffery, 1984). If Vg1 message is specifically associated with the cytoskeleton in these late-stage oocytes one would expect that Vg1 but not non-localized RNAs would be associated with the detergent-insoluble pellet. As shown in figure 3, Vg1 mRNA is highly associated with the cytoskeletal pellet, with less than 10 % of the total Vg1 mRNA in the soluble fraction. This association is not a result of non-specific trapping, because fibronectin mRNA, which is approximately twice the size of the Vg1 message, is found almost exclusively in the soluble fraction. Less than 2 % of the total oocyte poly(A)+ RNA is found in the detergent-insoluble pellet, and equal oocyte equivalents of pellet and soluble RNA are compared on the gel. Translatability of a message appears not to be important for its association with the cytoskeletal pellet because Vg1, fibronectin, and several other RNAs are all translated in oocytes but only Vg1 mRNA is found in the pellet (data not shown). These results are similar to those recently reported by Pondel and King (1988).

Microtubule and microfilament involvement at different stages of the localization process

The above results suggested that Vg1 mRNA is associated with cytoskeletal elements at the cortex in late-stage oocytes. In order to determine what these elements are and how they are interacting with Vg1 mRNA, we treated late-stage oocytes with various cytoskeletal inhibitors overnight and then looked at the localization of the Vg1 message by *in situ* hybridization. Cytochalasin B treatment, which depolymerizes microfilaments, had a dramatic effect on the distribution of Vg1 mRNA, releasing it from its tight shell and

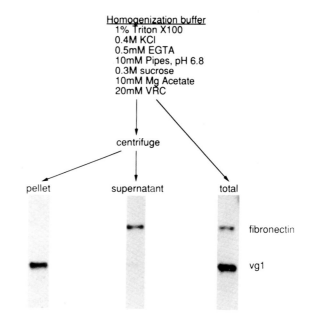

Fig. 3. Attachment of Vg1 mRNA to the detergent-insoluble pellet of extracts. Stage V/VI oocytes were homogenized in the indicated buffer at room temperature. After removing an aliquot and extracting the RNA (*total RNA*), the homogenate was centrifuged and RNA was prepared separately from the supernatant (*soluble*) and insoluble (*pellet*) fractions and analyzed by Northern blot hybridization. The positions of fibronectin and Vg1 messages on the blot are indicated at right. The RNA from two oocytes prepared in this way was run in each lane.

allowing it to diffuse (fig. 4); this distribution is very similar to that observed in unfertilized eggs (Weeks and Melton, 1987). Nocodazole and colchicine, drugs that bind tubulin and cause depolymerization of microtubules, have no effect on the localization of Vg1 message (fig. 4 and data not shown). Interestingly, analysis of the partitioning of RNA in detergent extracts of the treated oocytes only partially reflects the effects of the drugs. As expected from the *in situ* results, nocodazole treatment does not affect the association of Vg1 mRNA with the cytoskeletal pellet (fig. 4). Cytochalasin B treatment, however, despite releasing Vg1 mRNA from its cortical localization, has only a slight effect on Vg1 mRNA distribution in extracts. Presumably, although the depolymerization of microfilaments in late-stage oocytes allows Vg1 mRNA to diffuse away from the cortex, the mRNA remains bound with other factors that may cause it to be pelleted during the detergent extraction.

The experiments with late-stage oocytes address the question of how Vg1 mRNA is tethered at the vegetal cortex. To look at how the message is translocated to this site, we studied the effects of the cytoskeletal inhibitors on middle-stage oocytes undergoing localization. Cytochalasin B had little if any effect on the translocation of Vg1 mRNA, although the message seemed to accumulate further from the cortex than in untreated oocytes (fig. 5). Nocodazole, however, completely inhibits localization (fig. 5), and colchicine has

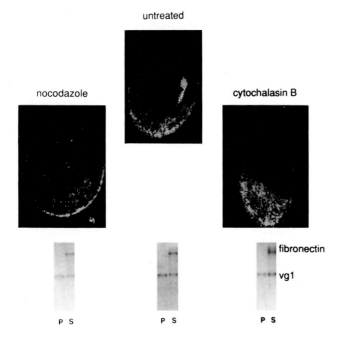

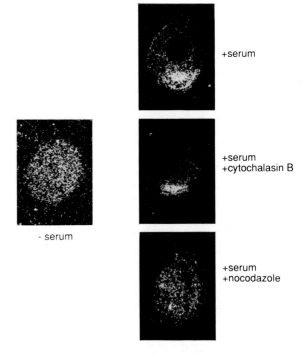

Fig. 4. Effect of cytoskeletal inhibitors on Vg1 mRNA in late-stage oocytes. Stage V/VI oocytes were incubated in saline (*untreated*), cytochalasin B (25 μg ml^{-1}, *cytochalasin B*), or nocodazole (10 μg ml^{-1}, *nocodazole*) overnight at 20°C and then analyzed by *in situ* hybridization for the localization of Vg1 mRNA. In addition, detergent extracts of the oocytes were performed for each treatment and the corresponding Northern blots are shown below each section. *p*, pellet; *s*, soluble fraction.

Fig. 5. Effect of cytoskeletal inhibitors on Vg1 mRNA in middle-stage oocytes. Late stage III oocytes were cultured for 5 days in the presence of medium and serum alone (*+serum*), medium and serum with cytochalasin B (*+serum +cytochalasin B*), and medium and serum with nocodazole (*+serum +nocodazole*). *In situ* hybridization visualized the location of the Vg1 mRNA in the oocyte sections. At left is a section from an oocyte cultured in medium alone for 5 days, showing no localization whatsoever (*−serum*).

an identical effect (data not shown). None of the drug treatments had any effect on the stability of Vg1 mRNA or on the synthesis of protein over the five day culture period (data now shown). All of the drugs severely inhibited growth of the oocytes in culture, perhaps by inhibiting the uptake of vitellogenin from the medium. Nonetheless, Vg1 mRNA was translocated in cytochalasin B-treated oocytes, indicating that growth and translocation are independent and separable phenomena, and that the inhibition of translocation by microtubule inhibitors is not a result of the lack of growth of the oocyte.

Discussion

The data presented here demonstrate that microtubule and microfilament inhibitors have different and stage-specific effects on the Vg1 localization machinery. The simplest model to explain these results is the two-step process diagrammed in figure 6, with microtubules involved in the translocation process and microfilaments involved in anchoring the message at the cortex. Although the data described above appear to argue against a specific degradation or instability of non-localized Vg1 mRNA, it is hard to distinguish between active, as opposed to passive, movement of Vg1 mRNA. The graded disappearance of Vg1 message during its localization both *in vivo* and *in vitro* in the

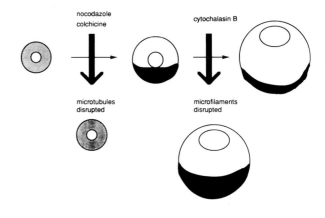

Fig. 6. A two-step model for the localization of Vg1 mRNA in oocytes. The horizontal arrows indicate the normal process of oogenesis, with the black dots and black shading indicating the location of Vg1 mRNA and its progressive localization. The larger, vertical arrows show where the various cytoskeletal inhibitors are thought to interrupt this process and point to the results of treating oocytes with these drugs. Thus, translocation of the Vg1 mRNA to the vegetal cortex is thought to be associated with microtubules and the anchoring of the message is thought to involve microfilaments.

animal to vegetal direction may be the result of an active localization of the message. Alternatively, reversible binding of Vg1 mRNA to a membrane-bound receptor would result in the same 'window shade' effect, even if movement of the mRNA were passive. The apparent involvement of microtubules in the translocation of the message may indicate an active movement of the message. A number of different types of cell make use of microtubule-mediated motors to actively direct the transport of macromolecules and organelles (see Vale, 1987). Indeed, calculated rates for slow axonal transport, which is mediated by microtubules, are similar to the estimated rate of localization of the Vg1 mRNA *in vitro* (0·1 mm/day; Lasek, 1982). Alternatively, however, microtubules may act simply as 'highways' or tracks, expediting the otherwise random movement of Vg1 mRNA without actually propelling it.

The model in figure 6 implies that cytoplasmic microtubules are disrupted in middle-stage oocytes by nocodazole or colchicine, and that cortical microfilaments are depolymerized by cytochalasin B in late-stage oocytes. Microtubule arrays begin to form early in oogenesis; tubulin staining appears first perinuclearly and then in radial arrays extending completely around the oocyte from the germinal vesicle (gv) to the cortex (Palecek *et al.* 1985; Dent and Klymkowsky, 1988; manuscript in preparation). As oogenesis proceeds and the gv migrates to the animal hemisphere, the microtubule arrays become less easily detectable in the vegetal hemisphere but remain radially aligned, emanating from the gv to the animal cortex. In both middle- and late-stage oocytes, these arrays are depolymerized by nocodazole and colchicine. Microfilaments, by comparison, appear mainly along the cortex early in oogenesis and remain there until maturation, when there is a reorganization of cytoskeletal elements throughout the oocyte (Franke *et al.* 1976; Dent and Klymkowski, 1988). Thus, the temporal and spatial organization of microtubules and microfilaments is precisely what would be expected from the two-step localization scheme outlined in figure 6.

The association of Vg1 mRNA with the detergent-insoluble fraction of extracts from late-stage oocytes is consistent with the release of Vg1 mRNA after cytochalasin B treatment. A similar detergent extract of oocytes has been shown to contain significant amounts of several intermediate filament proteins (Pondel and King, 1988), although there is no evidence at present for any Vg1 mRNA association with these proteins. The data presented here clearly indicate that Vg1 mRNA is somehow associated with microfilaments in the cortex but do not rule out interactions with other proteins as well. The association of Vg1 mRNA with the cytoskeletal pellet even in oocytes where the message has been released from its tight cortical shell by cytochalasin B may suggest a continued association of other detergent-insoluble proteins with the message. Presumably, the specificity for the localization process is a combination of the presence of *cis*-acting signals in the RNA itself, specific factors that recognize these sequences, and the cytoskeletal framework within which the RNA moves and is anchored properly. By more precisely defining the RNA signals and identifying the cytoskeletal elements involved in the localization, it should be possible more fully to understand how oocytes generate and interpret intracellular polarity.

References

AL-MUKHTAR, K. K. & WEBB, A. C. (1971). An ultrastructural study of primordial germ cells, oogonia, and early oocytes in *Xenopus laevis*. *J. Embryol. exp. Morph.* **26**, 195–217.

DANILCHIK, M. V. & GERHART, J. C. (1987). Differentiation of the animal-vegetal axis in *Xenopus laevis* oocytes: I. Polarized intracellular translocation of platelets establishes the yolk gradient. *Devl Biol.* **122**, 101–112.

DENT, J. A. & KLYMKOWSKY, M. W. (1988). Wholemount analyses of cytoskeletal reorganization and function during oogenesis and early embryogenesis in *Xenopus*. In *The Cell Biology of Fertilization* (eds H. Shatten and G. Shatten). Academic Press, Orlando Fl.

DUMONT, J. N. (1972). Oogenesis in *Xenopus laevis* (Daudin). I. Stages of oocyte development in laboratory maintained animals. *J. Morph.* **136**, 153–180.

FRANKE, W. W., RATHKE, P. C., SEIB, E., TRENDELENBURG, M. F., OSBORN, M. & WEBER, K. (1976). Distribution and mode of arrangement of microfilamentous structures and actin in the cortex of the amphibian oocyte. *Cytobiologie* **14**, 111–130.

GERHART, J. C. (1979). Mechanisms regulating pattern formation in the amphibian egg and early embryo. In *Biological Regulation and Development*. R. F. Goldberger, ed. New York, Plenum Press.

HEASMAN, J., QUARMBY, J. & WYLIE, C. C. (1984). The mitochondrial cloud of *Xenopus* oocytes: the source of germinal granule material. *Devl Biol.* **105**, 458–489.

JEFFERY, W. R. (1984). Spatial distribution of messenger RNA in the cytoskeletal framework of ascidian eggs. *Devl Biol.* **103**, 482–492.

KEEM, K., SMITH, L. D., WALLACE, R. A. & WOLF, D. (1979). Growth rate of oocytes in laboratory-maintained *Xenopus laevis*. *Gamete Res.* **2**, 125–135.

KING, M. L. & BARKLIS, E. (1985). Regional distribution of maternal messenger RNA in the amphibian oocyte. *Devl Biol.* **112**, 203–212.

KRIEG, P. A. & MELTON, D. A. (1987). *In Vitro* RNA synthesis with SP6 RNA polymerase. *Methods in Enzymology* **155**, 397–415.

LASEK, R. J. (1982). Translocation of the neuronal cytoskeleton and axonal locomotion. *Philos. Trans. R. Soc. Lond.* **29**, 313–327.

LENK, R., RANSOM, L., KAUFMANN, Y. & PENMAN, S. (1977). A cytoskeletal structure with associated polyribosomes obtained from HeLa cells. *Cell* **10**, 67–78.

MELTON, D. A. (1987). Translocation of a localized maternal mRNA to the vegetal pole of *Xenopus* oocytes. *Nature* **328**, 80–82.

PALECEK, J., HABROVA, V., NEDVIDEK, J. & ROMANOVSKY, A. (1985). Dynamics of tubulin structures in *Xenopus laevis* oogenesis. *J. Embryol. exp. Morph.* **87**, 75–86.

PONDEL, M. & KING, M. L. (1988). Localized maternal mRNA related to transforming growth factor β mRNA is concentrated in a cytokeratin-enriched fraction from *Xenopus* oocytes. *Proc. natn. Acad. Sci. USA* **85**, 7612–7616.

REBAGLIATI, M. R., WEEKS, D. L., HARVEY, R. P. & MELTON, D. A. (1985). Identification and cloning of localized maternal RNAs from *Xenopus* eggs. *Cell* **42**, 769–777.

VALE, R. D. (1987). Intracellular transport using microtubule-based motors. *A. Rev. Cell Biol.* **3**, 347–378.

VINCENT, J.-P. & GERHART, J. C. (1987). Subcortical rotation in *Xenopus* eggs: An early step in embryonic axis specification. *Devl Biol.* **113**, 484–500.

WALLACE, R. A., JARED, D. W. & NELSON, B. W. (1970). Protein incorporation by isolated amphibian oocytes I. Preliminary studies. *J. exp. Zool.* **175**, 259–270.

WALLACE, R. A., MISULOVIN, Z. & WILEY, H. S. (1980). Growth of anuran oocytes in serum-supplemented medium. *Reprod. Nutr. Develop.* **20**, 699–708.

WEEKS, D. L. & MELTON, D. A. (1987). A maternal mRNA localized to the vegetal hemisphere in *Xenopus* eggs codes for a growth factor related to TGF-β. *Cell* **51**, 861–867.

YISRAELI, J. K. & MELTON, D. A. (1988). The maternal mRNA Vg1 is correctly localized following injection into *Xenopus* oocytes. *Nature, Lond.* **336**, 592–595.

Development 1989 Supplement, 37–51 (1989)
Printed in Great Britain © The Company of Biologists Limited 1989

Cortical rotation of the *Xenopus* egg: consequences for the anteroposterior pattern of embryonic dorsal development

J. GERHART, M. DANILCHIK, T. DONIACH, S. ROBERTS, B. ROWNING and R. STEWART

Department of Molecular Biology, University of California, Berkeley CA 94720 USA

Summary

We first review cortical–cytoplasmic rotation, a microtubule-mediated process by which the *Xenopus* egg, like other amphibian eggs, transforms its polarized cylindrical symmetry into bilateral symmetry within the first cell cycle after fertilization. This transformation, the earliest of many steps leading to dorsal development, involves the displacement of the egg's cortex relative to its cytoplasmic core by 30° in an animal–vegetal direction. As rotation is progressively reduced by microtubule-depolymerizing agents, embryos develop with body axes progressively deleted for dorsal structures at the anterior end. With no rotation, ventralized embryos are formed. In an effort to comprehend this progressive effect on embryonic organization, we go on to review subsequent developmental processes depending on rotation, and we propose, with evidence, that reduced rotation leads to a reduced number of vegetal dorsalizing cells, which induce during the blastula stage a Spemann organizer region of smaller than normal size. The reduced organizer then promotes a reduced amount of cell rearrangement (morphogenesis) at gastrulation. Reduced morphogenesis seems the proximate cause of the incompleteness of axial pattern, as shown further by the fact that embryos that are normal until the gastrula stage, if exposed to inhibitors of morphogenesis, develop body axes that are progressively less complete in their anterior dorsal organization the earlier their gastrulation had been blocked. We discuss why axial pattern might depend systematically on morphogenesis.

Key words: cortical rotation, *Xenopus laevis*, mesoderm induction, microtubules, gastrulation, polarity, FGF, TGFβ, anteroposterior pattern, dorsoventral pattern, lithium, D₂O, organizer.

I. Organization and reorganization of the egg:

The egg's initial symmetry arises in oogenesis

The unfertilized *Xenopus* egg displays polarized cylindrical symmetry around an axis connecting the poles of the animal and vegetal hemispheres (these hemispheres henceforth abbreviated as AH and VH). The two hemispheres differ as the result of various localization mechanisms segregating materials during oogenesis, perhaps in relation to the oocyte's inherent axis comprising the nucleus, centrosome and division bridge (Tourte *et al.* 1984; Wylie *et al.* 1985; Danilchik & Gerhart, 1987; Yisraeli *et al.* this volume). The boundary between hemispheres (the 'equator') is roughly identified externally as the limit of dark pigment of the animal half, although this marking may not quite coincide with the internal interface of materials specific to the two hemispheres. Oocyte organization corresponds roughly to the germ layer organization of the embryo: ectodermal tissues arise from AH materials, endodermal tissues from VH materials, and mesoderm and archenteron roof endoderm from equatorial materials (reviewed in Gerhart & Keller, 1986).

All pole-to-pole meridians of the egg surface are indistinguishable before fertilization. Sperm can be applied at any point in the animal hemisphere (Elinson, 1980; K. Hara, unpublished; J. Gerhart, unpublished), and that point of entry identifies a meridian that coincides approximately but not perfectly with the eventual ventral midline of the embryo. The opposite meridian falls on the dorsal midline of the embryo, or more correctly, on the midline of the neural plate. Many experiments, some discussed later, indicate that the egg has an initial capacity to develop dorsally at any, several, or even all, meridians, and the same is true of ventral development. Normal embryonic development arises from the proportioned, patterned use of this potential, normally in relation to the sperm entry point.

Bilateralization of the egg after fertilization

The *Xenopus* egg reorganizes its cytoplasmic contents in an interval between 45 and 90 min after fertilization, a G₂-like period of the first cell cycle (100 min, 18°C), a period absent from the next 11 or 12 rapid cycles (35 min each). Within this interval, the egg behaves as if composed of two rigid units, a thin cortex (2–5 μm thick) and a large spherical core (1200 μm diameter). As diagrammed in Fig. 1, these *rotate* relative to one

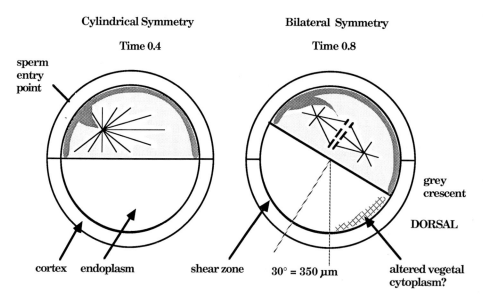

Fig. 1. Reorganization of the *Xenopus* egg cytoplasm by cortical rotation. On the left is shown a schematic cross section of an egg at time 0·4 (40% of the first cell cycle, lasting approximately 100 min at 18 °C), before cortical rotation has occurred. The sperm has entered at the left, forming a large aster and migrating towards the egg's center. The egg's cortex is shown as a rigid peripheral unit, 2–5 μm in depth, containing the plasma membrane, cortical actin, and materials that will travel with it during rotation. The core is shown as a rigid spherical unit, 1200 μm in diameter, containing yolk platelets and most cytoplasmic contents of the egg. Note that the cortex and core both differ in their animal and vegetal portions. Prior to rotation, the two units are in register along all pole-to-pole meridians, and the egg has polarized cylindrical symmetry.

On the right is shown an egg cross-section at time 0·8, after cortical rotation has occurred. The egg surface has been immobilized during rotation, and the core has undergone the entire displacement of 30° of arc, which is 350 μm of linear distance. The core has rotated in an animal–vegetal direction, downward on the right and upward on the left, separated from the cortex by a shear zone a few microns thick. The rotation axis is at the center of the section, pointing out of and into the page. Rotation destroys cylindrical symmetry and generates bilateral symmetry: contacts between core and cortical materials differ now on the right and left. Downward movement on the right activates dorsal development; the future dorsal embryonic midline will coincide with the meridian of greatest displacement. The opposite movement (on the left side of the section) has no consequence for dorsal development; ventral development ensues on the left side, but this kind of development occurs even without rotation. It is not known what cytoplasmic modifications are directly caused on the right side by rotation. They presumably occur in the shear zone or at the contact sites between the two rigid units, perhaps just in the vegetal hemisphere, but perhaps in both hemispheres. Some amphibian eggs (e.g. *Rana* but not *Xenopus*) show a grey crescent at the equatorial level; these species have black pigment in the animal hemisphere cortex and grey pigment in the animal hemisphere core. Where the core rotates downward, grey pigment can be seen as a crescent through the pigmentless vegetal cortex. The grey crescent may have importance for dorsal development (there is no convincing evidence of this, except for topographic correlation) or it may just be a convenient marker of the time and direction of cortical rotation.

If the egg were free to orient in the gravitational field (as when floating in pond water), the core would remain in gravitational equilibrium, weighted by its dense vegetal yolk platelets, and the cortex would undergo the entire displacement.

another in an animal–vegetal direction, for 30° of arc, (a distance of 350 μm) around a new axis perpendicular to the animal–vegetal axis. Movement can be observed by marking the cortex or core with dye spots (Nile blue, fluorescent lectins, photobleached fluoresceinated yolk proteins; see Vincent *et al.* 1986) or by tracking at high magnification the few pigment granules embedded in the core's vegetal surface (Rowning, 1989). It accelerates from rest to full speed (8 μm min^{-1}) within 7 min, remains almost constant for 40 min, and then abruptly stops. Spot patterns remain sharp and coherent for at least an hour, demonstrating the rigidity of the cytoplasm and cortex. The two units just seem to glide over one another, separated by a shear zone of less than 5 μm in depth. If the cortex is immobilized, as is the case for eggs embedded in gelatin or agarose (as in Fig. 1), the core makes all the displacement, even though work

must be done to lift its dense vegetal yolk mass out of gravitational equilibrium. If the cortex is free to move, as is the case for an egg floating in a pond, it makes all the displacement while the cytoplasmic core remains in gravitational equilibrium.

By this simple geometrical operation, the cylindrical symmetry of the egg transforms into bilateral symmetry (Fig. 1). Animal–vegetal organization is systematically modified by the slippage of concentric layers. Displacement is greatest on the midlines of rotation and decreases to zero at the rotation poles (located at opposite positions on the equator). On one rotation midline, the core moves in a vegetal direction relative to the cortex, or stated identically, the cortex moves animalward relative to the core. This midline coincides accurately (±10°) with the embryo's dorsal midline (Vincent *et al.* 1986). On the other rotation midline, which coincides with the embryonic ventral midline, displacement has the opposite sense, and, as discussed later, this sense has no consequence for development since ventral development occurs even without rotation. The ventral midline just seems by default the farthest position from the dorsal midline.

This reorganization process has received many names: subcortical rotation, the rotation of symmetrization or cortical/cytoplasmic rotation. We will call it cortical rotation for brevity. It was first inferred by Banki in 1929 for axolotl eggs and described in detail by Ancel & Vintemberger (1948) for *Rana fusca* eggs, who recognized it as the process forming the grey crescent, a lightly pigmented subequatorial region marking the embryo's future dorsal side, including its organizer region. Cortical rotation has also been inferred in *Rana pipiens* eggs from grey crescent formation and from displacement of the polar body spot (Elinson, 1980). Rotation was not detected in *Xenopus* eggs until our studies with artificially marked eggs because *Xenopus* eggs rarely form a grey crescent; this is simply because the pigment granules reside entirely in the core during rotation. Probably most amphibian eggs make use of cortical rotation, as do the eggs of some fish (ancient groups such as lungfish and sturgeons) which display grey crescents and complete cleavage.

Cortical rotation correlates well with embryonic dorsoventral organization

Rotation is normally oriented toward the sperm entry point (SEP), as is the dorsoventral organization of the embryo. Løvtrop (1965) has proposed that the true dorsalizing process in *Xenopus* eggs may not be cortical rotation but a contraction of cortical materials toward the sperm entry point. However, there is now abundant evidence that rotation is the more crucial rearrangement for embryonic dorsoventral development, and that the sperm only affects embryonic organization by influencing (*via* its sperm aster) the direction of rotation:

(1) Under normal conditions of fertilization and development, the direction of rotation more accurately predicts the embryonic dorsal midline than does the SEP (Vincent *et al.* 1986).

(2) Eggs can be tipped out of gravitational equilibrium, or squeezed laterally in various directions before or during cortical rotation, and these treatments randomize the relation of the SEP to the embryonic axes, whereas the direction of rotation still accurately correlates (Gerhart *et al.* 1980; Vincent *et al.* 1986; Black & Vincent, 1988).

(3) Dispermic and trispermic eggs initiate a single direction of rotation which predicts the dorsal midline (Vincent & Gerhart, 1987).

(4) Artificially activated eggs, which lack an SEP, rotate in a unique direction and, if later transplanted with a nucleus and centrosome, will develop an embryo having its dorsal midline at the position predicted by the rotation direction (Vincent & Gerhart, 1987; J. Roberts & B. Rowning, unpublished).

(5) When fertilized eggs fail to engage in cortical

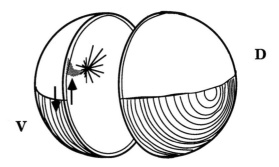

Fig. 2. Schematic diagram of parallel microtubules in the vegetal hemisphere of the *Xenopus* egg during cortical rotation. The egg is cut in the bilateral plane, showing the sperm aster in the animal hemisphere (upper half), and the parallel microtubules in the periphery of the vegetal hemisphere (lower half). The tubule array exists only in the interval from 0·4–0·9 of the first cell cycle, at the time of cortical rotation. The sheet of tubules is only 2–4 μm thick, starting approximately 2 μm from the egg surface. Tubules are aligned in the direction of rotation, shown by the arrows; their polarity is not known. Ventral (V) and dorsal (D) development will occur on opposite meridians, as indicated. Note that tubules describe tighter half-circles as the rotation poles ('hubs') are approached.

rotation, they develop no dorsal embryonic structures, as discussed later, despite their SEP.

Taken in its entirety, the evidence is strong that cortical rotation is an indispensable step in normal dorsal development. The need for it can be bypassed under certain experimental conditions (e.g. the use of lithium ion), and it is certainly not sufficient by itself for dorsal development; but it seems to be a normal, essential, early member of a series of processes leading to dorsal development. The role of the sperm in influencing the direction of rotation will be discussed later.

Microtubules serve as tracks for cortical rotation

At the start of rotation, a thin layer of parallel, slightly sinuous, microtubules (MTs) appears in the vegetal hemisphere, approximately 2–5 μm beneath the egg surface (Elinson & Rowning, 1988). The MTs align in the direction of rotation, describing tighter semicircles nearer the rotation hubs (Fig. 2). They are dynamic and perhaps associate laterally. They disappear at the end of rotation. The array is probably anchored to the core (B. Rowning and T. Mitchison, unpublished). If true, the cortex would then have anchored to it the motor molecules (e.g. kinesin or dynein), which presumably crawl along the tracks of parallel MTs and generate the force to displace the rigid cortex relative to the rigid core. The polarity of the MTs is not known, and so we cannot yet speculate on the need for kinesin as opposed to dynein. However, since movement is unaffected by injected sodium vanadate (10–100 μM) combined with long wavelength UV irradiation of the vegetal egg surface (365 nm), we currently disfavor the possibility of a dynein-like motor molecule.

Many agents depolymerize MTs of the array, and all of these inhibit cortical rotation. These include colchi-

cine, vinblastine, nocodazole, cold shock and hydrostatic pressure. Also, UV-irradiation (254 nm) of the
vegetal surface prevents MT polymerization (Grant &
Wacaster, 1972; Malacinski *et al.* 1977; Elinson &
Rowning, 1988), perhaps because GTP becomes covalently bound to tubulin (S. Roberts, 1989). Since all
these agents inhibit rotation, we can assert that MTs are
needed for rotation under normal conditions, probably
as aligned tracks for movement. Cytochalasin D, in
contrast, does not interfere with rotation, precluding a
continuous role for dynamic microfilaments. Finally,
cycloheximide doesn't inhibit rotation, even when applied before fertilization, indicating that the entire
process is post-translational, depending only on pre-
formed maternal proteins.

What aligns the microtubule array?

This is an important issue because as the array gains a
unique directionality (one selected from 360° of possibilities), rotation is committed to that direction, producing a unique bilateral symmetry retained throughout
the rest of development. Before rotation starts at 45 min
postfertilization, there is no detectable MT array.
Whatever controls the direction of MTs in the first few
minutes of their polymerization, controls the orientation of subsequent embryonic development, under
normal conditions.

We have had difficulty examining the earliest stages
of polymerization because the array builds up so
quickly. As rotation accelerates, a few short and poorly
aligned MTs can be seen, but within a few minutes,
rotation reaches full speed and the array is complete.
To explain the rapid transition from a disordered to
ordered array, we propose a *positive feedback model*
with two provisions, namely: microtubules orient rotation, and rotation orients microtubules (Fig. 3). The
first provision follows reasonably from what is known
about MT function, for as the first few tubules polym-
erize with poor alignment, a single direction of rotation
of the two rigid units (cortex *versus* core) must nonetheless emerge as the vector sum of forces generated along
all MTs (their lengths and directions considered). MTs
of opposed directions will cancel each other, while any
slight excess of MT polarity in one direction will dictate
the direction of rotation. At first rotation will be slow
because the vector sum is small.

The second provision is more controversial: can
rotation feed back on MT polymerization so that MTs
tend to arise or persist in the direction of rotation? As
background, we note evidence that the direction of MT
polymerization in the periphery of cultured cells responds to the arrangement of elongated tubes of
endoplasmic reticulum (Terasaki *et al.* 1986). Endoplasmic reticulum (ER) vesicles and tubes possess kinesin-
like MAPs which associate with MTs during their
transport and elongation (Vale, 1987), and these ves-
icle-associated MAPs could in principle stabilize the
walls (rather than ends) of MTs, thus disfavoring MT
depolymerization. If rotation could elongate and align
ER in the shear zone between the rigid cortex and core,
then the ER might in turn preferentially stabilize MTs

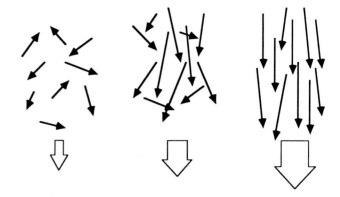

Fig. 3. Positive feedback model for the unidirectional
aligning of vegetal microtubules (MTs) during rotation. In
the left panel, MTs are first polymerizing in a small region
of the egg's vegetal periphery, and rotation is just starting
(approximately time 0·4). MTs are short and poorly
aligned. Tubule polarity is indicated by the solid arrow
heads. We assume MTs are anchored to the rigid core.
Since kinesin or dynein-like motor molecules, which are
assumed anchored to the cortex, must travel
unidirectionally along MTs and exert force in the direction
of each MT, rotation will start in whatever single direction
constitutes the vector sum of all tubules (tubule direction
and length considered). Only one rotation direction can
result (see large open arrow) since there are only two rigid
units. At first, rotation will be slow since the vector sum is
small. Then, as rotation starts, cytoplasmic materials of the
shear zone become partially aligned by shear flow (a
proposal, not a fact), and these materials stabilize MTs that
form in the direction of alignment, while other tubules
break down. The identity of these materials is unknown.
The center panel shows the MT array a few minutes later:
MTs are more numerous, longer on average, and more
aligned in the direction of movement. More force is
generated in the direction of rotation and now displacement
is faster (large open arrow). Faster rotation means more
shear, leading to still more alignment of cytoplasmic
materials, and still more stabilization of MTs in that
direction. In the right panel, a few minutes later, MTs are
still longer and better aligned, supporting full-speed
displacement in the original direction. Since MT orientation
defines the direction of rotation, and since rotation defines
the direction of MT orientation, polymerization and
rotation have a positive feedback relationship to one
another. Due to positive feedback, the egg amplifies a small
initial asymmetry (left panel) into a large one (right panel);
the polymerization–rotation process tends strongly to
disrupt cylindrical symmetry, as long as it starts in an
animal–vegetal direction.

in that direction. In this way, rotation might influence
the direction of MT polymerization, through the mediation of shear-aligned ER tubes and vesicles. With
increased MT alignment, rotation would then be faster,
leading to still more alignment of the ER and more
positive feedback on tubule polymerization. Soon MTs
would lie overwhelmingly in the rotation direction,
directing rotation and ensuring their own persistence in
that direction. The egg would be fully committed to one
direction of rotation, out of all directions initially
possible (Fig. 3 right panel).

The initial bias can be small

According to this model, any initial slight departure from a perfectly random array of MT (a vector sum of zero) will quickly amplify into a large departure, the unidirectional array. What initial bias might allow a few more MTs to form in one direction than in others, thereby controlling the orientation of later embryonic organization? To begin with, one could argue that, even if there were no bias, the first MTs are very unlikely to take up a perfectly random orientation, and therefore the egg will always be able to escape from cylindrical symmetry, due to positive feedback. A near-random condition may be approached in carefully manipulated eggs which are artificially activated by needle puncture or electric shock. In these, the direction of rotation can't be predicted beforehand. Usually they succeed in rotating for the full distance at the correct time, though occasionally they choose a skewed or equatorial path. A reliable bias can be introduced in such an egg simply by tipping it out of gravitational equilibrium for 5–10 min, at some time before rotation, to achieve a small displacement of the core relative to the cortex in an animal–vegetal direction (Ancel & Vintemberger, 1948; Rowning, 1989). Remarkably this forced displacement, which occurs in the absence of MTs, can be terminated long before rotation begins (15–30 min before), and nonetheless, when MTs appear, they align in the direction of the earlier forced displacement. MT-mediated rotation then continues what tipping had started. Materials of the egg periphery must have been oriented by the forced movement; these must have persisted and later biased the direction of MT polymerization and/or stability. In addition to demonstrating an experimentally imposed bias, this is our best evidence that similar displacements might influence the direction of MT polymerization during the normal cortical rotation period, as part of the positive feedback mechanism, and that the influence makes use of something other than MTs.

Under normal conditions, though, the sperm provides the dominant bias (Manes and Barbieri, 1977). MTs of the sperm aster extend through the AH long before vegetal cortical MTs appear (Stewart-Savage & Grey, 1982; Ubbels *et al.* 1983). Perhaps MTs of the aster enter the vegetal hemisphere at an early time and support a small amount of cortical displacement, leaving materials of the shear zone slightly oriented in the same way as can gravitationally forced displacement. Any slight orientation of materials with respect to the SEP would suffice to bias the whole MT array to build up in that direction. Actually, the sperm's effect is not strong; if gravity or centrifugal force is used to displace materials in another direction in a fertilized egg, that displacement easily comes to provide the dominant bias (Black & Gerhart, 1985).

In general, once the array of MT becomes aligned and rotation reaches full speed, it is difficult to change direction (Vincent & Gerhart, 1987), although this can occasionally happen in eggs briefly subjected to low temperatures to reversibly depolymerize the MT array during rotation (Vincent & Gerhart, 1987) or can

Fig. 4. Dorsalized and ventralized embryos of *Xenopus laevis*. The right embryo developed from an egg UV-irradiated (254 nm, 44 μW cm^{-2}, 2 min) at time 0·4 of the first cell cycle to prevent cortical rotation; that on the left from an egg treated with 60 % D$_2$O for 4 min at time 0·28. The right embryo lacks dorsal axial structures, but has differentiated a ciliated epidermis, red blood cells, coelomic compartments, and a short gut. The left embryo has a large heart, and circumferential bands of eye pigment and of cement gland. Both embryos retain the egg's cylindrical symmetry in their organization.

frequently happen in eggs compressed laterally during rotation to force movement into a new path (Black & Vincent, 1988). If the MT array is really dynamic and if positive feedback operates continuously to define MT directionality, these changes would be explicable.

Dorsal development requires rotation

Embryonic organization is drastically altered when rotation is prevented. The egg, after it has been treated briefly (2–4 min) with nocodazole, cold shock, hydrostatic pressure, or UV irradiation (of the vegetal surface only) to prevent MT polymerization and cortical rotation (Vincent *et al.* 1987; Elinson & Rowning, 1988), cleaves normally but then gastrulates abnormally, forming a ventral-type of blastopore lip which is late and synchronous around the gastrula circumference (Scharf & Gerhart, 1980, 1983). Although the embryo does not neurulate or form dorsal components of the body axis, it still develops a limited set of ventral structures at all meridians, preserving the cylindrically symmetric organization of the oocyte (Fig. 4, right). Tissues of all three germ layers are present in these ventralized 'limit forms': ciliated epidermis, coelomic mesoderm and blood islands (up to 15 times the normal amount of red blood cells; Cooke and Smith, 1987), and a short gut. The total amount of mesoderm is the same as that of normal embryos; but dorsal mesoderm is missing (Cooke & Smith, 1987). Dorsal development clearly depends on rotation whereas ventral development does not.

With intermediate amounts of rotation, the egg develops certain dorsal structures, in an interesting anteroposterior deletion series that depends on the amount of rotation. The more rotation, the more

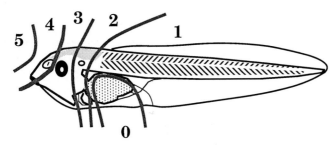

Fig. 5. Schematic diagram of the anteroposterior order of deletion of dorsal structures from the embryonic body axis as cortical rotation is reduced. Although the embryonic body axis can be truncated at any level, grades (or anatomical types) of embryos are defined to establish a scoring system, for the rough quantification of embryonic defects. This scale originated with Malacinski *et al.* (1977), was modified by Scharf & Gerhart (1980), and expanded to include excessively dorsalized embryos by Kao & Elinson (1988). Note that the scores described here are not interchangeable with those described in the earlier papers. A grade 5 embryo has all normal axial structures, whereas a grade 0 embryo lacks all dorsal structures, as well as some ventral ones such as the heart, gills, and probably some parts of the digestive system. However, grade 0 embryos still develop red blood cells and coelomic mesoderm (organized in two chambers), and are covered with ciliated epidermis (see Fig. 4). They digest their vegetal yolk in what may be a simple gut. Ventral structures of the normal belly region (i.e. excluding gills, heart, and anus) develop along all meridians of the egg, rather than just on the ventral-most. This is the 'limit form' obtained without cortical rotation, or without vegetal dorsalizing cells (a 'Nieuwkoop center'), or without a Spemann organizer. Intermediate grades have the structures of grade 0, plus more and more of the dorsal structures, as shown by the contour lines on the diagram. Embryonic structures are reduced and lost concertedly in the anteroposterior and dorsoventral directions. The pattern of progressive deletion can be more easily rationalized by examining the fate map of the early gastrula, than by examining the final larva.

anterior is the truncation level beyond which dorsal elements are missing from the body axis. Thus, while the direction of rotation defines the position of the dorsal midline, the extent of rotation defines the anterior extent of dorsal development. Fig. 5 shows the progression by which body parts are gained and lost.

While all eggs require rotation, they differ in the quantity required; some need at least 25° and others only 12° for development of the complete body axis (Fig. 6A). Normally eggs accomplish about 30° of rotation, an amount sufficient for the normal development of even the most insensitive members of the population. Presumably the difference reflects a variable effectiveness of rotation on its target, a component involved in a subsequent process of the series leading toward dorsal development.

Rotation without microtubules still allows dorsal development

When eggs are treated with anti-microtubule agents so that they have no tracks along which to effect rotation, they can nonetheless be forced to rotate artificially by tipping them out of gravitational equilibrium, while immobilizing the egg surface. The vegetally weighted core then slips relative to the cortex, driven by the artificial motive force of gravity. Tipped eggs, it turns out, are well rescued for dorsal development (Scharf and Gerhart, 1980), and the amount of forced displacement correlates with the amount of rescue. The anterior end of the body axis is rescued only in eggs experiencing the greatest displacements (Vincent & Gerhart, 1987). During the period of forced displacement in these eggs, MTs cannot be detected in the vegetal periphery. Rotation, driven by artificial means, seems sufficient to initiate dorsal development. Thus, we think that in normal eggs the parallel MT array functions only as tracks for cortical rotation in the first cell cycle, and that rotation itself, not the MTs, causes a dorsalizing change in the egg periphery.

What and where is the immediate target of rotation?

When rotation stops at time 0·85 of the first cell cycle, what cytoplasmic alteration persists, with consequences for later steps of dorsal development? Unfortunately we don't know, but we have considered two rather different possibilities: either a change of the contacts between the cortex and core of the egg, or an alignment and polarization of materials in the shear zone between the cortex and core.

Regarding the first, the animal core cytoplasm, for example, comes into contact with vegetal cortex on the prospective dorsal side during rotation. This kind of contact is not formed on the prospective ventral side. However, this contact may not be important since normal, and not excessively dorsalized, development is still obtained from eggs in which the core has been completely inverted at time 0·4 in the first cell cycle, bringing animal core cytoplasm into total contact with vegetal cortex (S. Black, unpublished). These eggs gastrulate normally from the hemisphere containing the vegetal yolk mass and animal cortex. The core alone may determine the animal–vegetal differences of development, and rotation-dependent modifications of the core may determine dorsoventral differences.

Regarding the second possibility, the zone between the core and cortex must experience high shear as the two rigid units move past one another for 350 μm while separated by only 2–5 μm. Shear could in principle lead to the alignment and deformation of materials within the zone. High voltage electron microscopy shows the shear zone to contain large numbers of membrane-bounded vesicles (Rowning, 1989). Perhaps these become elongated and aligned during rotation. If such vesicles are important in influencing the direction of tubule polymerization and hence the direction of rotation, as described earlier, shear forces would have to polarize them. Furthermore, aligned vesicles would have to retain different polarities on opposite sides of the egg if they are to promote dorsal development on just one side. To our knowledge, this proposal of polarized vesicles gains as yet no support from studies of other types of cells. Nonetheless, shear-dependent

Fig. 6. The anterior completeness of the embryonic body axis depends on the amount of cortical rotation, of vegetal dorsalizing induction and of the organizer.

Panel A: Cortical rotation. Details are in Vincent & Gerhart (1987), from which these data are replotted. *Xenopus* eggs were UV-irradiated at times before or during cortical rotation. The amount of rotation of each egg was measured as the angular displacement (degrees of arc, shown on the horizontal scale) of a hexagonal array of nile blue spots applied to the vegetal surface of the egg. The open circles report the movement of the cytoplasmic core. The egg surface was immobilized by resting the eggs in tight-fitting wells in agarose. Eggs were removed from the wells at gastrulation and allowed to develop to stage 40, for scoring of the dorsoanterior completeness of the body axis, recorded as the dorsoanterior grade, on the vertical scale of the figure. Each data point is an individual egg and embryo. Filled circles report the degree of cortical rotation of ten control eggs and the vertical arrow indicates the average, about 30°.

Panel B: Vegetal dorsalizing induction. Details are in Gimlich & Gerhart (1984), from which these data are replotted. Prospective host eggs were UV-irradiated early in the first cell cycle to prevent cortical rotation. Such eggs would develop to give mostly grade 0 embryos, lacking all dorsal axial structures. At the 64-cell stage, two cells were removed from the tier of cells nearest the vegetal pole (the D tier) and were replaced by two cells taken from the corresponding tier of a normal (non-irradiated) embryo of the same age. Donor cells came from the dorsal midline, the lateral position, or the ventral midline, as indicated in the inset. Dorsalmost cells were most effective at rescue, giving larvae with dorsal axial structures complete to the ear vesicle level or more anterior (Grades 3, 4, 5).

Panel C: The organizer. Details are in Stewart & Gerhart (1989) from which these data are replotted. Normal late blastula embryos (taken 30–60 min before stage 10) were cut in half in an animal–vegetal plane. The plane of cutting was chosen to split the embryo on the bilateral plane or at various angles from that plane. In this way a half embryo (called the 'test half') could be made to contain different amounts of the organizer region, which is centered on the prospective dorsal midline. (Eggs had been tipped and marked in the first cell cycle so that the prospective dorsal midline of the blastula was accurately known).

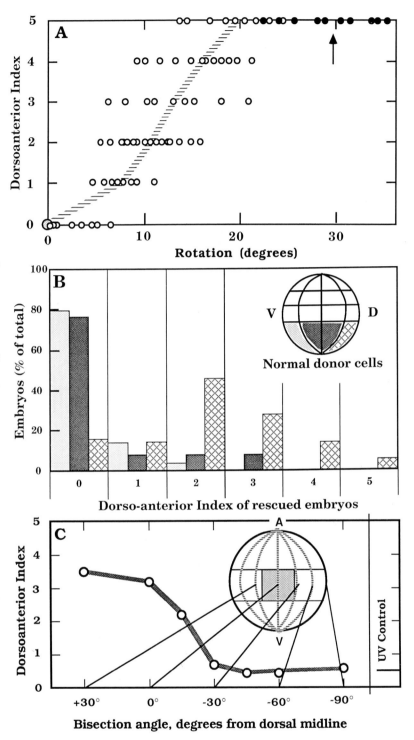

The test half was combined with a cut half of an embryo from an egg which had been UV-irradiated in the first cell cycle to prevent cortical rotation, and which therefore would lack an organizer. Such recombinates develop well and achieve bilateral symmetry in all cases, although the anterior truncation level of the embryo's body axis varies with the amount of organizer present. Half an organizer is usually sufficient for development of an entire body axis up to the level of the hindbrain or even further (Grades 3, 4, 5). At an angle of 30° from the bilateral plane, there is too little organizer in the test half to allow dorsal development, and the recombinate develops just as would an intact UVed embryo. Thus, the marginal zone of the normal late blastula, except for the 60°-wide organizer, lacks capability for autonomous dorsal development, although it is competent to produce somites, heart, and kidney if allowed to interact with the organizer during gastrulation.

polarization is worth mentioning as a very different possibility from that of altered core–cortex contacts.

In addition to our ignorance of what is affected, we don't know where the effect of rotation is first registered, namely, in the AH or VH, or both, even though we know that the effect must occur near the prospective dorsal midline, probably in the shear zone between the core and cortex. There are several indications that the vegetal hemisphere contains the target: Elinson & Pasceri (1989) have recently shown that UV-irradiated oocytes give rise to eggs that form vegetal microtubules and that rotate, but do not thereafter develop dorsal structures; these are presumably damaged in materials that rotation would normally activate. The target of irradiation is in the vegetal hemisphere of the oocyte. By the 16- or 32-cell stage, the vegetal hemisphere is certainly specialized for promoting dorsal development; it contains a dorsalizing inductive quadrant (discussed later) centered on the midline of greatest rotational displacement.

However, Cardellini (1988) has presented evidence that the animal hemisphere is initially specialized near the prospective dorsal midline, presumably by rotation, and that it passes its effect to the vegetal hemisphere at the 8- to 16-cell stage. Kageura & Yamana (1984) have also found cases where dorsal animal blastomeres, if transplanted at the 8-cell stage, can initiate dorsal development independent of the state of vegetal blastomeres. (We have unfortunately not been able to reproduce these results; in our hands, the animal hemisphere carries no dominant dorsalizing bias at the 8-cell stage, and the vegetal hemisphere is already fixed in its control of dorsal development.) Furthermore, London *et al.* (1988) report that AH cells at the 8-cell cleavage stage differ on the prospective dorsal and ventral sides: isolated and cultured AH prospective ventral cells can autonomously express at a later time an antigen characteristic of normal embryonic epithelium, whereas prospective dorsal AH cells cannot. Non-expression is characteristic of the neural plate region of the intact embryo, a region that normally develops from the AH prospective dorsal cells. However, the isolated AH prospective dorsal cells do not form a neural plate autonomously. Thus, there is evidence that the animal hemisphere is regionally modified at least to some extent by rotation.

At this time, the most inclusive interpretation would be that the entire dorsal meridian of the egg, in both hemispheres, is modified by rotation, and the particular local developmental expression of this modification will differ depending on the animal, equatorial, or vegetal level. Finally, rotation may only initiate a first transient cytoplasmic change, soon leading to other longer-lasting modifications. In this connection, it is observable that pigmentation differences continue to develop in the animal hemisphere until at least the 4-cell stage, that deep cytoplasmic materials of the AH circulate in relation to the direction of rotation, and that cortical materials ingress into the egg interior along new cleavage furrows which differ in detail on the prospective dorsal and ventral sides (Phillips, 1985; M. Danilchik

and J. Degnen, unpublished). It remains to be seen how many of these changes are indispensible for dorsal development, and how many are epiphenomena of rotation.

Excessive dorsoanterior development

When eggs are centrifuged twice in opposite directions, to achieve two forced displacements, they frequently develop as twins, with dorsal midlines at positions related to two force vectors (Black & Gerhart, 1986). A 10 min interval must separate the two centrifugations in order for both displacements to have effect; with shorter intervals only the second displacement initiates dorsal development. The existence of these twins shows that the egg has the capacity to initiate dorsal development in excess of the normal amount.

The egg can accomplish still more dorsoanterior development, at the expense of ventroposterior development, if treated with D_2O early in the first cell cycle (Scharf *et al.* 1989). In the extreme, such embryos possess a large heart, a core of unextended notochord, and circumferential bands of eye pigment and cement gland. They lack somites and red blood cells. They retain the cylindrical symmetry of the unfertilized egg, with dorsal development initiated on all meridians. In exaggerating dorsoanterior development, they define the opposite end of the anatomical spectrum from ventralized embryos (Fig. 4, left). Partially affected eggs develop as embryos with enlarged heads and trunks, but lacking tails, or as enlarged heads lacking trunks and tails (Scharf *et al.* 1989). As discussed later, similar embryos arise from blastulae treated with lithium ion at the 64- to 128-cell stage (Kao & Elinson, 1988). Cooke and Smith (1988) estimate that hyperdorsalized embryos contain the same total amount of mesoderm as normal embryos, but dorsal mesoderm has been increased at the expense of its ventral counterpart.

These hyperdorsal forms arise only if eggs are treated with D_2O before cortical rotation. Once rotation begins, D_2O has no effect. D_2O causes a precocious polymerization of MTs in the vegetal periphery, in a dense random array that persists into the rotation period. The D_2O-stabilized MTs are crucial since any subsequent treatment that eliminates them also eliminates hyperdorsal development. The action of D_2O remains a puzzle to us. Even though unified cortical rotation is strongly inhibited, probably because the random MT array cannot acquire unidirectionality, there may occur multiple local displacements of cortex and core materials. The egg behaves as if it had rotated in many directions, and among the mildly affected cases, twinning occurs frequently.

The existence of hyperdorsal embryos shows that the egg has maternal resources for more extensive dorsal development than it normally uses. Presumably this potential resides at all meridians of the egg's circumference, in a latent state, just as does the potential for ventral development. Unified cortical rotation normally activates the use of this potential in just one region, while leaving the remainder of the circumference for ventral development, thereby establishing the proportions of the normal embryonic pattern.

II. The quantitative dependence of later events on cortical rotation

Why does the *quantity* of cortical rotation in the first cell cycle delimit the anterior completeness of the embryonic body axis? To consider this relationship, we will sketch three steps of later development in which the same truncation series of embryos can be generated by experimental interference. We propose that the amount of cortical rotation determines: (1) the number of vegetal dorsalizing cells which in turn, by way of induction in the blastula period, determine (2) the number of the cells of the Spemann organizer region which in turn, by way of inductive interactions in the gastrula period, determine (3) the extent of morphogenesis and patterning during gastrulation.

Vegetal dorsalizing induction

As Nieuwkoop discovered (1973), cells of the vegetal hemisphere of the midblastula embryo (4000-cell stage) induce neighboring cells of the animal hemisphere to behave as marginal zone cells at gastrulation and to differentiate ultimately as many types of mesoderm and as archenteron roof endoderm. The dorsalmost quadrant of the vegetal hemisphere differs from other vegetal regions: it induces the organizer quadrant of the marginal zone, which initiates much of the morphogenesis of gastrulation, and which usually forms the notochord, a central mesodermal tissue of the embryonic dorsal midline. Dorsal development beyond the blastula stage depends on the presence of these special vegetal cells.

We extended these studies to earlier stages in an attempt to connect cortical rotation to the founding of this specialized vegetal quadrant. At the 32- to 64-cell blastula stage, two vegetal cells can be removed from the prospective dorsal midline, as predicted by the direction of cortical rotation, and these cells can be transplanted into another blastula of the same age, for example, replacing two vegetal cells of a blastula derived from a UV-irradiated egg, one that would on its own develop only ventral structures. From these grafted embryos arise well-rescued tadpoles, with nearly complete body axes containing normal dorsal structures of the head, trunk and tail. When graft cells are preloaded with a fluorescent lineage tracer, we see that progeny cells of the graft do not populate the rescued embryo's dorsal structures, but only the ventral yolk mass. Graft cells induce neighboring equatorial cells of the host to develop the entire body axis. Gastrulation begins near the graft, and the dorsal midline of the rescued embryo is centered on the meridian of grafting (Gimlich & Gerhart, 1964; Gimlich, 1986).

Rescuing graft cells can only be obtained from positions close to the prospective dorsal midline of the donor, within 45° or less of the midline; cells from lateral or opposite vegetal positions do not rescue (Figure 6B). The effective donor region includes the two vegetal tiers of cells present at the 32- to 64-cell stage, that is, from the equator to the vegetal pole. The inductive strength of cells of the two tiers differs from embryo to embryo, perhaps because cleavage furrows are variably related to the locus of specialized cytoplasm (Gimlich, 1986). In the absence of other names, we call this the 'vegetal dorsalizing region', or the 'organizer inducing region', or the 'Nieuwkoop center'.

The normal embryo requires cortical rotation for this region's formation, and the region arises on the meridian of greatest cytoplasmic displacement, on the side where the core moves vegetally *vis à vis* the cortex. While any part of the VH is latently capable of forming a dorsalizing center, only one region actually does in normal development: that part affected by the single, unidirectional rotation. As discussed before, rotation may directly activate cytoplasm of the vegetal dorsalizing center, presumably bordering the shear zone or at new contact regions between the cortex and core, or it may activate materials of the animal hemisphere, which secondarily activate the vegetal center, as suggested by Cardellini (1988). If the latter, the steps of transfer are probably complete by the 8- to 16-cell stage.

The rest of the vegetal hemisphere, unaffected by rotation, also engages in an induction of the marginal zone, but this does not lead to organizer formation or to differentiation of dorsal mesoderm. It leads to the formation of the 'indifferent' or 'ventral' portion of the marginal zone. This type of ventralizing induction does not depend on rotation, for it occurs in embryos prevented from rotation by MT depolymerizing agents. As discussed elsewhere in this Volume (see chapters by Slack *et al.*; Smith *et al.*; Yisraeli *et al.*), the VH may exert its inductive effects by secreting growth-factor-like proteins. By these accounts, cortical rotation might be expected to enable cells of the vegetal dorsalizing region to specifically release a TGF-β homolog, whereas all vegetal cells even without rotation would release an FGF-like material. At this time we have no idea how cortical rotation might alter the secretory properties of cells derived from one region. Since TGF-β and FGF homologs are present as proteins even in the unfertilized egg (Kimelman *et al.* 1988; Slack & Isaacs, 1989; Dale *et al.* 1989; Tannahill & Melton, 1989), their release could involve the region-specific activation of a step of processing or externalization, rather than of transcription or translation.

As an aside, lithium ion deserves special mention because it obviates the need for cortical rotation and for a Nieuwkoop center. Eggs that have failed to rotate can be rescued to form near-normal embryos by an injection of lithium chloride into equatorial cells at the 16- to 32-cell stage (tier C; Busa & Gimlich, 1989). Uniform exposure of such eggs to lithium solutions leads to the development of cylindrically symmetric hyperdorsalized forms resembling D_2O embryos (Kao & Elinson, 1988). Apparently lithium acts not by stimulating vegetal cells to release organizer inducing (dorsalizing) factors, but by sensitizing animal hemisphere cells to respond to the vegetal ventralizing inductors *as if* they were dorsalizing inductors, i.e. to an FGF homolog as if it were a TGF-β homolog (Nieuwkoop, 1970; Kao & Elinson, 1989; Slack *et al.* 1988; Cooke & Smith, 1988). Hence, the embryo circumvents the normal requirements for cortical rotation and the Nieuwkoop center. Given this interesting response to lithium ion, it seems plausible that the normal vegetal dorsalizing inductor, like lithium, just enhances the response of neighboring AH cells to the ubiquitous vegetal ventralizing inductor, and these responding cells become the organizer. In this regard, TGF-β1 is known to synergize the FGF-dependent response by explanted AH cells to produce dorsal mesoderm (Kimelman & Kirschner, 1987).

Rescue by cells of the Nieuwkoop center is often incomplete

Vegetal dorsalizing cells do not always promote complete rescue when grafted into UVed recipients. When the body axis is incomplete, it is always truncated from the anterior end, and the same scoring scale can be used as for embryos inhibited in cortical rotation (see Fig. 5 and 6B). Grafts with one, two, or four cells from the C and D tiers of the donor give increasingly frequent well-rescued embryos. Truncated embryos of the same types can also be produced from normal blastulae by eliminating cells from the Nieuwkoop center of the 32-cell blastula (Gimlich, 1986). The elimination of more cells leads to greater anterior defectiveness in the final embryos.

These results, while not well quantified yet, imply that later dorsal development depends systematically on the amount of Nieuwkoop center present in the blastula stage embryo. Since experimental perturbations of vegetal induction produce the same final body patterns as do perturbations of rotation, we suggest that the amount of rotation determines the amount of vegetal dorsalizing induction. With no rotation, there is no such induction. Intermediate rotation gives intermediate induction. Two opposite rotations lead to two opposite Nieuwkoop centers. And after D$_2$O treatment, most of the vegetal hemisphere becomes a fully active Nieuwkoop center. Presumably the amount of rotation determines the amount of secretion of a specific inductor protein from cells of the Nieuwkoop center. Despite this quantitative correspondence, however, we can't yet discern why the anterior end of the body axis is the end missing in deficient embryos.

The amount of organizer

By the end of the blastula period, the marginal zone is sufficiently patterned for the initiation of normal gastrulation. In *Xenopus*, the marginal zone's organizer region, which arises directly above the vegetal dorsalizing region, is approximately 60° wide; whereas the indifferent part of the marginal zone is 300° wide, arising above the non-Nieuwkoop part of the VH (Smith & Slack, 1983; Dale & Slack, 1987; Stewart & Gerhart, 1989).

The organizer can be reduced in size by surgery at the late blastula stage. This allows us to test the effects on development of subnormal amounts of organizer. As one way to do this, the late blastula (stage 9, approx. 15 000 cells, 30–60 min before blastopore formation) is cut vertically on the bilateral plane (i.e. in the animal–vegetal direction through the organizer region), and the left or right half is recombined with half an embryo of equal age, cut from an egg which had been UV-irradiated in the first cell cycle to prevent its rotation and to preclude its formation of a Nieuwkoop center. This latter half, lacking an organizer, would on its own be incapable of any dorsal development. Although such recombinates have each just half an organizer, they develop remarkably well and produce near-perfect bilateral embryos, in many cases with near-complete body axes containing normal dorsal structures of the head, trunk and tail. One side of the body is contributed by the would-be ventralized half, as shown by lineage tracing. Still, some recombinates give bilateral embryos with incomplete body axes (Fig. 6C), and when dorsal structures are missing, the body axis is truncated from the anterior end, just as we have seen before, and the same scoring system can be used.

In the same kind of operation, the organizer can be intentionally cut off center (e.g. 15° from the midline), to include a still smaller amount of organizer in the rescuing normal half embryo used to make a recombinate with a UVed half. When this is done, the recombinate tends to have still fewer anterior structures (Fig. 6C), though always in a bilateral arrangement to which the UVed half contributes one side. The relationship seems monotonic: the less organizer, the less anterior development.

Finally, when the cut departs 30° or more from the bilateral plane, the piece lacking the dorsal meridian has no capacity for rescue; the recombinate develops as a cylindrically symmetric ventralized embryo. The organizer, at least in its capacity to initiate dorsal axial development, apparently extends just 30° to either side of the dorsal meridian, i.e. it is 60° wide. The remaining marginal zone material of a normal late blastula resembles the marginal zone of a ventralized embryo, with no autonomy for dorsal development, even though this part is destined in normal development to produce the bulk of the mesodermal tissues of the embryo, namely, the somites, kidney and heart, in fact, almost all mesoderm except the notochord and some head mesenchyme. This indifferent region must interact with organizer cells during gastrulation to generate its substantial part of the normal embryo's axial organization. The major share of definitive embryonic organization, along both the dorsoventral and anteroposterior axes, must be established during and/or after gastrulation, as shown by the performance of UVed halves brought into contact with an organizer, and by the performance of normal indifferent marginal zone regions deprived of an organizer.

We can now extend our causal chain of quantitative relationships by one more step since progressive reductions in the amount of organizer material in the late blastula result in embryonic body axes progressively truncated from the anterior end. We suggest that the amount of rotation defines the amount of Nieuwkoop center, which defines the amount of organizer. With no rotation, there is no vegetal dorsalizing induction and no organizer. Partial rotation leads to partial induction and a reduced organizer. However, despite our causal chain, we haven't answered why, when the organizer is reduced in size, the anterior end of the embryonic axis is missing.

Definitive axis formation

Gastrulation transforms egg organization into embryonic organization. In this process, cells of the marginal zone generate the dorsoventral and anteroposterior dimensions of the body axis as the result of their migration, repacking and manifold interactions (Keller & Danilchik, 1988; Wilson & Keller, 1989). In undisturbed development, the first cells to gastrulate are those of the organizer region, which comprises the 'dorsal lip' of the blastopore. Cells of the organizer region are special in their ability, as a population, to converge toward the prospective dorsal midline and to extend in the anteroposterior direction. They induce neighboring cells of the indifferent marginal zone to undertake similar movements and they induce ectodermal cells to undertake neurulation. Eventually they contribute to dorsoanterior elements of the body axis, such as pharyngeal endoderm, head mesenchyme, archenteron roof, notoplate and notochord (see Gerhart & Keller, 1986, for a review).

Because organizer cells are so special, we initially assumed that they are fully determined at the start of gastrulation, not only for their gastrulation movements and induction abilities, but also for their ultimate cell type differentiations. Fate maps show that the first invaginated cells of the organizer tend to populate the most anterior parts of the body, and later ones contribute more posteriorly. The organizer might have within it a cryptic anteroposterior and a dorsoventral pattern of cellular differences, a pattern that would propagate to the rest of the embryo during morphogenesis. By this view, the organizer would itself be already fully organized at the start of gastrulation, a miniature mosaic of the future embryo's axial organization. In many respects, this interpretation could explain the series of systematically truncated embryos produced by our experimental interventions just described. For example, reduced rotation and reduced vegetal induction of the organizer might just lead to the formation of an organizer lacking the most anterior–dorsal parts of its cryptic pattern, if we assume that qualitative differences within the organizer originate from quantitative differences set up by vegetal induction. In such manipulated embryos, gastrulation does in fact start later, and cells accomplish less convergence and extension. Thus, we thought it plausible that the diminished organizer just lacked cells for organizing the most anterior dorsal parts of the body axis. Of course, it must be admitted that the results on reducing the size of the organizer by surgery at the start of gastrulation would not readily fit this interpretation.

The situation is considerably more subtle, though, as

shown by the results of experiments in which embryos are allowed to develop normally up to and into the gastrula stage (so as to have a well-organized organizer), and then at various times are prevented from continuing gastrulation. Inhibitors of *Xenopus* gastrulation are not easy to find: there is no significant effect from RGD peptides, *p*-nitrophenyl-xylosides, or β-aminopropionitrile, agents that arrest gastrulation in sea urchins (Wessel & McClay, 1987; Lane & Solursh, 1988) and *Pleurodeles* (Boucaut *et al.* 1984). However, polysulfonated compounds such trypan blue and suramin (germanin) are very effective (Waddington & Perry, 1956). These are powerful teratogens in mammals, acting at the primitive streak stage; they animalize sea urchins by arresting gastrulation (Beck & Lloyd, 1966). Suramin disrupts the binding of protein ligands to cell surface receptors, the examples including growth factors (FGF and TGF-β, Coffey *et al.* 1987), vitellogenin, and LDL (Peacock *et al.* 1988). High doses of trypan blue or suramin (20 μM in the blastocoel) stop convergent extension movements *in vivo*, though allowing the blastopore to close. The agents effectively arrest these same movements of cells in explanted preparations of the organizer (Danilchik *et al.* 1989).

The clearest demonstration of their systematic effect on axis formation comes when these agents are injected into the blastocoel *at different times* during the 6 h period of gastrulation (stages 10 to 13): embryos thereafter develop body axes truncated at different anteroposterior levels depending on the time of injection (Figure 7 and 8). If injected when the dorsal lip is first invaginating, the resulting embryo develops no head or trunk, and sometimes no tail as well (Fig. 8B). Somites and notochord are absent; the embryo resembles the cylindrically symmetric ventralized forms seen when rotation fails or when the Nieuwkoop center or organizer is ablated. If the agents are injected midway in gastrulation, embryos develop without heads, but with trunks and tails (Fig. 8A). Finally, if injected at the end of gastrulation, the embryo is completely unaffected, even though the agents are present throughout the periods of neurulation and cell differentiation. Thus, the polysulfonated agents are not indiscriminately toxic, but act in a stage-specific way during gastrulation, inhibiting some process perhaps unique to gastrulation, or most exaggerated or critical at that time.

Gastrulation is the latest stage at which we have been able to produce the familiar series of truncated anatomies for which we can use the same dorsoanterior index scoring system (Fig. 5). In preliminary experiments with injected fluorescent lineage tracers, we find that the leading cells of the dorsal marginal zone (the organizer region) differentiate into whatever parts of the body axis are most anterior in the truncated embryo. Also, in preliminary experiments, the extent of gastrulation (the length of the archenteron) correlates with the completeness of the body axis. In contradiction to the expectations of the miniature mosaic model, organizer cells do not seem to have a fixed fate at the start of gastrulation but seem to undergo a progressive dorsoanteriorization in relation to the time

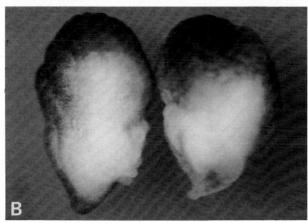

Fig. 7. Embryos blocked in gastrulation by polysulfonated compounds develop truncated body axes similar to those developed by UV-irradiated eggs. Eggs were allowed to develop normally until the gastrula stage, and were then injected with trypan blue (TB; 40 µM stock, 30 nl injected in the blastocoel). Panel A: Two grade 2 embryos at the equivalent of stage 32 are shown. The lower one is from a midgastrula (stage 11) injected with TB, the upper from a UVed egg. Panel B: Two grade 0 to 1 embryos. The left embryo is from a UVed egg and the right, from an early gastrula (stage 10) injected with TB. The similarities allow us to use the DAI scoring scale (Fig. 5) for TB-injected embryos.

and/or extent of morphogenesis (Gerhart *et al.* 1984). At the start of gastrulation, organizer cells seem determined only in their potentiality for starting a series of steps leading eventually to anterior dorsal development, steps that can be inhibited experimentally by polysulfonated compounds. If the steps are not completed, the potential is not fulfilled and the cells differentiate as posterior ventral tissues.

As further evidence that cell fates change during gastrulation, we find that trypan blue and suramin, injected at the gastrula stage, can even reverse the dorsoanteriorizing effects of lithium ion (applied at the 64- to 128-cell stage). Doubly treated embryos develop trunks and tails, and usually not heads; whereas with lithium alone they develop heads, but not trunks and tails (Doniach *et al.* 1989).

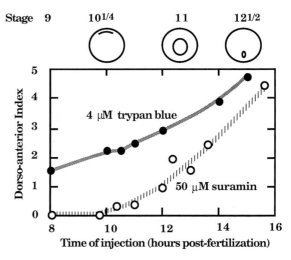

Fig. 8. The later gastrulation is blocked, the more anteriorly complete is the embryo's body axis. Eggs developed normally until the late blastula stage (8 h postfertilization, approx. 10 000 cells) and thereafter were each injected at various times with 30 nl of stock solutions of either 40 µM-trypan blue or 500 µM-suramin, delivered into the blastocoel. Estimated intrablastocoelic concentrations of the agents are indicated on the figure. Suramin (at a high dose) abruptly stops convergent extension movements, although the blastopore succeeds in closing. Trypan (at an intermediate dose) reduces but does not stop these movements. When control embryos reached stage 35–40, experimental embryos were scored. The dorsoanterior index for the treated populations (10 embryos averaged per data point) is shown on the vertical scale, graphed against the time of injection. Note that at stage 10, the embryos are still sensitive to the agents but by stage 12½ to 13 (the start of neurulation), they are completely resistant. The sensitive period to these agents falls exactly in the period of gastrulation. During gastrulation (hours 10–16), the later the injection, the more anterior will be the completeness of the eventual body axis. Across the top of the figure are shown vegetal views of embryos at the stage injected, to indicate the progress of blastopore closure.

In comparing embryos from all our different stage-specific interferences with development, we see that the completeness of the embryonic body axis always correlates well with the extent of the morphogenetic movements of gastrulation; anteriormost parts of the axis emerge only when morphogenesis is most extensive, as diagrammed in Fig. 9. This is true no matter whether gastrulation is incomplete because it starts late and stops on time (as is the case with rotation-deficient embryos), or because it starts on time but ends early (as in the case with trypan and suramin-injected embryos). Gastrulation itself is the last developmental process that we can connect quantitatively to the amount of cortical rotation in the first cell cycle. During gastrulation, quantity seems finally converted to quality.

The organizer of the early gastrula is probably *not* a mosaic of terminally determined cell types. It may instead be a mosaic of cells of different potentials for arriving at the external and/or internal conditions needed for the differentiation of the different antero-posterior cell types predicted by fate maps. Cells of high

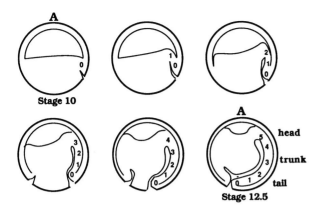

Fig. 9. Progressive anteriorization of the embryonic body axis during *Xenopus* gastrulation. In all our experimentally perturbed embryos (excluding D_2O effects), the truncation level of the final body is related to the extent of gastrulation movements, regardless of whether gastrulation starts normally at stage 10 but is then ended at different times (by trypan blue or suramin), or whether gastrulation starts later (due to reduced amounts of organizer in the marginal zone, due to inhibited rotation, or reduced numbers of vegetal dorsalizing cells, or surgical removal of parts of the organizer), while ending at the same time (probably stage 13).

The six panels are schematic cross-sections of embryos, showing different stages of the 6 h period of gastrulation, from stage 10 (upper left) and to stage 12·5–13 (lower right). The animal pole (A) is at the top of all figures. The blastocoel is the space in the animal hemisphere. At the start of gastrulation, some cells of the organizer part of the marginal zone (right subequatorial level) begin invaginating first, followed in sequence by cells more distant laterally and vertically. The '0' in the upper left section indicates that cells of the organizer, if their morphogenesis were stopped at that point, would differentiate ventral structures, like the parts of a grade 0 embryo (see Fig. 5). In the top center panel, leading cells of the organizer have moved farther inward, followed by dorsal marginal zone cells which were initially farther from the blastopore. The leading cells are now in a condition to differentiate as posterior dorsal structures, which they would do if gastrulation were stopped at this point, while cells behind them have just reached the '0' condition. These conditions, which may reflect internal or external (or both) states of the cells, change progressively with the time and/or distance of morphogenesis (see subsequent panels). Leading cells are unique in that they have the potential for progressing through the full range of conditions, finally reaching condition '5' (lower right) sufficient for anterior dorsal differentiation. Cells farther back in the migration series make less progress, because they start later and are less active. While cells of the marginal zone would be initially graded in their potential for progress toward anterior dorsal development, all would need to accomplish extensive morphogenesis to fulfill this potential. Thus, inhibitors of morphogenesis always have a posteroventralizing effect on the final pattern.

potential would initiate morphogenesis earlier and more vigorously than those of low potential, the latter not having the option to progress very far in the series of conditions for dorsoanterior differentiation; they would be limited to producing posterior parts of the

pattern, although even in this they would fail if morphogenesis were inhibited.

Why is the extent of gastrulation related to the anterior completeness of the axial pattern?

This inquiry dates back to Spemann (1938) and Vogt who considered the connection between dynamic determination (a cell's morphogenetic behavior at gastrulation) and its material determination (its final cell type differentiation). We don't know the answer, but have considered two possibilities, for each of which we will give an example:

(1) Morphogenesis does not itself accomplish patterning but creates conditions upon which a separate patterning process operates. This possibility is inherent in the double gradient idea of Saxen and Toivonen (1961). All cells would have an intrinsic capacity for anterior differentiation, but many are suppressed by a posteriorizing (or caudalizing or tail-inducing) center located in those regions of the marginal zone gastrulating last. Suppression, and therefore fates, would be graded with distance from the center: the closest cells becoming tail, and more distant ones, trunk. Only the earliest, farthest advancing marginal zone cells and the most distant neurectoderm would escape the effects of the center and would become anterior. According to this view, if we inhibit gastrulation movements by any means, we should expect to prevent cells from escaping the posteriorizing center, i.e. from acquiring the external conditions needed for their anterior differentiation. The head end of the body axis would be deleted and the completeness of the axial pattern would be quantitatively related to morphogenesis, just as we find.

(2) Morphogenesis and axial patterning may depend jointly on yet another agency such as intercellular signalling. This possibility resembles ones for cell aggregation and slug migration in *Dictyostelium* (see chapter by Johnson *et al.* this Volume). At the start of gastrulation, organizer cells might be unique in their high intensity of intercellular signalling, due to prior stimulation from the Nieuwkoop center. Such a cell might have three responses to signals: to move, to emit more signal, and to keep a running sum of the amount of received signal, a sum that would determine the cell's anteroposterior–dorsoventral fate. If the response duration were short, repeated signal reception would be needed by cells to keep signalling and responding. Cell fate would change during gastrulation in concert with movement, both depending on continued intercellular signalling. The earliest invaginating cells would have the greatest potential for movement and anterior fates since they could maintain the longest period of signalling. Non-organizer cells of the marginal zone might receive enough signals from organizer cells to begin signalling, moving, and changing fates. Signalling could propagate through the marginal zone and neurectoderm. By this view, polysulfonated inhibitors of gastrulation would be inhibitors of signalling; they would terminate both morphogenesis and progress towards anterior fates since these jointly depend on continued signalling. Parenthetically, another agent that affects

signal transduction, namely lithium ion, also reduces morphogenetic movements and gives headless embryos, if applied in the gastrula stage (Hall, 1942; J. Slack, personal communication; an effect not to be confused with hyperdorsalization by treatment of the blastula). By this view, reduced rotation and vegetal induction would lead to a diminished organizer, one with a lowered level of signalling, and morphogenesis and anterior patterning would consequently diminish in concert.

These rather different interpretations have equal plausibility at present. Both confer to gastrulation, as a process, an inherent dynamic organization by which anterior dorsal fates arise in relation to the increasing quantity of morphogenesis, and both give to the early steps of development, such as cortical rotation and vegetal induction, the significance of setting the initial conditions of gastrulation, conditions that may limit its operation.

This work was supported by USPHS grant GM 19363 and NSF grant DCB-8517548.

References

ANCEL, P. & VINTEMBERGER, P. (1948). Recherches sur le determinisme de la symetrie bilaterale dans l'oeuf des Amphibiens. *Bull. Biol. Fr. Belg.* **31 (Suppl.)**, 1–182.

BECK, F. & LLOYD, J. B. (1966). The teratogenic effect of azo dyes. *Adv. Teratol.* **1**, 133–191.

BLACK, S. D. & GERHART, J. C. (1985). Experimental control of the site of embryonic axis formation in *Xenopus laevis* eggs centrifuged before first cleavage. *Devl Biol.* **108**, 310–324.

BLACK, S. D. & GERHART, J. C. (1986). High frequency twinning of *Xenopus laevis* embryos from eggs centrifuged bidirectionally before first cleavage. *Devl Biol.* **116**, 228–240.

BLACK, S. D. & VINCENT, J.-P. (1988). The first cleavage plane and the embryonic axis are determined by separate mechanisms in *Xenopus laevis. Devl Biol.* **128**, 65–71.

BOUCAUT, J. C., DARRIBERE, T., POOLE, T. J., AOYAMA, H., YAMADA, K. M. & THIERY, J.-P. (1984). Biologically active synthetic peptides as probes of embryonic development. *J. Cell Biol.* **99**, 1822–1830.

BUSA, W. B. & GIMLICH, R. L. (1989). Lithium-induced teratogenesis in frog embryos prevented by a polyphosphoinositide cycle intermediate or a diacylglycerol analog. *Devl Biol.* **132**, 315–324.

CARDELLINI, P. (1988). Reversal of dorsoventral polarity in *Xenopus laevis* embryos by 180° rotation of the animal micromeres at the 8 cell stage. *Devl Biol.* **128**, 428–434.

COFFEY, R. J., LEOF, E. B., SHIPLEY, G. D. & MOSES, H. L. (1987). Suramin inhibition of growth factor receptor binding and mitogenecity in AKR-2B cells. *J. cell. Physiol.* **132**, 143–148.

COOKE, J. & SMITH, E. J. (1988). The restrictive effect of early exposure to lithium upon body pattern in *Xenopus* development, studies by quantitative anatomy and immunofluorescence. *Development* **102**, 85–100.

COOKE, J. & SMITH, J. C. (1987). The midblastula cell cycle transition and the character of mesoderm in UV-induced nonaxial *Xenopus* development. *Development* **99**, 197–210.

DALE, L., MATTHEWS, G., TABE, L. & COLMAN, A. (1989). Developmental expression of the protein product of Vg1, a localized maternal mRNA in the frog *Xenopus laevis. EMBO J.* **8**, 1057–1065.

DALE, L. & SLACK, J. M. W. (1987). Regional specification within the mesoderm of early embryos of *Xenopus laevis. Development* **100**, 279–295.

DANILCHIK, M., DONAICH, T. & GERHART, J. C. (1989). Patterning

of the embryonic body axis during *Xenopus* gastrulation: experimentally reduced morphogenesis leads to anteriorially truncated embryos. In preparation.

DANILCHIK, M. V. & GERHART, J. C. (1987). Differentiation of the animal-vegetal axis in *Xenopus laevis* oocytes. I. Polarized translocation of platelets establishes the yolk gradient. *Devl Biol.* **122**, 101–112.

DONIACH, T., DANILCHIK, M. & GERHART, J. C. (1989). Patterning of the embryonic body axis during *Xenopus* gastrulation: the progressive anteriorization of cell fates. In preparation.

ELINSON, R. P. (1980). The amphibian egg cortex in fertilization and development. *Symp. Soc. Devl Biol.* **38**, 217–234.

ELINSON, R. P. & PASCERI, P. (1989). Two UV-sensitive targets in dorsoanterior specification of frog embryos. *Development* **106**, 00–00.

ELINSON, R. P. & ROWNING, B. (1988). A transient array of parallel microtubules in frog eggs: Potential tracks for a cytoplasmic rotation that specifies the dorso-ventral axis. *Devl Biol.* **128**, 185–197.

GERHART, J. & KELLER, R. (1986). Region-specific cell activities in amphibian gastrulation. *A. Rev. Cell Biol.* **2**, 201–229.

GERHART, J., UBBELS, G., BLACK, S., HARA, K. & KIRSCHNER, M. (1980). A reinvestigation of the role of the grey crescent in axis formation in *Xenopus laevis. Nature, Lond.* **292**, 511–516.

GERHART, J. C., VINCENT, J.-P., SCHARF, S. R., BLACK, S. D., GIMLICH, R. L. & DANILCHIK, M. (1984). Localization and induction in early development of *Xenopus. Phil. Trans. R. Soc. Lond.* B **307**, 319–330.

GIMLICH, R. L. (1986). Acquisition of developmental autonomy in the equatorial region of the *Xenopus* embryo. *Devl Biol.* **115**, 340–352.

GIMLICH, R. L. & GERHART, J. C. (1964). Early cellular interactions promote embryonic axis formation in *Xenopus laevis. Devl Biol.* **104**, 117–130.

GRANT, P. & WACASTER, J. F. (1972). The amphibian grey crescent-a site of developmental information? *Devl Biol.* **28**, 454–471.

HALL, T. S. (1942). The mode of action of lithium salts in amphibian development. *J. exp. Zool.* **89**, 1–30.

KAGEURA, H. & YAMANA, K. (1984). Pattern regulation in defect embryos of *Xenopus laevis. Devl Biol.* **101**, 410–415.

KAO, K. R. & ELINSON, R. P. (1988). The entire mesodermal mantle behaves as a Spemann's Organizer in dorsoanterior enhanced *Xenopus laevis* embryos. *Devl Biol.* **127**, 64–77.

KAO, K. R. & ELINSON, R. P. (1989). Dorsalization of mesoderm induction by lithium. *Devl Biol.* (in press).

KELLER, R. E. & DANILCHIK, M. (1988). Regional expression, pattern and timing of convergence and extension during gastrulation of *Xenopus laevis. Development* **103**, 193–210.

KIMELMAN, D. & KIRSCHNER, M. (1987). Synergistic induction of mesoderm by FGF and TGF-β and the identification of an mRNA coding for FGF in the early Xenopus embryo. *Cell* **51**, 869–877.

KIMELMAN, D., ABRAHAM, J. A., HAAPARANTA, T., PALISI, T. M. & KIRSCHNER, M. W. (1988). The presence of fibroblast growth faster in the frog egg: its role as a natural mesoderm inducer. *Science* **242**, 1053–1056.

LANE, M. C. & SOLURSH, M. (1988). Dependence of sea urchin primary mesenchyme cell migration on xyloside and sulfate sensitive cell surface associated components. *Devl Biol.* **127**, 78–87.

LONDON, C., AKERS, R. & PHILLIPS, C. R. (1988). Expression of epi 1, an epidermal specific marker, in *Xenopus laevis* embryos is specified prior to gastrulation. *Devl Biol.* **129**, 380–389.

LØVTRUP, S. (1965). Morphogenesis in the amphibian embryo: Fertilization and blastula formation. *Wilhelm Roux' Arch. EntwMech. Org.* **156**, 204–248.

MALACINSKI, G. M., BROTHERS, A. J. & CHUNG, H.-M. (1977). Destruction of components of the neural induction system of the amphibian egg with ultraviolet irradiation. *Devl Biol.* **56**, 24–39.

MANES, M. E. & BARBIERI, F. D. (1977). On the possibility of sperm aster involvement in dorso-ventral polarization and pronuclear migration in the amphibian egg. *J. Embryol. exp. Morph.* **40**, 187–197.

NIEUWKOOP, P. D. (1970). The formation of mesoderm in urodelan amphibians. III. The vegetalizing action of the Li ion. *Wilhelm Roux' Arch. EntwMech. Org.* **166**, 105–123.

NIEUWKOOP, P. D. (1973). The "organization center" of the amphibian embryo: its spatial organization and morphogenetic action. *Adv. Morphogen* **10**, 1–39.

PEACOCK, S. L., BATES, M. P., RUSSELL, D. W., BROWN, M. S. & GOLDSTEIN, J. L. (1988). Human low density lipoprotein receptor expressed in *Xenopus* oocytes. *J. biol. Chem.* **263**, 7838–7845.

PHILLIPS, C. R. (1985). Spatial changes in polyA concentrations during early embryogenesis in *Xenopus laevis*: analysis by in situ hybridization. *Devl Biol.* **109**, 299–310.

ROBERTS, S. (1989). Crosslinking of GTP to tubulin in *Xenopus* eggs: the possible basis of UV inactivation of dorsal development. In preparation.

ROWNING, B. (1989). Microtubule-mediated cortical rotation in the *Xenopus* egg. Thesis, University of California, Berkeley CA., 156 pp.

SAXEN, L. & TOIVONEN, S. (1961). The two gradient hypothesis in primary induction. The combined effect of two types of inductors in different ratios. *J. Embryol. exp. Morph.* **9**, 514–528.

SCHARF, S. R. & GERHART, J. C. (1980). Determination of the dorso-ventral axis in eggs of *Xenopus laevis*: Complete rescue of UV-impaired eggs by oblique orientation before first cleavage. *Devl Biol.* **79**, 181–198.

SCHARF, S. R. & GERHART, J. C. (1983). Axis determination in eggs of *Xenopus laevis*: A critical period before first cleavage, identified by the common effects of cold, pressure, and ultraviolet irradiation. *Devl Biol.* **99**, 75–87.

SCHARF, S. R., ROWNING, B., WU, M. & GERHART, J. C. (1989). Hyperdorsoanterior embryos from *Xenopus* eggs treated with D_2O. *Devl Biol.* (in press).

SLACK, J. M. W. & ISAACS, H. V. (1989). Presence of basic fibroblast growth factor in the early *Xenopus* embryo. *Development* **105**, 147–154.

SLACK, J. M. W., ISAACS, H. V. & DARLINGTON, B. G. (1988). Inductive effects of fibroblast growth factor and lithium ion on *Xenopus* blastula ectoderm. *Development* **103**, 581–590.

SMITH, J. C. & SLACK, J. M. W. (1983). Dorsalization and neural induction: Properties of the organizer in *Xenopus laevis*. *J. Embryol. exp. Morph.* **78**, 299–317.

SPEMANN, H. (1938). *Embryonic Development and Induction*, Yale University Press, New Haven, 401pp.

STEWART, R. & GERHART, J. C. (1989). The organization of the marginal zone of the late blastula stage of *Xenopus laevis*. *Devl Biol.* (submitted).

STEWART-SAVAGE, J. & GREY, R. (1982). The temporal and spatial relationship between cortical contraction, sperm trail formation, and pronuclear migration in fertilized *Xenopus* eggs. *Wilhelm Roux' Arch. devl Biol.* **191**, 241–245.

TANNAHILL, D. & MELTON, D. A. (1989). Localized synthesis of Vg1 protein during early *Xenopus* development. *Development*, in press.

TERASAKI, M., CHEN, L. B. & FUJIWARA, K. (1986). Microtubules and the endoplasmic reticulum are highly independent structures. *J. Cell Biol.* **103**, 1557–1568.

TOURTE, M., MIGNOTTE, F. & MOUNOLOU, J.-C. (1984). Heterogeneous distribution and replication activity of mitochondria in *Xenopus laevis* oocytes. *Eur. J. Cell Biol.* **34**, 171–178.

UBBELS, G. A., HARA, K., KOSTER, C. H. & KIRSCHNER, M. W. (1983). Evidence for a functional role of the cytoskeleton in determination of the dorsoventral axis in *Xenopus laevis* eggs. *J. Embryol. exp. Morph.* **77**, 15–37.

VALE, R. D. (1987). Intracellular transport using microtubule based motors. *A. Rev. Cell Biol.* **3**, 347–378.

VINCENT, J.-P. & GERHART, J. C. (1987). Subcortical rotation in *Xenopus* eggs: an early step in embryonic axis specification. *Devl Biol.* **123**, 526–539.

VINCENT, J.-P., OSTER, G. F. & GERHART, J. C. (1986). Kinematics of grey crescent formation in *Xenopus* eggs: The displacement of subcortical cytoplasm relative to the egg surface. *Devl Biol.* **113**, 484–500.

VINCENT, J.-P., SCHARF, S. R. & GERHART, J. C. (1987). Subcortical rotation in *Xenopus* eggs: a preliminary study of its mechanochemical basis. *Cell Mot. & Cytoskel.* **8**, 143–154.

WADDINGTON, C. H. & PERRY, M. M. (1956). Teratogenic effects of trypan blue on amphibian embryos. *J. Embryol. exp. Morph.* **4**, 110–119.

WESSEL, G. & McCLAY, D. R. (1987). Gastrulation in the sea urchin requires deposition of cross linked collagen within the extracellular matrix. *Devl Biol.* **103**, 235–245.

WILSON, P. A., OSTER, G. & KELLER, R. (1989). Cell rearrangement and segmentation in *Xenopus*: direct observation of cultured explants. *Development* **105**, 155–166.

WYLIE, C. C., BROWN, D., GODSAVE, S. F., QUARMBY, J. & HEASMAN, J. (1985). The cytoskeleton of *Xenopus* oocytes and its role in development. *J. Embryol. exp. Morph.* **89 Supplement**, 1–15.

Development 1989 Supplement, 53–57
Printed in Great Britain © The Company of Biologists Limited 1989

Genetics of intercellular signalling in *C. elegans*

JUDITH AUSTIN[1,3], ELEANOR M. MAINE[1] and JUDITH KIMBLE[1,2]

[1]*Laboratory of Cell and Molecular Biology, Graduate School* and [2]*Department of Biochemistry* and [3]*Department of Genetics,*
College of Agricultural and Life Sciences, University of Wisconsin-Madison, Madison, Wisconsin 53706, USA

Summary

Cell–cell interactions play a significant role in controlling cell fate during development of the nematode *Caenorhabditis elegans*. It has been found that two genes, *glp-1* and *lin-12*, are required for many of these decisions. *glp-1* is required for induction of mitotic proliferation in the germline by the somatic distal tip cell and for induction of the anterior pharynx early in embryogenesis. *lin-12* is required for the interactions between cells of equivalent developmental potential, which allow them to take on different fates. Comparison of these two genes on a molecular level indicates that they are similar in sequence and organization, suggesting that the mechanisms of these two different sets of cell–cell interactions are similar.

Key words: *Caenorhabditis elegans*, cell–cell interaction, cell fate, *glp-1*, *lin-12*.

Introduction

Interactions between cells have been shown to be crucial to the determination of cell fate in a variety of organisms. These interactions were first observed in classical experiments with sea urchin and frog embryos (e.g. Driesch, 1891; Spemann and Mangold, 1924). More recently, cell interactions that influence the determination of cell fate have been described in the nematode *Caenorhabditis elegans*. In this brief review, we describe several cellular interactions that influence development in *C. elegans* and two genes, *glp-1* and *lin-12*, that are required for these interactions. Remarkably, these two genes, which are required in different sets of cell–cell interactions, appear to encode similar proteins, indicating that diverse regulatory interactions during development may rely on a similar underlying biochemical mechanism.

Cell interactions in *C. elegans*

The evidence for cell–cell interactions in *C. elegans* has come primarily from experiments in which particular cells were physically removed, by laser ablation or puncture with a needle, and the effect on development of other cells was monitored (Sulston and White, 1980; Kimble and White, 1981; Kimble, 1981; Sulston *et al.* 1983; Priess and Thomson, 1987). Three of the regulatory interactions that have been identified by these experiments are summarized in Table 1. They include control of germline proliferation by the distal tip cell (Kimble and White, 1981), induction of pharyngeal mesoderm in the embryo (Priess and Thomson, 1987),

and regulation among precursor cells of equivalent developmental potential so that they adopt different fates (Sulston and White, 1980; Kimble, 1981; Sulston *et al.* 1983). We have focused on the interaction that takes place between the distal tip cell and the germline. In *C. elegans*, proliferation of germline cells occurs throughout the lifetime of the animal; germ cells located close to the distal tip cell are in the mitoic cell cycle while more proximal germ cells enter meiosis. [The germline tissue is actually a syncytium. However, each germline nucleus occupies its own membrane-bound alcove of cytoplasm located at the edge of a common anuclear cytoplasm (Hirsh *et al.* 1976). Each germline nucleus and its cytoplasm is called a germ cell for simplicity.] If the distal tip cell is destroyed at any time during postembryonic development, germ cells leave the mitotic cell cycle, enter meiosis and undergo gametogenesis (Kimble and White, 1981). Thus the distal tip cell must signal cells of the germline to continue dividing mitotically. By isolating loss-of-function mutations whose phenotypes mimic the effect of disrupting the interaction between distal tip cell and germline, we hope to identify the gene products that mediate this interaction. So far, we have identified one gene, *glp-1*, required for this interaction.

glp-1 affects cell interactions needed for germline and pharynx development

The *glp-1* locus was identified in a screen for mutations affecting germline development (Austin and Kimble, 1987). Six recessive alleles of *glp-1* were isolated in a screen of 20 000 mutagenized chromosomes; this fre-

Table 1. *Regulatory cell interactions in* C. elegans *development**

Signalling cell	Receiving cell	Normal fate of receiving cell	Fate of receiving cell after removal of signal	Deduced interaction
Distal tip cell (dtc)	Germline	Continued mitotic proliferation	Germ cells enter meiosis	Dtc induces germline to continue mitosis
P₁ blastomere	AB blastomere	AB gives rise to anterior pharynx	AB does not produce anterior pharynx	P₁ induces AB to produce anterior pharynx
1° cell	2° cell	2° fate	Cell that would be 2° becomes 1°	1° cell inhibits 2° cell from becoming 1°

* Only cell interactions discussed in this review are listed.

quency suggests that these mutations result in a loss of *glp-1* activity. Other alleles of *glp-1* were independently identified in a screen for mutations that result in defective embryogenesis (Priess *et al.* 1987). In wild-type animals, two germline precursor cells give rise to approximately 2000 germ cells in the adult hermaphrodite. In *glp-1(−)* animals only 4–8 germ cells are produced in all; they undergo meiosis and form a small number of gametes (Table 2). This switch of the germ cells from mitosis to meiosis is similar to the effect of ablating the distal tip cell early in larval development (Kimble and White, 1981). Experiments using temperature-sensitive alleles have shown that there is a continuous requirement for *glp-1* activity. This result parallels the observation seen for the distal tip cell–germline interaction: the presence of the distal tip cell is required throughout germline development for continued germ cell proliferation (Kimble and White, 1981).

In addition to their effect on germline development, mutations in *glp-1* result in an embryonic phenotype that indicates a requirement for maternal *glp-1* product during embryogenesis (Priess *et al.* 1987; Austin and Kimble, 1987). This embryonic phenotype can be observed using conditional mutations in *glp-1*. At permissive temperature, *glp-1(ts)* homozygotes produce a normal number of germ cells, but when shifted as adults to restrictive temperature, their progeny do not survive. Moreover, the *glp-1(ts)/glp-1(+)* heterozygous cross-progeny of a *glp-1(ts)* mother do not survive. Therefore, *glp-1* product must be contributed by the mother for survival of her progeny. The lethal phenotype of *glp-1(−)* embryos includes defects in hypodermal morphogenesis and pharyngeal development (Priess *et al.*

1987). The embryos have a near normal number of cells, but they are missing the anterior half of their pharynx and they do not undergo the morphogenesis that normally changes a ball of cells into an elongated worm during embryogenesis (Table 2). It has been shown that, while development of the posterior pharynx occurs in a cell-autonomous manner, formation of the anterior pharynx requires an inductive interaction between the AB blastomere (or its descendants) and the P1 blastomere (or its descendants) (Table 1). Temperature-shift experiments have shown that maternal *glp-1* product is required between the 4-cell and 28-cell stages of embryogenesis. Cell destruction experiments have shown that induction of the anterior pharynx occurs during this same early period of embryogenesis (Priess *et al.* 1987). It is not presently known whether inductive interactions are also required for proper formation of the hypodermis.

What role does *glp-1* play in the cell–cell interactions controlling development of the germline and the pharynx; is it, for example, a component of the signalling mechanism or the receiving mechanism? To address this question, we examined genetic mosaic animals where either the distal tip cell or the germline was *glp-1(−)* (Austin and Kimble, 1987). Our results are summarized in Table 3. They indicate that the *glp-1* activity necessary for continued proliferation of the germline is produced by the germline and not by the distal tip cell. This implies that *glp-1* encodes a component of the receiving machinery for the distal tip cell–germline interaction rather than the distal tip cell signal. It is not possible to use these genetic mosaics to determine where maternally derived *glp-1* gene product

Table 2. *Mutant phenotypes of* glp-1 *and* lin-12

gene	genotype	phenotype	defective interaction
glp-1*	m(+/−);z(−/−) m(−/−);z(+/−) or m(−/−);z(−/−)	all germ cells enter meiosis anterior pharynx not formed	distal tip cell–germline P₁/AB
lin-12†	lf/lf gf/gf or gf/+	both cells follow 1° fate both cells follow 2° fate	signalling between cells in equivalence groups

m, maternal genotype; z, zygotic genotype; lf, loss-of-function; gf, gain-of-function.
* Austin and Kimble (1987); Priess *et al.* (1987). † Greenwald *et al.* (1983).

Table 3. *Genetic mosaic experiments with* glp-1*

	Genotype		Phenotype
Animal	Distal tip cell	Germline	No. germline nuclei
Wild-type	*glp-1(+)*	*glp-1(+)*	~2000
Mutant	*glp-1(−)*	*glp-1(−)*	4–8
Mosaic	*glp-1(+)*	*glp-1(−)*	~2000
Mosaic	*glp-1(−)*	*glp-1(+)*	4–8

*The results summarized here are from Austin and Kimble (1987).

is required for induction of the pharynx during embryogenesis, but we think it likely that *glp-1* acts on the receiving end of this interaction as well.

lin-12 and equivalence groups

The *lin-12* locus was identified in a general screen for mutations that produced defects in the cell lineages of the vulva (Greenwald *et al.* 1983). Mutations in this gene cause changes in cell fate similar to the results of laser ablation experiments, suggesting that this gene product is necessary for cell–cell signalling (Table 1 and Table 2) (Greenwald *et al.* 1983; Sternberg, 1988). In particular, *lin-12* appears to be involved in the interactions that occur between cells in equivalence groups. Such sets of cells have equivalent developmental potential, but, as a result of cell–cell interactions, take on different cell fates. Normally, one of a pair of equivalent cells adopts a primary fate while the other cell adopts a secondary fate. If either of the two cells is destroyed by laser ablation, the remaining cell will adopt the primary fate, suggesting that an interaction takes place between these cells in which the cell adopting the primary fate prevents the other cell from also adopting this fate (Kimble, 1981). Two types of *lin-12* alleles have been isolated. In *lin-12(lf)* (loss-of-function) mutants, both cells adopt the primary fate, while in *lin-12(gf)* (gain-of-function) mutants both adopt the secondary fate (Greenwald *et al.* 1983). Analysis of animals that are genetic mosaics for *lin-12(+)* indicates that *lin-12* acts on the receiving end of these cell interactions (Seydoux and Greenwald, 1989).

Molecular analyses of glp-1 and lin-12

We were able to identify the *glp-1* gene on a molecular level by making use of its proximity to *lin-12* (Austin and Kimble, 1989). *glp-1* is located 0·02 map units to the right of *lin-12* on LGIII (Austin and Kimble, 1987). Comparisons of genetic and molecular distances in the region surrounding *lin-12* (Greenwald *et al.* 1987) indicated that this genetic distance would correspond to 20–40 kb. *lin-12* has been cloned (Greenwald, 1985) and the region of the *C. elegans* genome surrounding *lin-12* has been placed in a series of overlapping cosmids (Greenwald *et al.* 1987). Using these cosmids as hybridization probes, we examined the pattern of restriction

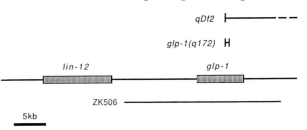

Fig. 1. Map of the *lin-12 – glp-1* region showing the relative positions of the two genes. The extent of the genomic region contained in the cosmid ZK506 is shown below the map. The extent of the deletions in *glp-1(q172)* and *qDf2* is shown above the map. The right endpoint of *qDf2* has not been determined but it is to the right of the region contained in ZK506.

fragments produced by DNA isolated from wild-type animals and animals carrying mutations in *glp-1*. We found that the cosmid ZK506 detected DNA alterations associated with three different *glp-1* mutations (Fig. 1) (Austin and Kimble, 1989). Two of these mutations, *glp-1(q172)* and *qDf2*, contain deletions while *glp-1(q339)* contains a complex rearrangement. We have identified a single transcript produced from the region identified by these three *glp-1* mutations. This transcript is altered in size by *glp-1(q172)*, confirming that it is the *glp-1* transcript.

Fortuitously, a search of the *C. elegans* genome for *lin-12* homologues identified one such homologue in the cosmid ZK506 (Yochem and Greenwald, 1989). The region of *lin-12* homology was centered on the transcription unit that we had identified as *glp-1*. Subsequent sequence analysis has shown that *glp-1* is similar both in sequence and organization to *lin-12* (Yochem and Greenwald, 1989). *lin-12* is also homologous to a *Drosophila* gene, *Notch* (Greenwald, 1985; Yochem *et al.* 1988). *Notch* has been shown to be required for the decision between differentiation as an epidermal precursor or a neuroblast which takes place during *Drosophila* embryogenesis (Poulson, 1937). Thus all three homologous genes, *glp-1*, *lin-12* and *Notch*, influence a developmental decision of cell fate. In each case, it is thought that this developmental decision occurs as the result of cell–cell interactions. The deduced amino acid sequences of all three genes have the molecular characteristics predicted for membrane proteins (Yochem and Greenwald, 1989; Yochem *et al.* 1988; Wharton *et al.* 1985). Although the functions of *glp-1*, *lin-12* and *Notch* in mediating cell interactions are not known, a simple possibility is that each encodes a receptor. In the case of *glp-1*, its product might be the receptor that binds the signal emitted by the distal tip cell.

Mode of action of glp-1

Fig. 2 presents one model for the molecular function of *glp-1* in the germline. We show the *glp-1* product as a receptor located in the membrane of the germline syncytium. Upon binding of the signalling molecule

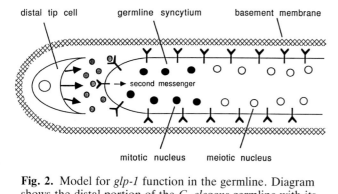

distal tip cell   germline syncytium   basement membrane

second messenger

mitotic nucleus   meiotic nucleus

Fig. 2. Model for *glp-1* function in the germline. Diagram shows the distal portion of the *C. elegans* germline with its associated distal tip cell and basement membrane. The distal tip cell is a somatic cell that signals to the germline syncytium. Germline nuclei at the distal end of the syncytium remain in mitosis; germline nuclei further proximal enter meiosis. In this figure, the distal tip cell is shown at some distance from the germline in order to allow the drawing of signal molecules in the intercellular space. In the animal, the membrane of the distal tip cell is closely juxtaposed to the membrane of the germline. No basement membrane separates the distal tip cell from the germline; instead a basement membrane encapsulates both and separates the gonad from the surrounding pseudocoelom (Kimble and Ward, 1988).

Based on the genetic mosaic experiments of Austin and Kimble (1987) and the predicted *glp-1* molecular structure (Yochem and Greenwald, 1989), we propose that *glp-1* encodes a component of the membrane receptor for the signal produced by the distal tip cell. In this figure we show the *glp-1* product as a receptor (**Y**) that is present throughout the germline; this is one possibility but there is no evidence to date of its localization. We propose that the distal tip cell emits a signal (◯) that binds the *glp-1* receptor locally. Since the distal tip cell signal appears to act over a distance (Kimble and White, 1981), we propose that the ligand-activated *glp-1* generates a second messenger that diffuses in the germline syncytium. Experiments that show that mutations in collagen genes can suppress the phenotypes of mutations in *glp-1* suggest a role for the basement membrane in the distal tip cell–germline interaction; whether *glp-1* interacts directly with the basement membrane is not presently known.

produced by the distal tip cell, this receptor transduces the signal to direct continued mitotic divisions in the germline. The *glp-1* protein may be present throughout the germline. In this case, it might be the position of the distal tip cell and its signal that determines where *glp-1* will actively direct germline proliferation.

One approach to the identification of genes that interact with *glp-1* and *lin-12* is the isolation of mutations that act as phenotypic suppressors of mutations in these genes. A set of recessive suppressors of both the *glp-1* germline and embryonic phenotypes has been identified (Table 4) (Maine and Kimble, 1989). These mutations suppress hypomorphic and conditional alleles of *glp-1* but not putative null alleles, indicating that they do not simply bypass the requirement for *glp-1* activity. In addition to suppressing the *glp-1* phenotype, these mutations cause an alteration in body morphology: suppressor homozygotes (*sup/sup*) are

Table 4. *Suppression of the* glp-1 *phenotype by mutations that affect body morphology**

Suppressor	*glp-1* genotype	germline phenotype: presence of mitotic germ cells in adult†	embryonic phenotype % hatching‡
−	*glp-1(+)*	+	>99
−	*glp-1(−)*	−	0
dpy-1(e1)	*glp-1(−)*	+	15
dpy-2(q292)	*glp-1(−)*	+	15
dpy-3(e27)	*glp-1(−)*	+	38
dpy-7(q288)	*glp-1(−)*	+	12
dpy-8(q287)	*glp-1(−)*	+	19
dpy-9(e12)	*glp-1(−)*	+	11
dpy-10(q291)	*glp-1(−)*	+	15
sqt-1(e1350)	*glp-1(−)*	+	2

* Results summarized here are from Maine and Kimble (1989). All animals grown at 20°C.
† Presence of mitotically dividing germline nuclei in *sup/sup*; *glp-1(−)/glp-1(−)* hermaphrodites was assayed two days after they became young adults.
‡ Percentage of hatching was measured for eggs laid by *sup/sup;glp-1(−)/glp-1(−)* hermaphrodites. Data shown here include all embryos produced by each animal. In general, the percentage of eggs that hatched was much higher at the beginning of the egg-laying period than at the end of it.

shorter than normal [a Dumpy (Dpy) phenotype]. The suppressor mutations have all turned out to be located in previously identified genes. Alleles of these genes, isolated in screens for mutations that alter body morphology, also suppress mutations in *glp-1*, indicating that the suppression is not due to unusual mutations in these genes. It has been shown that the change in body morphology is not sufficient for suppression, as mutations in other *dpy* genes do not have this effect. Two of the suppressor genes, *sqt-1* and *dpy-10*, have been shown to encode collagens (Kramer *et al.* 1988; J. Kramer, personal communication). Suppression of the *glp-1(−)* phenotype by mutations in genes encoding collagen suggests that there is a role for extracellular matrix in the interaction between distal tip cell and germline. One possibility is that suppression of the *glp-1* phenotype is caused by effects on the basement membrane surrounding both the germline and the distal tip cell (Fig. 2).

Conclusions

The identification of *glp-1* and *lin-12* is an important first step towards understanding the mechanism of cell–cell interactions in *C. elegans*. Several major questions remain unanswered. Does the same *glp-1* product mediate both its germline and embryonic functions? If so, what are the signals and are they the same? Are the *glp-1* and *lin-12* proteins actually receptors for intercellular signals or do they serve some other function that is critical to transduction of the signal? Although the *glp-1* and *lin-12* genes code for similar proteins, genetic data suggest that these two proteins are required for different sets of cell–cell interactions. Is this difference in function due to differences in biochemical specificity or in the pattern of expression for these two genes? Finally, the suppression of mutations in *glp-1* by mutations in at least two collagen genes suggests a possible role for extracellular matrix in cell–cell interactions. Does *glp-1* interact directly with the basement membrane surrounding the germline and, if so, how is this interaction changed by mutations in collagen genes? The answers to these questions are now accessible. Starting with the cloned *glp-1* and *lin-12* genes, it will be possible to analyze the regulation and function of their products

We are grateful to Geraldine Sedoux, John Yochem, Iva Greenwald and Jim Kramer for sharing unpublished results. This research was supported by a U.S. Public Health Service grant GM31816 and a Research Career Development Award HD00630 to J.K. J.A. is a trainee of the NIH Predoctoral Training Program in Genetics GM07133. E.M. is supported by Public Health Service Grant GM11569.

References

AUSTIN, J. & KIMBLE, J. (1987). *glp-1* is required in the germ line for regulation of the decision between mitosis and meiosis in *C. elegans*. *Cell* **51**, 589–599.

AUSTIN, J. & KIMBLE, J. (1989). Transcript analysis of *glp-1* and *lin-12*, homologous genes required for cell interactions during development of *C. elegans*. *Cell* (in press).

DRIESCH, H. (1891). Entwicklungsmechanische Studien. I. Der Werth der beiden ersten Furchungszellen in der Echinodermenentwicklung. Experimentelle Erzeugung von Theil und Doppelbidungen. II. Uber die Beziehunger des Lichtes zur ersten Etappe der thierischen Formbildung. *Z. Wiss. Zool.* **53**, 160.

GREENWALD, I. (1985). *lin-12*, a nematode homeotic gene, is homologous to a set of mammalian proteins that includes epidermal growth factor. *Cell* **43**, 583–590.

GREENWALD, I., COULSON, A., SULSTON, J. & PRIESS, J. (1987). Correlation of the physical and genetic maps in the *lin-12* region of *Caenorhabditis elegans*. *Nucleic Acids Res.* **15**, 2295–2307.

GREENWALD, I. S., STERNBERG, P. W. & HORVITZ, H. R. (1983). The *lin-12* locus specifies cell fates in *Caenorhabditis elegans*. *Cell* **24**, 435–444.

HIRSH, D., OPPENHEIM, D. & KLASS, M. (1976). Development of the reproductive system of *C. elegans*. *Devl Biol.* **49**, 200–219.

KIMBLE, J. (1981). Alterations in cell lineage following laser ablation of cells in the somatic gonad of *Caenorhabditis elegans*. *Devl Biol.* **87**, 286–300.

KIMBLE, J. & WARD, S. (1988). Germ-line development and fertilization. In *The nematode* Caenorhabditis elegans, (ed. W. B. Wood), pp. 191–213. Cold Spring Harbor, New York: Cold Spring Harbor Press.

KIMBLE, J. E. & WHITE, J. G. (1981). On the control of germ cell development in *Caenorhabditis elegans*. *Devl Biol.* **81**, 208–219.

KRAMER, J. M., JOHNSON, J. J., EDGAR, R. S., BASCH, C. & ROBERTS, S. (1988). The *sqt-1* gene of *C. elegans* encodes a collagen critical for organismal morphogenesis. *Cell* **55**, 555–565.

MAINE, E. & KIMBLE, J. (1989). Identification of genes that interact with *glp-1*, a gene required for inductive cell interactions in *Caenorhabditis elegans*. *Development* **106**, 133–143.

POULSON, D. F. (1937). Chromosomal deficiencies and embryonic development of *Drosophila melanogaster*. *Proc. natn. Acad. Sci. U.S.A.* **23**, 133–137.

PRIESS, J. R., SCHNABEL, H. & SCHNABEL, R. (1987). The *glp-1* locus and cellular interactions in early *C. elegans* embryos. *Cell* **51**, 601–611.

PRIESS, J. R. & THOMSON, J. N. (1987). Cellular interactions in early *C. elegans* embryos. *Cell* **48**, 241–250.

SEYDOUX, G. & GREENWALD, I. (1989). Cell autonomy of *lin-12* function in a cell fate decision in *C. elegans*. *Cell* **57**, 1237–1245.

SPEMANN, H. & MANGOLD, H. (1924). Uber Induktion von Embryonalanlagen durch Implantation artfremder Organisatoren. *Wilhelm Roux's Arch. EntwMech. Org.* **100**, 599.

STERNBERG, P. W. (1988). Lateral inhibition during vulval induction in *Caenorhabditis elegans*. *Nature, Lond.* **335**, 551–554.

SULSTON, J. E., SCHIERENBERG, E., WHITE, J. G. & THOMSON, N. (1983). The embryonic cell lineage of the nematode *Caenorhabditis elegans*. *Devl Biol.* **100**, 64–119.

SULSTON, J. E. & WHITE, J. G. (1980). Regulation and cell autonomy during postembryonic development of *Caenorhabditis elegans*. *Devl Biol.* **78**, 577–597.

WHARTON, K. A., JOHANSEN, K. M., XU, T. AND ARTAVANIS-TSAKONAS, S. (1985). Nucleotide sequence from the neurogenic locus Notch implies a gene product that shares homology with proteins containing EGF-like repeats. *Cell* **43**, 567–581.

YOCHEM, J. & GREENWALD, I. (1989). *glp-1* and *lin-12*, genes implicated in distinct cell-cell interactions in *C. elegans*, encode similiar transmembrane proteins. *Cell* (in press).

YOCHEM, J., WESTON, K. & GREENWALD, I. (1988). The *Caenorhabditis elegans lin-12* gene incodes a transmembrane protein with overall similarity to *Drosophila Notch*. *Nature, Lond.* **335**, 547–550.

Development 1989 Supplement, 59–63
Printed in Great Britain © The Company of Biologists Limited 1989

Short-range positional signals in the developing *Drosophila* eye

ANDREW TOMLINSON

MRC Laboratory of Molecular Biology, Hills Road, Cambridge CB2 2QH

Summary

Positional signals provided by immediate neighbours appear to direct developmental decisions in the eye of *Drosophila*. By a combined genetic and molecular approach the biochemical bases of the signal and reception mechanisms are being systematically dissected. Three key gene products have now been identified. *sevenless* is a transmembrane tyrosine kinase probably transducing positional signals that direct the R7 cell to its fate. The *bride of sevenless* gene product is on the signalling side of the mechanism and is required in R8 for R7 to develop. The type of protein *bride of sevenless* encodes is not yet known. The *rough* gene encodes a transcription factor on the signalling side required in R2 and R5 for positional signals to be transmitted to neighbouring cells.

Key words: *Drosophila*, compound eye, positional signals, tyrosine kinase transmembrane receptor, homeobox.

Introduction

Cells within a developing organism can be directed to their fate by positional cues. These can be long range in nature with cells being developmentally directed by signals from a distant source. Until recently few long-range diffusable signals had been identified, however some good examples have now been demonstrated. Perhaps the best example is the *bicoid* protein which is translated in the anterior region of the *Drosophila* embryo and redistributes posteriorly. A gradient of protein concentration is then established along the anterior–posterior axis of the embryo, to which the *hunchback* gene is thought to respond (Driever and Nüsslein-Volhard, 1989). Many developmental phenomena are difficult to explain with models using long-range diffusable molecules and positional signals which operate over smaller distances local to the source itself are expected. Spatially restrained positional signalling could occur when cues are communicated between immediate neighbours. There have been few descriptions of this but there are some good examples in the vertebrate immune response where signals are passed through the MHC complexes of cells contacting each other. Strong evidence is accumulating from analyses of ommatidial development in the compound eye of the fruit fly for positional signals that are of short-range nature and are presented by directly adjacent cells.

The compound eye is made from many hundred identical subunit ommatidia each of which is a simple assembly of 20 cells (Fig. 1). Each cell can be identified both by its position in the unit and its cell type, and the many hundred fold reiteration of the structure allows large numbers to be sampled in a single preparation.

Cell lineage directed developmental decisions do no occur in assembling ommatidia (Ready *et al.* 1976; Lawrence and Green, 1979) and examinations of cell-fate choices occurring in this system therefore focus upon the nature of the positional cues. The specific questions that are being addressed are the nature and transmission of the signals, the mechanisms the cells use to receive them, and the molecular events that follow reception and lead to developmental decisions.

Ommatidia develop in a monolayer epithelium, contained within the eye–antennal imaginal disc (Fig. 1D), in which cells extend from the apical surface to the basal membrane. Each ommatidium is built from a foundation precluster made from five cells destined to form photoreceptors R2, R3, R4, R5 and R8. The nuclei of these cells are positioned within the apical regions of the epithelium and the nuclei of all other cells destined to join the ommatidium are placed in the basal regions. Cells are systematically incorporated into the cellular unit and the ommatidium grows in a radial manner. As a cell joins the ommatidium it first establishes a precise set of contacts with cluster cells in the apical regions. Subsequently these cellular contacts extend throughout the entire apical/basal depth of the ommatidium and the nucleus of the cell rises from its basal position into the apical clustering. Following this the cell shows evidence of differentiation such as expression of neural antigens recognisable by specific antibodies and axon out-growth. The five cell unit grows to eight cells with the incorporation of the cells destined to become R1, R6 and R7, completing the photoreceptor complement of the ommatidium. Lens-secreting cone cells are the next to be added and in this manner the ommatidium carries on growing. Using antibodies that recognise neural epitopes a developmental sequence can be

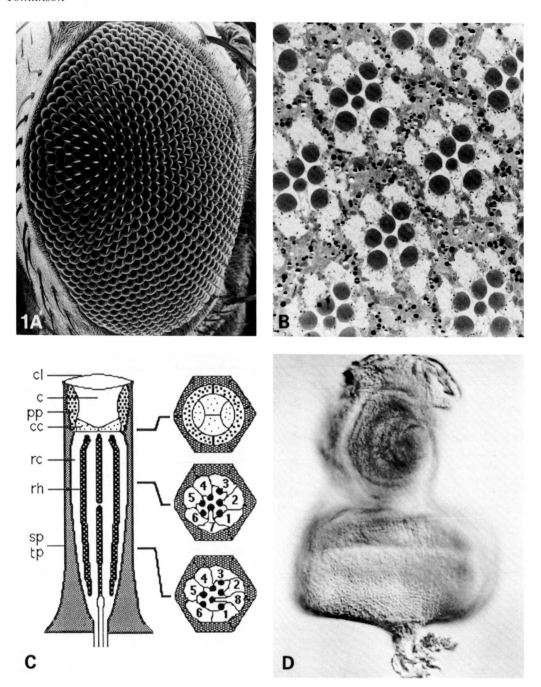

Fig. 1. (A) A smooth array of 700–800 ommatidia forms a Drosophila compound eye. Anterior is to the right. Small mechanosensory bristles project between ommatidia. (B) Tangential section of the eye; anterior is to the right. In any cross section, ommatidia present an asymmetric, trapezoidal pattern of seven rhabdomeres. (C) A schematic ommatidium, anterior is to the right. Below the corneal lens (cl) is a second lens element, the pseudocone (c), which is a refractile extracellular secretion of the four underlying cone cells (cc). The accessory cone cells meet in the centre occluding the principal cells from contact. The cone cells are collared by the two primary pigment cells (pp). Photoreceptors or retinuala cells (rc) are elongated sensory neurons that carry rhabdomeres (rh), dense stacks of rhodopsin-loaded microvilli. Rhabdomeres of photoreceptors R1–R6 extend the depth of the ommatidium. The rhabdomere of R7 lies above that of R8 on the central axis. A sheath of secondary and tertiary pigment cells (sp, tp) optically insulates each ommatidium. (D) A late third instar eye-antennal disc; anterior is to the top. The upper portion is the antennal disc which is folded into a series of concentric rings, and below it the briad slightly cupped eye disc. The morphogenetic furrow (indentation visible in eye disc) lies dorsoventrally and moves across the eye disc from posterior to anterior. Ommatidial patterning occurs posterior to the furrow. At the posterior of the eye disc is the optic stalk which carries the axons to the brain (not shown). Reprinted from Tomlinson and Ready (1987a), with permission.

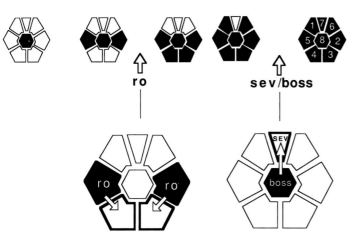

Fig. 2. Sequential development of the ommatidium. Upper panel shows the differentiation sequence of the eight photoreceptors. R8 differentiates first followed by the pair R2 and R5, next come R3 and R4, followed by R1 and R6 and lastly R7. The cells are shown in the positions they come to occupy rather than the position they hold at any particular stage. Below shows where mutations have identified gene products involved in the inductive sequence. *rough* (ro) breaks the sequence after the addition of R2 and R5 but before the determination of R3 and R4, the gene product is required in R2 and R5 to communicate a signal to R3 and R4. *sevenless* (sev) and *bride of sevenless* (boss) prevent the differentiation of R7. *boss* is required in R8 to signal and *sev* is required in R7 to receive.

detected in the five cells of the precluster. R8 is the first to differentiate followed by the pair R2 and R5 followed by the pair R3 and R4. R1 and R6, and R7 follow in the sequence as to be expected from the description above (Fig. 2; Ready *et al.* 1976; Tomlinson, 1985; Tomlinson and Ready, 1987*a*).

Mutants in which perfectly normal ommatidia form, even though they are surrounded by aberrantly patterned ones indicate the positional cues directing the cells to their fate in the developing ommatidium are local to the ommatidium itself. Since cells differentiate as pairs (R2/5, R3/4, R1/6) then the positional cues directing the cells of a pair to their fate must be presented simultaneously on opposite sides of the ommatidium. A model was proposed to account for these features (Tomlinson and Ready, 1987*a*) in which undetermined cells are cued to their fate by the combination of differing cell types they contact. The model envisages that differentiating cells express cell-type-specific signals and undetermined cells, which occupy a precise position in the developing unit, would be in contact with a specific subset of differentiating types, the combination of which specify the developmental pathway of the undetermined cell (Tomlinson and Ready, 1987*a*). A prediction made from this model is that mutations should be recoverable that interfere with cells' abilities to express signals and others that prevent cells from receiving the signals. Both types of mutation would be expected to cause cells to be developmentally misdirected. In any particular mutant the pattern formation should be normal up to the point when the

particular gene product is used and then the developmental error should occur. Once mutations have been identified mosaic analysis can be used to assess whether the mutation is in a gene used on the signalling or reception side of the mechanism, and to determine in which cells of the ommatidium the gene product is required. Mosaic analysis is performed by inducing a patch of mutant tissue in an otherwise wild-type eye. Where the two tissue types meet the cells of the different genotypes mix freely and ommatidia containing cells of both types form. The questions that can be asked by mosaic and other analyses are: (1) Can surrounding wild-type cells rescue mutant cells from their inappropriate developmental pathway, indicating a role of the gene product on the signalling side of the mechanism? (2) Which specific cells must carry the gene product for the ommatidium to form correctly and do these correspond to the cells that behave wrongly in the mutant? After cloning the gene, its nucleotide sequence may indicate the type of protein encoded, and antibodies raised against the protein can be used to establish in which cells and where in these cells the protein is found. The developmental analysis of the mutant, the mosaic analysis, the nucleotide sequence of the gene and the spatial and temporal localisation of the protein can be collectively assessed for indications of the gene's function in the communication mechanism.

To date there are three genes identified that have been shown to have a role in the communication of the developmental directives between the cells. *sevenless* and *bride of sevenless* are genes used in determining the R7 cell type and *rough* is used to establish R3 and R4.

sevenless

sevenless is a mutation that causes each ommatidium to specifically lack R7 (Harris *et al.* 1976). Analysis of the developmental phenotype showed that, although a cell occupies the position in the developing ommatidium that normally generates R7, it fails to differentiate as that cell type, becoming instead a lens-secreting cone cell. Occupation of the correct developmental position by a cell which then fails to differentiate as the type normal to that position is the phenotype expected of mutations in genes used in the communication mechanism. From mosaic analysis, it has been shown that genetically *sevenless* cells in the R7 position cannot be rescued from transformation to the cone cell by surrounding wild-type cells (Harris *et al.* 1976; Campos-Ortega *et al.* 1979; Tomlinson and Ready, 1987*b*). This indicates that the cell in the R7 position is supplied with the correct positional signals but is incapable of receiving or interpreting them. The nucleotide sequence of the gene correlates well with this, showing that the gene encodes a putative *trans* membrane protein with a large extracellular domain and an intracellular tyrosine kinase, similar in general structure to hormone receptors such as the EGF receptor and insulin receptor (Hafen *et al.* 1987). This led to the proposal that the *sevenless* protein transduces signals for the R7 developmental pathway by binding of a signalling ligand to the large extracellular domain and subsequent modulation of the tyrosine kinase activity internally within the cell. A single amino acid substitution within the tyrosine kinase domain of the protein (known in similar proteins to abolish kinase activity) eliminates *sevenless* gene function, indicating that the signal transduction operates through the kinase domain (Basler and Hafen, 1988). Localisation of the protein indicates it is expressed in many cells (including the presumptive R7) in their apical plasma membranes (Bannerjee *et al.* 1987; Tomlinson *et al.* 1987). Expression of a receptor protein in more cells than those in which it is required is expected of a positional signalling system since prior to occupying a specific position a cell must be able to differentiate as one of many cell types, including the R7 type, which requires the *sevenless* protein. In cells that express the *sevenless* protein and contact R8, an accumulation of the protein is seen where the cells meet R8 in the apical cell junctions (Tomlinson *et al.* 1987). This suggested that a ligand for the *sevenless* protein is expressed by R8, and a requirement for signals from R8 for R7 to develop will be described below. By reintroducing the *sevenless* gene under an inducible (heat shock) promoter it has been demonstrated that *sevenless* protein is required in a short temporal window of ommatidial development, correlating well with the few hours that the protein is detected in the presumptive R7 by antibody analysis (Basler and Hafen, 1989). Blanket expression of the protein using heat shock does not interfere with the R7 developmental decision, neither does it affect the development of the rest of the fly, indicating that *sevenless* activation is achieved by a precise spatial restriction of its ligand(s).

bride of sevenless

bride of sevenless is a mutation with a similar phenotype to *sevenless* in that each ommatidium specifically lacks R7. Mosaic analysis has shown that unlike *sevenless*, R7 can be rescued by surrounding wild-type cells. More specifically, the *bride of sevenless* gene product is required in R8, and only R8, for the ommatidium to generate R7 (Reinke and Zipursky, 1988). This clearly indicates developmental communication occurring between R8 and R7, and correlates well with the interaction between these two cells indicated by the *sevenless* antibody analysis. The *bride of sevenless* gene is not yet cloned so the type of protein it encodes remains to be established.

rough

In developing *rough* ommatidia, the initial stages appear identical to wild type. R8 begins to differentiate normally, followed by R2 and R5 with cells correctly positioned to differentiate as R3 and R4. However, the cells in the R3/4 positions fail to behave correctly and ommatidial development passed this point is aberrant. Again, this is the expected phenotype of a mutation in a gene involved in the communication mechanism, with cells correctly positioned to become specific cell types but failing to do so. Mosaic analysis indicates that the *rough* gene product is required only in R2 and R5 for the ommatidium to develop normally. All other cells in a wide variety of combinations can be mutant without affecting ommatidial development. However, the developmental analysis indicates that R2 and R5 probably develop normally in the mutant, R3 and R4 are the cells that clearly behave inappropriately. This then indicates a developmental communication between R2/5 and R3/4. After R3 and R4 misbehave the ommatidia carry on building in variable and uninterpretable ways. Cells joining the ommatidia later than R3 and R4 may also need R2 and R5 to have the *rough* gene product, but from the analyses performed these requirements would remain undetected.

The nucleotide sequence of the *rough* gene shows it contains a homeobox which suggests a role for the protein in DNA binding and transcriptional regulation. Since the cells in which the protein is required appear normal in the mutant, neighbouring cells being the ones affected, then it is suggested that the *rough* protein acts as a transcription factor regulating the expression of signals by R2 and R5 communicated to the cells destined to become R3 and R4 (Tomlinson *et al.* 1987).

From these analyses it is becoming clear that developmental cues can be presented by directly adjacent cells. Whether these signals are held on the expressing cells' plasma membranes or whether they are short-range diffusable molecules is not clear. The question to be addressed is how applicable very short-range communication is to development generally. There are a large number of developmental phenomena that could be explained by positional signals being passed between directly neighbouring cells, but in general this has yet to be demonstrated. The power of the genetic and mosaic analyses in *Drosophila* has allowed this short range communication to be detected, but finding similar signalling mechanisms in animals lacking experimental advantages will be difficult.

References

BANERJEE, U., RENFRANZ, P. J., HINTON, D. R., RABIN, B. A. AND BENZER, S. (1987*b*). The sevenless protein is expressed apically in cell membranes of developing Drosophila retina; it is not restricted to cell R7. *Cell* **51**, 151–158.

BASLER, K. AND HAFEN, E. (1988). Control of photoreceptor cell fate by the *sevenless* protein requires a functional tyrosine kinase domain. *Cell* **54**, 299–311.

BASLER, K. AND HAFEN, E. (1989). Ubiquitous Expression of sevenless: Position dependent specification of cell fate. *Science* **243**, 931–934.

CAMPOS-ORTEGA, J. A., JURGENS, G. AND HOFBAUER, A. (1979). Cell clones and pattern formation: Studies on sevenless a mutant of Drosophila melanogaster. *Wilhelm Roux' Arch. devl Biol.* **186**, 27–50.

DRIEVER, W. AND NÜSSLEIN-VOLHARD, C. (1989). The bicoid protein is a positive regulator of hunchback transcription in the early Drosophila embryo. *Nature (Lond)* **337**, 138–143.

HAFEN, E., BASLER, K., EDSTROM, J. E. AND RUBIN, G. M. (1987). sevenless, a cell-specific homeotic gene of Drosophila, encodes a putative transmembrane receptor with a tyrosine kinase domain. *Science* **236**, 55–63.

HARRIS, W. A., STARK, W. S. AND WALKER, J. A. (1976). Genetic dissection of the photoreceptor system in the compound eye Drosophila melanogaster. *J. Physiol. (Lond)* **256**, 415–439.

LAWRENCE, P. A. AND GREEN, S. M. (1979). Cell lineage in the developing retina of Drosophila. *Devl Biol.* **71**, 142–152.

READY, D. F., HANSON, T. E. AND BENZER, S. (1976). Development of the Drosophila retina, a neurocrystalline lattice. *Devl Biol.* **53**, 217–240.

REINKE, R. AND ZIPURSKY, S. L. (1988). Cell-cell interactions in the Drosophila retina: The bride of sevenless gene product is required in photoreceptor cell R8 for R7 cell development. *Cell* **55**, 321–330.

TOMLINSON, A. (1985). The cellular dynamics of pattern formation in the eye of Drosophila. *J. Embryol. exp. Morph.* **89**, 313–331.

TOMLINSON, A. AND READY, D. F. (1986). Sevenless: A cell specific homeotic mutation of the Drosophila eye. *Science* **231**, 400–402.

TOMLINSON, A. AND READY, D. F. (1987a). Neuronal differentiation in the Drosophila ommatidium. *Devl Biol.* **120**, 366–376.

TOMLINSON, A. AND READY, D. F. (1987b). Cell fate in the Drosophila ommatidium. *Devl Biol.* **123**, 264–275.

TOMLINSON, A., BOWTELL, D. D. L., HAFEN, E. AND RUBIN, G. M. (1987). Localization of the sevenless protein, a putative receptor of positional information in the eye imaginal disc of Drosophila. *Cell* **51**, 143–150.

Development 1989 Supplement, 65–74
Printed in Great Britain © The Company of Biologists Limited 1989

The *decapentaplegic* gene: a TGF-*β* homologue controlling pattern formation in *Drosophila*

WILLIAM M. GELBART

Department of Cellular and Developmental Biology, Harvard University, 16 Divinity Avenue, Cambridge, MA 02138-2097, USA

Summary

The type *β* transforming growth factor (TGF-*β*) family of secreted factors encompasses a wide range of structurally related proteins that control the state of determination or differentiation in a wide variety of cell types. For all members of the family that have been studied at the protein level, the active moieties arise as dimers of the *C*-terminal ~110 amino acid fragment derived from much longer precursor polypeptides. The hallmark of the family is a series of 7 completely conserved cysteine residues in the *C*-terminus; other conserved amino acid sequences generally cluster in the vicinity of 6 of these 7 cysteines. This report focuses on our current understanding of the genetic structure and developmental role of the *decapentaplegic* (*dpp*) gene in *Drosophila*, the only member of the TGF-*β* family thus far identified in invertebrates. The *dpp* polypeptide bears a sufficiently close relationship to two bone morphogenesis proteins (BMP-2A and BMP-2B) identified in mammals (Wozney *et al.* 1988, *Science* 242, 1528–1534) to warrant the suggestion that *dpp* and the BMP-2s are the descendants of a common ancestral gene. The protein-coding information for *dpp* is contained within a 6 kb DNA segment. An elaborate *cis*-regulatory apparatus, encompassing a >55 kb DNA segment, has evolved to control expression of the *dpp* gene, which is required for determination of dorsal ectoderm in the early embryo, for normal distal outgrowth of the adult appendages, and for sundry other developmental events, which are currently less well-defined. Studies of chimeric individuals and observations of transcript accumulation *in situ* have demonstrated that the *dpp* gene is expressed along the A/P boundary of the imaginal disks. A possible role of *dpp* in elaborating positional information in imaginal disk development is discussed.

Key words: intercellular communication, pattern formation, positional information, TGF-*β*, *Drosophila*, *decapentaplegic* gene, imaginal disk development.

Introduction

The TGF-*β* family comprises a diverse set of 12 polypeptides having profound (generally inhibitory) effects on the growth and/or differentiation of many cell types. Typically, there are no obvious common physiological themes which would have predicted the relationship of these polypeptides to one another, but rather their homology has been revealed through searches of available protein data bases. In the four years following the reported sequencing of the prototypical member of the family, now called TGF-*β*1 (Derynck *et al.* 1985), the family has grown to include one polypeptide identified in the amphibian *Xenopus laevis* [a vegetal pole specific maternal transcript, Vg1 (Weeks and Melton, 1987)], 9 other polypeptides identified in humans and other mammals [a Vg1 cross-homologous gene, Vgr-1 (Lyons *et al.* 1989), TGF-*β*2 (Marquardt *et al.* 1987), TGF-*β*3 (Dijke *et al.* 1988), the inhibin *α* and *β* subunits (Mason *et al.* 1985; Mayo *et al.* 1986), Müllerian inhibiting substance, MIS (Cate *et al.* 1986), three bone morpho-genesis proteins BMP-2A, BMP-2B and BMP-3 (Wozney *et al.* 1988)], and the decapentaplegic product in *Drosophila* [dpp (Padgett *et al.* 1987)].

The mammalian polypeptides are processed to generate secreted dimeric proteins which are thought to bind to cell surface receptors on target cells (Cheifetz *et al.* 1986). The first functional demonstration of a biologically active receptor for TGF-*β*1 and TGF-*β*2 has recently been reported (Boyd and Massagué, 1989). No definitive information is available on signal transduction systems which are activated in target cells in response to ligand-receptor binding. Several members of the TGF-*β* family have been implicated as key factors in determinative or differentiative decisions, and therefore, this family of intercellular signalling molecules is of special interest to developmental biologists. In this report, I will briefly review the current state of information regarding the TGF-*β* family, and will then focus on our current view of the one member of the family thus far identified in invertebrates: the decapentaplegic gene in *Drosophila*.

The biological effects of the vertebrate members of the TGF-β family

In general, the members of the TGF-β family have been isolated on the basis of specific *in vitro* assays: growth inhibition, differentiation inhibition, asymmetric distributions of transcripts. Upon further study, however, it has been found that at least some of these polypeptides have profound and singular effects on the growth or differentiation of many other cell types. Furthermore, by *in situ* localization of transcripts or by immunohistochemistry, it has been shown that at least some TGF-β family gene products are localized in many discrete sites during vertebrate development. However, in most cases, specific *in vivo* roles remain uncertain.

TGF-β1, TGF-β2 and TGF-β3

TGF-β1 was discovered as one of two proteins (the other being TGF-α, which is a member of the EGF family of growth factors) present in conditioned medium of transformed mammalian cell lines which would cause phenotypic transformation of the immortalized NRK (normal rat kidney) cell line, such that it would now exhibit anchorage-independent growth in soft agar (Roberts *et al.* 1985). Since its initial discovery based on this phenotypic transformation assay, TGF-β1 activity and responsiveness have been found in many normal cell types *in vivo* and in cell culture. It is especially abundant in bone and platelets (Roberts *et al.* 1981; Assoian *et al.* 1985). Its physiological functions *in vivo* have not been established. In addition, its effects *in vitro* have proven quite wide ranging. Under many conditions of treatment, it turns out to be growth inhibitory rather than growth promoting (Roberts *et al.* 1985). In other circumstances, it leads to the differentiation of particular cell lines in culture (Ignotz and Massagué, 1985). In part, the effects of TGF-β1 seem to depend upon the profile of other factors which are added along with it (Assoian *et al.* 1984). Many of the actions of TGF-β1 can be explained as the indirect consequences of changes in the architecture of the extracellular matrix (Ignotz and Massagué, 1986; Allen-Hoffmann *et al.* 1988; Montesano and Orci, 1988).

Recent observations have uncovered two proteins (TGF-β2 and TGF-β3) which are close relatives of TGF-β1. Both TGF-β1 and TGF-β2 homodimers have been identified. They are somewhat different in their binding to putative TGF-β receptors (Cheifetz *et al.* 1987), suggesting that they might have different biological activities. TGF-β3 was recovered on the basis of its cross-homology to TGF-β1 and TGF-β2 (Dijke *et al.* 1988). No information is available on its structure or biological effects.

Inhibin/activin

Inhibin, a secretion found in ovarian fluid, suppresses the release of follicle-stimulating hormone (FSH) by the pituitary gland (Ramasharma *et al.* 1984), thereby interfering with ovulation. It is an α/β heterodimer in which both subunits bear structural homologies to the TGF-β's (Mason *et al.* 1985). In pigs, two genes encoding related β-chains have been found (Mason *et al.* 1985). β-chain homodimers, or heterodimers of these β-chains, have been found to have the opposite effect of promoting FSH release; these proteins have been termed 'activins' (Ling *et al.* 1986; Vale *et al.* 1986).

Müllerian inhibiting substance

Müllerian inhibiting substance (MIS) is a homodimer secreted by the fetal testis that contributes to conversion of the indifferent urogenital system into the male reproductive system, by causing regression of the Müllerian ducts (Picon, 1969). It is thus a key factor in the determination of the somatic sexual phenotype of the mammalian fetus. Molecular analysis has revealed it to be a divergent member of the TGF-β family (Cate *et al.* 1986).

Bone morphogenesis proteins

These proteins were identified as products that have the ability to induce bone growth, using the ability to induce infiltration and differentiation of osteoblasts in demineralized bone as an assay system (Wang *et al.* 1988). Two of the proteins, BMP-2A and BMP-2B, are highly conserved (and hence their names), while BMP-3 is more divergent (Wozney *et al.* 1988). No information is available on the *in vivo* roles of these three proteins.

The vegetal pole specific transcript, Vg1

The sequencing of Vg1 cDNAs has revealed that the protein encoded by Vg1 transcripts is a member of the TGF-β family (Weeks and Melton, 1987). Vg1 RNA was first identified as the only transcript that was highly concentrated at the vegetal pole of unfertilized *Xenopus* oöcytes (Melton, 1987; Pondel and King, 1988). As the embryo begins development, the maternal Vg1 RNA becomes incorporated into vegetal cells, which will eventually form the endoderm. At this stage of gastrulation, endodermal cells induce ectoderm to form mesoderm. A TGF-β-like molecule has been implicated in this induction process (Slack *et al.* 1987; Kimelman and Kirschner, 1987; Rosa *et al.* 1987), using TGF-β1 and TGF-β2 polypeptides from mammalian sources. Given the distribution of Vg1 RNA, it has been suggested that Vg1 protein is a strong candidate to be the natural mesoderm-inducing factor (Weeks and Melton, 1987). Characterizations of Vg1 and of mesoderm-inducing factor are the subjects of other reports in this volume.

Recently, using Vg1 probes, Lyons *et al.* (1989) were able to isolate a cross-homologous mammalian gene from a mouse cDNA library. This gene, called Vgr-1 (Vg1-related), is expressed in numerous tissues throughout development. No information is available on the structure of the Vgr-1 protein, or on its biological role.

A structural comparison of the polypeptides of the TGF-β family

In every case in which the protein has been characterized, TGF-β family members are active as secreted dimers. The subunits of these dimers are about 110–130 amino acids in length and derive from longer precursors, ranging in size from approximately 300–600 amino acids. These precursors share several structural features. They all have N-terminal secretion signal sequences and several internal potential N-glycosylation sites; both of these features are consistent with the secreted nature of the polypeptides. No transmembrane domains are apparent in the protein sequences. The precursors all contain several basic residue pairs (arginine–arginine, arginine–lysine, lysine–lysine), at least some of which are the sites of cleavage in the processing of the precursor (*e.g.* Derynck *et al.* 1985). The amino acid conservations that characterize the TGF-β family are confined to the C-terminal 110 amino acid residues. As noted above, it is this C-terminal region that dimerizes to form the mature secreted product. In general, the extensive regions N-terminal to the mature product are poorly conserved between different family members. Nonetheless, if the same member is examined in different vertebrate species, strong homologies in more N-terminal regions are identified as well (*e.g.* Derynck *et al.* 1986). In the case of TGF-β1, a cleavage product of the N-terminal domain remains noncovalently associated with the C-

terminal dimer in a latent form of the secreted molecule (Lyons *et al.* 1988).

With the recent expansion of the membership of the TGF-β family, it has been possible to discern subgroups on the basis of conserved or divergent structural features of the C-terminal portion of the polypeptides. The conservations among the members of the family generally reside in three domains surrounding six of the seven conserved cysteines present in each polypeptide. TGF-β1, TGF-β2, TGF-β3 and inhibin-β have two additional conserved cysteines, placing these molecules in a different subfamily from the others. MIS and inhibin-α show only a low level of conservation to the other polypeptides and to each other (~20–25 %). BMP-2A, BMP-2B, BMP-3, Vg1, Vgr-1 and dpp exhibit at least 45 % conservation (at the level of amino acid identities), and appear to be in their own subfamily. Below, we will discuss evidence that BMP-2A, BMP-2B and dpp are very closely related, and may actually represent the dipteran and mammalian derivatives of the same ancestral gene. The relationships of the different TGF-β family members to one another are demonstrated by a comparison of primary amino acid sequences of their C-termini (Fig. 1).

In summary, in the course of the four years since the first of these sequences – TGF-β1– was published, this vertebrate polypeptide family has come to include a diverse and physiologically unrelated set of factors with a range of very intriguing developmental effects. The homology of the decapentaplegic (dpp) polypeptide,

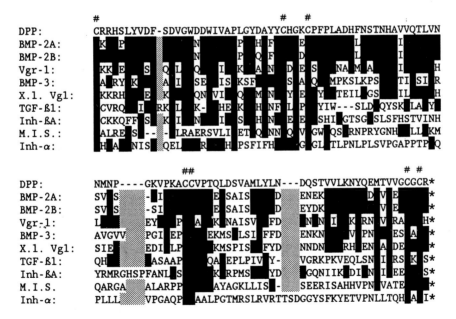

Fig. 1. A comparison of the C-terminal sequences (~100 amino acids) of the decapentaplegic polypeptide and several of the vertebrate members of the TGF-β family. The dpp polypeptide from *Drosophila melanogaster* is presented in the top line of the figure. Other members of the family, described in the text are listed below, in approximate rank order of amino acid similarity. The Vg1 sequence is from *Xenopus laevis*. All other sequences are from mammals. Origins of sequences are given in the text. Amino acid positions that are blacked out (■) are identical to the dpp amino acid. Positions that are shaded (□) represent gaps shared with a gap in the dpp sequence. Thus, the more a sequence is blacked out or shaded, the more similar it is to the dpp polypeptide. A # symbol identifies the 7 completely conserved cysteines in the C-termini of all TGF-β family members. The asterisk at the end of each sequence indicates the presence of a stop codon at aligned positions for each polypeptide.

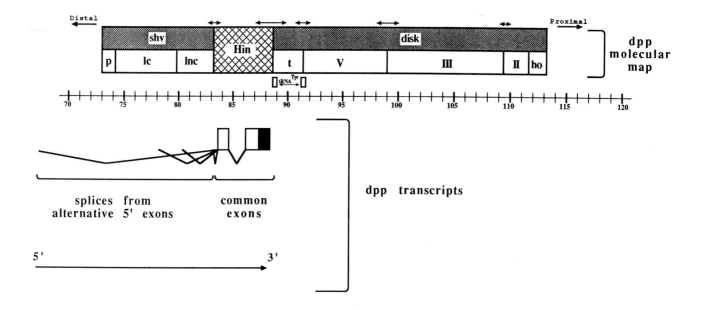

Fig. 2. The molecular map of the *dpp* gene. This map summarizes information presented by St. Johnston *et al.* (1989). The positions of the major segments of the *dpp* gene (**shv-Hin-disk**) and of the subdivisions of the **shv** and **disk** regions are depicted, and are based on the molecular mapping of mutant breakpoints. Double- headed arrows above the molecular map indicate uncertainties in the positions of these boundaries. Distal and proximal indicate the orientation of the *dpp* gene relative to the chromosome 2 (left arm) telomere and centromere, respectively. Below the molecular map are noted the positions of two tRNA^{Tyr} genes within *dpp* (Suter *et al.* 1990). A standard molecular scale, from 70–120 kb, is depicted. The positions of the two exons common to all *dpp* transcript species, falling within the **Hin** region, are shown. The open boxes within these exons represents the extent of the open reading frame of the *dpp* transcripts, and the black box represents 3′ untranslated material (Padgett *et al.* 1987; Padgett *et al.* in preparation). At least 5 different 5′ exons have been identified in different *dpp* cDNAs.

which will be described in the next section, demonstrates that at least one ancestor of this gene family predates the divergence of arthropods from vertebrates, and provides yet another set of important developmental functions controlled by a representative of the TGF-β family.

The *decapentaplegic* polypeptide

We have now characterized several cDNAs corresponding to 5 different classes of overlapping *dpp* transcripts (Padgett *et al.* 1987; St. Johnston *et al.* 1989; Padgett *et al.* in preparation). Each transcript appears to encode the same polypeptide. We have not addressed the questions of possible heterogeneity among the transcripts in terms of stability or translational efficiency. The structures of the cDNAs that correspond to these transcripts are depicted in Fig. 2. These five transcript classes have three exons apiece, and they differ only in their first (*i.e.* 5′) untranslated exon. These untranslated exons appear to be initiated by different promoters and range in size from about 150 bases up to 2 kb. Each transcript class utilizes the same splice acceptor site in the second exon. There is only a single pattern of splicing between the second and third exons.

The first AUG in the open reading frame (ORF) of each transcript is located near the beginning of the common second exon. The ORF extends through the middle of the third exon. If translation initiated with the first AUG, the polypeptide that was produced would be 588 amino acids in length (Padgett *et al.* 1987). We think it likely that the first AUG of the ORF does indeed represent the actual translation initiation codon because (a) it conforms to the consensus sequence for *Drosophila* initiation codons and (b) unlike other AUGs in the ORF, it is followed by a consensus N-terminal signal secretion sequence (Watson, 1984), as expected for a secreted TGF-β-like polypeptide.

Several potential glycosylation sites can be found within the *dpp* ORF, consistent with the view that the *dpp* polypeptide is itself a secreted protein. Several dibasic residues are found within the ORF, suggesting that the primary polypeptide product might be proteolytically cleaved to generate a smaller mature product. The positions of these sites are diagrammed in Fig. 3.

The relationship of the *dpp* polypeptide to other members of the TGF-β family

The *C*-terminal ~110 amino acids of the *dpp* polypep-

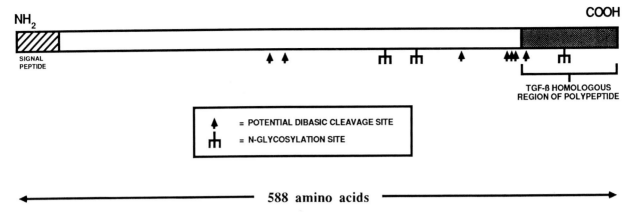

Fig. 3. A schematized view of the dpp polypeptide. The full-length product of the dpp ORF is a 588 amino acid protein containing an *N*-terminal signal peptide and a *C*-terminal region exhibiting high conservation with other members of the TGF-β family. Positions of dibasic residues, some of which may serve as cleavage sites for serine proteases, and *N*-glycosylation sites are shown as indicated. While the dpp polypeptide is the longest member of the family, the basic structure of the molecule parallels the structures of the other family members.

tide show extensive similarity to the comparable regions of the vertebrate TGF-β family members (Fig. 1). Three arginine–arginine dipeptides reside just *N*-terminal to this region of high conservation; these potential proteolytic cleavage sites are thus positioned analogously to the known cleavage sites in most of the other family members. The dpp polypeptide contains the same seven cysteines in its putative *C*-terminal fragment as are shared by the vertebrate family members. The locations of the similarities between the *dpp* polypeptide and the vertebrate members of the TGF-β family conform to the regions of similarity among the vertebrate family members themselves. These conservations reside in three domains surrounding six of the seven *C*-terminal cysteines. We presume this pattern of conservation reflects a common structural motif in this family of molecules.

With the recent report of the primary sequences of human BMP-2A and BMP-2B (Wozney *et al.* 1988), we now have two very strong candidates for the vertebrate analogues of *dpp*. The *C*-termini of BMP-2A and BMP-2B are each 75% identical in amino acid sequence to the corresponding region of the *dpp* polypeptide. Moreover, within the *N*-terminal precursor region, there is 25–30% amino acid identity. The only other polypeptides in the family which show any significant conservation in the *N*-termini are between BMP-2A and BMP-2B themselves, and among TGF-β1, TGF-β2 and TGF-β3. Based on these considerations, we think it very likely that the *dpp* gene of *Drosophila* and the BMP-2A and BMP-2B genes of humans are the modern highly conserved derivatives of a gene which was present in an ancestor common to the arthopod and vertebrate lineages.

The *dpp* gene

The organization of the dpp locus

Numerous observations on the structure and function of the *dpp* gene have coalesced into a clear picture of its

organization. In brief, the *dpp* gene (map location 2–4.0; 22F1,2) is a rather large genetic unit (>55 kb), which produces a single TGF-β-homologous polypeptide (St. Johnston *et al.* 1990; Padgett *et al.* in preparation). This polypeptide is encoded by at least 5 overlapping transcripts (St. Johnston *et al.* 1990; Padgett *et al.* in preparation). These transcripts are initiated by different promoters and contain different 5′ untranslated exons. Each transcript has its own temporal (and presumably spatial) pattern of expression (Gelbart *et al.* 1985; St. Johnston and Gelbart, 1987; St. Johnston *et al.* 1989; Posakony *et al.* 1990). The bulk of the genetic information contained in the >55 kb of *dpp* DNA consists of *cis*-regulatory elements controlling the timing, location and quantity of *dpp* transcription (Gelbart *et al.* 1985; St. Johnston *et al.* 1990; Blackman *et al.* in preparation). These *cis*-regulatory elements must drive a very complex pattern of expression, as the *dpp* gene is required for numerous developmental events, including determination of dorsal ectoderm along the dorsoventral axis of the early embryo (Irish and Gelbart, 1987; St. Johnston and Gelbart, 1987), proper morphogenesis of the adult appendages derived from the imaginal disks (Spencer *et al.* 1982; Posakony *et al.* 1990; Spencer *et al.* in preparation), and other, less well-defined events necessary for proper development of the larva and adult (Segal and Gelbart, 1985).

Some mutations in the *dpp* gene interfere with the production of an active dpp polypeptide product. They are identified as lesions that affect all developmental events controlled by *dpp* (Irish and Gelbart, 1987). Null (amorphic) mutations are called *dpp^{Hin}* alleles, because they are Haplo-insufficient that is, *dpp^{Hin}*/+ animals are lethal, apparently because there is too little *dpp* product in the early embryo to produce proper determination along the dorsoventral axis. Most of these are likely to act by altering the structure of the dpp polypeptide, while the remainder probably derange the structure of all of the transcripts. Some *dpp^{Hin}* alleles have lesions that can be identified by restriction mapping; these lesions cluster in a region of about 6 kb

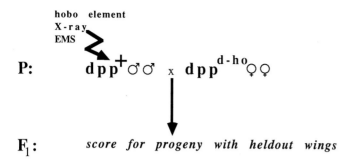

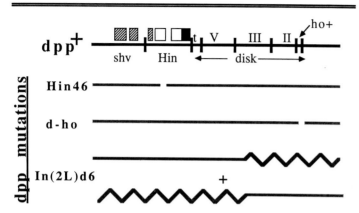

which we term the **Hin** region (St. Johnston *et al.* 1990). This region also contains the two exons encoding the open reading frame for the *dpp* polypeptide. Leaky (hypomorphic) mutations are not haplo-insufficient; because they map to the **Hin** region but are recessive, they are called *dpp*^*hin-r* alleles. All *dpp*^*hin-r* alleles have normal restriction maps in the **Hin** region. We think it likely that some of the *dpp*^*Hin* and many of the *dpp*^*hin-r* lesions are point mutations altering the amino acid sequence of the dpp polypeptide.

Other *dpp* mutations affect only a subset of the diverse array of *dpp* functions. We think that these mutations (virtually all of which are inversions, translocations or deletions: Spencer *et al.* 1982; Segal and Gelbart, 1985; St. Johnston *et al.* 1990) represent lesions disrupting batteries of *cis*-regulatory elements necessary for the proper spatial and temporal deployment of *dpp* transcripts. This is best exemplified by a consideration of the **disk** region, which is a >25 kb untranscribed region 3' to the polyadenylation sites of all *dpp* transcripts.

Mutations in the **disk** region are recessive lesions that disrupt proper *dpp* expression in the imaginal disks, leading to the production of distally incomplete appendages. Several classes of such mutations have been described, with the most severe removing all but the most proximal regions of each appendage. All mutations of the **disk** region are recessive to wild-type.

The mildest alleles of the **disk** region are defective only in wing posture. These 'heldout' (*dpp*^*d-ho*) mutations cause the wings to be held out laterally and perpendicular to the body axis; this phenotype is associated with the loss of specific pattern elements (a group of 25 sensory structures called the sensilla campaniformia-25 or Sc25) on the dorsal base of the wing

Fig. 4. The origins and types of mutations recovered in heldout mutagenesis screens. TOP: The basic scheme for generating *dpp* mutations as alleles of the original heldout (*dpp*^*d-ho*) lesion is shown. Several permutations of this screen, in which different mutagens (X-rays, *hobo* transposon mobilization, ethyl methanesulfonate [EMS]) were employed, extra copies of the **Hin** region were included to recover *dpp*^*null* alleles, and/or rearrangements were included on the *dpp*^*d-ho* tester chromosome to obviate *dpp* transvection effects (Gelbart, 1982). BOTTOM: Specific examples of the three major types of *dpp* lesions recovered as heldout alleles are depicted below a molecular map of the *dpp* region (St. Johnston *et al.* 1990). On the molecular map, the subdivisions of the **disk** region are included. The boxes above the map indicate the position of relevant *dpp* exons. The two common exons are indicated in open and black boxes, as in Fig. 2. The striped boxes indicate the positions of some of the alternative 5' exons containing untranslated information. The *dpp*^*d-ho* mutation is a ~2.8 kb deletion from molecular position 112–114.8 on the molecular map of *dpp*. It presumably deletes a *cis*-regulatory element necessary to elaborate the portion of the dorsal base of the wing which includes a group of mechanoreceptors called the sensilla campaniformia-25 (Sc25) (Spencer *et al.* 1982). Other lesions which delete this region of the gene also confer the heldout phenotype and lack the Sc25. The *dpp*^*Hin46* lesion is a ~0.5 kb deletion within the first of the two common exons, and hence within the *dpp* ORF. It behaves as a null allele of *dpp* (although it is transvection-sensitive) and hence was recovered as a heldout allele (Irish and Gelbart, 1987). *In(2L)dpp*^*d6* is an example of the largest class of heldout alleles recovered by X-irradiation. It is a cytologically visible inversion of the *dpp*^*disk-III* class, and has one breakpoint at ~102 on the molecular map. *In(2L)dpp*^*d6* splits the *dpp* gene into two pieces. The fragment containing the **shv-Hin** region retains its residual activities of the **shv**, **Hin** and **disk-V** regions. The fragment containing the **disk-III**, **disk-II** and **disk-ho** *cis*-regulatory regions is no longer adjacent to the *dpp* transcription unit, and is thus are inactive. Hence, this inversion was recovered as a heldout allele. Most *dpp*^*disk* mutations recovered as heldout alleles are such rearrangement breakpoints falling between the **disk-ho** *cis*-regulatory element and the *dpp* transcription unit.

(Spencer *et al.* 1982). Most mutations of the **disk** region have been recovered as *dpp*^*d-ho* alleles (Fig. 4). When examined in homozygotes, most have a more severe array of mutant phenotypes (Spencer *et al.* 1982; Irish and Gelbart, 1987; Blackman *et al.* 1987). These mutations are generally associated with gross chromosomal rearrangements. Mutant homozygotes lack structures derived from distal portions of the adult appendages. Mild alleles (*dpp*^*disk-II*) only affect the wing, halter and male genital derivatives. Intermediate alleles (*dpp*^*disk-III*) affect all major appendages (wing, halter, leg, eye, antenna, proboscis, male and female genitalia), but sufficient appendages remain to permit *dpp*^*disk-III* homozygotes to survive to adulthood. Severe alleles (*dpp*^*disk-V*) cause such severe defects in all of the appendages that they engender death early in pupation. The defects in the adult structures are due to corresponding abnormalities in the imaginal disks (the precursors of the adult appendages). Distal structures of adult appendages are known to derive from central regions of the imaginal disks (Bryant, 1978). These central regions are defective in these *dpp* homozygotes. The amount of imaginal disk material lacking in these mutant individuals parallels the severity of the adult defects (Spencer *et al.* 1982).

We have several lines of indirect evidence that the **disk** region is *cis*-regulatory in nature. (a) When duplications covering the **Hin** region, but not the **disk** region are used to rescue pseudopoint *dpp*^{Hin} mutations past the Haplo-lethal embryonic period, *dpp*^{Hin} mutations exhibit a phenotype indistinguishable from the most severe **disk** region phenotype, exhibited by *dpp*$^{disk-V}$ homozygotes. (b) The pattern of expression of the *dpp* transcripts emerging from the **shv-Hin** region is indistinguishable from the location of imaginal disk cells requiring normal **disk** region expression for proper appendage formation (Spencer *et al.* in preparation; Posakony *et al.* 1990). (c) We have no clear evidence of transcriptional activity within the **disk** region (St. Johnston *et al.* 1989). (d) The closer to the transcribed **shv-Hin** region that mutant breakpoints in the **disk** region fall, the more severe are their mutant phenotypes (Fig. 2). All of these mutations break within the **disk** region, and can be viewed as removing all **disk** region *cis*-regulatory DNA proximal to the breakpoint from the neighborhood of the *dpp* transcription unit (Fig. 4).

Based on these observations, we conclude that the **disk** region acts by controlling the expression patterns of **shv-Hin** transcripts in the imaginal disks. Similar considerations lead us to conclude that the **Hin** region must contain *cis*-regulatory elements for the embryonic ectodermal expression of the *dpp* transcripts (St. Johnston and Gelbart, 1987; Irish and Gelbart, 1987; Hoffmann and Goodman, 1987), and the **shv** region must contain *cis*-regulatory elements driving still other spatial and temporal patterns of *dpp* expression (Segal and Gelbart, 1985; St. Johnston *et al.* 1990).

On the contribution of *dpp* to imaginal disk development

The nature of the dpp protein product, combined with the developmental effects of *dpp* mutations, has led us to speculate that *dpp* contributes to *Drosophila* development at the level of intercellular signalling of positional information (Padgett *et al.* 1987). By analysis of chimeric individuals containing marked *dpp*$^-$ tissue, we have made several observations (chiefly on wing disks and their derivatives) which bear on possible models of *dpp*'s developmental role (Spencer *et al.* in preparation; Posakony *et al.* 1990). (1) In mosaics that are mixtures of genotypically *dpp*$^+$ and *dpp*$^{d-III}$ tissue, each imaginal disk solely determines the *dpp* phenotype of its consequent adult appendage. (2) In those mosaics in which a single imaginal disk contains a mixture of genotypically wild-type and mutant cells, the derivative adult appendages may be fully normal, even though 50 % or more of the pattern elements that would be lacking in wholly mutant appendages are of the mutant genotype. (3)

Alternatively, such disks of mixed *dpp* genotype can sometimes give rise to appendages that are partially or fully mutant in phenotype. (4) The *dpp* phenotype of a genotypically mixed imaginal disk depends solely upon the genotype of the cells in the region of the disk just anterior to, and abutting, the anterior–posterior (A/P) compartment boundary. We term this region the 'focus' of *dpp* disk expression. (5) *dpp* transcripts accumulate in a pattern concordant with the position of the *dpp* focus, *i.e.* along the A/P compartment boundary.

Based on these results, we conclude that *dpp* cannot act as an exocrine function, secreted from one organ to act on distant target tissues. However, within an imaginal disk primordium, we cannot determine if the primary action of *dpp* is strictly local, or if it acts on target cells throughout the disk.

One surprising aspect of our observations on *dpp* expression within the imaginal disks is its dissimilarity to the phenotypes *dpp* elicits in adult appendages. While the basic phenotype engendered by *dpp*^{disk} mutations are the loss of tissue in a center to peripheral (radial) direction within the disk, transcript accumulation and localization of the *dpp* focus occur as a stripe cutting across the entire disk at the level of the A/P compartment boundary. In other words, there is no apparent asymmetry of *dpp* expression along the radial axis of the imaginal disk. How then does *dpp* cause pattern deletions along the radial axis, leading to distally incomplete appendages?

One possible explanation is suggested by Meinhardt (1982). Based on theoretical considerations, he supposed that intersections of compartment boundaries (A/P and dorsal/ventral) would identify unique sets of cells, which would then serve as point sources of radial positional information. Given our observations on *dpp* expression in disks, I suggest that the strip of expression of *dpp* (which is constrained by the position of the A/P compartment boundary) serves as a reference line for a series of intersections which lead to the elaboration of radial positional information (detailed in Fig. 5). A gradient of *dpp* product within the disk may be one component of this positional signalling system, or alternatively, the localized expression of *dpp* along the A/P boundary may contribute to the activation of a different positional signalling molecule. In either case, it would be the integrated information from the intersection of *dpp* expression and the expression of other localized molecules within the disk that would lead to the elaboration of radial positional information. The *wingless* gene, which encodes an apparent secreted factor and which is expressed in a different but also highly localized pattern in all disks, is an intriguing candidate for another component of the positional signalling system (Cabrera *et al.* 1987; Rijsewijk *et al.* 1987; Baker, 1988).

In essence, then, I am proposing that *dpp* contributes to the establishment of central positions within developing imaginal disks. The establishment of these central positions would then, directly or indirectly, lead to the elaboration of radial positional information. Perhaps the establishment of central positions, together with the

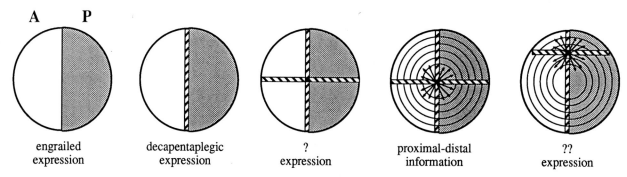

engrailed
expression

decapentaplegic
expression

?
expression

proximal-distal
information

??
expression

Fig. 5. A possible sequence of events in the elaboration of radial positional information within developing imaginal disks. In this scheme, first the disk primordium is divided into anterior (A) and posterior (P) compartments by the differential expression of the *engrailed* gene (Lawrence and Morata, 1976; Kornberg *et al.* 1985). *dpp* expression then occurs just anterior to the A/P boundary, forming a reference line running from the dorsal to the ventral margin of the disk proper. Another gene product is then locally activated in another orientation within the disk, such that it intersects the *dpp* reference line. The cells at the intersection point have the unique property of expressing both gene products. These cells might then elaborate a radially graded positional signal involving some third molecule, or radial information may be transmitted as direct gradients of the products of *dpp* and this other, undefined gene. In the last frame, another, developmentally later product intersecting the *dpp* reference line is shown, to indicate that multiple rounds of intersections and graded signals are likely to be necessary to elaborate the structures typical of an asymmetric primordium such as the wing disk. The basic idea for this model derives from the suggestions of Meinhardt (1982) and from the observations on *dpp* expression by Posakony *et al.* (1990).

pre-existence of peripheral positional values, could lead to the elaboration of intermediate positions through a process of intercalation. While there are some difficulties in fitting the range of *dpp* adult appendage phenotypes into such a model, it does have the attractive feature of relating to observations coming from so-called 'competence' experiments in imaginal disk development. As first noted by Schubiger (1974) in transplantation experiments in which immature leg disks were forced to metamorphose precociously, there is a regional hierarchy in the abilities of disk cells to differentiate adult cuticular structures. In the youngest disks at all competent to elaborate adult structures, structures from the very periphery and the very center of the disk differentiate. In somewhat older disks, larger swatches of peripheral and of central tissue differentiates. As the age of the disk increases, the size of the swatches increases until finally, in mature disks, the entire radial pattern is differentiated. A similar scenario holds for the wing disk (Bownes and Roberts, 1979). It is as if the cells forming center and periphery are first specified during development, and as if further specification occurs by intercalation. Curiously, the first structures from the leg and the wing that are removed by the mildest *dpp* alleles affecting those tissues are *precisely* the first structures competent to be differentiated from the central regions of those disks (the tarsal claws of the leg in dpp^{d-III} homozygotes, and the Sc25 of the dorsal base of the wing in dpp^{d-ho} homozygotes). Thus, *dpp* mutations and competence experiments appear to identify the same set of structures as central within the developing disk. Whether this relationship is of importance in understanding the molecular basis of positional specification within the developing disks must await future experimentation.

This work summarizes the excellent and invaluable intellectual and technical contributions of many investigators over a ten year period, most notably (in alphabetical order) Ronald Blackman, F. Michael Hoffmann, Vivian Irish, Richard W. Padgett, Leila Posakony, Laurel Raftery, Daniel Segal, Forrest Spencer and R. Daniel St. Johnston. This work has been supported by research grants from the Public Health Service and from the American Cancer Society.

References

ALLEN-HOFFMANN, B. L., CRANKSHAW, C. L. AND MOSHER, D. F. (1988). Transforming growth factor β increases cell surface binding and assembly of exogenous (plasma) fibronectin by normal human fibroblasts. *Molec. cell. Biol.* **10**, 4234–4242.

ASSOIAN, R. K., GROTENDORST, G. R., MILLER, D. M. AND SPORN, M. B. (1984). Cellular transformation by coordinated action of three peptide growth factors from human platelets. *Nature, Lond.* **309**, 804–806.

ASSOIAN, R. K., KOMORIGA, A., MEYERS, C. A., MILLER, D. M. AND SPORN, M. B. (1985). Transforming growth factor-β in human platelets: Identification of a major storage site, purification and characterization. *J. biol. Chem.* **258**, 7155–7160.

BAKER, N. E. (1988). Transcription of the segment-polarity gene *wingless* in the imaginal discs of *Drosophila*, and the phenotype of a pupal-lethal *wg* mutation. *Development* **102**, 489–497.

BLACKMAN, R. K., GRIMAILA, R., KOEHLER, M. M. D. AND GELBART, W. M. (1987). Mobilization of hobo elements residing within the *decapentaplegic* gene complex: Suggestion of a new hybrid dysgenesis system in *Drosophila melanogaster*. *Cell* **49**, 497–505.

BOWNES, M. AND ROBERTS, S. (1979). Acquisition of differentiative capacity in imaginal wing discs of *Drosophila melanogaster*. *J. Embryol. exp. Morph.* **49**, 103–113.

BOYD, F. T. AND MASSAGUÉ, J. (1989). Transforming growth factor-β inhibition of epithelial cell proliferation linked to the expression of a 53-kDa membrane receptor. *J. biol. Chem.* **264**, 2272–2278.

BRYANT, P. J. (1978). Pattern formation in imaginal discs. In *Genetics and Biology of Drosophila*, vol. 2c (ed. M. Ashburner and T.R.F. Wright), pp. 230–335. London: Academic Press.

CABRERA, C. V., ALONSO, M. C., JOHNSTON, P., PHILLIPS, R. G. AND LAWRENCE, P. A. (1987). Phenocopies induced with antisense RNA identify the *wingless* gene. *Cell* **50**, 659–663.

CATE, R. L., MATTALIANO, R. J., HESSION, C., TIZARD, R., FARBER, N. M., CHEUNG, A., NINFA, E. G., FREY, A. Z., GASH, D. J., CHOW, E. P., FISHER, R. A., BERTONIS, J. M., TORRES, G., WALLNER, B. P., RAMACHANDRAN, K. L., RAGIN, R. C., MANAGANARO, T. F., MACLAUGHLIN, D. T. AND DONAHOE, P. K. (1986). Isolation of the bovine and human genes for Müllerian inhibiting substance and expression of the human gene in animal cells. *Cell* **45**, 685–698.

CHEIFETZ, S., LIKE, B. AND MASSAGUÉ, J. (1986). Cellular distribution of type I and II receptors for transforming growth factor-β. *J. biol. Chem.* **261**, 9972–9978.

CHEIFETZ, S., WEATHERBEE, J. A., TSANG, M. L.-S., ANDERSON, J. K., MOLE, J. E., LUCAS, R. AND MASSAGUÉ, J. (1987). The transforming growth factor-β system, a complex pattern of cross-reactive ligands and receptors. *Cell* **48**, 409–415.

DERYNCK, R., JARRETT, J. A., CHEN, E. Y., EATON, D. H., BELL, J. R., ASSOIAN, R. K., ROBERTS, A. B., SPORN, M. B. AND GOEDDEL, D. V. (1985). Human transforming growth factor-β complementary DNA sequence and expression in normal and transformed cells. *Nature, Lond.* **316**, 701–705.

DERYNCK, R., JARRETT, J. A., CHEN, E. Y. AND GOEDDEL, D. V. (1986). The murine transforming growth factor-β precursor. *J. biol. Chem.* **261**, 4377–4379.

DIJKE, P. T., HANSEN, P., IWATA, K. K., PIELER, C. AND FOULKES, J. G. (1988). Identification of another member of the transforming growth factor type β gene family. *Proc. natn. Acad. Sci. U.S.A.* **85**, 4715–4719.

GELBART, W. M. (1982). Synapsis-dependent allelic complementation at the *decapentaplegic* gene complex in *Drosophila melanogaster. Proc. natn. Acad. Sci. U.S.A.* **79**, 2636–2640.

GELBART, W. M., IRISH, V. F., ST JOHNSTON, R. D., HOFFMANN, F. M., BLACKMAN, R. K., SEGAL, D., POSAKONY, L. M. AND GRIMAILA, R. (1985). The *decapentaplegic* gene complex in *Drosophila melanogaster. Cold Spring Harbor Symp. quant. Biol.* **50**, 119–125.

HOFFMANN, F. M. AND GOODMAN, W. (1987). Identification in transgenic animals of Drosophila decapentaplegic sequences required for embryonic dorsal pattern formation. *Genes & Devel.* **1**, 615–625.

IGNOTZ, R. A. AND MASSAGUÉ, J. (1985). Type β transforming growth factor controls the adipogenic differentiation of 3T3 fibroblasts. *Proc. natn. Acad. Sci. U.S.A.* **82**, 8530–8534.

IGNOTZ, R. A. AND MASSAGUÉ, J. (1986). Transforming growth factor-β stimulates the expression of fibronectin and collagen and their incorporation into the extracellular matrix. *J. biol. Chem.* **261**, 4337–4345.

IRISH, V. F. AND GELBART, W. M. (1987). The *decapentaplegic* gene is required for dorsal-ventral patterning in *Drosophila* embryos. *Genes & Devel.* **1**, 868–879.

KIMELMAN, D. AND KIRSCHNER, M. (1987). Synergistic induction of mesoderm by FGF and TGF-β and the identification of an mRNA coding for FGF in the early xenopus embryo. *Cell* **51**, 869–877.

KORNBERG, T., SIDEN, I., O'FARRELL, P. AND SIMEN, M. (1985). The *engrailed* locus of *Drosophila: In situ* localization of transcripts reveals compartment-specific expression. *Cell* **40**, 45–53.

LAWRENCE, P. A. AND MORATA, G. (1976). Compartments in the wing of *Drosophila*: A study of the *engrailed* gene. *Devl Biol.* **50**, 321–337.

LING, N., YING, S-Y., UENO, N., SHIMASAKI, S., ESCH, F., HOTTA, M. AND GUILLEMIN, R. (1986). Pituitary FSH is released by a heterodimer of the β-subunits from the two forms of inhibin. *Nature, Lond.* **321**, 779–782.

LYONS, K., GRAYCAR, J. L., LEE, A., HASHMI, S., LINDQUIST, P. B., CHEN, E. Y., HOGAN, B. L. M. AND DERYNCK, R. (1989). *Vgr-1*, a mammalian gene related to *Xenopus Vg-1*, is a member of the transforming growth factor β gene superfamily. *Proc. natn. Acad. Sci. U.S.A.* **86**, 4554–4558.

LYONS, R. M., KESKI-OJA, J. AND MOSES, H. L. (1988). Proteolytic activation of latent transforming growth factor-β from fibroblast-conditioned medium. *J. Cell Biol.* **106**, 1659–1665.

MARQUARDT, H., LIOUBIN, M. N. AND IKEDA, T. (1987). Complete amino acid sequence of human transforming growth factor type β2. *J. biol. Chem.* **262**, 12 127–12 131.

MASON, A. J., HAYFLICK, J. S., LING, N., ESCH, F., UENO, N., YING, S-Y., GUILLEMIN, R., NAILL, H. AND SEEBURG, R. H. (1985). Complementary DNA sequences of ovarian follicular fluid inhibin show precursor structure and homology with transforming growth factor-β. *Nature, Lond.* **318**, 659–663.

MAYO, K. E., CERELLI, G. M., SPIESS, J., RIVIER, J., ROSENFELD, M. G., EVAND, R. M. AND VALE, W. (1986). Inhibin A-subunit cDNAs from porcine ovary and human placenta. *Proc. natn. Acad. Sci. U.S.A.* **83**, 5849–5853.

MEINHARDT, H. (1982). Generation of structures in a developing organism. In *Developmental Order: Its Origin and Regulation* (ed. S. Subtelny and P.B. Green), pp. 439–461. New York: Alan Liss.

MELTON, D. A. (1987). Translocation of a localized maternal mRNA to the vegetal pole of *Xenopus* oocytes. *Nature, Lond.* **328**, 80–82.

MONTESANO, R. AND ORCI, L. (1988). Transforming growth factor β stimulates collagen-matrix contraction by fibroblasts: Implications for wound healing. *Proc. natn. Acad. Sci. U.S.A.* **85**, 4894–4897.

PADGETT, R. W., ST JOHNSTON, R. D. AND GELBART, W. M. (1987). The *decapentaplegic* gene complex of *Drosophila* encodes a protein homologous to the transforming growth factor-β gene family. *Nature, Lond.* **325**, 81–84.

PICON, R. (1969). Action du testicule foetal sur le development in vitro des canaux de Müller chez le rat. *Arch. Anat. Micro. Morph. exp.* **58**, 1–19.

PONDEL, M. D. AND KING, M. L. (1988). Localized maternal mRNA related to transforming growth factor β mRNA is concentrated in a cytokeratin-enriched fraction from Xenopus oocytes. *Proc. natn. Acad. Sci. U.S.A.* **85**, 7612–7616.

POSAKONY, L. M., RAFTERY, L. A., ST JOHNSTON, R. D. AND GELBART, W. M. (1990). Wing formation in Drosophila melanogaster requires decapentaplegic gene function along the anterior-posterior compartment boundary. *Genes & Devel.* (submitted).

RAMASHARMA, K., SAIRAM, M. R., SEIDAK, N. G., CHRETIEN, M., MARJUNATH, P., SCHILLER, P. W., YAMASHIRA, D. AND LAI, C. H. (1984). Isolation, structure, and synthesis of a human seminal plasmis peptide with inhibin-like activity. *Science* **223**, 1199–1202.

RIJSEWIJK, F., SCHUERMANN, M., WAGENAAR, E., PARREN, P., WEIGEL, D. AND NUSSE, R. (1987). The *Drosophila* homolog of the mouse mammary oncogene int-1 is identical to the segment polarity gene *wingless. Cell* **50**, 649–657.

ROBERTS, A. B., ANZANO, M. A., LAMB, L. C. AND SPORN, M. B. (1981). New class of transforming growth factors potentiated by epidermal growth factor: isolation from non-neoplastic tissues. *Proc. natn. Acad. Sci. U.S.A.* **78**, 5339–5343.

ROBERTS, A. B., ANZANO, M. A., WAKEFIELD, L. M., ROCHE, N. S., STERN, D. F. AND SPORN, M. B. (1985). Type β transforming growth factor: A bifunctional regulator of cellular growth. *Proc. natn. Acad. Sci. U.S.A.* **82**, 119–123.

ROSA, F., ROBERTS, A. B., DANIELPOUR, D., DART, L. L., SPORN, M. B. AND DAWID, I. B. (1987). Mesoderm induction in Amphibians: The role of TGF-β2-like factors. *Science* **239**, 783–785.

SCHUBIGER, G. (1974). Acquisition of differentiative competence in the imaginal leg disc of *Drosophila. Wilhelm Roux' Arch. EntwMech. Org.* **174**, 303–311.

SEGAL, D. AND GELBART, W. M. (1985). Shortvein, A new component of the *decapentaplegic* gene complex in *Drosophila melanogaster. Genetics* **109**, 119–143.

SLACK, J. M. W., DARLINGTON, B. G., HEATH, J. K. AND GODSAVE, S. F. (1987). Mesoderm induction in early *Xenopus* embryos by heparin-binding growth factors. *Nature, Lond.* **326**, 197–200.

SPENCER, F. A., HOFFMANN, F. M. AND GELBART, W. M. (1982).

Decapentaplegic: a gene complex affecting morphogenesis in *Drosophila melanogaster. Cell* **28**, 451–461.

ST JOHNSTON, R. D. AND GELBART, W. M. (1987). *decapentaplegic* transcripts are localized along the dorsal-ventral axis of the *Drosophila* embryo. *EMBO J.* **6**, 2785–2791.

ST JOHNSTON, R. D., HOFFMANN, F. M., BLACKMAN, R. K., SEGAL, D., GRIMAILA, R., PADGETT, R. W., IRICK, H. A. AND GELBART, W. M. (1990). The molecular organization of the *decapentaplegic* gene in *Drosophila melanogaster. Genes & Devel.* (in press).

SUTER, B., DÖRIG, R. E., HOFFMANN, F. M., GELBART, W. M. AND KUBLI, E. (1990). A tRNA gene located in the *decapentaplegic* gene of *Drosophila melanogaster* is expressed stage specifically. *Molec. Cell Biol.* (submitted).

VALE, W., RIVIER, J., VAUGHAN, J., MCCLINTOCK, R., CORRIGAN, A., WOO, W., KARR, D. AND SPIESS, J. (1986). Purification and characterization of an FSH releasing protein from porcine ovarian follicular fluid. *Nature, Lond.* **321**, 776–779.

WANG, E. A., ROSEN, V., CORDES, P., HEWICK, R. M., KRIZ, M.-J., LUXENBERG, D. P., SIBLEY, B. S. AND WOZNEY, J. M. (1988). Purification and characterization of novel bone-inducing factors. *Proc. natn. Acad. Sci. U.S.A.* **85**, 9484–9488.

WATSON, M. E. E. (1984). Compilation of published signal sequences. *Nucl. Acids Res.* **12**, 5145–5163.

WEEKS, D. L. AND MELTON, D. A. (1987). A maternal mRNA localized to the vegetal hemisphere in *Xenopus* eggs codes for a growth factor related to TGF-β. *Cell* **51**, 861–867.

WOZNEY, J. M., ROSEN, V., CELESTE, A. J., MITSOCK, L. M., WHITTERS, M. J., KRIZ, R. W., HEWICK, R. M. AND WANG, E. A. (1988). Molecular cloning of novel regulators of bone formation. *Science* **242**, 1528–1534.

Development 1989 Supplement, 75–80 (1989)
Printed in Great Britain © The Company of Biologists Limited 1989

G-protein-linked signal transduction systems control development in

Dictyostelium

R. L. JOHNSON, R. GUNDERSEN, P. LILLY, G. S. PITT, M. PUPILLO, T. J. SUN, R. A. VAUGHAN
and P. N. DEVREOTES

Department of Biological Chemistry, Johns Hopkins University School of Medicine, 725 N. Wolfe Street, Baltimore, MD 21205, USA

Summary

G-protein-linked cAMP receptors play an essential role in *Dictyostelium* development. The cAMP receptors are proposed to have seven transmembrane domains and a cytoplasmic *C*-terminal region. Overexpression of the receptor in cells, when the endogenous receptor is not present, results in a 10- to 50-fold increase in cAMP-binding sites. Antisense cell lines, which lack cAMP receptors, do not enter the developmental program. Ligand-induced phosphorylation is proposed to occur on serine and threonine residues in the receptor *C*-terminus. The kinetics of receptor phosphorylation and dephosphorylation correlate closely with the shift of receptor mobility and the adaptation of several cAMP-induced responses. Two *α*-subunits, G-*α*-1 and G-*α*-2, have been cloned and specific antisera developed against each. Both subunits are expressed as multiple RNAs with different developmental time courses. The mutant *Frigid A* has a functional defect in G-*α*-2 which prevents it from entering development. We propose that G-protein-linked receptor systems will be a major component in the development of many organisms.

Key words: G-protein, *Dictyostelium*, cAMP receptors, phosphorylation.

Role of cAMP signaling in morphogenesis and pattern formation

Dictyostelium is an elegant system for studying the role of cell–cell signaling in development. During vegetative growth, this organism exists as single amoebae that phagocytose bacteria. However, upon starvation, aggregation centers begin to secrete cAMP spontaneously at six minute intervals. Concentric or spiral waves of cAMP propagate from the centers and direct the formation of multicellular aggregates (Tomchik and Devreotes, 1981). As aggregates form 'slugs', cell-type-specific differentiation occurs and a pattern appears. Prestalk cells are found in the anterior region while prespore cells arise from the posterior of the cell mass (see chapter by Williams *et al.*). The prestalk cells become vacuolated to form a stalk, which holds a sporehead aloft in the fruiting body (Gerisch, 1987).

Aggregation is organized by closely coordinating cell–cell signaling and chemotaxis. As a wave of cAMP approaches, randomly oriented cells become polarized and move up the chemical gradient. As they move, the cells secrete additional cAMP which relays the signal outward. Cells continue to respond until the peak of the cAMP wave passes. They do not react to cAMP on the declining edge of the wave since they have become adapted. Hence secretion ceases and migration becomes random. During the interlude between cAMP stimuli, the system deadapts in preparation for the next wave. Approximately 30 waves are needed to complete aggregation (Devreotes, 1983).

Extracellular cAMP also plays a critical role in gene regulation. Expression of early genes such as the surface cAMP receptor, membrane-bound phosphodiesterase, and CSA (a cell adhesion protein) are induced by intermittent, but inhibited by persistent, application of cAMP (Figure 1). Transcripts of these early genes begin to accumulate within two hours and peak between six to eight hours of development (Mann and Firtel, 1987). In contrast, prestalk and prespore gene expression require continual, rather than intermittent, stimulation by cAMP. In addition, the morphogen DIF (Differentiation-Inducing Factor, see chapter by Kay *et al.*) is needed for prestalk gene expression in the tip where it also inhibits the induction of prespore genes (Schaap, 1983). Most prestalk genes are induced late in aggregation, while prespore gene expression begins somewhat later (Gerisch, 1987, see chapter by Williams *et al.*).

The molecular components involved in this signaling system include cAMP receptors, G-proteins, adenylate cyclase, and phosphodiesterase (Figure 2). These developmentally regulated proteins allow the establishment of the cAMP oscillator. Exogenous cAMP binds to surface membrane receptors which activate G-proteins and stimulate the formation of intracellular cAMP by adenylate cyclase. Each cell secretes cAMP which activates its

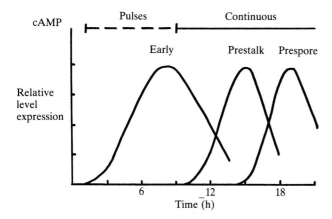

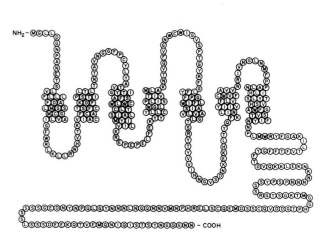

Fig. 1. Gene expression is controlled by cAMP stimulation. Many early genes are induced by intermittent stimulation by cAMP. In later development, prestalk gene markers are induced by persistent exposure to cAMP with prespore expression beginning a few hours later.

Fig. 3. The cAMP receptor consists of seven transmembrane domains with the *N*-terminus facing the extracellular and the *C*-terminus facing the cytoplasmic side of the membrane. Multiple stretches of serine residues in the *C*-terminal region are the proposed sites of phosphorylation.

own receptors as well as those of nearby cells. After several minutes of stimulation, ligand occupancy triggers desensitization (Janssens and Van Haastert, 1987). Removal of cAMP by extracellular and cell surface phosphodiesterase allows the system to resensitize and return to its prestimulus state (Gerisch, 1987).

Studies in our laboratory have focused on defining and characterizing the components involved in signal transduction. Recently, we have cloned surface cAMP receptors and proposed a model of their structure. We have also investigated ligand-induced phosphorylation. Two α- and one β-subunit of G-proteins have been cloned as well. Mutation and overexpression of these genes have helped to establish their essential roles in development.

Cell surface cAMP receptors

A structural model of the cAMP receptor was derived from its primary sequence (Figure 3). It is postulated to span the membrane seven times with the *N̈*-terminus facing the extracellular and *C*-terminal domain facing the cytoplasmic side of the membrane (Klein *et al.* 1988). The model is topologically similar to other

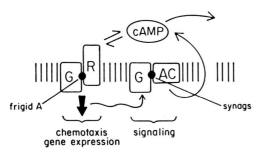

Fig. 2. The cAMP oscillator controls development. cAMP binds to cell surface receptors to activate adenylate cyclase and cause secretion of cAMP. *Frigid A*, which lacks a functional G α-subunit, is defective in chemotaxis and induction of gene expression. In *Synag 7*, receptors are unable to couple to adenylate cyclase.

G-protein linked receptors such as rhodopsin (Hargrave, 1986) and the β-adrenergic receptor (Dolhman *et al.* 1987). Although the *N*-terminus has a potential site for *N*-linked glycosylation, there is no biochemical evidence that the protein is glycosylated. The *C*-terminal region contains multiple stretches of serine residues which are the proposed sites of ligand-induced phosphorylation.

Multiple criteria demonstrate that this cDNA encodes the cAMP receptor. Antisera against the purified receptor identify several fusion proteins derived from the cDNA; RNA blot analysis, using the receptor cDNA as a probe, identifies a 2 kb message that is developmentally regulated in the same manner as the receptor protein; complementary receptor RNA specifically hybrid arrests *in vitro* translation of a 37 kD protein that is immunoprecipitated by receptor antiserum (Klein *et al.* 1988). Most conclusively, vegetative cells, which do not contain endogenous cAMP receptors, acquire cAMP binding sites when transformed with the cDNA. Transformed cells have seven to fifty times the amount of cAMP-binding compared to wildtype ($1-8 \times 10^5$ *vs* 1.5×10^4 sites per cell, Johnson *et al.* in prep.).

To examine the function of the cAMP receptor in development, an antisense cell line that blocked production of receptor was created. A construct was designed to transcribe the receptor cDNA in the antisense orientation using a strong constitutive promoter. Antisense cell lines, which failed to express receptor RNA or protein, did not enter the developmental program. As shown in Figure 4, antisense cells remain as a smooth monolayer after eight hours of starvation while wild-type cells have developed into aggregates. By 36 hours, however, the antisense cells begin to show signs of weak aggregation (Sun *et al.* in prep.).

The cAMP receptor exists in two interchangeable forms designated R (40 kD) and D (43 kD). This

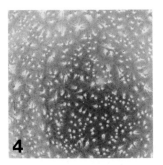
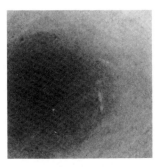

Fig. 4. Antisense cell lines, which lack cAMP receptors, do not enter the developmental program. The left panel shows wild-type cells forming aggregates after eight hours of starvation while antisense cells, shown in the right panel, are a smooth monolayer.

reversible shift of electrophoretic mobility is coupled to the spontaneous oscillations in cAMP synthesis in developing cells (Klein *et al.* 1985*a*). The R form is predominant in unstimulated cells and converts to the D form upon stimulation with cAMP (Devreotes and Sherring, 1985). Phosphorylation of both forms of receptor has been demonstrated *in vitro* and *in vivo*. Upon stimulation with cAMP, the phosphorylation increases by several-fold to a level of about four moles phosphate/mole receptor. It is likely that this phosphorylation underlies the shift in electrophoretic mobility (Klein *et al.* 1985*b*).

The kinetics of receptor phosphorylation and dephosphorylation correlate closely with the shift of receptor mobility and the adaptation of several cAMP-induced responses (Figures 5 and 6). Phosphorylation is detectable in five seconds, has a half time of 30 s, and reaches a steady state within five minutes. When cells are freed of cAMP, both the shift in receptor mobility and phosphorylation decay. Dephosphorylation is detectable in 30 s, has a half time of 2·5 min, and is complete within 15 min (Figure 6). The kinetics of receptor phosphorylation and dephosphorylation match those of adaptation and deadaptation of cAMP-stimulated activation of adenylate cyclase and myosin phosphorylation. The half-maximal responses of these events all occur with concentrations of 5 nM-cAMP (Vaughan and Devreotes, 1988). Receptor phosphorylation is probably essential in the adaptation response as demonstrated in other G-protein-linked receptor systems (Sibley *et al.* 1988). Isolation of a cAMP-receptor kinase mutant would directly test if receptor desensitization requires phosphorylation.

Predominately serine and some threonine residues of the cAMP receptor are phosphorylated (Klein *et al.* 1985*b*). Two serines are present on the third cytoplasmic loop and an additional 18 are found in the *C*-terminal domain (Figure 3). When membranes containing the phosphorylated receptor are trypsinized, a soluble fragment is released. This peptide has an apparent molecular weight of 19 kD and appears to contain all of the ligand-induced phosphorylation sites. Studies are now underway to isolate this fragment and

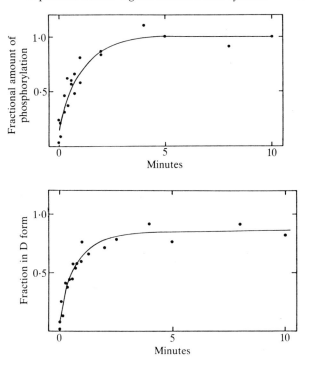

Fig. 5. The kinetics of phosphorylation (top panel) correlate closely with the receptor shift to the D form (bottom panel) during stimulation with cAMP. Both increase exponentially and reach a steady state by five minutes.

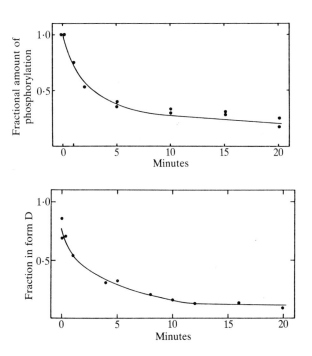

Fig. 6. The kinetics of dephosphorylation (top panel) and the shift to the R form of receptor (bottom panel) are similar after removal of cAMP.

map the sites of phosphorylation (Vaughan and Devreotes, in prep.).

Multiple G-proteins and signal transduction pathways

Two G-protein α-subunits, designated G-α-1 and G-α-2, have been isolated from cDNA libraries using oligonucleotide probes based on the highly conserved GTP-binding and GTPase sites of the α-subunits in mammals. The nucleotide sequences of both subunits encode polypeptides of approximately 41 kD. Both subunits are 45 % identical to each other and to the mammalian α-subunits, G$_i$, G$_o$, and transducin, while only 35 % identical to G$_s$ and yeast GPA-1. When compared to the other α-subunits, some highly conserved regions are notable (Figure 7). Region A is almost 100 % identical among all seven subunits and is the proposed GTPase site by analogy to c-Ha-ras and EF-Tu. Regions C, E and G are also highly conserved and are believed to form the GTP-binding site. A fifth domain, designated T, contains an almost completely conserved sequence of TCATDT and is near the C-terminus (Pupillo *et al.* 1989). This region may interact with receptor (Hamm *et al.* 1988).

Both G-α-1 and G-α-2 are expressed as multiple RNAs with different developmental time courses (Figure 8). The predominant 1·7 kb band of G-α-1 is present during vegetative growth, increases several-fold until the 'loose aggregate' stage and then decreases. In contrast, the major 2·7 kb RNA of G-α-2 is almost completely absent during vegetative growth and is induced during early development with peak expression in the aggregation state. The developmental regulation of G-α-2 is similar to those genes involved in cell aggregation that require intermittent cAMP stimulation for induction.

Peptide antisera were developed that specifically recognize each α-subunit as well as a common domain of both proteins (Figure 9). When visualized by immunoblot, G-α-1 migrates as a 38 kD protein, while G-α-2 has an apparent molecular weight of 40 kD. The time course of protein expression is consistent with the transcription of the major mRNA for each subunit. G-α-1 is present in both vegetative growth and throughout development, while G-α-2 is expressed in early development, peaking around 6–8 hours in shaking cultures (Figure 9, Kumagai *et al.* 1989).

Characterization of the mutant *Frigid A* has helped to establish a function for G-α-2. *Frigid A* mutants bind cAMP, but appear to be blocked in subsequent steps of signal transduction (Coukell *et al.* 1983). Activation of adenylate cyclase and early gene expression fails to occur even when cells are stimulated with cAMP. However, adenylate cyclase can be activated by GTP *in vitro* (Kesbeke and Van Haastert, 1988; Kumagai *et al.* 1989). Both RNA blot and immunoblot analysis show

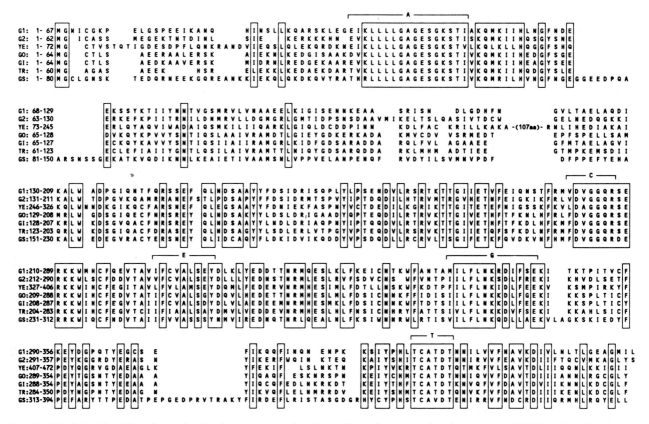

Fig. 7. All of the identified G α-subunits share conserved regions. Domain A contains the proposed GTPase site. Regions C, E, and G comprise the putative GTP-binding site. The T domain is thought to interact with receptors. (G1 – *Dictyostelium* G-α-1. G2 – *Dictyostelium* G-α-2. YE – Yeast GPA1. GO – Bovine G$_o$. GI – Rat G$_i$. TR – Bovine transducin. GS – Bovine G$_s$.

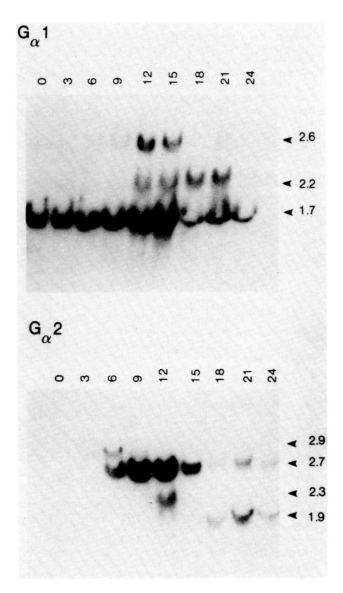

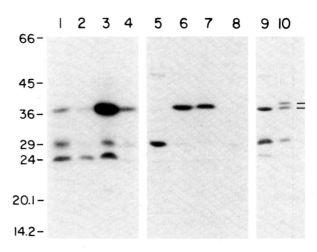

Fig. 9. Antibodies specifically recognize G-α-1 (lanes 1–4) and G-α-2 (lanes 5–8). In vegetative growth, G-α-1 is present (lane 1 & 9) but G-α-2 is absent (lane 5 & 9). Both α-subunits are present at six hours of development (lanes 2, 6, and 10). A cell line overexpressing G-α-1 shows a high increase in the staining of this protein (lane 3) while G-α-2 staining is normal at six hours of development (lane 7). *Frigid A* allele, HC 85, lacks G-α-2 (lane 8) when developed six hours. Both antibodies were mixed to stain G-α-1 and G-α-2 (lanes 9 & 10). The two bars show where G-α-2 (top bar) and G-α-1 (bottom bar) migrate.

Fig. 8. The time course of G-α-1 and G-α-2 mRNA expression reveals multiple transcripts. The major 1·7 kb band of G-α-1 is present throughout development with peak expression between 12–15 h. The predominant 2·7 kb band of G-α-2 is developmentally regulated and expressed maximally at 12 h.

most alleles to have a strong reduction or absence of G-α-2 mRNA and protein at all stages of cell development. Most conclusively, one *Frigid A* allele, HC 85, contains a deletion in the G-α-2 gene (Kumagai *et al.* 1987). Hence both biochemical and genetic evidence suggest that the *Frigid A* allele is the G-α-2 subunit. One *Frigid A* mutant, HC 112, however, has near normal levels of both mRNA and protein. The G-α-2 gene in this mutant was cloned by PCR (Polymerase Chain Reaction) and sequenced. It carries a point mutation within the coding sequence. Further characterization of HC 112 is in progress (Pitt and Devreotes, in prep.).

To investigate the function of the G-α-1 subunit, this protein was overexpressed. Both G-α-1 mRNA and protein levels are approximately 20-fold higher than wild-type as detected by RNA blot and immunoblots (Figure 9). Transformed cells grown on surfaces are large and multinucleate. When these cells are developed, most fail to aggregate but those that do, produce small and abnormal fruiting bodies. This phenotype suggests a role for G-α-1 in cytokinesis during growth (Kumagai *et al.* 1989).

A G-protein β-subunit has also been cloned using probes based on conserved sequences of *Drosophila* and human β-subunits. It is expressed as a constitutive 1·9 kb mRNA. The amino acid sequence has 63 % identity to the human β-2-subunit. The first 50 residues share only 30 % identity, with the remainder of the protein being 70 % identical. The significance of these different domains is under investigation. Work is in progress to examine the function of the β-subunit by creating antisense and overexpression cell lines (Lilly and Devreotes, in prep.)

G-protein linked signaling pathways in development

Our studies of *Dictyostelium* show that G-protein-linked signal transduction pathways play a central role in the development of a multicellular organism. The cAMP receptors we have identified are essential to development; antisense cell lines do not enter the developmental program. The G-α-2 subunit is critical for cAMP chemotaxis and induction of gene expression; *Frigid A*, which lacks a functional G-α-2, is unable to differentiate. We propose that G-protein-linked receptor systems will be a major component in the development of many organisms.

The oscillatory nature of cAMP-receptor activation and inactivation plays a critical role in cell–cell signaling, aggregation and gene expression in *Dictyostelium*. Positional signaling, *via* a cAMP oscillator, underlies cell aggregation in early development and establishes cell differentiation in later stages. Perhaps higher organisms such as *C. elegans*, *Drosophila*, or vertebrates use this type of cellular communication during embryogenesis. One could envision progenitor cells creating organization centers by establishing gradients or oscillations of a signaling molecule. These organization centers could influence local cell differentiation or act in concert to institute larger changes. Hence cAMP signaling may not just be limited to slime molds, but utilized in more complex organisms as well.

References

COUKELL, M. B., LAPPANO, S. & CAMERON, A. M. (1983). Isolation and characterization of cAMP unresponsive (frigid) aggregation-deficient mutants of *Dictyostelium discoideum*. *Dev. Genet.* **3**, 283–297.

DEVREOTES, P. N. (1983). Cyclic nucleotides and cell-cell communication in *Dictyostelium discoideum*. *Adv. Cyclic Nucl. Res.* **15**, 55–96.

DEVREOTES, P. N. & SHERRING, J. A. (1985). Kinetics and concentration dependence of reversible cAMP-induced modification of the surface cAMP receptor in *Dictyostelium*. *J. biol. Chem.* **260**, 6378–6384.

DOHLMAN, H. G., CARON, M. G. & LEFKOWITZ, R. J. (1987). A family of receptors coupled to guanine nucleotide regulatory proteins. *Biochem.* **26**, 2657–2664.

GERISCH, G. (1987). Cyclic AMP and other signals controlling cell development and differentiation in *Dictyostelium*. *Annu. Rev Biochem.* **56**, 853–879.

HAMM, H. E., DERETIC, D., ARENDT, A., HARGRAVE, P. A., KOENIG, B. & HOFMANN, K. P. (1988). Site of G-protein binding to rhodopsin mapped with synthetic peptides from the α-subunit. *Science* **241**, 832–835.

HARGRAVE, P. A. (1986). Molecular dynamics of the rod cell. In *The Retina*, (ed. R. Adler & D. Farber), pp. 207–237. New York: Academic Press.

JANSSENS, P. M. W. & VAN HAASTERT, P. J. M. (1987). Molecular basis of transmembrane signal transduction in *Dictyostelium discoideum*. *Microbiol. Rev.* **51**, 396–418.

KESBEKE, F., SNAAR-JAGALSKA, B. E. & VAN HAASTERT, P. J. M. (1988). Signal transduction in *Dictyostelium fgd* A mutants with a defective interaction between surface cAMP receptors and a GTP-binding regulatory protein. *J. Cell Biol.* **107**, 521–528.

KLEIN, P., FONTANA, D., KNOX, B., THEIBERT, A. & DEVREOTES, P. (1985b). cAMP receptors controlling cell-cell interactions in the development of *Dictyostelium*. *Cold Spring Harbor Symp. Quant. Biol.* **50**, 787–799.

KLEIN, P., SUN, T. J., SAXE, C. L., KIMMEL, A. R., JOHNSON, R. L. & DEVREOTES, P. N. (1988). A chemoattractant receptor controls development in *Dictyostelium discoideum*. *Science* **241**, 1467–1472.

KLEIN, P., THEIBERT, A., FONTANA, D. & DEVREOTES, P. N. (1985a). Identification and cyclic AMP-induced modification of the cyclic AMP receptor in *Dictyostelium discoideum*. *J. biol. Chem.* **260**, 1757–1764.

KUMAGAI, A., PUPILLO, M., GUNDERSON, R., MIAKE-LYE, R., DEVREOTES, P. N. & FIRTEL, R. A. (1989). Regulation and function of G-α-1 protein subunits in *Dictyostelium*. *Cell* **57**, 265–275.

MANN, S. K. O. & FIRTEL, R. A. (1987). Cyclic AMP regulation of early gene expression in *Dictyostelium discoideum*: mediation via the cell surface cyclic AMP receptor. *Molec. cell. Biol.* **7**, 458–469.

PUPILLO, M., KUMAGAI, A., PITT, G., FIRTEL, R. A. & DEVREOTES, P. N. (1989). Multiple α subunits of G-proteins in *Dictyostelium*. *Proc. natn. Acad. Sci.* (in press).

SCHAAP, P. (1986). Regulation of size and pattern in the cellular slime molds. *Differentiation* **33**, 1–16.

SIBLEY, D. R., BENOVIC, J. L., CARON, M. G. & LEFKOWITZ, R. J. (1987). Regulation of transmembrane signaling by receptor phosphorylation. *Cell* **49**, 913–22.

TOMCHIK, K. J. & DEVREOTES, P. N. (1981). cAMP waves in *Dictyostelium discoideum*: demonstration by a novel isotope dilution fluorography technique. *Science* **212**, 443–446.

VAUGHAN, R. A. & DEVREOTES, P. N. (1988). Ligand-induced phosphorylation of the cAMP receptor from *Dictyostelium discoideum*. *J. biol. Chem.* **263**, 14538–14543.

Development 1989 Supplement, 81–90
Printed in Great Britain © The Company of Biologists Limited 1989

Morphogen hunting in *Dictyostelium*

ROBERT R. KAY, MARY BERKS and DAVID TRAYNOR

Medical Research Council, Laboratory of Molecular Biology, Hills Road, Cambridge, CB2 2QH, UK

Summary

A highly regulative pattern of prestalk and prespore tissue is formed during *Dictyostelium* development, starting from separate amoebae. Potential morphogens controlling this process have been hunted biochemically, using bioassays to monitor activity. All those discovered to date are low MW diffusible compounds: cAMP, adenosine, NH_3 and DIFs 1–3. The DIFs are assayed by their ability to induce isolated amoebae to differentiate into stalk cells and have been identified as a family of chlorinated phenyl alkanones.

The diversification of amoebae into prestalk and prespore cells seems to be brought about by cAMP and DIF-1. cAMP is necessary for both pathways of differentiation but DIF-1 specifically induces the differentiation of prestalk cells while suppressing that of prespores.

When DIF-1 is added to intact slugs, it causes a substantial enlargement of the prestalk tissue at physiological concentrations in the time previously shown to be required for pattern regulation.

DIF-1 is a dynamic molecule and we have found that it is metabolized along a pathway involving at least 8 compounds. Metabolism is developmentally regulated and may be important in producing DIF gradients or other effector molecules from DIF.

Although we almost certainly have some of the central actors, it is difficult to formulate a satisfactory theory of pattern formation in *Dictyostelium* at the moment. We suspect that at least one important actor is missing.

Key words: *Dictyostelium discoideum*, DIF-1, cell differentiation, morphogen.

Introduction

During *Dictyostelium* development, order is literally created out of chaos. A teeming mass of separate amoebae at the start of development is transformed over 24 h into a population of discrete fruiting bodies, each one consisting of a basal disc on the substratum stabilizing a cellular stalk that in turn supports a mass of spores in the air (Raper, 1940; for recent reviews see Loomis, 1982; Gerisch, 1987; Williams, 1988). Because of this life style there can be no spatially organized input of maternal information to the embryo, as is so important in creatures such as *Drosophila*. Instead the patterning process in *Dictyostelium* must rely on the intrinsic properties of the cells and environmental inhomogeneities to produce reference points and morphogen gradients in the aggregate. In this respect *Dictyostelium*, a part-time multicellular organism, resembles mammals, where there is also thought to be little input of maternal positional information to the embryo.

Amputation and grafting experiments suggest that development in the *Dictyostelium* aggregate is organized by long-range signalling (in this context 1–2 mm) and, since the organism lacks intercellular junctions (Johnson *et al.* 1977) and the cells are not electrically coupled (Weijer and Durston, quoted in Loomis, 1982), it seems likely that this signalling proceeds *via* extra-cellular diffusible molecules. This paper describes first some of the *Dictyostelium* biology that is relevant to pattern formation, then the ways in which potential morphogens have been hunted in this organism (especially the DIFs) and finally what is known of the roles of these molecules in controlling cell differentiation and patterning.

Outline of development

Development is triggered by starvation and thereafter proceeds without external nutrients or essential cell divisions. After a few hours the amoebae start to gather toward collecting centers guided by cAMP signals relayed out from these centers. The number of amoebae gathered into each center is a function of the cell density and the density of signalling centers. In many cases large mounds of around 10^6 cells can form, but invariably these become subdivided into smaller mounds of no more than about 10^5 cells (see later). Each small mound becomes surrounded by a slime sheath, thereby isolating it from its neighbours. As this happens a protruding tip appears on the top of the mound (Fig. 1) and it elongates upwards to form a first finger, which can fall on its side to form the well-known migrating slug. Fate mapping reveals that the anterior 25 % of the slug is normally destined to become the stalk of the fruiting body and that the spores derive from the posterior 75 % (Raper, 1940). At this stage the anterior prestalk and the posterior prespore cells have clearly differentiated from each other. For instance, prespore cells express various components of the eventual spore coat, prepackaged into prespore vesicles (Hohl and Hamamoto, 1969; Maeda and Takeuchi, 1969). By staining these vesicles with antibodies, the prestalk/prespore pattern can readily be visualized (see Fig. 6). Definitive markers for prestalk cells have been much harder to obtain but recently we have isolated two genes whose expression is prestalk-specific and which code for proteins of the extracellular matrix (Williams *et al.* 1987; Jermyn *et al.* 1987). Using markers derived from these genes, an unexpected heterogeneity has been revealed in the prestalk zone of the slug (Jermyn *et al.* 1989; see Williams *et al.* this volume). There appear

to be at least 3 types of prestalk cell: pstA cells express pDd63 mRNA and form an anterior cortex of the prestalk zone, pstB cells express pDd56 mRNA and form a central core of the prestalk zone and pstO cells express neither of these markers and form the rear of the prestalk zone. Finally as an added complication there are prestalk-like cells scattered in the prespore zone (Sakai and Takeuchi, 1971; Sternfeld and David, 1981). It is not known whether these cells should be regarded as a fifth cell type or merely as circulating prestalk cells, with a possible role in slug movement (Williams *et al.* 1987). The slug is an arrested stage of development which can persist for days. For this reason of experimental convenience, most work on patterning has focussed on the slug. However, it is now clear from using molecular markers that prestalk and prespore cells first arise earlier, in the mound, at, or shortly

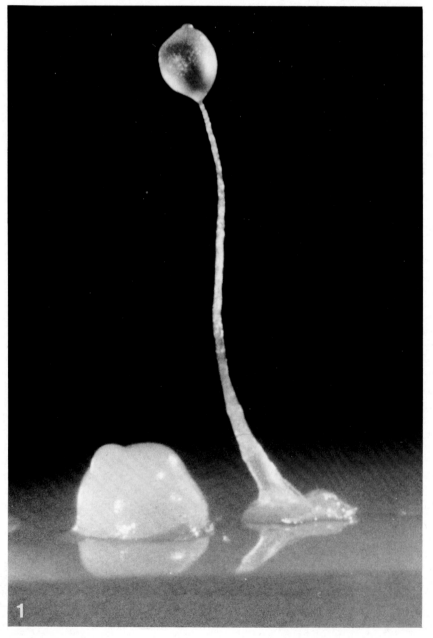

Fig. 1. Tipped mound and mature fruiting body of *Dictyostelium discoideum*. Starvation of *Dictyostelium* triggers development and after a few hours the amoebae aggregate together by chemotaxis to relayed cAMP signals to form a mound of cells. The size of the mound is initially indeterminate but there is an unknown mechanism whereby large mounds are partitioned into aggregates of about 10^5 cells. These aggregates surround themselves in a sort primitive extracellular matrix (the slime) and develop a protruding tip (shown just emerging, left) which thereafter leads the morphogenetic movements. The mound elongates upwards to form the standing slug and this can fall on its side to form the migrating slug which is photo- and thermo-tactic. In suitable environmental conditions, the slug transforms into the mature fruiting body (right) in which a basal disc and stalk support a mass of spores. Depending on strain, the entire process can be completed in 24 h with tips forming at about 11 h. Fruiting bodies can be up to 5 mm tall. Photograph reproduced by permission of The Company of Biologists.

before, the time when a tip forms (Hayashi and Takeuchi, 1976; Takeuchi *et al.* 1978; Krefft *et al.* 1984; Williams *et al.* 1987; Jermyn *et al.* 1987) and it follows that this stage of development is the primary seat of pattern formation. The slug is eventually triggered to transform into the final fruiting body by suitable environmental conditions, such as overhead light. During this process there are complicated movements of the prestalk and prespore tissues, which rival any described in higher embryos, before terminal differentiation into dead vacuolated stalk cells and viable, resistant spores.

Patterning, regulation and gradients

The patterning process in *Dictyostelium* has features that echo those in many other organisms. The regulative properties are perhaps the most extravagant known. Reasonably proportioned fruiting bodies can be constructed consisting of from 10^3 to 10^5 cells (Stenhouse and Williams, 1977). There are even reports of a minute fruiting body consisting of just 7 cells (see Hohl and Raper, 1964). Similarly it is well known that, given time, fragments of slugs can regulate to give properly proportioned fruiting bodies (Raper, 1940; Sampson, 1976). The impression gained from these experiments, that cell-type proportions are regulated by a supracellular signalling system, is confirmed by mixing cells of different physiology and showing that the probability of any cell becoming a spore depends on the nature of the cells it develops with (MacWilliams *et al.* 1985). Though many experimenters have wished for them, giant fruiting bodies have never been reported. There appears to be some mechanism for sub-dividing large aggregates or slugs into smaller ones, of no more than about 10^5 cells. Each entity develops a tip and then behaves independently (Hohl and Raper, 1964; Kopachik, 1982). The sizing mechanism in mounds appears to involve a diffusible tip inhibitor that can penetrate an agar membrane (Kopachik, 1982) and a similar conclusion has been reached from transplantation experiments with slugs (Durston, 1976; MacWilliams, 1982). In these experiments, the frequency with which a standard transplant will form a tip (and hence a separate organism) is measured when it is placed at various positions down a slug. The tip-formation inhibitor gradient thus detected is labile and has its high point at the anterior: the signal probably comes from the tip. When tissue from various positions down a slug is transplanted to a standard site in the host slug, the most anterior tissue is the most likely to form a secondary tip. The tip-activator gradient so revealed is most likely a stable cellular property as it can be measured in small transplants, where a diffusible morphogen would be expected to rapidly equilibrate with the host tissue. The explanation for size-control in terms of gradients of tip inhibitor and activator with high points at the tip is reminiscent of that offered for *Hydra* head formation (Hicklin *et al.* 1973).

Although various schemes can be advanced to explain cell-type proportioning and size-control, it has not

been possible to prove any of them by experiments at the organismal level. To do this it is necessary to know about the signalling mechanisms involved, with the first step being the identification of the signal substances themselves.

Morphogen hunting

In *Drosophila* morphogens have been hunted very successfully by molecular genetics. Mutants affecting patterning are isolated, sifted in various ways and the most promising genes cloned by conventional techniques. By good fortune the protein product of a gene such as *bicoid* has turned out to be the morphogen itself, rather than, say, an enzyme that makes the morphogen (Driever and Nüsslein-Volhard, 1988; see St. Johnston *et al.* this volume). This genetic approach is also feasible in *Dictyostelium*, given the ease with which developmental mutants can be isolated, but it has not been used to date. Morphogens have instead been hunted by biochemical means. The key to success is to have a good assay for the morphogen: with this in hand, and a ready supply of material to purify, modern techniques of purification and identification should allow almost any molecule to be identified eventually. The most desirable assay would be one in which some aspect of pattern was affected but in practice less direct, but more convenient, assays have been used. For instance cAMP and adenosine were first implicated at the aggregation stage of development, cAMP as a chemoattractant for amoebae (Konijn *et al.* 1967), adenosine as a factor that reduced the number of spontaneous signalling centers during aggregation (Newell and Ross, 1982). Similarly ammonia was recognised as a factor that promoted the continued migration of slugs (Schindler and Sussman, 1977). Only later were these three compounds implicated in the patterning process.

Our hunt for *Dictyostelium* morphogens has been based on cell differentiation assays, on the assumption that the morphogens must ultimately control the positionally dependent differentiation of prestalk and prespore cells in the mound and later the positionally dependent maturation of prestalk cells as the stalk of the fruiting body is formed. This work started from an observation of John Bonner (1970), who found that cells plated on cAMP–agar remained as a monolayer but nevertheless some of them differentiated into stalk cells. We repeated this experiment with a particularly susceptible strain called V12M2 and also managed to devise conditions in which mature spores differentiated too. Spore formation required either a particular mutation or treatment of the cells with high concentrations of a penetrating cAMP analogue, to overcome a late block to spore maturation in the *in vitro* conditions (Town *et al.* 1976; Kay *et al.* 1978; Kay, 1989). Conditions were modified from those of Bonner, by allowing cells to differentiate as monolayers, submerged in a simple salts solution in tissue culture dishes, and we set out to discover the inducers necessary to make isolated

DIF ASSAY

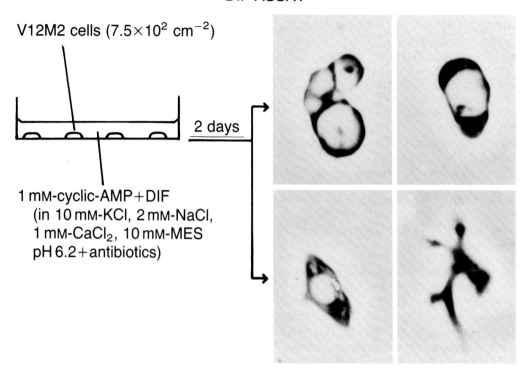

Fig. 2. Bioassay for DIF. The principle of the assay is that cells incubated at low cell density with cAMP in a simple salts solution (in which conditions they accumulate insignificant amounts of DIF) can be induced to form stalk cells by DIF. The proportion of stalk cells is scored by phase-contrast microscopy after 2 days and this gives a measure of the DIF concentration. The fully vacuolated cells (upper panels) are scored as stalk cells, the amoeba and partially vacuolated cell (lower panels) are scored as non-stalk cells. 10^{-10} M-DIF-1 induces approximately 27 % stalk cells in the assay. With a standard 2 ml assay volume 0.1 pmole DIF-1 can be detected.

amoebae differentiate into either stalk cells or spores. Here we concentrate on the DIFs, which specifically induce stalk cell differentiation and have been our major interest.

The DIFs: a new class of effector molecules

The DIFs are assayed by their ability to induce isolated amoebae to differentiate into stalk cells in the presence of cAMP (Fig. 2, Town *et al.* 1976; Town and Stanford, 1978; Brookman *et al.* 1982). At least 5 different DIFs have been resolved by HPLC of the medium collected from developing cells (Kay *et al.* 1983). Of these DIF-1 accounts for about 96 % of the recovered activity, DIF-2 for 3 %, DIF-3 and the others for 1 %. DIF-1 is active in the bioassay at 10^{-11} M and correspondingly minute amounts can be gathered from developing cells: from 2 years of accumulation using 40001 of medium and producing 16 kg of amoebae only about 100 μg of purified DIF-1 was available for identification. Power-ful physical techniques such as ^{13}C-n.m.r. were there-fore precluded and most information came from mass spectroscopy, with the isomeric possibilities being finally resolved by chemical synthesis. DIF-1 is a phenyl hexanone with di-chloro, di-hydroxy and methoxy sub-stitution of the benzene ring; DIFs 2 and 3 are closely related molecules (Fig. 3; Morris *et al.* 1987, 1988). Chemically the DIFs are quite stable and their solubility

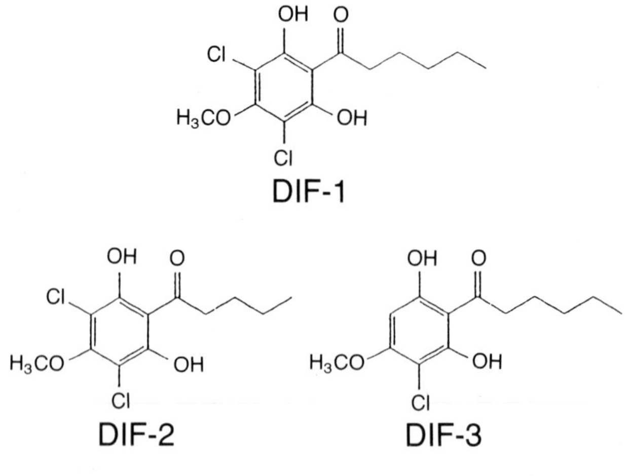

Fig. 3. Chemical structures of DIFs 1, 2, and 3. The structures were established largely by mass spectroscopy from less than 100 μg of purified material in each case.

in both hexane and water suggests that they are membrane permeable, opening the possibility that they have an intracellular receptor in the steroid/thyroid/retinoic acid super-family.

It is not known whether the DIFs and related molecules are unique to slime moulds or could be more widespread in nature. DIF activities have been detected in two other slime mould species, which use different chemoattractants in their aggregation stage (Brookman *et al.* 1982), but a systematic search has yet to be made in other organisms. Certainly something as scarce as DIF would have eluded the sort of chemical analysis that has been used to classify major cellular lipids and metabolites in the past.

Role of the DIFs

The main role of the DIFs that we know about at the moment is in controlling cell differentiation during the multicellular stages of development. Most work has concentrated on DIF-1 because it is the most potent and most abundant DIF species in the slug (Masento *et al.* 1988; Brookman *et al.* 1987), but it remains quite possible that DIFs 2 and 3 also have important roles.

The fact that DIF-1 (together with cAMP) can induce a vegetative amoeba to differentiate into a stalk cell does not necessarily implicate DIF-1 in the patterning process. For instance, DIF-1 could just be stimulating some very early or very late step in the differentiation pathway and not be effective at the time when the prestalk/prespore pattern is laid down. We initially sought to address this problem in several ways: by determining when DIF is made during development, by isolating mutants with reduced DIF levels and examining their phenotypes, by isolating genes whose expression is induced by DIF and examining their regulation and finally by determining the effects of DIF-1 on spore cell differentiation.

The DIFs can be extracted from cells with organic solvents and estimated using the stalk cell bioassay. Growing cells do not contain detectable DIF, there is a small but definite rise during aggregation but the major rise occurs at the end of aggregation when the prestalk/prespore is formed (Fig. 4; Brookman *et al.* 1982; Sobolewski *et al.* 1983). DIF-1 can reach 0.2 μM in the slug (from Brookman *et al.* 1987), which is ample to bring about all the effects to be described in later sections.

Mutants making reduced amounts of DIF, but still responsive to it, were isolated using a stalk cell differentiation assay as the screen. At high density, wild-type cells incubated with cAMP accumulate their own DIF and so are induced to become stalk cells. Mutants impaired in DIF accumulation would not become stalk cells in these conditions but, if no other process was impaired, they should become stalk cells when DIF-1 was added. Three strains producing less than 10% of the peak wild-type levels of DIF but still responsive to it were recognised in this way (Kopachik *et al.* 1983). These mutants had several important properties: they arrested in development as tip-less mounds, suggesting a role for DIF beyond this point, they synergised with wild-type, suggesting a defect in signal production but not reception (as expected from the screen used in their isolation), and they made prespore products but not a prestalk product, suggesting that DIF was required for prestalk but not prespore cell differentiation. Thus the properties of these mutants strongly suggest an essential role for DIF at the time of pattern formation and that

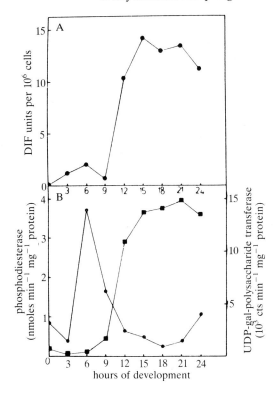

Fig. 4. Developmental regulation of DIF activity. DIF was extracted from developing cells using a standard lipid extraction procedure and assayed with the stalk cell differentiation bioassay (upper panel). There is little if any DIF detectable in growing cells but during aggregation there is a small but definite rise which might reflect a role at this stage of development. However, the major rise in levels occurs during the mound stage of development when the prestalk–prespore pattern is established. For comparison, the developmental regulation of an aggregative (cAMP phosphodiesterase) and a post-aggregative enzyme (glycogen phosphorylase) are also shown (lower panel). Reproduced from Brookman *et al.* (1982), with permission.

this role may be to induce prestalk cell differentiation. There are however a number of caveats. The mutants have not been subjected to an extensive genetic analysis, in no case has their basic lesion been tracked down and we cannot explain why they do make small, but definite, amounts of DIF.

The 'reduced-DIF' mutants allowed us to take the next step of identifying gene products whose expression is induced by DIF-1, by comparing DIF-1-treated and control cells. In this way a number of DIF-1-induced protein spots were recognised on 2D gels (Kopachik *et al.* 1985) and three cDNA species cloned by differential screening (Williams *et al.* 1987; Jermyn *et al.* 1987). The satisfying thing about these experiments was that all of the markers so identified could be shown independently to be prestalk or stalk cell specific. In the case of the pDd56 and pDd63 mRNAs, these markers actually identified a cryptic heterogeneity in the prestalk cell population, as described by Williams *et al.* (this volume).

Finally it could be shown in several ways that DIF-1 repressed prespore and spore differentiation. For instance, wild-type prespore cells are converted to stalk cells under the influence of DIF-1 (Kay and Jermyn, 1983) and expression of prespore markers is repressed (Kopachik *et al.* 1985; Early and Williams, 1988). Likewise monolayer amoebae, which would otherwise become spores, are diverted almost quantitatively to stalk cell differentiation by DIF-1 (Kay and Jermyn, 1983; Kay, 1989).

All of these results strongly indicate that DIF (presumably DIF-1) is the endogenous inducer of prestalk cell differentiation that is active as the prestalk/prespore pattern is generated. It is easy to see that an appropriate gradient of DIF-1 in the aggregate could account for the formation of the prestalk/prespore pattern.

Before taking the patterning problem further, it is important to assess the roles of other *Dictyostelium* signal molecules in controlling cell differentiation. Again we are most interested in signals with a pathway-specific effect, since if these were correctly localized in the aggregate they could help create the prestalk/prespore pattern.

The origin of prestalk and prespore cells

The signal molecules that have been chemically identified and proposed to play some role in controlling cell differentiation are DIFs 1–3, cAMP, its breakdown product adenosine, and ammonia, a product of cellular catabolism during development. The effects of these compounds on cell differentiation can be examined under two basic circumstances designed either to minimize cell interaction so as to detect direct effects on cell differentiation (single cell and short-term assays) or to permit interaction so as to detect also indirect effects that work by modulating the levels of some other factor such as DIF (high cell density, longer term assays).

A scheme for the regulation of cell-type specific differentiation is given in Fig. 5 and is based on the following points:

1. The basic bifurcation between prestalk and prespore differentiation is made by DIF-1 which directly induces prestalk and inhibits prespore differentiation (last section).

2. cAMP directly induces prespore (Kay *et al.* 1978; Kay, 1979, 1982; Barklis and Lodish, 1983; Mehdy *et al.* 1983) and prestalk A differentiation (provided DIF is present; Berks and Kay unpublished). After the tipped mound stage cAMP represses prestalk B differentiation (Berks and Kay, 1988; and unpublished) and may therefore be responsible for maintaining the distinction between prestalk A and B cells in the slug.

3. Adenosine inhibits prespore cell differentiation (Weijer and Durston, 1985; Schaap and Wang, 1986) probably indirectly by an inhibition of cAMP signalling (Newell and Ross, 1982; Thiebert and Devreotes, 1984).

4. Ammonia may inhibit prestalk cell differentiation (Gross *et al.* 1983; Bradbury and Gross, 1989) by an unknown mechanism and its abrupt removal can trigger

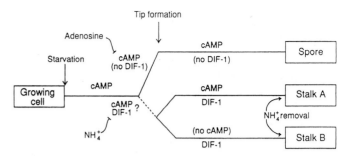

Fig. 5. Control of cell differentiation by diffusible signals. This provides a summary of a large body of work. After starvation the initial differentiation of all cells through aggregation is driven by cAMP signalling. It then appears that cell diversification is brought about by cAMP and DIF-1 acting combinatorially, with DIF-1 being necessary for the differentiation of both types of stalk cell. The dotted line on the stalk lineage indicates an uncertainty as to whether the prestalk A and prestalk B cells share a common prestalk precursor or come directly from aggregative amoebae. Adenosine is envisaged as working by inhibiting cAMP signalling though some direct effect on gene expression cannot be totally excluded. Ammonia antagonises DIF-1 by a mechanism that might involve intracellular pH (see Gross *et al.* 1988; Inouye, 1988).

stalk cell maturation (Schindler and Sussman, 1977; Wang and Schaap, 1989). probably by causing a drop in intracellular pH (Inouye, 1988).

There are a number of holes in this scheme: it is not clear how the division of prestalk cells into prestalk A and B is first brought about, nor how prestalk O cells (not shown in the diagram) originate, nor how the final maturation of prestalk and prespore cells is controlled. However, Fig. 5 does re-emphasise the central role of DIF-1 in bringing about the basic bifuraction of aggregated amoebae into prestalk and prespore cells. Finally, it is interesting to note that in the slug cAMP and DIF-1 might be acting combinatorily to define cell states: plus cAMP no DIF-1, plus cAMP plus DIF-1 and no cAMP plus DIF-1 each define a distinct cell type (no cAMP no DIF-1 probably corresponds to a state of dedifferentiation toward the aggregative state).

DIF-1 and patterning

Measurement of the distribution of DIF in migrating slugs by dissection, extraction and bioassay raised a puzzle. The gradient is the reverse of that expected (Brookman *et al.* 1987), with the concentration of DIF in the prespore zone (where it is not active) approximately twice that in the prestalk zone (where it is active). There are many possible explanations for the reverse DIF-1 gradient. Two technical doubts are firstly that it was only possible to measure total DIF, not the fraction which is actually active, and secondly that the experiments were performed on slugs, several hours after the primary patterning process in the mound. In this time, as a way of stabilizing the differentiated states, the prespore cells could have become relatively

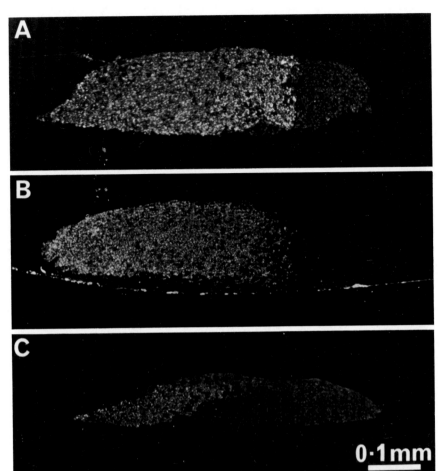

Fig. 6. DIF-1 treatment of slugs causes the prestalk zone to become enlarged. Longitudinal sections of slugs are stained with an antibody recognising prespore cells. (A) Control slug; (B) typical DIF-1-treated slug; (C) extreme example of a DIF-1-treated slug. The effect of DIF-1 is to increase the relative sizes of both the prestalk zone and of the platform zone adjacent to the agar and to blur the prestalk–prespore boundary. Slugs migrating on cellophane were transferred to fresh agar containing 0.2 μM-DIF-1 as indicated. After 4 h slugs were fixed, sectioned and stained by conventional techniques. Reproduced from Kay *et al.* (1988) with permission.

insensitive to DIF-1 and so not be affected by the DIF-1 in the prespore zone. Clearly the dissection experiments need repeating on mounds. Alternatively the results might indicate the involvement of an additional morphogen: either an activator formed from DIF-1 and localized to the prestalk zone (Meinhardt, 1983) or a DIF-1 antagonist in the prespore zone (see below).

In contrast, evidence that DIF-1 does act as a morphogen comes from experiments in which slugs or aggregates were transferred to agar containing DIF-1. The general effect of DIF-1 is to cause enlargement of the prestalk zone and of the 'platform' zone of prestalk cells adjacent to the agar (Fig. 6, Kay *et al.* 1988). Significant changes are produced by 0.1 μM-DIF-1 (Fig. 7). which is less than estimated physiological concentrations in the slug of 0.2 μM. Patterning changes are detectable after 1 h and complete by 4 h of incubation with DIF-1, times comparable to those required for prespore to prestalk conversion in isolated prespore fragments (Sakai, 1973). However, even here there is a complication because the extent of conversion induced by DIF-1 is always limited. In strain V12M2 the proportion of prestalk cells can be increased from 33 % to 53 % but no further (Fig. 7). Other strains, such as X22, behave in a similar way. This lack of responsiveness to DIF-1 of prespore cells in intact slugs is surprising because isolated prespore cells respond

readily (Kay and Jermyn, 1983). We do not think the problem is one of DIF-1 penetration; more likely we suggest that there is a DIF-1 antagonist in the slug, produced in response to DIF-1, which limits its effects. To date searches for DIF antagonists have turned up ammonia (Gross *et al.* 1983) and cAMP itself (Berks and Kay, 1988), but neither fits the bill exactly. For instance, neither cAMP nor ammonia (except at very high concentrations) represses the induction of the pDd63 mRNA by DIF-1 (Berks and Kay, unpublished). It may now be necessary to start hunting for a factor that does.

DIF-1 metabolism

It is important to understand DIF-1 metabolism for several reasons. First, this is likely to be an important way in which DIF-1 levels are regulated in the aggregate and provide a target for control of DIF-1 levels by other morphogens. Second, an understanding of how DIF-1 is metabolised should allow us to manipulate DIF-1 levels in the aggregate and thereby learn more of its role in development. Finally, it is possible that some metabolites may turn out to be morphogens in their own right: possibilities include a short-range activator as suggested by Meinhardt (1983) or the inhibitor mentioned above.

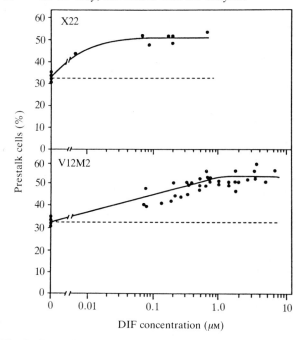

Fig. 7. Dose dependence of patterning changes caused by DIF-1. Slugs of strain V12M2 or X22, migrating on cellophane, were transferred to agar containing various concentrations of DIF-1. After a further 4–6 h, the slugs were harvested, disaggregated to single cells and stained with an antibody against prespore cells (Takeuchi, 1963) and the proportion of non-staining (=prestalk) cells determined.

Radioactive DIF-1, with ^{3}H or ^{14}C label of the ring methoxy group was synthesised chemically and fed to cells. DIF-1 metabolites were then recovered from the medium or cells and examined by reverse-phase HPLC or TLC. It was immediately apparent that DIF-1 is metabolized in a surprisingly complicated way and we have so far recognised at least 8 significant metabolites (Traynor and Kay, unpublished). By following the flow of counts from one compound to another and by determining the fate of purified intermediates refed to cells, we have been able to deduce a tentative pathway for DIF-1 metabolism, in which the first component is largely cell-associated and the other metabolites are found mainly in the medium. Little is yet known of their chemical nature.

DIF metabolism is developmentally regulated, reaching a maximum at about the mound stage, when DIF-1 levels are rapidly rising and the prestalk/prespore pattern is being established. At this stage or in the slug the cellular DIF-1 metabolizing capacity is such that DIF-1 must be rapidly metabolized with a half-life of only a few minutes. Thus DIF-1 is probably a dynamic molecule that is made and degraded rapidly.

Most of the DIF-1 metabolites are active in the stalk cell induction bioassay, but none has more than 5% of the specific activity of DIF-1. To date none synergise with DIF-1 or inhibits its activity. Thus so far none of the metabolites is a candidate morphogen in its own right: what, if anything, do all these compounds do?

Prospects

The study of pattern formation in *Dictyostelium* is at a tantalizing stage, where candidate morphogens have been identified but a coherent scheme for their action is still lacking. We cannot yet explain how the prestalk/prespore pattern is generated, how a large aggregate is partitioned into discrete entities or the nature of the tip inhibitory gradient emanating from the tip. Several factors impede, or have until recently impeded, progress in this area. At a conceptual level, too great an emphasis has in the past been devoted to patterning in the migrating slug. This is several hours removed from the mound stage, which is the primary seat of patterning, and in this time cell differentiation could complicate the analysis. Perhaps the greatest technical problem here, and in other organisms using small, diffusible morphogens, is that of visualizing morphogen gradients. Even with suitable antibodies it is unlikely that the fixation procedures used to reveal the distribution of a large morphogen like the bicoid protein would be of any use for cAMP or DIF-1. An additional problem is that we probably do not have the complete inventory of *Dictyostelium* morphogens: the nature of the tip inhibitor is obscure (though it could be adenosine; Schaap and Wang, 1986) and we have been forced here to postulate the existence of a new DIF-antagonist. Perhaps some of the DIF metabolites or other factors recently described will complete the story (Gibson and Hames, 1988; Kumagai and Okamato, 1986; Mehdy and Firtel, 1985)?

Thus the main consequence of knowing the structure of DIF-1 seems not to have been an immediate understanding of the biological processes in which it participates, but instead the ability to do more and better experiments. DIF-1, which was once scarce, can now be synthesised chemically along with radioactive DIF-1 and various analogues. Work on DIF-1 has led to the identification of new markers for prestalk cells, which in turn have revealed the existence of a new anatomy in the prestalk zone. It is clear that the basic diversification of developing amoebae toward stalk or spore cell differentiation can be brought about by DIF-1. With this rate of progress and because *Dictyostelium* is now such a favourable organism to work with, one must be optimistic of obtaining quite soon a working outline of the patterning process.

References

BARKLIS, E. AND LODISH, H. F. (1983). Regulation of *Dictyostelium discoideum* mRNAs specific for prespore or prestalk cells. *Cell* **32**, 1139–1148.

BERKS, M. AND KAY, R. R. (1988). Cyclic AMP is an inhibitor of stalk cell differentiation in *Dictyostelium discoideum*. *Devl Biol.* **126**, 108–114.

BONNER, J. T. (1970). Induction of stalk cell differentiation by cyclic AMP in the cellular slime mold *Dictyostelium discoideum*. *Proc. natn. Acad. Sci. U.S.A.* **65**, 110–113.

BRADBURY, J. M. AND GROSS, J. G. (1989). The effect of ammonia on cell type specific enzyme accumulation in *Dictyostelium discoideum*. *Cell Diff. & Development*, (in press).

BROOKMAN, J. J., JERMYN, K. A. AND KAY, R. R. (1987). Nature and distribution of the morphogen DIF in the *Dictyostelium* slug. *Development* **100**, 119–124.

BROOKMAN, J. J., TOWN, C. D., JERMYN, K. A. AND KAY, R. R. (1982). Developmental regulation of a stalk cell differentiation inducing factor in *Dictyostelium discoideum*. *Devl Biol.* **91**, 191–196.

DRIEVER, W. AND NÜSSLEIN-VOLHARD, C. (1988). A gradient in bicoid protein in *Drosophila* embryos. *Cell* **54**, 83–93.

DURSTON, A. J. (1976). Tip formation is regulated by an inhibitory gradient in the *Dictyostelium discoideum* slug. *Nature, Lond.* **263**, 126–129.

EARLY, A. E. AND WILLIAMS, J. G. (1988). A *Dictyostelium* prespore-specific gene is transcriptionally repressed by DIF *in vitro*. *Development* **103**, 519–524.

GERISCH, G. (1987). Cyclic AMP and other signals controlling cell development and differentiation in *Dictyostelium*. *A. Rev. Biochem.* **56**, 853–879.

GIBSON, F. P. AND HAMES, B. D. (1988). Characterization of a spore protein inducing factor from *Dictyostelium discoideum*. *J. Cell Sci.* **89**, 387–395.

GROSS, J. D., PEACEY, M. J. AND POGGE-VON STRANDMANN, R. P. (1988). Plasma membrane proton pump inhibition and stalk cell differentiation in *Dictyostelium discoideum*. *Differentiation* **38**, 91–98.

GROSS, J. D., BRADBURY, J., KAY, R. R. AND PEACEY, M. J. (1983). Intracellular pH and the control of cell differentiation in *Dictyostelium discoideum*. *Nature, Lond.* **303**, 244–245.

HAYASHI, M. AND TAKEUCHI, I. (1976). Quantitative studies on cell differentiation during morphogenesis of the cellular slime mold *Dictyostelium discoideum*. *Devl Biol.* **50**, 302–309.

HICKLIN, J., HORNBRUCH, A., WOLPERT, L. AND CLARKE, M. (1973). Positional information and pattern regulation in hydra: the formation of boundary regions following axial grafts. *J. Embryol. exp. Morph.* **30**, 701–725.

HOHL, H. R. AND HAMAMOTO, S. T. (1969). Ultrastructure of spore differentiation in *Dictyostelium*: the prespore vacuole. *J. Ultrastruct. Res.* **26**, 442–453.

HOHL, H. R. AND RAPER, K. B. (1964). Control of sorocarp size in the cellular slime mold *Dictyostelium discoideum*. *Devl Biol.* **9**, 137–153.

INOUYE, K. (1988). Induction by acid load of the maturation of prestalk cells in *Dictyostelium discoideum*. *Development* **104**, 669–681.

JERMYN, K. A., BERKS, M., KAY, R. R. AND WILLIAMS, J. G. (1987). Two distinct classes of prestalk-enriched mRNA sequences in *Dictyostelium discoideum*. *Development* **100**, 745–755.

JERMYN, K. A., DUFFY, K. T. I. AND WILLIAMS, J. G. (1989). A new anatomy of the prestalk zone in *Dictyostelium*. *Nature, Lond.* **340**, 144–146.

JOHNSON, G., JOHNSON, R., BORYSENKO, J. AND REVEL, J. P. (1977). Do cellular slime molds form intercellular junctions? *Science* **197**, 1300.

KAY, R. R. (1979). Gene expression in *Dictyostelium discideum*: mutually antagonistic roles of cyclic-AMP and ammonia. *J. Embryol. exp. Morph.* **52**, 171–182.

KAY, R. R. (1982). cAMP and spore differentiation in *Dictyostelium discoideum*. *Proc. natn. Acad. Sci. U.S.A.* **79**, 3228–3231.

KAY, R. R. (1989). Evidence that elevated intracellular cyclic AMP triggers spore maturation in *Dictyostelium*. *Development* **105**, 753–759.

KAY, R. R., BERKS, M., TRAYNOR, D., TAYLOR, G. W., MASENTO, M. S. AND MORRIS, H. R. (1988). Signals controlling cell differentiation and pattern formation in *Dictyostelium*. *Dev. Genet.* **9**, 579–587.

KAY, R. R., DHOKIA, B. AND JERMYN, K. A. (1983). Purification of stalk-cell-inducing morphogens from *Dictyostelium discoideum*. *Eur. J. Biochem.* **136**, 51–56.

KAY, R. R., GARROD, D. AND TILLY, R. (1978). Requirements for cell differentiation in *Dictyostelium discoideum*. *Nature, Lond.* **271**, 58–60.

KAY, R. R. AND JERMYN, K. A. (1983). A possible morphogen

controlling differentiation in *Dictyostelium*. *Nature, Lond.* **303**, 242–244.

KONIJN, T. M., VAN DE MEENE, J. G. C., BONNER, J. T. AND BARKLEY, D. S. (1967). The acrasin activity of adenosine-3′,5′ cyclic phosphate. *Proc. natn. Acad. Sci. U.S.A.* **58**, 1152–1154.

KOPACHIK, W. (1982). Size regulation in *Dictyostelium*. *J. Embryol. exp. Morph.* **68**, 23–35.

KOPACHIK, W., DHOKIA, B. AND KAY, R. R. (1985). Selective induction of stalk-cell-specific proteins in *Dictyostelium*. *Differentiation* **28**, 209–216.

KOPACHIK, W., OOHATA, A., DHOKIA, B., BROOKMAN, J. J. AND KAY, R. R. (1983). *Dictyostelium* mutants lacking DIF, a putative morphogen. *Cell* **33**, 397–403.

KREFFT, M., VOET, L., GREGG, J. H., MAIRHOFER, H. AND WILLIAMS, K. L. (1984). Evidence that positional information is used to establish the prestalk-prespore pattern in *Dictyostelium discoideum* aggregates. *EMBO J.* **3**, 201–206.

KUMAGAI, A. AND OKAMOTO, K. (1986). Prespore-inducing factors in *Dictyostelium discoideum*. Developmental regulation and partial purification. *Differentiation* **31**, 79–84.

LOOMIS, W. F. (1982). *The Development of* Dictyostelium discoideum. Academic Press, New York.

MACWILLIAMS, H. (1982). Transplantation experiments and pattern mutants in cellular slime mold slugs. In *Developmental Order: Its Origin and Regulation* pp. 463–483. Alan Liss New York.

MACWILLIAMS, H., BLASCHKE, A. AND PRAUSE, I. (1985). Two feedback loops may regulate cell-type proportions in *Dictyostelium*. *Cold Spring Harbor Symp. quant. Biol.* **50**, 779–785.

MAEDA, Y. AND TAKEUCHI, I. (1969). Cell differentiation and fine structures in the development of the cellular slime molds. *Develop. Growth and Diff.* **11**, 232–245.

MASENTO, M. S., MORRIS, H. R., TAYLOR, G. W., JOHNSON, S. J., SKAPSKI, A. AND KAY, R. R. (1988). Differentiation-inducing factor from the slime mould *Dictyostelium discoideum* and its analogues. *Biochem. J.* **256**, 23–28.

MEHDY, M. C. AND FIRTEL, R. A. (1985). A secreted factor and cyclic AMP jointly regulate cell-type-specific gene expression in *Dictyostelium discoideum*. *Mol. & Cell. Biol.* **5**, 705–713.

MEHDY, M. C., RATNER, D. AND FIRTEL, R. A. (1983). Induction and modulation of cell-type-specific gene expression in *Dictyostelium*. *Cell* **32**, 763–771.

MEINHARDT, H. (1983). A model for the prestalk/prespore patterning in the slug of the slime mold *Dictyostelium discoideum*. *Differentiation* **24**, 191–202.

MORRIS, H. R., MASENTO, M. S., TAYLOR, G. W., JERMYN, K. A. AND KAY, R. R. (1988). Structure elucidation of two differentiation inducing factors (DIF-2 and DIF-3) from the cellular slime mould *Dictyostelium discoideum*. *Biochem. J.* **249**, 903–906.

MORRIS, H. R., TAYLOR, G. W., MASENTO, M. S., JERMYN, K. A. AND KAY, R. R. (1987). Chemical structure of the morphogen differentiation inducing factor from *Dictyostelium discoideum*. *Nature, Lond.* **328**, 811–814.

NEWELL, P. C. AND ROSS, F. M. (1982). Inhibition by adenosine of aggregation centre initiation and cyclic AMP binding in *Dictyostelium*. *J. gen. Microbiol.* **128**, 2715–2724.

RAPER, K. B. (1940). Pseudoplasmodium formation and organization in *Dictyostelium discoideum*. *J. Elisha Mitchell Scient. Soc.* **56**, 241–282.

SAKAI, Y. (1973). Cell type conversion in isolated prestalk and prespore fragments of the cellular slime mold *Dictyostelium discoideum*. *Devl. Growth & Differentiaton* **15**, 11–19.

SAKAI, Y. AND TAKEUCHI, I. (1971). Changes of the prespore specific structure during dedifferentiation and cell type conversion of a slime mold cell. *Devl. Growth & Diff.* **13**, 231–240.

SAMPSON, J. (1976). Cell patterning in migrating slugs of *Dictyostelium discoideum*. *J. Embryol. exp. Morph.* **36**, 663–668.

SCHAAP, P. AND WANG, M. (1986). Interactions between adenosine and oscillatory cAMP signaling regulate size and pattern in *Dictyostelium*. *Cell* **45**, 137–144.

SCHINDLER, J. AND SUSSMAN, M. (1977). Ammonia determines the choice of morphogenetic pathways in *Dictyostelium discoideum*. *J. molec. Biol.* **116**, 161–169.

SOBOLEWSKI, A., NEAVE, N. AND WEEKS, G. (1983). The induction of stalk cell differentiation in submerged monolayers of *Dictyostelium discoideum*. *Differentiation* **25**, 93–100.

STENHOUSE, F. O. AND WILLIAMS, K. L. (1977). Patterning in *Dictyostelium discoideum*: the proportions of the three differentiated cell types (spore, stalk and basal disc) in the fruiting body. *Devl Biol.* **59**, 140–152.

STERNFELD, J. AND DAVID, C. N. (1981). Cell sorting during pattern formation in *Dictyostelium*. *Differentiation* **20**, 10–21.

TAKEUCHI, I. (1963). Immunochemical and immunohistochemical studies on the development of the cellular slime mold *Dictyostelium mucoroides*. *Devl Biol.* **8**, 1–26.

TAKEUCHI, I., OKAMOTO, K., TASAKA, M. AND TAKEMOTO, S. (1978). Regulation of cell differentiation in slime mold development. *Bot. Mag. Tokyo Special Issue* **1**, 46–60.

THEIBERT, A. AND DEVREOTES, P. N. (1984). Adenosine and its derivatives inhibit the cAMP signalling response in *Dictyostelium discoideum*. *Devl Biol.* **106**, 166–173.

TOWN, C. AND STANFORD, E. (1979). An oligosaccharide-containing factor that induces cell differentiation in *Dictyostelium discoideum*. *Proc. natn. Acad. Sci. U.S.A.* **76**, 308–312.

TOWN, C. D., GROSS, J. G. AND KAY, R. R. (1976). Cell differentiation without morphogenesis in *Dictyostelium discoideum*. *Nature, Lond.* **262**, 717–719.

WANG, M. AND SCHAAP, P. (1989). Ammonia depletion and DIF trigger stalk cell differentiation in intact *Dictyostelium discoideum* slugs. *Development* **105**, 569–574.

WEIJER, C. J. AND DURSTON, A. J. (1985). Influence of cyclic AMP and hydrolysis products on cell type regulation in *Dictyostelium discoideum*. *J. Embryol. exp. Morph.* **86**, 19–37.

WILLIAMS, J. G. (1988). The role of diffusible molecules in regulating the cellular differentiation of *Dictyostelium discoideum*. *Development* **103**, 1–16.

WILLIAMS, J. G., CECCARELLI, A., McROBBIE, S., MAHBUBANI, H., KAY, R. R., EARLY, A., BERKS, M. AND JERMYN, K. A. (1987). Direct induction of *Dictyostelium* prestalk gene expression by DIF provides evidence that DIF is a morphogen. *Cell* **49**, 185–192.

WILLIAMS, K. L., VARDY, P. H. AND SEGEL, L. A. (1986). Cell migrations during morphogenesis: Some clues from the slug of *Dictyostelium discoideum*. *BioEssays* **5**, 148–152.

Development 1989 Supplement, 91–97
Printed in Great Britain © The Company of Biologists Limited 1989

Formation and anatomy of the prestalk zone of *Dictyostelium*

J. G. WILLIAMS, K. A. JERMYN and K. T. DUFFY

Imperial Cancer Research Fund, Clare Hall Laboratory, Blanche Lane, South Mimms, Potters Bar, Herts., EN6 3LD, UK

Summary

The pDd63 and pDd56 genes encode extracellular matrix proteins which, respectively, surround the migratory slug and mature stalk cells. Both genes are dependent for their expression upon, and rapidly induced by, DIF, the stalk cell inducer. Using these genes as cell-autonomous markers, we have defined three distinct kinds of 'prestalk' cells localized to different parts of the anterior region of the slug. At least one, and probably both, prestalk cell types initially differentiates at the base of the aggregate. The most abundant of the two prestalk cell types then migrates into the tip, the precursor of the prestalk zone which arises at the apex of the aggregate. Thus we believe that morphogenesis of the prestalk zone,

the primary pattern-forming event in *Dictyostelium* development, involves a combination of positionally localized differentiation and directed cell migration. To account for the positionally localized differentiation of prestalk cells, we invoke the existence of gradients of the known antagonists of DIF – cAMP and NH3. We further suggest that differences in the motility of pstA and pstB cells might result from differences in their chemotactic responsiveness to cAMP signals propagated from the tip.

Key words: *Dictyostelium*, prestalk zone, extracellular matrix, DIF, inducer.

Introduction

At the end of aggregation, which in *D. discoideum* occurs in response to pulsatile emissions of cAMP from a signalling centre, a hemispherical cell mass, known as the tight aggregate, is formed. A nipple-shaped tip then forms atop the tight aggregate. This elongates to form a structure known as the standing slug, or first finger. Under conditions inappropriate for culmination, a migratory slug is formed. This is exquisitely phototactic and thermotactic and these sensitivities direct it to the surface where culmination occurs. The tip of the aggregate is retained at the anterior of the slug where it displays many of the properties of an embryonic organizer (Raper, 1940; Rubin and Robertson, 1975). The front 20 % of the slug is composed of prestalk cells. The rear 80 % is predominantly composed of prespore cells but there are also scattered cells, throughout the prespore zone, with the characteristics of prestalk cells. These are termed anterior-like cells. (Sternfeld and David, 1982).

In one sense *D. discoideum* is an exception amongst slime moulds, in that the migratory slug contains a population of prestalk cells which act as the direct precursors of stalk cells. In other species the majority of cells in the slug express prespore markers and the stalk is formed by 'transdifferentiation' of cells as they reach the extreme tip of the slug (Gregg and Davis, 1982; Schaap *et al.* 1985). In these situations it is clear that differentiation occurs in response to positional signals at the tip which direct cells to differentiate into stalk

cells. However, in *D. discoideum* it has been a matter of great debate whether initial differentiation, to form prestalk cells, occurs randomly throughout the aggregate, with subsequent cell sorting to form a distinct prestalk zone.

Cells sort when morphogenesis is subverted (Sternfeld and David, 1981; MacWilliams, 1982; Oyama *et al.* 1983) and it is possible to generate populations of cells biased to one or other pathway of differentiation, by manipulation of the growth conditions (Leach *et al.* 1973; Tasaka and Takeuchi, 1981) or by selecting cells at defined phases of the cell cycle. (MacDonald and Durston, 1984; Van Lookeren Campagne *et al.* 1984). In an analysis using an antibody directed against a prespore marker, prespore cells were first detected, at the time of tip formation, in the lower part of the aggregate (Krefft *et al.* 1984). This was taken to indicate that prespore cell differentiation occurs in response to positionally localized, morphogenetic signals. However, spore cells are essentially passive participants in *Dictyostelium* pattern formation and it is the differentiation and directed movement of prestalk cells that primarily shapes the fruit. In order to understand *Dictyostelium* morphogenesis, it is therefore necessary to determine how the expression of stalk-specific markers is induced and to use these markers to study the differentiation of individual prestalk cells. We have isolated definitive prestalk cell markers by identifying genes responsive to an inducer specific for stalk cell differentiation.

The stalk cell morphogen, DIF-1 (Morris *et al.* 1987)

acts rapidly to induce the expression of two closely related proteins, ST430 and ST310 (Jermyn *et al.* 1987; McRobbie *et al.* 1988*a,b*; Williams *et al.* 1987). They were first identified by two-dimensional gel electrophoresis of total cellular proteins (Morrissey *et al.* 1984) and are composed of tandem repeats of a twenty four amino acid, cysteine-rich sequence (Ceccarelli *et al.* 1987; Williams *et al.* 1987). They are extracellular proteins of the slime sheath and stalk tube (McRobbie *et al.* 1988), the protein–cellulose matrices which respectively surround the migrating slug and stalk cells of the mature fruit. We have shown, using the 'DIF-less' mutant HM44 (Kopachik *et al.* 1983), that the pDd63 gene and the pDd 56 genes, which encode these two proteins, are dependent upon DIF for their expression (Jermyn *et al.* 1987). Both genes are induced at the transcriptional level and expression of the pDd63 gene is detectable within fifteen minutes of the addition of DIF (Williams *et al.* 1987; Ceccarelli *et al.* 1987). The speed of this induction suggests it is mediated by a pre-existing receptor, or second-messenger pathway, directly responsive to DIF. Consistent with their induction by DIF, both mRNA sequences first appear just before the time a tip forms on the aggregate and both mRNA sequences persist into mature stalk cells (Jermyn *et al.* 1987; Williams *et al.* 1989).

Within the limits of purity achieved when prestalk and prespore cells are separated by gradient centrifugation, the pD56 and pD63 mRNA species appear to be completely prestalk-specific (Jermyn *et al.* 1987). As such they differ from most previously described 'prestalk' markers, which are also expressed in prespore cells (Jermyn *et al.* 1987). With the exception of the recently described cDt100 cDNA clone of Ozaki *et al.* 1988, which is as highly enriched in prestalk cells as pDd63 and pDd56, these other markers seem likely to be expressed in all cells and selectively stabilized in prestalk cells. They cannot, therefore, be used as cell-autonomous markers. The pDd56 and pDd63 provide such markers but, because they encode extracellular proteins, we are unable directly to identify cells expressing them. We have created cell-autonomous markers from them, by fusing their promoters to a 'reporter' gene containing a nuclear translocation signal, and transforming the constructs into *Dictyostelium* cells (Jermyn *et al.* 1989). We have shown there to be multiple classes of prestalk cells located in different parts of the anterior zone whose ontogeny and fate we have investigated (Williams *et al.* 1989). Here we outline these results and discuss their significance.

Discussion

(1) Multiple prestalk cell types in the migrating slug
The pDd63-Tag-CAt and pDd56-Tag-CAT constructs contain the pDd63 and pDd56 promoters (Ceccarelli *et al.* 1987; Early *et al.* 1988) coupled to reporter genes (Fig. 1). They display correct temporal, cell-type-specific and DIF-inducible expression after transformation into *Dictyostelium*. We have therefore been able

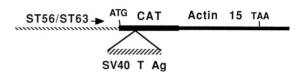

Fig. 1. Structure of the reporter gene constructs used to establish cell autonomous markers. The pDd56 and pDd63 genes were fused at a point just downstream of their ATG initiation codons to the chloramphenicol acetyl transferase (CAT) gene. Termination and polyadenylation signals are provided by the *Dictyostelium* actin15 gene. After transformation into *Dictyostelium* the fusion genes were correctly regulated (Ceccarelli *et al.* 1987; Early *et al.* 1988). They were further modified by the insertion of a fragment of the SV40 T antigen gene containing the nuclear localization signal (Jermyn *et al.* 1989). The fusion proteins are efficiently transported to the nucleus of *Dictyostelium* cells expressing the two genes.

to use them to monitor expression of the endogenous pDd56 and pDd63 genes. Cells expressing the pDd63 gene are restricted to the front 10 % of the length of the slug (Fig. 3A and Jermyn *et al.* 1989). The prestalk zone, defined using vital dyes that selectively stain prestalk cells (Bonner, 1951), occupies the front 20 % of the length of the slug. Hence there is a region, between the anterior 10 % and the prespore zone which does not contain cells expressing the pDd63 gene. In slugs derived from pDd56 transformants there is an anterior, central 'funnel' of staining cells, which occupies about one fifth to one tenth of the length of the slug (Fig. 3B and Jermyn *et al.* 1989).

Thus the slug has a more complex organization than hitherto suspected, with two kinds of prestalk cells, located in different parts of the anterior 10 % of the slug (Fig. 3C). We term these prestalk A (pstA) and prestalk B (pstB) cells. The pstA cells express the pDd63 gene but there is no detectable level of the pDd56 gene product. The pstB cells express the pDd56 gene and possibly also the pDd63 gene. We call the cells in the region immediately posterior to the front 10 %, which express neither marker, prestalk 0 (pst0) cells.

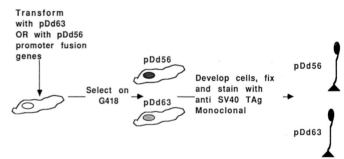

Fig. 2. Use of the reporter genes as cell autonomous markers. The pDd56 and pDd63 gene fusions contain a region of the SV40 genome recognized by four potent monoclonal antibodies and staining nuclei are detected by secondary incubation with an antibody coupled to horse radish peroxidase (Jermyn *et al.* 1989).

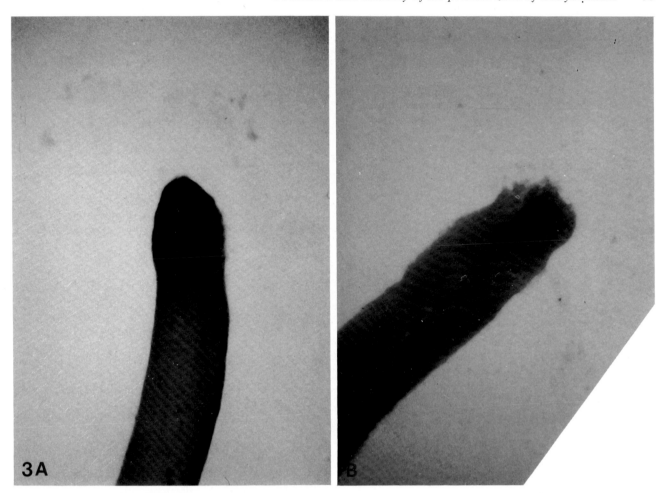

3A

B

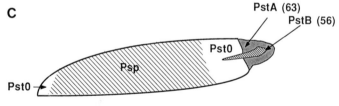

C

PstA (63)
PstB (56)
Pst0
Psp
Pst0

Fig. 3. Expression of the pDd63 and pDd56 fusion genes in different parts of the slug. (A) Expression of the pDd63 fusion gene. Migrating slugs, transformed with the pDd63–Tag–CAT construct were fixed as whole mounts and stained as described in the legend to Fig. 2. (B) Expression of the pDd56 fusion gene. This figure shows the front portion of a whole mount of pDd56 transformant slug. (C) Schematic representation of the distribution of prestalk and prespore cells in the slug. The pDd56 gene is expressed only in the central core (pstB cells) while the pD63 gene is expressed in cells surrounding them (pstA cells) and possibly also in the pstB cells. (Jermyn *et al.* 1989). The pstO cells in the zone behind the front 10 % of the length of the slug express neither marker. The prespore (psp) cells constitute the major fraction of cells. The rearguard cells, which express neither marker are classed here as pstO cells.

(2) Ontogeny and fate of prestalk cells during slug formation

We have recently shown that initial pstA and pstB cell differentiation occurs prior to appearance of the tip and that pstA cells move to it (Williams *et al.* 1989 and Fig. 4). Furthermore, quite contrary to expectation, pstB cells are predominantly localized to, and pstA cells become enriched at, the base of the tipped aggregate. Expression of the pDd56 gene, which defines a cell as pstB, is totally dependent upon DIF (Jermyn *et al.* 1987). Since pstB cells appear initially to differentiate at the base of the tight aggregate, this strongly implies the base to be a region of high effective DIF concentration from the very earliest stages of morphogenesis. Ex-

pression of the pDd63 gene is also dependent upon DIF (Jermyn *et al.* 1987) and we would therefore expect expression of the pDd63 gene to be initiated in the base of the aggregate. Because pstA cells rapidly migrate to the tip, we are unable to determine whether they also initially differentiate there but their enrichment in the basal zone of the tipped aggregate is certainly consistent with this idea.

PstA cells are the majority population and their behaviour presumably reflects the fact that prestalk cells are more chemotactically responsive and have a higher intrinsic motility than prespore cells (Bonner, 1951; Mee *et al.* 1986; Durston and Vork, 1979). We think that pstB cells may remain at the base because

Tight Aggregate

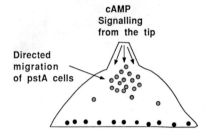

Tipped Aggregate

Fig. 4. A model for pstA and pstB cell differentiation. The pstA and pstB cells are proposed to differentiate in the base of the aggregate. PstA cells then migrate to the tip while pstB cells are left at the base to be lost in the slime trail as the slug migrates away from its site of formation (Williams *et al.* 1989). PstA cells within the tip then differentiate further to give the central core of pstB cells found in the slug tip.

they are chemotactically inactive (Fig. 5). We further believe that pstB cells are cells more advanced in their differentiation than pstA cells and that these are not two mutually exclusive states of differentiation – that there is potential progression, from pstA to pstB when the effective DIF concentration becomes high enough (Fig. 6).

Both cell sorting and positionally localized differentiation contribute to tip formation

Our observations suggest both models for morphogenesis to be partially correct. There *is* positionally localized differentiation but it initially occurs in the base of the aggregate and not, as logic would have suggested, in the tip. There is directed migration, of pstA cells, but pstB cells differentiate entirely *in situ* – an initial population in the base of the aggregate and a second population in the tip of the standing slug.

Characteristics of stalk cell precursors?

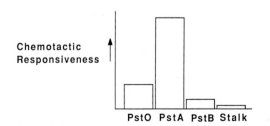

Fig. 5. A possible explanation for the different behaviour of pstA and pstB cells during slug formation.

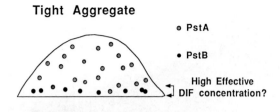

Fig. 6. Proposed stages in stalk cell differentiation. Terminal stalk cell differentiation is known to require a higher level of DIF than pstA cell differentiation, i.e. expression of the pDd63 gene (Jermyn *et al.* 1987). The evidence that a higher level of DIF is required for pstB cell differentiation derives from unpublished studies by Mary Berks and Rob Kay.

By showing that prestalk differentiation occurs prior to tip formation and that one of the two classes of prestalk cell, pstA cells, migrate into it, we have provided direct proof that directed prestalk cell migration plays a role in normal development. While we have confirmed its involvement, we do not believe that our observations show cell-sorting to play the primary role in patterning. We certainly do not subscribe to the view that cells are determined to one or other pathway of differentiation at the time they enter development by virtue of their position in the cell cycle (Gomer and Firtel, 1987). A critical property of the pDd56 and pDd63 genes is their dependence upon, and rapid induction by, DIF. Cells are inevitably heterogeneous and may, for example, differ in their sensitivity to DIF. This could affect the probability that they will form prestalk cells. However, the fact that cells transcribing these two genes constitute the two definitive prestalk cell populations, provides compelling evidence that exposure to DIF, or some active metabolite of it (Meinhardt, 1983), is the over-riding signal directing cells into the stalk cell pathway.

How is the initial positionally localized differentiation achieved and how are the cell types regulated during slug migration? There are a host of potential explanations and the eventual distinction between them will require a knowledge of the effective concentrations of all of the potential morphogens and their antagonists. However, it is worthwhile to attempt to formulate a model if only to serve as the basis for further experiment.

Molecules regulating the differentiation of pstA and B cells

Both the DIF inducible genes require DIF for their expression but the pDd56 gene may require a higher level of DIF for activation than the pDd63 gene (Mary Berks and Rob Kay personal communication). Presumably, therefore, the effective DIF concentration is highest at the base. We do not believe this is likely to be due to a higher level of DIF itself. Rather, we favour an alternative explanation; that an antagonist of DIF is present at a lower concentration and we suggest that this might be ammonia (Fig. 4). This is produced in large amounts because of the very active catabolism accompanying development. Ammonia acts as a DIF antagonist *in vitro*, acting to prevent stalk cell differentiation (Gross *et al.* 1983). There is also good evidence for it playing a similar role *in vivo*. A reduction in ammonia levels appears to be the normal trigger for culmination (Schindler and Sussman, 1977) and depletion of ammonia, induced artificially within the slug (Inouye, 1988; Wang and Schaap, 1989), leads to stalk cell differentiation *in situ*. We suggest that loss of ammonia might occur selectively at the base of the aggregate, perhaps because it has a higher rate of loss to, or inactivation in, the substratum than DIF. The formation of a stable, prestalk zone in the slug is more difficult to explain. First we must account for the existence of the pst0 cells.

There is abundant evidence to show that prespore gene expression is induced and maintained by cAMP signalling (reviewed by Schaap, 1986; Gerisch, 1987; Williams, 1988). Cyclic AMP signalling is amplified in a relay reaction and, in principle, all cells in the slug should respond. How then are cells at the front of the slug prevented from expressing prespore genes? DIF may play a part in this, since it represses the expression of prespore markers. (Kay and Jermyn, 1983; Early and Williams, 1988; Wang *et al.* 1986). However, adenosine, a competitive inhibitor of cAMP signalling and prespore cell differentiation (Newell, 1982; Newell and Ross, 1982; Schaap and Wang, 1986; Theibert and Devreotes, 1984; Schaap and Wang, 1986), appears very likely to be the primary repressor *in vivo*. The enzymes generating adenosine from cAMP are present at a higher concentration in the prestalk zone (Brown and Rutherford, 1980; Armant and Stetler, 1980; Armant and Rutherford, 1979) and enzymatic depletion of adenosine from the intact slug leads to prespore gene expression in the anterior, prestalk region (Schaap and Wang, 1986). We suggest that the pst0 zone is composed of cells blocked in prespore gene expression because of the presence of a high adenosine concentration (Fig. 7A,B). They are prevented from progressing into pstA cells because they are not exposed to a sufficiently high DIF concentration. They would therefore correspond in their properties to cells late in aggregation, i.e. they would be uncommitted to either pathway of differentiation. On this model adenosine would act only as an inhibitor of prespore differentiation. One prediction is that cells in the anterior zone should simultaneously express prespore and prestalk markers, when adenosine levels in the slug are depleted, and we are testing this.

The occurrence of pstA and pstB cells in the tip indicates that the effective DIF concentration must be relatively high there (Fig. 7A). The concentration of DIF has been determined in sub-sections of migrating slugs, with the apparently paradoxical observation of a higher concentration in the rear of migrating slugs than in the front. This has been suggested to indicate that the active species is not DIF itself but a metabolite produced from it (Meinhardt, 1983). However, the known breakdown products of DIF are much less active in stalk cell induction than DIF (Kay *et al.* this volume) and this model, therefore, remains unproven. Our results might appear to have some bearing on this paradox. The rear of the slug derives from the basal zone and, given the observation that prestalk cell differentiation appears to

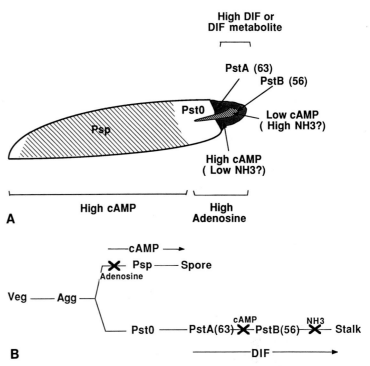

Fig. 7A,B. A scheme for the interactions between inducers of cellular differentiation and of their antagonists in the slug. The evidence supporting parts of this scheme has been presented elsewhere (Williams, 1988). The major new feature is the inclusion of pstA cells as an intermediate stage in prestalk differentiation and the suggestion that the progression from pstA to pstB is repressed by cAMP.

initiate there, DIF might also be expected to be present at a higher concentration in the base. However, metabolic studies show DIF to have a half-life *in vitro* of only minutes (Kay *et al.* this volume) and it therefore seems very unlikely that slugs, which had migrated for several days, would retain any vestiges of the distribution present in the aggregate.

What of the relative distribution of pstA and pstB cells? We believe that there is a progression from pstA to pstB and that this occurs when the DIF concentration reaches a critical threshold (Fig. 6). It is therefore tempting to believe that the effective DIF concentration is higher in the core at the centre of the migrating slug. The distribution of pstB cells suggests the existence of a radially distributed antagonist. Loss from the outer layers of the tip, of a highly diffusible substance such as ammonia, would establish a radial gradient but, on the model presented above where DIF and ammonia are held to be directly antagonistic, the effective concentration of DIF would be higher in the outer part of the tip. Hence differentiation of pstB cells would occur to give the reverse distribution to that actually observed. There is a potential explanation but it requires invoking a more complex set of interactions:

Cyclic AMP is required in the early stages of an *in vitro* induction in order that cells become competent to respond to DIF (Sobolewski *et al.* 1983) but it then acts to repress accumulation of the pDd56 protein (Berks and Kay, 1988). Ammonia is known to repress the intracellular accumulation of cAMP in response to an extracellular cAMP pulse (Schindler and Sussman, 1977). Hence it may be that, in the slug tip, ammonia is acting as a cAMP antagonist leading to a low effective cAMP concentration (Fig. 7A). It may also play a role as a DIF antagonist, preventing the progression of pstB cells into stalk cells (Fig. 7B). This would be consistent with the fact that depression of ammonia levels is the signal for terminal differentiation (Schindler and Sussman, 1977). Again, however, the speculative nature of these proposed interactions emphasizes the importance of establishing the effective concentrations of all of the signalling molecules involved in both chemotaxis and cellular differentiation.

Evolutionary considerations

The Dictyostelids present a fascinating opportunity to study the evolution of multicellularity, cellular differentiation and morphological diversification (Bonner, 1982; Schaap *et al.* 1985). The most remarkable feature of our results is the demonstration that prestalk cell differentiation appears to be initiated at the base of the aggregate and not at the tip, as logic would have suggested. How might this have arisen?

Primitive relatives of *Dictyostelium*, such as *Protostelium mycophaga*, form a single spore, supported by an acellular stalk (Fig. 8). In a more advanced species, such as *Actyostelium leptosomum*, a mass of spores is formed but again it is supported by an acellular stalk (Fig. 8). Thus *D. discoideum* presumably evolved from organisms in which stalk material, possibly containing a protein similar to ST310 the product of the pDd56 gene, was secreted down onto the substratum. We suggest that the initial burst of pDd56 gene expression in pstB cells at the base of the aggregate may reflect an intermediate stage in the evolution of the Dictyostelids, where cells were diverted into the stalk cell pathway of differentiation only at the base of the aggregate. Consistent with this hypothesis is our finding of a second wave of pDd56 gene expression during culmination at the base of the mexican hat (K. A. Jermyn and J. G. Williams, unpublished results). This is the stage at which the migrating slug re-enters the culmination pathway. Thus it is logical that the pstB cells, which are lost from the base when a migratory slug is formed, should be replaced as the slug sits down at culmination.

At the point in time when a migratory slug stage evolved, it may have been necessary to provide a continuously generated source of slime sheath material at the front of the slug. Therefore, cells were arrested in prestalk cell differentiation at some equivalent of the present day pstA stage and endowed with enhanced chemotactic responsiveness to cAMP and the capacity to produce a pDd63-like protein. This gave the further possibility of producing a stalk tube internal to the spore cell mass, by the reverse fountain movement characteristic of culmination in present day Dictyostelids. The further differentiation of these pstA cells into pstB cells in the centre of the slug tip may then have evolved in order to facilitate the initial production of the stalk tube, which occurs at this point. Consistent with this suggestion is the observation that this group of pstB cells is the first to enter the stalk tube and that they form part of the basal disc, the expanded base of the stalk tube, which gives *D. discoideum* its name (K. A. Jermyn and J. G. Williams, unpublished results). Again, this model is speculative but it will be informative to seek the equivalents of the pDd63 and pDd56 proteins in other Dictyostelids and to compare their patterns of expression.

References

ARMANT, D. R. AND RUTHERFORD, C. L. (1979). 5′ nucleotidase is localized in the area of cell contact of the prespore and prestalk region during culmination of *Dictyostelium discoideum*. *Mech. Ageing Dev.* **10**, 199–217.

ARMANT, D. R. AND STETLER, D. A. (1980). Cell surface localization of 5′ AMP nucleotidase in prestalk cells of *Dictyostelium discoideum*. *J. Cell Sci.* **45**, 119–129.

BERKS, M. AND KAY, R. R. (1988). Cyclic AMP is an inhibitor of prestalk cell differentiation in *Dictyostelium discoideum*. *Devl Biol.* **126**, 108–114.

BONNER (1951). The pattern of differentiation in amoeboid slime moulds. *Am. Naturalist* **86**, 79–89.

BONNER, J. T. (1982). Evolutionary strategies and developmental constraints in the cellular slime moulds. *Am. Naturalist* **119**, 530–552.

BROWN, S. S. AND RUTHERFORD, C. L. (1980). Localization of cyclic nucleotide phosphodiesterase in the multicellular stages of *Dictyostelium discoideum*. *Differentiation* **16**, 173–184.

CECCARELLI, A., McROBBIE, S. J., JERMYN, K. A., DUFFY, K., EARLY, A. AND WILLIAMS, J. G. (1987). Structural and functional characterization of a *Dictyostelium* gene encoding a DIF inducible, prestalk-enriched mRNA sequence. *Nucleic Acids Res.* **15**, 7463–7476.

DURSTON, A. J. AND VORK, F. (1979). A cinematographical study of the development of vitally stained *Dictyostelium discoideum*. *J. Cell Sci.* **35**, 261–279.

EARLY, A., McROBBIE, S. J., DUFFY, K. T., JERMYN, K. A., TILLY, R., CECCARELLI, A. AND WILLIAMS, J. G. (1988). Structural and functional characterization of genes encoding *Dictyostelium* prestalk and prespore cell-specific proteins. *Devl Genet.* **9**, 383–402.

EARLY, A. E. AND WILLIAMS, J. G. (1988). A *Dictyostelium* prespore-specific gene is transcriptionally repressed by DIF *in vitro*. *Development* **103**, 519–524.

GERISCH, G. (1987). Cyclic AMP and other signals controlling cell

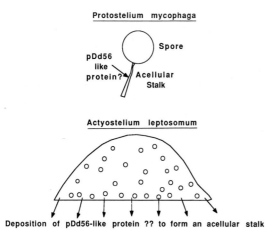

Protostelium mycophaga

Spore

pDd56
like
protein?

Acellular
Stalk

Actyostelium leptosomum

Deposition of pDd56-like protein ?? to form an acellular stalk

Fig. 8. Possible early stages in the evolution of the Dictyostelids.

development and differentiation in *Dictyostelium. A. Rev. Biochem.* **56**, 853–879.

GOMER, R. H. AND FIRTEL, R. A. (1987). Cell autonomous determination of cell-type choice in *Dictyostelium* development by cell cycle phase. *Science* **237**, 758–762.

GREGG, J. H. AND DAVIS, R. W. (1982). Dynamics of cell redifferentiation in *Dictyostelium mucoroides. Differentiation* **21**, 200–205.

GROSS, J. D., BRADBURY, J., KAY, R. R. AND PEACEY, M. (1983). Intracellular pH and the control of cell differentiation in *Dictyostelium discoideum. Nature, Lond.* **303**, 244–245.

INOUYE, K. (1988). Induction by acid load of the maturation of prestalk cells in *Dictyostelium. Development* **104**, 669–681.

JERMYN, K. A., BERKS, M., KAY, R. R. AND WILLIAMS, J. G. (1987). Two distinct classes of prestalk-enriched mRNA sequences in *Dictyostelium discoideum. Development* **100**, 745–755.

JERMYN, K. A., DUFFY, K. T. AND WILLIAMS, J. G. (1989). A new anatomy of the prestalk zone of *Dictyostelium. Nature, Lond.* **340**, 144–146.

KAY, R. R. AND JERMYN, K. A. (1983). A possible morphogen controlling differentiation in *Dictyostelium. Nature, Lond.* **303**, 242–244.

KOPACHIK, W., OOHATA, A., DHOKIG, B., BROOKMAN, J. J. AND KAY, R. R. (1983). *Dictyostelium* mutants lacking DIF, a putative morphogen. *Cell* **33**, 397–403.

KREFFT, M., VOET, L., GREGG, J. H., MAIRHOFER, H. AND WILLIAMS, K. L. (1984). Evidence that positional information is used to establish the prestalk-prespore pattern in *Dictyostelium discoideum* aggregates. *EMBO. J.* **3**, 201–206.

LEACH, C. K., ASHWORTH, J. M. AND GARROD, D. R. (1973). Cell sorting out during the differentiation of mixtures of metabolically distinct populations of *Dictyostelium discoideum. J. Embryol. exp. Morph.* **29**, 647–661.

MACDONALD, S. A. AND DURSTON, A. J. (1984). The cell cycle and sorting behaviour in *Dictyostelium discoideum. J. Cell Sci.* **66**, 195–204.

MACWILLIAMS, H. K. (1982). Transplantation experiments and pattern mutants in cellular slime mould slugs. In Developmental order: its origin and regulations (ed. S. Subtelny and P. B. Green). Alan R. Liss, New York. 463–483.

McROBBIE, S. J., JERMYN, K. A., DUFFY, K., BLIGHT, K. AND WILLIAMS, J. G. (1988*a*). Two DIF-inducible, prestalk-specific mRNAs of *Dictyostelium* encode extracellular matrix proteins of the slug. *Development* **104**, 275–284.

McROBBIE, S. J., TILLY, R., BLIGHT, K., CECCARELLI, A. AND WILLIAMS, J. G. (1988*b*). Identification and localization of proteins encoded by two DIF-inducible genes of *Dictyostelium. Devl Biol.* **125**, 59–63.

MEE, J. D., TORTOLO, C. AND COUKELL, M. B. (1986). Chemotaxis associated properties of isolated prestalk and prespore cells of *Dictyostelium discoideum. Biochem. Cell Biol.* **64**, 722–732.

MEINHARDT (1983). A model for the prestalk/prespore patterning in the slug of the slime mould *Dictyostelium discoideum. Differentiation* **24**, 191–202.

MORRIS, H. R., TAYLOR, G. W., MASENTO, M. S., JERMYN, K. A. AND KAY, R. R. (1987). Chemical structure of the morphogen differentiation inducing factor from *Dictyostelium discoideum. Nature, Lond.* **328**, 811–814.

MORRISSEY, J. H., DEVINE, K. M. AND LOOMIS, W. F. (1984). The timing of cell-type specific differentiation in *Dictyostelium discoideum. Devl Biol.* **103**, 414–424.

NEWELL, P. C. (1982). Cell surface binding of adenosine to *Dictyostelium* and inhibition of pulsatile signaling. *FEMS Microbiol. Lett.* **13**, 417–421.

NEWELL, P. C. AND ROSS, F. M. (1982). Inhibition by adenosine of

aggregation centre initiation and cyclic AMP binding in *Dictyostelium. J. gen. Microbiol.* **128**, 2715–2724.

OYAMA, M., OKAMOTO, K. AND TAKEUCHI, I. (1983). Proportion regulation without pattern formation in *Dictyostelium discoideum. J. Embryol. exp. Morph.* **75**, 293–301.

OZAKI, T., HASEGAWA, M., TASAKA, M., IWABUCHI, I. AND TAKEUCHI, I. (1988). Molecular cloning of cell-type specific cDNAs exhibiting new types of developmental regulation in *Dictyostelium discoideum. Cell Differ.* **23**, 119–124.

RAPER, K. B. (1940). Pseudoplasmodium formation and organization in *Dictyostelium discoideum. J. Elisha Mitchell Sci. Soc.* **56**, 241–282.

RUBIN, J. AND ROBERTSON, A. (1975). The tip of the *Dictyostelium discoideum* pseudoplasmodium as an organizer. *J. Embryol. exp. Morph.* **33**, 227–241.

SCHAAP, P. (1986). Regulation of size and pattern in the cellular slime moulds. *Differentiation* **33**, 1–16.

SCHAAP, P., PINAS, J. E. AND WANG, M. (1985). Patterns of cell differentiation in several cellular slime mould species. *Devl Biol.* **111**, 51–61.

SCHAAP, P. AND WANG, M. (1986). Interactions between adenosine and oscillatory cAMP signalling regulate size and pattern in *Dictyostelium. Cell* **45**, 137–144.

SCHINDLER, J. AND SUSSMAN, M. (1977). Ammonia determines the choice of morphogenetic pathways in *Dictyostelium discoideum. J. molec. Biol.* **116**, 161–170.

SCHINDLER, J. AND SUSSMAN, M. (1977). Effect of NH3 on c-AMP associated activities and extracellular c-AMP production in *Dictyostelium discoideum. Biochem. biophys. Res. Commun.* **79**, 611–617.

SOBOLEWSKI, A., NEAVE, N. AND WEEKS, G. (1983). The induction of stalk cell differentiaton in submerged monolayers of *Dictyostelium discoideum. Differentiation* **25**, 93–100.

STERNFELD, J. AND DAVID, C. N. (1981). Cell sorting during pattern formation in *Dictyostelium. Differentiation* **20**, 10–20.

STERNFELD, J. AND DAVID, C. N. (1982). Fate and regulation of anterior-like cells in *Dictyostelium* slugs. *Devl Biol.* **93**, 111–118.

TASAKA, M. AND TAKEUCHI, I. (1981). Role of cell sorting in pattern formation in *Dictyostelium discoideum. Differentiation* **18**, 191–196.

THEIBERT, A. AND DEVREOTES, P. N. (1984). Adenosine and its derivatives inhibit the cAMP signalling response in *Dictyostelium discoideum. Devl Biol.* **106**, 166–173.

VAN LOOKEREN CAMPAGNE, M. M., DUSCH, G. AND DAVID, N. C. (1984). Dependence of cell type proportioning and sorting on cell cycle phase in *Dictyostelium discoideum. J. Cell Sci.* **70**, 133–145.

WANG, M. AND SCHAAP, P. (1989). Ammonia depletion and DIF trigger stalk cell differentiation in intact slugs. *Development* **105**, 569–575.

WANG, M., VAN HAASTERT, P. J. M. AND SCHAAP, P. (1986). Multiple effects of differentiation-inducing factor on prespore differentiation and cyclic-AMP signal transduction in *Dictyostelium. Differentiation* **33**, 24–28.

WILLIAMS, J. G. (1988). The role of diffusible molecules in regulating the cellular differentiation of *Dictyostelium discoideum. Development* **103**, 1–16.

WILLIAMS, J. G., CECCARELLI, A., McROBBIE, S., MAHBUBANI, H., KAY, R. R., EARLY, A., BERKS, M. AND JERMYN, K. A. (1987). Direct induction of *Dictyostelium* prestalk gene expression by DIF provides evidence that DIF is a morphogen. *Cell* **49**, 185–192.

WILLIAMS, J. G., DUFFY, K. T., LANE, D. P., McROBBIE, S. J., TRAYNOR, D., KAY, R. R. AND JERMYN, K. A. (1989). Origins of prestalk and prespore cells in *Dictyostelium* development. (Ms submitted).

Development 1989 Supplement, 99–107 (1989)
Printed in Great Britain © The Company of Biologists Limited 1989

Role of the neuropeptide head activator for growth and development in hydra and mammals

H. CHICA SCHALLER, SABINE A. H. HOFFMEISTER and STEFAN DÜBEL

Zentrum für Molekulare Biologie, Im Neuenheimer Feld 282, 6900 Heidelberg, FRG

Summary

In hydra, HA is produced by nerve cells and released into the intercellular space bound to large-molecular-weight carrier(s). By additional interaction with extracellular matrix components and selfinactivation by dimerisation, a local action is ensured. HA acts as a mitogen on all dividing cell types in hydra forcing them to pass through G_2, divide, and either start a new round of cell division or terminally differentiate. In addition, HA is required for head-specific determination and differentiation processes. To become a head-specific nerve cell, for example, an interstitial stem cell requires HA in early S-phase to become determined to the nerve cell pathway, in late G_2 to progress through mitosis, and/or in G_1 to differentiate to a head-, and not to a foot-, specific nerve cell.

HA (with identical amino acid sequence) occurs in other animals including mammals. In mammals, it is produced by nerve or endocrine cells and it probably acts, as in hydra, on nerve-precursor cells. On the neural cell line NH15-CA2 and on the pituitary cell line AtT20, HA acts as mitogen by stimulating cells arrested in G_2 to enter mitosis. The presence of HA early in neural development and in abnormal neural development, such as in brain and neuroendocrine tumors, are consistent with a function in growth control for HA in mammals.

Key words: head activator, morphogen, mitogen, cell differentiation, extracellular matrix.

Introduction

Intercellular communication is important for the ordered spatial and temporal pattern of cellular differentiations that results in morphogenesis. Two types of signals are required for communication, positive signals that induce specific, local differentiation events, and negative signals that inhibit the spread of inductive events to larger areas. By definition, substances responsible for induction should have restricted diffusion properties to ensure local action, whereas inhibitors should be easily diffusible to be able to communicate with cells at greater distances (Gierer and Meinhardt, 1972; Kemmner, 1984). To study such substances, we originally used hydra as a model system. When we found that one of our inducing substances, the head activator, is present also in other animals including mammals, we extended our investigations to them. The role of the hydra head activator (HA) in the development and cellular differentiation of both hydra and mammals is described. The special molecular properties of the HA, namely binding to large molecular weight carriers and selfinactivation by dimerisation, suit it for its function as a locally acting growth and differentiation signal.

Hydra, a small freshwater coelenterate about 1 cm in length (Fig. 1), is suited as a model system because it is simple, contains few cell types with short differentiation pathways, and is very amenable to experimental manipulations such as tissue grafting, regeneration and reaggregation of cells. For developmental studies, the central part of hydra, the gastric column, is the most interesting, since it contains undetermined, undifferentiated tissue. The structures at the ends, the head with hypostome and tentacles, and the foot with peduncle and basal disk contain predominantly committed cells in the process of or in terminal differentiation. With daily feeding, hydra reproduces asexually by budding, having a 3-day doubling time. Under starvation conditions and in the cold, the animal enters a sexual cycle in which gonads are formed instead of buds (reviewed in Lenhoff, 1982).

Hydra consists of only two cell layers, ectoderm and endoderm, separated by a collagenous extracellular structure, the mesoglea (Fig. 2). Ectoderm and endoderm are made up of epithelio-muscular cells, which in the gastric region contain cells able to differentiate to head- or foot-specific epithelial cells. Thus, if a hydra is cut horizontally into two parts, gastric cells will differentiate into the specific cells of the missing structure, head or foot, and this occurs within a single cell cycle. Thus, foot-specific ectodermal epithelial cells, characterised by the production of a peroxidase-like enzyme as a marker (Hoffmeister and Schaller, 1985), become

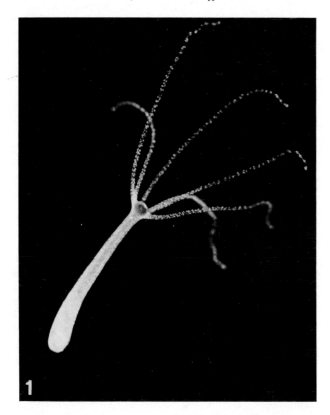

Fig. 1. *Hydra attenuata:* Animal before it produces its first bud.

cells are stem cells for nerve cells, nematocytes, endo-dermal gland and mucous cells, and, in the sexual cycle, also for oocytes and sperm cells (David and Gierer, 1974; David and Murphy, 1977; Bode and David, 1978; Bode *et al.* 1987; Bosch and David, 1987). Nerve cells differentiate from stem cells in a single cell cycle, nematocytes require two to four cell cycles giving rise from one stem cell to (4), 8, 16, (32) clonally derived nematocytes. The differentiation of interstitial stem cells is, like that of epithelial cells, dependent on their position within the animal. Close to the end structures, interstitial stem cells differentiate preferentially to nerve cells whereas commitment to the nematocyte cell lineage occurs in a graded fashion along the gastric column. Under steady-state conditions, a constant ratio between stem cells and differentiating cells is strictly maintained (Bode and Flick, 1976; Bode *et al.* 1976).

Purification and chemical analysis of inducers and inhibitors of differentiation and morphogenesis in hydra

We found that two sets of substances regulate head- and foot-specific differentiation events in hydra, an activator and an inhibitor of head formation and a second set for foot formation. The effect of substances influencing head- and foot-specific differentiation events can most easily be measured as acceleration or inhibition of head or foot regeneration (for a review see Schaller *et al.* 1979). For that purpose, heads or feet are removed from intact animals, and the head- or footless parts incubated in medium with and without the factors to be assayed. In the presence of inhibitors, regeneration is retarded or at higher concentrations completely inhibited. In the presence of the activators, regeneration is accelerated. The effects are specific such that, for example, the head activator accelerates the rate of head regeneration, but not that of foot regeneration (Schaller *et al.* 1979). Underlying these gross morphogenetic effects are changes at the cellular level which can also be used to assay the respective substance. The

visible 20–24 h after cutting. Similarly, head-specific ectodermal epithelial cells characterised by a head-specific monoclonal antibody (Javois *et al.* 1986), appear at about the same time, each marker restricted to the appropriate half (Dübel *et al.* 1987). Ectodermal and endodermal epithelial cells do not interconvert and must therefore derive from different gastric stem cells (Smid and Tardent, 1982).

The most interesting stem-cell population in hydra are interstitial cells which, as their name implies, are located between epithelial cells (Fig. 2). Interstitial

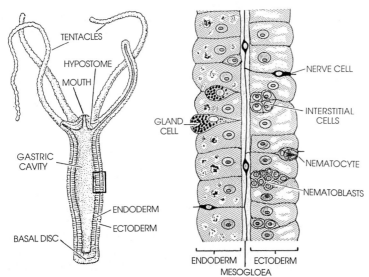

Fig. 2. Schematic representation of a hydra (left) and expanded view of gastric tissue (right).

Table 1. *Properties of head and foot factors from hydra*

Morphogen	Molecular mass (D)	Purification (x-fold)	Active concentration	Gradient	$T_{\frac{1}{2}}$	Range of action
Head activator	1124	10^9	10^{-13} M	head→foot	4 h	local
Head inhibitor	<500	10^5	<10^{-9} M	head→foot	$\frac{1}{2}$ h	global
Foot activator	~1000	10^8	<10^{-12} M	foot→head	Long	local
Foot inhibitor	<500	10^4	<10^{-8} M	foot→head	Short	global

appearance of foot-specific ectodermal epithelial cells is thus accompanied by the production of a peroxidase activity which can easily be utilised to quantify foot-specific cellular differentiation (Hoffmeister and Schaller, 1985).

By means of such quantifiable assays, we separated the four substances and purified the two activators extensively, the two inhibitors to a lesser extent (Table 1). The two activators are small peptides with relative molecular masses of around 1000. The sequence of the head activator (HA) was determined to be pGlu-Pro-Pro-Gly-Gly-Ser-Lys-Val-Ile-Leu-Phe (Schaller and Bodenmüller, 1981). The analysis of the foot activator (FA) is close to completion. The two inhibitors, both nonpeptide, hydrophilic molecules of relative molecular masses lower than 500 are difficult to purify, since so far no special property has distinguished them from other small molecules. For purification, in general, a crude extract is subjected to an organic solvent extraction with 90 % methanol to remove large molecules and to separate the active components from possible carriers or substances to which they adhere. Lipids are removed by ether and chloroform extraction, and the active components separated by ion-exchange, molecular-sieve and other conventional chromatographic procedures. As a last step, HPLC methods allow final purification. Both activators can be purified by using reverse-phase columns from which FA elutes under neutral conditions at 25 % methanol, whereas 60 % methanol is required for HA elution indicating that FA is a more polar molecule than HA. The inhibitors do not adsorb to such reverse-phase columns and require separation on nonreverse-phase material such as silica. From such silica HPLC columns, the head inhibitor (HI) elutes faster than the foot inhibitor (FI) when solvent gradients with decreasing hydrophobicity are applied indicating that FI is more polar than HI. This purification of the inhibitors is sufficient for biological experiments but not yet for chemical analysis.

The crux of the problem as shown in Table 1 is the low molar activity of all four substances. The activators are active at picomolar and the inhibitors at nanomolar concentrations. This means that a hydra needs, and contains, low amounts of the respective substance. A hydra contains, for example, less than one femtomole (10^{-15} moles) of HA. For analysis at least one nanomole of purified peptide is required. With an optimistic 10 % yield this implies that at least 10^7 hydra have to be extracted. For the purification of HA, we made use of the fact that other coelenterates also contain HA. We thus processed 200 kg of the sea anemone, *Anthopleura*

elegantissima, to obtain 20 nanomoles (20 μg) of pure HA (Schaller and Bodenmüller, 1981).

Biological and morphogenetic properties of activators and inhibitors in hydra

In hydra, all four substances occur in gradients with maximal concentrations for the head factors in the hypostomal region and the foot factors in the basal disk (Fig. 3). Copurification with nerve cells was taken as evidence that in normal hydra all four factors are products of nerve cells (Schaller and Gierer, 1973; Berking, 1977; Grimmelikhuijzen, 1979; Schmidt and Schaller, 1980). For HA this was confirmed by copurification with neurosecretory granules (Schaller and Gierer, 1973) and, as shown in Fig. 4, by immunocyto-chemical localisation of HA in developing nerve cells (Schawaller *et al.* 1988).

All four factors are released from nerve cells into the intercellular space where they act on target cells. The inhibitors control where a certain structure is induced

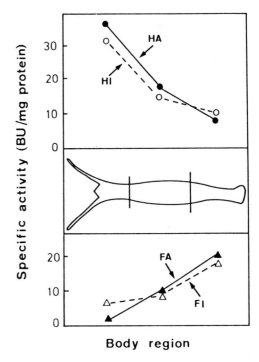

Fig. 3. Concentration of head activator (HA), head inhibitor (HI), foot activator (FA), and foot inhibitor (FI) in different body regions of hydra. The concentration is expressed in biological units (BU) as defined by respective bioassays per mg of protein (Schaller *et al.* 1979; Hoffmeister and Schaller, 1985).

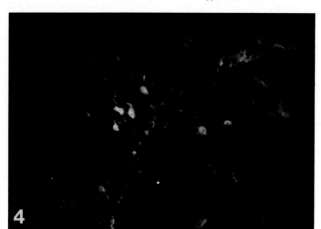

Fig. 4. Immunocytochemical localisation of head activator in interstitial cells developing to nerve cells in hydra. Cryosections of hydra were fixed with 1 % carbodiimide and 1 % formaldehyde and reacted with the antibody 12/4 ($1:10^3$) (Schawaller *et al.* 1988). Enlargement ×250.

Fig. 5. *Mini* and *maxi* mutant of hydra showing the influence of head inhibitor on size regulation (Schaller *et al.* 1977).

primarily by regulating the release of the activator and also their own release. Thus we found that HI at very low concentrations inhibits the release of HA and at 20-fold higher concentrations it also inhibits its own release (Schaller, 1976; Kemmner and Schaller, 1984). The morphological action of HI is best illustrated by mutants of hydra which differ in HI content and consequently in size. Under normal feeding conditions, hydra asexually reproduce by budding, maintaining a constant growth rate and size. A young animal after detachment from the parent animal grows to a certain size, then growth stops, and newly arising cells form buds. The location where a bud is induced is regulated predominantly by the head and to a lesser extent by the foot through the mediation of the respective inhibitors. In mutants with high HI content, the distance between head and bud becomes very large resulting in a *maxi* phenotype; in mutants with low HI content, the distance shrinks to produce *mini* animals (Fig. 5). This indicates that the larger HI concentration in *maxi* over *mini* results in a greater inhibited area (Schaller *et al.* 1977). It also shows that HI is able to diffuse over long distances.

In the absence of inhibitors induction occurs. If a hydra is cut horizontally into two pieces of equal size, in the upper half the head inhibits the release of HA at the cut surface, whereas, in the lower half release of HA is allowed. Vice versa, in the lower half the foot inhibits FA release, whereas, in the upper half FA release is allowed. This results in a local induction of head or foot regeneration leading to complete restoration of the missing structure within 2 days.

Corelease of activators with carrier molecules

HA and HI are both small molecules with very similar molecular masses. It was unclear why they should have different diffusion properties. As an explanation we found that HI is released in its naked low molecular

mass form, whereas HA is bound to a large molecular mass carrier (Schaller *et al.* 1986). If HA is extracted from hydra tissue with aqueous solvents or if medium is collected from animals regenerating a head, all HA activity elutes from S-300 columns with an apparent relative molecular mass of $600–800×10^3$ (Fig. 6). Binding is noncovalent as demonstrated by quantitative extractability with organic solvents such as methanol and/or high salt (2 M-NaCl). The complex binds to heparin (Scheerer, unpublished results) suggesting an additional barrier to diffusion by a possible interaction with extracellular matrix components. This carrier-bound HA is active at 10^{-13} M indicating that binding to the carrier does not inhibit the biological effect. HA either binds to its receptor as HA-carrier complex and/or the affinity of the free HA for its receptor is higher than that for the carrier. The free HA peptide, once released from the carrier or offered as synthetic HA, has little chance of long persistence, since it either inactivates itself rapidly by dimerisation (Fig. 7) or is degraded by enzymes. We found that dimeric HA has no biological action on hydra (Bodenmüller *et al.* 1986). The rapid inactivation fulfils an additional prerequisite for local action, namely that a molecule once released cannot diffuse far. The head inhibitor is not associated

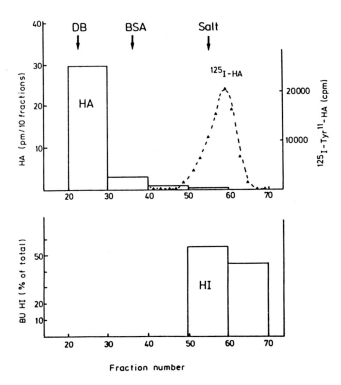

Fig. 6. Gel filtration of medium collected from hydra during the first 3 h of head regeneration on Sephacryl S-300 columns equilibrated with 25 mM-ammonium bicarbonate, pH 7·5, at 4°C. Total volume: 40 ml, fraction size: 0·95 ml. ^{125}I-Tyr^{11}-HA was added to monitor the position of free HA.

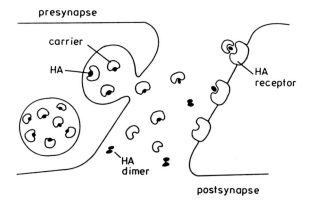

Fig. 7. Diagram depicting release of HA bound to a carrier molecule from producer cell and subsequent interaction with HA receptors on target cells or selfinactivation by dimerisation.

with carrier molecules (Fig. 6) and is therefore not hindered in its free diffusion over long distances. Likewise the foot inhibitor is also released in a low molecular mass form, whereas the foot activator is bound to a large molecular mass carrier. We therefore assume that this represents a general principle. Binding to carrier fulfils two functions: it inhibits diffusion and it prevents degradation thus ensuring the longer half-life (Table 1) of activators over inhibitors. It also explains

why substances of low molecular mass, by definition diffusible, can nevertheless be morphogens with local action.

Action of HA at the cellular level in hydra

At the cellular level, HA has two effects in hydra. It stimulates cells to divide, and it is responsible for head-specific differentiations (Schaller, 1976a,b; Holstein *et al.* 1986; Hoffmeister and Schaller, 1987). The effects as a growth factor can most easily be demonstrated by adding HA to 24 h starved animals and counting mitotic cells 1–2 h later. In hydra this can be monitored as an effect on mitotic index shown in Fig. 8 for interstitial cells. The effect is dose dependent (Hoffmeister and Schaller, 1987), and it is used in our laboratory as a convenient, fast biological assay for determining HA concentrations. The effect of HA is not cell-type specific. All dividing cell types in hydra arrested in the G_2 phase of the cell cycle respond in this way (Schaller, 1976a). HA thus acts as a true mitogen in contrast to growth factors in higher animals, which usually act in the transition from G_0 to G_1.

Differentiation pathways in hydra are short. From stem cell to fully differentiated cells only one or a few cell cycles are required. Hydra contains two main stem cell populations, epithelial cells, which are the main structural components of the two cell layers ectoderm and endoderm, and interstitial cells from which, as main differentiation products, nerve cells and nemato-cytes derive.

Epithelial cell differentiation occurs in one cell cycle, as evidenced by the appearance of head- or foot-specific epithelial cells in head or foot regenerating tissue one day after cutting (Dübel *et al.* 1987). After treatment of gastric tissue with foot activator, foot-specific epithelial cells appear (Hoffmeister and Schaller, 1987). In analogy, HA is required for head-specific epithelial cell differentiation.

The decision which pathway is chosen may be a multistep process. Interstitial cells require HA at least twice, first for the determination to enter the nerve-cell

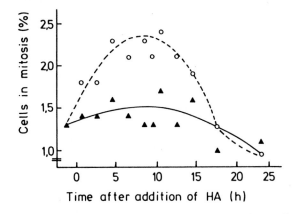

Fig. 8. Effect of HA stimulating mitosis of interstitial cells in hydra. ○---○ cells treated with HA (10^{-12}M), ▲——▲ non-treated controls. For each time point 8000 cells were counted.

pathway, and second for the decision to differentiate to a head-, as opposed to a foot-, specific nerve cell. Using pulse labeling with [³H]thymidine applied before or after treatment with head activator and assaying for labeled nerve cells, we could show that head activator is required in early S-phase to allow the determination of stem cells to nerve cells (Schaller, 1976*b*). In C. N. David's laboratory a convenient method to assay determination was developed. After treatment with head activator, a piece of tissue from the gastric region is removed from the inhibitory influence of head and foot by isolation. In such isolates up to 50 % of all the stem cells differentiated to nerve cells compared to only 10 % in an intact animal (Holstein *et al.* 1986). Head inhibitor at high concentrations could antagonise the effect on nerve cell determination (Berking, 1977). After determination in S-phase, such a cell will traverse through the G_2-phase and its final mitosis only if head activator or foot activator is present (Fig. 9). The differentiation is inhibited in the presence of relatively low concentrations of head inhibitor. Thus, for the determination to the nerve cell pathway, head activator is absolutely necessary, head inhibitor is able to antagonise this effect and foot activator has no influence. For the final differentiation, both head activator and foot activator may be used as signals, but both can be antagonised by head and maybe also by foot inhibitor.

From these data, the following model is derived: close to the head region where head activator concentration is highest many stem cells become determined to nerve cells and differentiate to nerve cells fast and in a head-specific manner. In the gastric region, fewer stem cells become determined to nerve cells, and most of them are prevented from differentiation to nerve cells by the head inhibitor. During the gradual tissue dis-

placement from the subhypostomal to the basal region, these cells reach the foot where, under the influence of foot activator, they differentiate to nerve cells, now in a foot-specific manner. Head activator and head inhibitor are produced by nerve cells of the head, foot activator and foot inhibitor by nerve cells of the foot. This nerve cell differentiation scheme represents a very complicated autocrine control loop which in the end ensures that head-specific growth and differentiation is maintained in the head region, that foot-specific processes occur in the foot, and that the head system dominates over the foot system as postulated from other biological experiments (Bode *et al.* 1980).

Occurrence of HA in mammals

HA was originally isolated and sequenced from two main mammalian sources, hypothalamus and intestine. Its amino sequence was found to be identical to the hydra peptide (Bodenmüller and Schaller, 1981). Using immunological assays in combination with reverse-phase high-pressure liquid chromatography (Bodenmüller and Roberge, 1985), we discovered that HA is present in other animals (insects, amphibia, birds, crustaceans) and, in addition to brain (Table 2), in other tissue of neural or endocrine origin. High amounts of HA were found in tumors of such origins (Fig. 10), in cell lines derived from such tumors, and in blood of patients with such tumors (Schaller *et al.* 1988).

HA is not only present in tumor tissue and in tumor cell lines, but also in developing tissue. Thus we found that in human and rat embryos HA is present in the developing brain and in the developing intestine (Schaller *et al.* 1977). In addition, elevated levels were produced by human placental cells at 3–4 months of gestation and found in the milk of lactating mothers. This suggests that HA also acts as a growth factor in normal development.

To study which cell types in mammals produce HA, we made use of the teratoma cell line P19 which by treatment with retinoic acid and cell clumping can differentiate after several cell divisions and a 8- to 14-day lag phase into different cell types including nerve cells (McBurney *et al.* 1982). Such early nerve cells produce high amounts of HA as shown by direct extraction from the cells and by immunocytochemistry (Fig. 11).

Determination to nerve cells

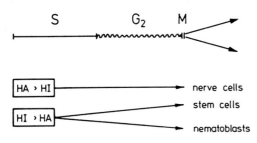

Differentiation to nerve cells

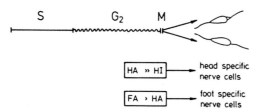

Fig. 9. Influence of HA, HI, and FA on the determination and differentiation of interstitial stem cells to nerve cells.

Table 2. *Occurrence of head activator in human tissue*

Source of tissue	Concentration of HA (fm mg^{-1} protein)
Cerebral cortex	12
Cerebellum	22
Pons	18
Medulla	65
Thalamus	65
Hypothalamus	1670
Retina	800

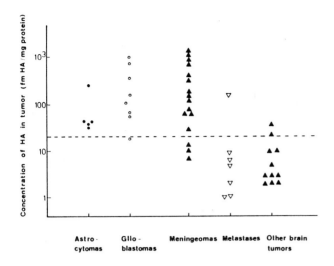

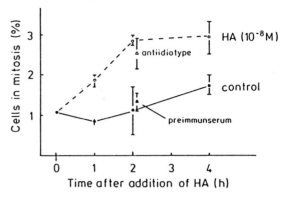

Fig. 12. Effect of HA stimulating mitosis in the neural cell line NH15-CA2. Cells were incubated either with HA (10^{-8} M), with the anti-idiotypic protein-A purified HA antiserum 64/10 (1:100), with protein-A purified preimmune serum 64/0 (1:100), and with medium as control. Three×2000 cells were counted for each time point.

Fig. 10. Occurrence of HA in human brain tumors. Broken line indicates upper limit of HA concentration found in nonhypothalamic nontumor brain tissue.

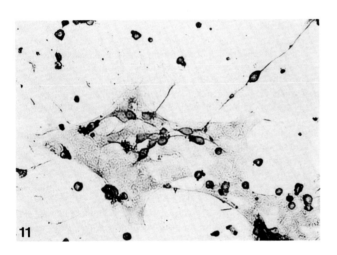

Fig. 11. Immunocytochemical localisation of HA in the teratoma cell line P19 induced to nerve cell differentiation by treatment with retinoic acid (5×10^{-7} M). Reaction with the monoclonal HA antibody E 21 (1:200) (Schawaller *et al.* 1988).

Action of HA as a growth factor in mammals

To investigate HA's action on mammalian cells, we used the cell lines NH15-CA2 and AtT20. We found that, in both cases, the presence of HA leads to an increase in cell number. This is due to the mitogenic action of HA, stimulating cells to pass through G_2 and enter mitosis. This is shown in Fig. 12, where the action of HA was monitored as an increase in mitotic index on NH15-CA2 cells. Fig. 12 also demonstrates that the effect of HA can be mimicked by anti-idiotypic antibodies produced against monoclonal HA antibodies. Localisation of HA receptors on cells in mitosis confirms HA's action as a growth factor acting in the transition from G_2 to mitosis (Schawaller *et al.* 1988). This effect seems to be specific for neural cell lines since no other cells responded in this way.

Other possible functions of HA in mammals

In mammals, the head activator is not only found in growing tissue like embryos and tumors but also later in differentiated tissue, such as in the hypothalamus of an 85-year-old man, and in blood samples of all ages. We therefore assume that the head activator not only acts as a growth factor but, like other mammalian neuropeptides, also has additional functions in intercellular communication.

Neuropeptides in general may act as neurotransmitters or modulators directly at synapses, at target sites nearby or as neurohormones over long distances following release into the blood. We found that the head activator is present in the blood of all mammals including humans. When trying to analyse its action in the blood, we discovered that injected head activator was degraded within minutes (Roberge *et al.* 1984). Most of this degradation was due to the angiotensin-converting enzyme. An astonishing finding was that endogenous head activator was stable and unavailable for degradation by angiotensin-converting enzyme. As M. Roberge in our laboratory could show this was due to the fact that HA, in the blood, like in hydra, is bound to a high molecular weight carrier from which it can be released by salt treatment or methanol extraction indicating that HA is not covalently bound, but only attached to the carrier. Angiotensin-converting enzyme is a dipeptidyl carboxypeptidase which cuts off dipeptides from the carboxy end. The fact that carrier-bound head activator is not degraded by angiotensin-converting enzyme shows that the carboxy end of the head activator, which is very hydrophobic, is hidden in or protected by the carrier. Likewise antibodies directed against the amino terminus of HA also do not recognize the carrier-bound HA suggesting that the amino end is also hidden by, or buried in, the carrier.

In human blood, the HA level increased 30- to 200-fold within 15–30 min after a meal (Bodenmüller and Roberge, 1985). Since the gastrointestinal tract is the highest source of HA besides the brain, we assume that HA is released from there.

As a possible action, we found that HA, like many other neuropeptides, stimulates exocrine pancreatic secretion as measured by amylase release from isolated pancreatic lobules. This may suggest a role for HA in digestion control processes (Bodenmüller and Roberge, 1985).

In the brain, HA is most concentrated in the hypothalamus. Like other neuropeptides HA may therefore be a mediator in the hypothalamo-pituitary axis. Preliminary evidence suggests that HA specifically inhibits the basal and CRF-stimulated release of β-endorphin from isolated neurointermediate lobes (C. Kordon, unpublished results). By inhibiting β-endorphin, HA may have a gross activating effect justifying its name as head activator.

We are supported by the Deutsche Forschungsgemeinschaft (SFB 317), by the Bundesministerium für Forschung und Technologie (BCT 365/1), and by the Fonds der Deutschen Chemischen Industrie.

References

BERKING, S. (1977). Bud formation in hydra: inhibition by an endogenous morphogen. *Wilhelm Roux's Arch. devl Biol.* **181**, 215–225.

BODE, H. R. & DAVID, C. N. (1978). Regulation of a multipotent stem cell, the interstitial cell of hydra. *Progr. Biophys. molec. Biol.* **33**, 198–206.

BODE, H. R., HEIMFELD, S., CHOW, M. A. & HUANG, L. W. (1987). Gland cells arise by differentiation from interstitial cells in *Hydra attenuata. Devl Biol.* **122**, 577–585.

BODE, H. R., FLICK, K. M. & SMITH, G. S. (1976). Regulation of interstitial cell differentiation in *Hydra attenuata.* I. Homeostatic control of interstitial cell population size. *J. Cell Sci.* **20**, 29–46.

BODE, H. R. & FLICK, K. M. (1976). Distribution and dynamics of nematocyte populations in *Hydra attenuata. J. Cell Sci.* **21**, 15–34.

BODE, P. M. & BODE, H. R. (1980). Formation of patterns in regenerating tissue pieces of *Hydra attenuata.* I. Head-body proportion regulation. *Devl Biol.* **78**, 484–496.

BODENMÜLLER, H., SCHILLING, E., ZACHMANN, B. & SCHALLER, H. C. (1986). The neuropeptide head activator loses its biological activity by dimerisation. *EMBO J.* **5**, 1825–1829.

BODENMÜLLER, H. & SCHALLER, H. C. (1981). Conserved amino acid sequence of a neuropeptide, the head activator, from coelenterate to humans. *Nature* **293**, 579–580.

BODENMÜLLER, H. & ROBERGE, M. (1985). The head activator: discovery, characterisation, immunoassays, and biological properties in mammals. *Biochim. Biophys. Acta* **825**, 261–267.

BOSCH, T. & DAVID, C. N. (1987). Stem cells of *Hydra magnipapillata* can differentiate somatic cells and germ line cells. *Devl Biol.* **121**, 182–191.

DAVID, C. N. & GIERER, A. (1974). Cell cycle kinetics and development of *Hydra attenuata.* III. Nerve and nematocyte differentiation. *J. Cell Sci.* **16**, 359–375.

DAVID, C. N. & MURPHY, S. (1977). Characterisation of interstitial stem cells in hydra by cloning. *Devl Biol.* **58**, 373–383.

DÜBEL, S., HOFFMEISTER, S. A. H. & SCHALLER, H. C. (1987). Differentiation pathways of ectodermal epithelial cell in hydra. *Differentiation* **35**, 181–189.

GIERER, A., BERKING, S., BODE, H., DAVID, C. N., FLICK, K., HANSMANN, G., SCHALLER, H. & TRENKNER, E. (1972). Regeneration of hydra from reaggregated cells. *Nature* **239**, 98–101.

GIERER, A. & MEINHARDT, H. (1972). A theory of biological pattern formation. *Kybernetik* **12**, 30–39.

GRIMMELIKHUIJZEN, C. J. P. (1979). Properties of the foot activator from hydra. *Cell Differ.* **8**, 267–273.

HOFFMEISTER, S. A. H. & SCHALLER, H. C. (1985). A new biochemical marker for foot-specific cell differentiation in hydra. *Wilhelm Roux's Arch. devl Biol.* **194**, 433–461.

HOFFMEISTER, S. A. H. & SCHALLER, H. C. (1987). Head activator and head inhibitor are signals for nerve cell differentiation in hydra. *Devl Biol.* **122**, 72–77.

HOLSTEIN, T., SCHALLER, H. C. & DAVID, C. N. (1986). Nerve cell differentiation in hydra requires two signals. *Devl Biol.* **115**, 9–17.

JAVOIS, L., WOOD, R. D. & BODE, H. R. (1986). Patterning of the head in hydra as visualised by a monoclonal antibody. *Devl Biol.* **117**, 607–618.

KEMMNER, W. (1984). A model of head regeneration in hydra. *Differentiation* **26**, 83–90.

KEMMNER, W. & SCHALLER, H. C. (1984). Actions of head activator and head inhibitor during head regeneration in hydra. *Differentiation* **26**, 91–96.

LENHOFF, H. M. (1982). *Hydra: Research Methods.* New York and London: Plenum Press.

McBURNEY, M. W., JONES-VILLENEUVE, E. M. V., EDWARDS, M. K. S. & ANDERSON, P. J. (1982). Control of muscle and neuronal differentiation in a cultured embryonal carcinoma cell line. *Nature* **299**, 165.

ROBERGE, M., ESCHER, E., SCHALLER, H. C. & BODENMÜLLER, H. (1984). The hydra head activator in human blood circulation. Degradation of the synthetic peptide by plasma angiotensin-converting enzyme. *FEBS Lett.* **173**, 307–313.

SCHALLER, H. C., SCHMIDT, T. & GRIMMELIKHUIJZEN, C. J. P. (1979). Separation and specificity of action of four morphogens from hydra. *Wilhelm Roux's Arch. devl Biol.* **186**, 139–149.

SCHALLER, H. C. & BODENMÜLLER, H. (1981). Isolation and amino acid sequence of a morphogenetic peptide from hydra. *Proc. natn. Acad. Sci. U.S.A.* **78**, 7000–7004.

SCHALLER, H. C. & GIERER, A. (1973). Distribution of the head activating substance in hydra and its localisation in membranous particles in nerve cells. *J. Embryol. exp. Morph.* **29**, 39–52.

SCHALLER, H. C. (1976). Head regeneration is initiated by the release of head activator and head inhibitor. *Wilhelm Roux's Arch. devl Biol.* **180**, 287–295.

SCHALLER, H. C., SCHMIDT, T., FLICK, K. & GRIMMELIKHUIJZEN, C. J. P. (1977). Analysis of morphogenetic mutants of hydra. III. *Maxi* and *mini. Wilhelm Roux's Arch. devl Biol.* **183**, 215–222.

SCHALLER, H. C., SCHMIDT, T., FLICK, K. & GRIMMELIKHUIJZEN, C. J. P. (1977). Analysis of morphogenetic mutants of hydra. II. The non-budding mutant. *Wilhelm Roux's Arch. devl Biol.* **183**, 207–214.

SCHALLER, H. C., ROBERGE, M., ZACHMANN, B., HOFFMEISTER, S., SCHILLING, E. & BODENMÜLLER, H. (1986). The head activator is released from regenerating hydra bound to a carrier molecule. *EMBO J.* **5**, 1821–1824.

SCHALLER, H. C. (1976a). Action of the head activator as a growth hormone in hydra. *Cell Diff.* **5**, 1–11.

SCHALLER, H. C. (1976b). Action of the head activator on the determination of interstitial cells in hydra. *Cell Diff.* **5**, 13–20.

SCHALLER, H. C. (1975). Head activator controls head formation in reaggregated cells of hydra. *Cell Diff.* **4**, 265–272.

SCHALLER, H. C., SCHILLING, E., THEILMANN, L., BODENMÜLLER, H. & SACHSENHEIMER, W. (1988). Elevated levels of head activator in human brain tumors and in serum of patients with brain and other neurally derived tumors. *J. Neurooncology* **6**, 251–258.

SCHALLER, H. C., FLICK, K. & DARAI, G. (1977). A neurohormone from hydra is present in brain and intestine of rat embryos. *J. Neurochem.* **29**, 393–394.

SCHAWALLER, M., SCHENK, K., HOFFMEISTER, S. A. H., SCHALLER,

H. & SCHALLER, H. C. (1988). Production and characterisation of monoclonal antibodies recognizing head activator in precursor form and immunocytochemical localisation of head activator precursor and head activator peptide in the neural cell line NH15-CA2 and in hydra. *Differentiation* **38**, 149–160.

SCHMIDT, T. & SCHALLER, H. C. (1980). Properties of the foot

inhibitor from hydra. *Wilhelm Roux's Arch. devl Biol.* **188**, 133–139.

SMID, I. & TARDENT, P. (1982). The influences of ecto- and endoderm in determining the axial polarity of *Hydra attenuata* Pall. (*Cnidaria, Hydrozoa*). *Wilhelm Roux's Arch. devl Biol.* **191**, 64–67.

Development 1989 Supplement, 109–119
Printed in Great Britain © The Company of Biologists Limited 1989

The role of retinoid-binding proteins in the generation of pattern in the developing limb, the regenerating limb and the nervous system

M. MADEN[1], D. E. ONG[2], D. SUMMERBELL[1] and F. CHYTIL[2]

[1]*National Institute for Medical Research, The Ridgeway, Mill Hill, London, NW7 1AA UK*
[2]*Department of Biochemistry, Vanderbilt University School of Medicine, Nashville, Tennessee, USA*

Summary

We summarise existing data and describe new information on the levels and distribution of cellular retinoic acid-binding protein (CRABP) and cellular retinol-binding protein (CRBP) in the regenerating axolotl limb, the developing chick limb bud and the nervous system of the chick embryo in the light of the known morphogenetic effects of retinoids on these systems. In the regenerating limb, levels of CRABP rise 3- to 4-fold during regeneration, peaking at the time when retinoic acid (RA) is most effective at causing pattern duplications. The levels of CRBP are low. The potency of various retinoids in causing pattern respecification correlates well with the ability of these compounds to bind to CRABP. In the chick limb bud, the levels of CRABP are high and the levels of CRBP are low. Again the binding of various retinoids to CRABP correlates well with their ability to cause pattern duplications. By immunocytochemistry, we show that CRABP is present at high levels in the progress zone of the limb bud and is distributed across the anteroposterior axis in a gradient with the high point at the anterior margin. In the chick embryo,

CRABP levels are high and CRBP levels are low. By immunocytochemistry, CRABP is localised primarily to the developing nervous system, labelling cells and axons in the mantle layer of the neural tube. These become the neurons of the commissural system. Also sensory axons label intensely with CRABP whereas motor axons do not and in the mixed nerves at the brachial plexus sensory and motor components can be distinguished on this basis. In the neural tube, CRBP only stains the ventral floor plate. Since the ventral floor plate may be a source of chemoattractant for commissural axons, we suggest on the basis of these staining patterns that RA may fulfill this role and thus be involved morphogenetically in the developing nervous system.

Key words: retinoic acid-binding protein, retinol-binding protein, retinoic acid, retinol, chick limb bud, chick embryo, pattern formation, axolotl, limb regeneration, neural tube, sensory nerves, ventral floor plate, nervous system.

Introduction

Vitamin A has been the subject of extensive research since its discovery as a fat-soluble vitamin in the first part of this century. Because of the importance of vitamin A in nutrition, its involvement in vision, the maintenance of epithelial differentiation and spermatogenesis was soon established. Any deficiency or excess of vitamin A in the diet leads to a disturbance in these tissues and organs. Retinol is the parent vitamin A molecule and the many derivatives of this structure are known collectively as retinoids.

Uptake of vitamin A by the body

β-carotene, a plant pigment, and retinyl esters in animal tissues such as liver, oils and egg yolk are the major dietary sources of vitamin A. These esters are hydrolysed in the gut to retinol which is absorbed into the lining and reesterified. The transport of retinyl esters

from the small intestine is accomplished *via* chylomicrons released into the lymph and these esters are stored in the liver. When needed by the tissues of the body the esters are hydrolysed to retinol and then transported in the blood bound to serum retinol-binding protein (RBP), a 21K ($K=10^3 M_r$) protein (Ong, 1985). Cellular uptake of retinol is dependent upon a specific membrane receptor that recognises RBP and transfer to the cytoplasmic retinol-binding protein involves a further cycle of esterification (Otonello *et al.* 1987). Thus cells receive vitamin A in the form of retinol.

Cellular retinoid-binding proteins

Cellular retinol-binding protein (CRBP) is a 14.6K protein present in the cytosol of a wide variety of cell types (Chytil and Ong, 1984) and as just described is responsible for receiving the retinol delivered to the cell. It has a single binding site with a high degree of specificity for retinol which is its endogenous ligand

(Saari *et al.* 1982). CRBP has been shown to be capable of transferring retinol to specific binding sites in isolated rat nuclei or chromatin (Takase *et al.* 1979).

The other cytoplasmic binding protein widely distributed in cells is cellular retinoic-acid-binding protein (CRABP) which also has a relative molecular mass of 14.6×10^3 (Chytil and Ong, 1984). Like CRBP, CRABP has very specific binding properties and its endogenous ligand is RA (Saari *et al.* 1982). It too has been shown to transfer RA to specific binding sites in nuclei (Takase *et al.* 1986). The source of this retinoic acid (RA) is almost certainly oxidation of retinol as little or no RA is found in the diet. Thus if a cell needs RA it will synthesise it for itself (Napoli and Race, 1987), suggesting that, if RA is found in restricted regions of the embryo, it may be playing an important morphogenetic role.

Retinoic acid receptors

It was therefore assumed that the function of CRBP and CRABP was to behave like steroid hormones and deliver their ligands to the nucleus to produce a change in the pattern of gene activity (Chytil and Ong, 1984). However, upon sequencing, no DNA binding domains were found in these proteins and the situation was somewhat enlightened when a higher molecular weight nuclear protein, specific for RA, was detected in F9 cells (Daly and Redfern, 1987). Subsequently, two nuclear receptors with high affinity for RA were cloned on the basis of their homology to steroid receptors (Petkovich *et al.* 1987; Giguere *et al.* 1987; Brand *et al.* 1988; Benbrook *et al.* 1988). Thus it now seems likely that CRABP is a cytoplasmic protein which passes RA on to the nuclear retinoic acid receptors (RARs). In the absence of a retinol receptor, the function of CRBP remains uncertain.

Retinoids and the embryo

Until very recently the only information about retinoids and embryonic development came from nutritional studies in which pregnant mammals were fed on vitamin A-deficient diets or fed excess vitamin A. Embryos born to mothers raised on vitamin A-deficient diets, if they survive at all, have a variety of congenital abnormalities such as anophthalmia, microphthalmia, defects of the retina, cleft palate, hydrocephalus, malformed hind legs, cryptorchidism, cardiovascular malformations and urinogenital tract malformations (Kalter and Warkany, 1959). Retinoids are highly teratogenic and the embryonic defects produced under conditions of hypervitaminosis A are surprisingly similar to those described above, namely anophthalmia, microphthalmia, cleft palate, defects of the retina, hydrocephalus, spina bifida and limb defects (Kalter and Warkany, 1959).

Retinoids and the developing limb

Direct evidence for the role of retinoids in development must depend on their identification and quantification in individual organ systems within the embryo. The first such analysis by HPLC of the developing chick limb bud produced exciting results (Thaller and Eichele, 1987).

Upon dissecting the limb bud into two, it was found that, whereas retinol was in equal amounts in the two parts, RA was enriched in the posterior part. They interpreted this result to mean that there is a gradient of RA across the anteroposterior (AP) axis of the limb bud with the high point on the posterior side.

The reason for looking at RA in the limb bud in particular was because this compound had been shown to have remarkable effects on pattern formation in the AP axis. When RA is applied locally to the anterior side of the limb bud, it causes mirror-image duplications in the AP axis such that 6-digit double posterior limbs develop instead of the normal 3-digit ones (Tickle *et al.* 1982; Summerbell, 1983). The behaviour of RA precisely mimics the effects of grafting the zone of polarizing activity (ZPA), a group of cells at the posterior margin, which organises pattern across the AP axis of the limb (Tickle *et al.* 1975). This coincidence led to the suggestion that RA may be the natural morphogen that the ZPA uses to generate pattern (Eichele *et al.* 1985) and the data on its endogenous distribution (Thaller and Eichele, 1987) provide powerful support for this notion.

Retinoids and limb regeneration

It had earlier been shown in the regenerating limbs of toads that, instead of regenerating just the foot after amputation through the shank, extra limb segments were produced if the animal was treated with retinyl palmitate (Niazi and Saxena, 1978). In newts and axolotls, the same specific effects on the proximodistal (PD) axis were observed such that complete limbs could be regenerated from amputations through the hand (Maden, 1982; 1983*a*; Thoms and Stocum, 1984). In addition to these effects on the PD axis, pattern duplication in the AP axis can also be demonstrated (Maden, 1983*b*; Kim and Stocum, 1986) as well as in the dorsoventral axis (Stocum, unpublished). In the light of these effects on each of the three cardinal limb axes, it is difficult to see how RA could be a morphogen in the way that it is believed to be in the chick limb bud. But we still need to know the biochemical and molecular mechanisms of action of RA in the cells of the regenerating limb because it is clearly acting on the endogenous pattern generating mechanisms.

CRABP and CRBP in the limb and embryo

As a first step towards understanding the mode of action of RA either as a morphogen or as a chemical that specifically disturbs pattern generating mechanisms, we describe here our recent experiments on the levels and distribution of CRABP and CRBP. In the first section, we consider the regenerating axolotl limb and the developing chick limb bud in the light of the effects of RA on the two systems. In the second section, we have examined other regions of the chick embryo for the presence of retinoid-binding proteins and find them to be most interestingly localised in the developing nervous system. Because of this distribution we suggest that RA is acting as a morphogen in the nervous system as well as the limb.

The regenerating amphibian limb

CRABP

The presence of retinoid-binding proteins can be detected in high-speed supernatants of homogenised tissues by a variety of means. We have used sucrose gradient centrifugation assays in which a fixed volume of protein preparation is incubated with [³H]RA either in the presence or absence of a 100× molar excess of cold RA. The incubations are then dialysed to get rid of the excess radioactivity and spun on 5–20% sucrose gradients. If CRABP is present a peak of radioactivity appears at the point on the gradient which corresponds to its known molecular weight (approx. 16K) and if the binding is specific then there should be a drop in activity when excess cold RA is present (Fig. 1). By this means we determined that CRABP is present at low levels in some of the tissues of the larval axolotl, such as skin and muscle, and undetectable in liver and serum (Keeble and Maden, 1986). The latter two results were expected from data on mammals (Chytil and Ong, 1984) and confirmed that the assays were working and that axolotls did not have abnormal vitamin A metabolism.

When the level of CRABP in unamputated limbs and regeneration blastemas were compared a 3- to 4-fold rise was observed (Fig. 1; Table 1). This rise was

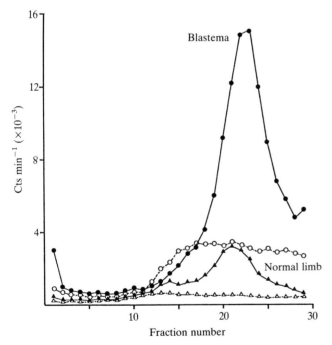

Fig. 1. Sucrose density gradient profile of axolotl limb and blastema cytosol to detect the presence of CRABP. Equivalent amounts of protein incubated with 66 nM-[³H]all-*trans*-retinoic acid (NEN, specific activity 55 Ci mmol⁻¹) alone (●——●, ▲——▲) or in the presence of 100× M excess cold all-*trans*-retinoic acid (○---○, △---△). ●——●, ○---○ cytosol from cone stage regeneration blastemas. ▲——▲, ▲---▲ cytosol from normal, unamputated limbs. The drop in cts min⁻¹ in the presence of cold RA is a measure of relative activity levels. The peak of activity is in the part of the gradient to which a myoglobin marker (17K) sediments.

Table 1. *Levels of CRABP and CRBP in various developing and regenerating tissues measured by sucrose density centrifugation assays*

Tissue	Concentration (fmoles per mg cytosolic protein)	
	CRABP	CRBP
Axolotl unamputated limb	700±30	162±44
Axolotl regeneration blastema	2600±100	471±117
Chick limb bud	9100±1200	805±79
Mouse limb bud	9780±1780	1075±325
Chick embryo	6700±400	660±300

maximal in the cone-stage blastema and as regeneration progressed so the level decreased to that found in unamputated limbs (Keeble and Maden, 1986). The early blastemal stage is also the period when exogenously administered RA has the most profound effect on pattern (Maden *et al.* 1985), a coincidence that suggests a role for CRABP in the mechanism of action of RA. When cone-stage blastemas were treated with a dose of RA sufficient to cause proximodistal duplications, no increase in CRABP could be detected so the levels of this protein do not seem to be regulated by the concentration of its ligand.

CRABP has also been detected in axolotl limbs by a different method, that of high-performance size-exclusion chromatography (McCormick *et al.* 1988). In this work the results obtained are, at first sight, somewhat different from those described above because no substantial difference in total CRABP was detected between unamputated and regenerating limbs. However, stage-dependent differences were detected in the levels of apo-CRABP (CRABP without any endogenous RA bound) and holo-CRABP (CRABP with RA bound). Apo-CRABP was highest at the blastemal stage and as regeneration proceeded it became saturated with endogenous RA such that only holo-CRABP could be detected at the 2-digit regenerate stage. Since the sucrose gradient method (Fig. 1) would be expected to measure apo-CRABP plus some fraction of the holo-CRABP due to ligand exchange, the two sets of data seem to show a similar stage-dependent rise and then decline in the availability of CRABP, implying a role for this molecule in limb regeneration (see below).

Competition and potency studies

In an effort to examine the role of CRABP in more detail, we have compared the ability of a range of retinoids to respecify the proximodistal pattern of the regenerate with their ability to bind to CRABP. If retinoids that do not affect pattern do not bind to CRABP and, conversely, those that do affect pattern do bind to CRABP then this would provide strong support for the involvement of CRABP in the mechanism of pattern respecification. We have tested a total of nine retinoids with different polar end groups or altered ring or side chain structures compared to the basic RA molecule (Keeble and Maden, 1989).

With regard to their effect on pattern formation, when administered locally in a silastin implant (see

Table 2. *Relative potencies (ability to respecify pattern) and binding affinities to CRABP (measured as IC₅₀) of nine different retinoids tested on axolotl regeneration blastemas and chick limb buds*

Retinoid	Structure	Axolotl		Chick	
		Potency	Affinity	Potency	Affinity
Retinoic acid		1	4×10^{-7}	1	2×10^{-7}
Ro 13–7410		100+	2×10^{-7}	2	1×10^{-7}
Arotinoid		10	1.2×10^{-6}	2	0
Ro 10–1670		0.1	6.7×10^{-7}	0.7	1.8×10^{-6}
Etretinate		0	0	0	0
Retinal		0	1.4×10^{-5}	0	2.2×10^{-6}
Retinol		0	0	0	0
Retinyl acetate		0	0	0	0
Retinyl palmitate		0	0	0	0

Potencies are assessed relative to all-*trans*-retinoic acid. Ro numbers refer to Hofmann-La Roche code numbers.

Maden *et al.* 1985) retinyl palmitate, retinyl acetate, retinol, retinal and etretinate were inactive (Table 2). Each of these compounds has an altered polar end group compared to the acid moiety of RA (see Table 2 for structural details), thus it is clear that this part of the molecule is crucial in determining biological activity. The compound Ro 10–1670, which has an acid end group like RA but an altered ring structure, has considerably less activity than RA. Arotinoid, which has an ester end group but 2 additional ring structures in the side chain, is 5–10× more potent than RA. Ro 13–7410, which has an acid end group and 2 additional ring structures in the side chain, is at least 100× more potent than RA (Table 2). Thus the addition of rings into the side chain of the RA molecule dramatically increases its potency at respecifying pattern.

Concerning their ability to bind to CRABP, similar principles emerged. Ro 13–7410 had twice the affinity for CRABP compared to RA, suggesting that the addition of rings into the side chain increased binding. Ro 10–1670 had only two thirds the affinity, suggesting that altering the parent ring structure decreased binding. Arotinoid and retinal had decreased affinity and retinol, retinyl acetate and retinyl palmitate had no affinity for CRABP, suggesting that the polar end group is important for binding.

Thus, in order to bind to CRABP, a retinoid needs an acid end group and such compounds are most effective in altering pattern. The addition of extra ring structres into the molecule increases binding and increases pattern respecification potency. These correlations imply a role for CRABP in pattern respecification. Arotinoid, however, does not strictly fit with these rules (Table 2) because its binding to CRABP is less avid than RA, but it is more potent than RA in respecifying pattern. This may be the exception that disproves the thesis or arotinoid may be metabolised by esterases in the limb to the more potent compound Ro 13–7410 and its potency at respecifying pattern thus exaggerated.

CRBP

The other retinoid-binding protein which is known to exist in mammalian tissues and is specific for retinol is CRBP. It is important to know whether this is present in the axolotl limb and during regeneration. By sucrose

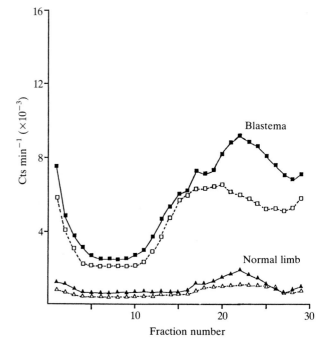

Fig. 2. Sucrose density gradient profile of axolotl limb and blastema cytosol to detect the presence of CRBP. Equivalent amounts of protein incubated with 66 nM-[³H]all-*trans*-retinol (Amersham, specific activity 60 Ci mmol⁻¹) alone (■——■, ▲——▲) or in the presence of 500× M excess cold all-*trans*-retinol (□---□, △---△). ■——■, □---□ cytosol from cone-stage regeneration blastemas. ▲——▲, △---△ cytosol from normal, unamputated limbs. The drop in cts min⁻¹ in the presence of cold retinol is a measure of relative activity levels. The peak of activity is in the part of the gradient to which a myoglobin marker (17K) sediments.

gradient assay CRBP was virtually undetectable in the unamputated limb, but clearly present in the cone-stage regeneration blastema (Fig. 2). However, the level was only one quarter of that of CRABP (Table 1).

The role of CRBP in regeneration is not clear. The lower levels of this protein could imply a lesser significance. Indeed retinol applied locally does not cause pattern respecification (Keeble and Maden, 1989). When applied systemically, however, retinol is active (Maden, 1983), but this may be due to the metabolic conversion of retinol to RA. Nevertheless, it would be unwise to rule out this molecule in the process of limb regeneration until more data such as its immunocyto-chemical distribution become available.

Speculations

The observations described above permit several interesting speculations about the mechanisms involved in pattern formation during limb regeneration. First, since RA is the endogenous ligand for CRABP (Saari *et al.* 1982) and CRABP levels rise and fall during regeneration it is highly likely that RA is involved in the process of limb regeneration. Whether it is a morphogen, as it is thought to be in the developing limb (Thaller and Eichele, 1987), is not at all clear. In the chick limb bud only the anteroposterior (AP) axis is affected by RA, but in the regenerating limb all three axes (PD, AP and DV) can be respecified (see Introduction). Classically, a Cartesian coordinate system such as this would be expected to be organised by gradients of three different morphogens (Wolpert, 1969) and it is difficult to see how only one could do the job.

Second, McCormick *et al.* (1988) have suggested from their data on apo- and holo-CRABP that the effects of exogenous RA on pattern respecification could be mediated by two different mechanisms. It was established early on in the analysis of retinoid effects on regenerating limbs that there was a stage dependency (Maden, 1983; Niazi *et al.* 1985; Maden *et al.* 1985). When RA is administered at early to midblastemal stages the effect is to proximalise the regenerate. At this stage, apo-CRABP is at its highest level and thus available for binding the exogenously administered RA which could then mediate proximalisation *via* an interaction with the genome. When RA is administered at later stages, by which time redifferentiation is already well under way (e.g. 2-digit stage) then only inhibitory effects such as missing phalanges or missing digits are produced. At these stages all the CRABP is in the form of holo-CRABP and thus the exogenous RA remains free and could directly inhibit biosynthetic processes such as cartilage formation (Hassell *et al.* 1978).

Thirdly, McCormick *et al.* (1988) also consider the possibility that a differing spatial distribution of apo- and holo-CRABP could explain the effects of RA on the anteroposterior axis of the regenerating limb. As described in the Introduction when double-anterior half limbs are treated with RA the regenerate is proximalised *and* mirror-imaged in the AP axis. RA thus induces posteriorisation of anterior cells. But when double-posterior half limbs are similarly treated regeneration is inhibited. This could be explained if the anterior region of the blastema was rich in apo-CRABP and thus exogenous RA could be bound, interact with the genome and posteriorise the cells. If CRABP in the posterior region were virtually all in the holo- form then exogenous RA could not be bound, would thereby remain free and thus inhibit biosynthetic process directly. Alternatively there may be an AP gradient of total CRABP with the high point on the anterior side as

has been found in the chick limb bud (Maden *et al.* 1988).

Clearly, we need to find out a lot more about the precise cellular and spatial distribution of CRABP and CRBP in the regenerating limb. Immunocytochemistry would be extremely valuable as it has been in the chick limb bud (see below), although this technique is unlikely to provide a full description as it cannot, for example, distinguish between apo- and holo-CRABP. It will also be important to establish the distributional relationship between CRABP and the retinoic acid receptors (see Introduction) both within the cell and within the blastema during the process of limb regeneration.

The developing chick limb bud

CRABP

We found high levels of CRABP in the chick limb bud in sucrose gradient assays (Fig. 3, Table 1) which remained high at all the stages examined (Maden and Summerbell, 1986). The total specific binding capacity was estimated to be 14–28 pmoles mg^{-1} protein and the K_d 140–280 nM. This estimate of dissociation constant is at the upper end of the range of values from other tissues which varies from 2 nM for mouse limb buds (Kwarta *et al.* 1985) and 4.2 nM for rat testis (Ong and Chytil, 1978) to 318 nM for rat testis (Bonelli and

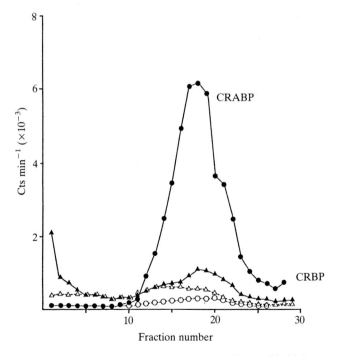

Fig. 3. Sucrose density gradient profiles of stage 24 chick limb bud cytosol to detect the relative levels of CRABP (●——●, ○---○) and CRBP (▲——▲, △---△). Equivalent amounts of protein incubated with: 66 nM-[^{3}H]all-*trans*-retinoic acid (●——●), [^{3}H]RA plus 100× M excess cold RA (○---○), 66 nM-[^{3}H]all-*trans*-retinol (▲——▲), [^{3}H]retinol plus 500× M excess cold retinol (△---△).

DeLuca, 1985) and 400 nm for human skin (Siegen-thaler and Saurat, 1985).

Competition and potency studies

As described above for axolotl blastemal CRABP, we have examined the binding affinities of various retinoids for chick limb bud CRABP and compared this with the ability of these compounds to respecify pattern in the AP axis of the limb bud.

A similar sequence of affinities was found (Maden and Summerbell, 1986) indicating similar structural requirements for binding when compared to axolotl blastemal CRABP (Table 2). Thus Ro 13–7410 had twice the affinity for chick limb bud CRABP than did its natural ligand all-*trans*-RA. Ro 10–1670 was about 10× less effective at binding than RA and retinal was about 12× less effective. The remaining analogues – aroti-noid, etretinate, retinol, retinyl palmitate and retinyl acetate – did not show any affinity for CRABP. Thus the primary structural requirement was an acid end group and the presence of two additional rings in the side chain increased binding affinity.

Regarding the effect of these retinoids on pattern formation, it is known that Ro 13–7410 is more potent than RA (Eichele *et al.* 1985) and we have confirmed that result (Table 2). Thus the two additional rings in the side chain increase potency as well as binding affinity. Arotinoid, which also has two additional rings, is nearly twice as potent as RA although it does not bind to CRABP. Ro 10–1670 is less potent than RA despite having an acid end group and does not bind to CRABP as well as RA. The remaining analogues – etretinate, retinol, retinal, retinyl palmitate and retinyl acetate – were inactive (Table 2). Thus the sequence of binding affinities is the same as the sequence of potencies with the exception of arotinoid, which is active but does not bind to CRABP. As discussed above for the axolotl data, it is possible that arotinoid is metabolised to Ro 13–7410 by endogenous esterases in the limb thus causing the potency score to be exaggerated. Alterna-tively arotinoid may be the exception that demonstrates that these compounds do not have to bind to CRABP to be biologically active. We are currently examining the metabolism of retinoids in the chick embryo in an attempt to solve this problem.

CRBP

In sucrose gradient assays CRBP is barely detectable in the chick limb (Fig. 3), having only about 1/10th of the level of CRABP (Table 1). We have failed to detect CRBP immunocytochemically in the limb bud (see below) and therefore presume that this protein does not play a significant role in the establishment of pattern in this system.

Immunocytochemistry

A great deal of valuable information has been obtained with the use of antibodies to these binding proteins. To look at the distribution of CRABP, we have used an affinity-purified rabbit polyclonal antibody made from rat CRABP. This antibody reacts with a single protein

of the same size as rat CRABP on a Western blot of stage 24 chick limb buds (Maden *et al.* 1988).

Sections through the flank of stage 18 embryos in nonlimb regions show virtually no labelling of the mesodermal cells (Fig. 4). The epidermis is also un-labelled except for nonspecific reactivity on the surface. Sections through the region of the early limb bud, however, show intense labelling of the mesodermal cells, particularly those at the distal tip of the limb bud (Fig. 5). By stage 24, when the limb bud has elongated considerably and differentiation of the upper arm has begun proximally, several discrete regions of CRABP immunoreactivity can easily be distinguished (Fig. 6). At the tip, the apical ectodermal ridge is unlabelled (Fig. 7). The progress zone, which is the distalmost mesenchyme, is heavily immunoreactive. The cells in this location have a high rate of mitosis and are responsible for generating the complex pattern of elements that emerge sequentially during development (Wolpert *et al.* 1975). Most importantly, only such distal cells are able to respond to exogenously administered RA by duplicating their pattern (Tickle and Crawley, 1988). Behind the progress zone is undifferentiatied mesenchyme which does not label so intensely. In this region cells have begun to withdraw from the cell cycle in preparation for differentiation. Further proximally, differentiation can be seen to have commenced. In the central region, the humerus has begun to differentiate in the absence of CRABP immunoreactivity whereas the muscle and connective tissue on the periphery stain intensely.

The high levels of CRABP in the progress zone are likely to be of significance for the establishment of pattern in the limb bud. To examine this in further detail, we looked at the distribution of CRABP immu-noreactivity across the AP axis, particularly with regard

Figs 4–8. Sections of chick embryos treated with an affinity-purified rabbit anti-rat CRABP antibody to reveal areas of specific immunoreactivity which are shown by the brown HRP reaction product. 4, section through the flank of a stage 18 embryo adjacent to the forelimb. There is no staining of the mesenchymal cells beneath the epidermis. Bar = 100 μm. 5, section through the limb bud of a stage 18 embryo. In contrast to Fig. 4, these mesenchymal cells are CRABP immunoreactive particularly at the distal tip. Bar = 100 μm. 6, stage 24 limb bud, longitudinal section, showing several areas of varying intensity of immunoreactivity. At the tip is the apical ectodermal ridge (aer) which does not label (see Fig. 7). The distalmost mesenchyme is the progress zone (pz) which is intensely CRABP reactive. Behind that is a weakly staining region consisting of undifferentiated mesenchyme (um). Further proximal the humerus (h) has differentiated in the absence of CRABP whereas the muscle, connective tissue and dermis (ct) stain intensely, particularly the dermis on the periphery. Bar = 150 μm. 7, high power view of the AER (arrow) showing the absence of staining in the epidermis compared to the mesenchyme of the progress zone beneath. Bar = 25 μm. 8, transverse section through the progress zone of a stage 21 limb bud. The anterior margin on the right is more intensely labelled than the posterior margin on the left. Bar = 100 μm.

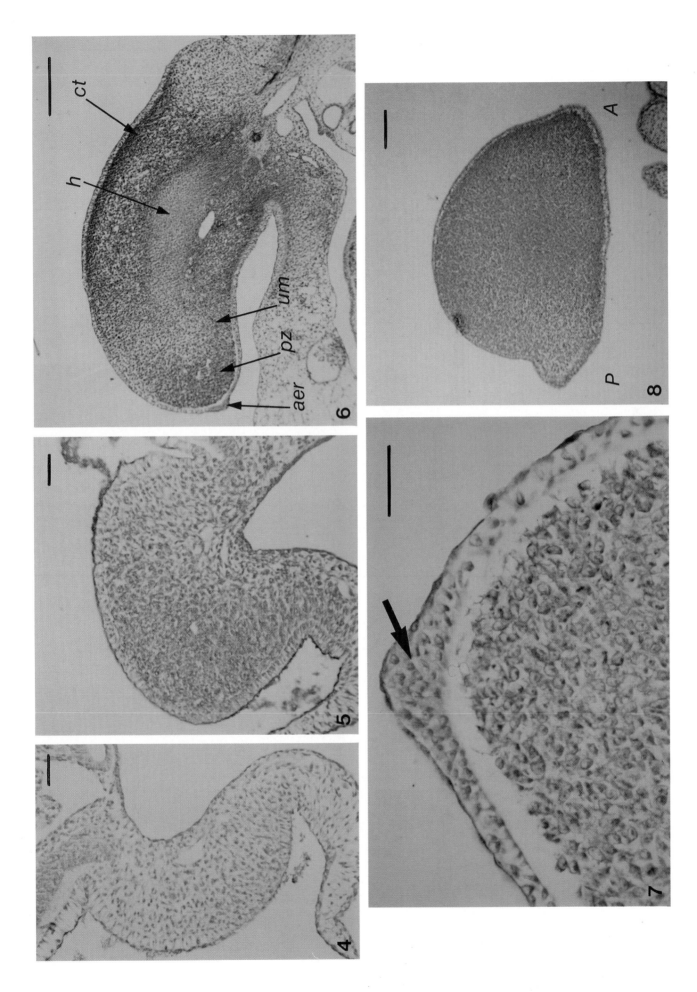

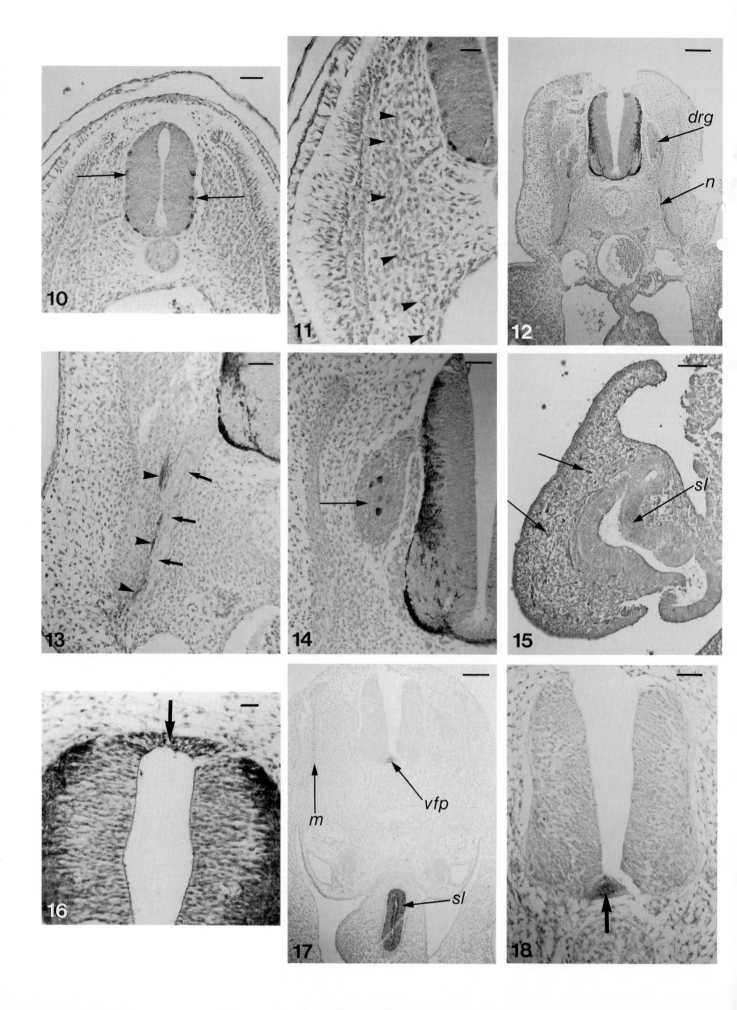

to the endogenous gradient of RA which has its high point at the posterior side of the limb bud (Thaller and Eichele, 1987). In transverse sections, a gradient of CRABP was indeed detected, but to our surprise it was

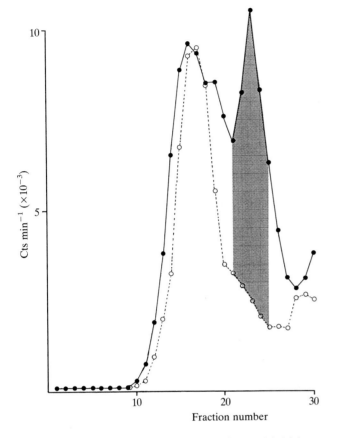

Fig. 9. Sucrose density gradient profile of stage 24 chick embryo cytosol to detect the presence of CRABP. 375 μg protein was incubated with 66 nM-[³H]all-*trans*-retinoic acid (NEN, specific activity 55 Ci mmol⁻¹) alone (●——●) or in the presence of 100× M excess cold all-*trans*-retinoic acid (○‑‑‑○). In these preparations, there are two peaks of radioactivity. The right-hand peak at approx. 17K which disappears in the presence of excess cold RA measures CRABP (hatched area). The left-hand peak at approx. 66K is non-specific.

of the opposite polarity to that of RA, namely the high point was at the anterior margin and the low point at the posterior margin (Fig. 8). We have quantified the levels of CRABP using a false colour-image analysis system which gives a ratio of peroxidase label from anterior to posterior of 3.5:1.

It is important to note that these distributions of CRABP immunoreactivity are not caused by local variations in cell density. The two areas at the tip of the limb bud (progress zone and undifferentiated mesenchyme) have the same cell density, yet have a twofold variation in immunoreactivity and the anterior and posterior sides have similar densities despite a 3.5-fold difference in immunoreactivity.

Regarding the immunocytochemical distribution of CRBP, we cannot detect any in the limb bud. Coupled with the observation that only very low levels are present on sucrose gradient assays (Fig. 3) and that retinol is not an active compound when administered locally (Table 2), this suggests that CRBP may not be involved in the establishment of pattern in the chick limb bud.

Speculations

The levels of CRABP in a limb bud cell from birth to differentiation are thus strictly regulated. At birth in the progress zone CRABP levels are high in the rapidly dividing population of cells. As a cell leaves this zone, division slows down in preparation for differentiation and CRABP levels decline. As the developmental decision to become either cartilage or connective tissue/dermis is made CRABP levels are either extinguished (cartilage) or rise again (connective tissue/ dermis). These fluctuations suggest that CRABP is playing a role in the generation of pattern in the limb bud.

In the proximodistal axis, CRABP may be responsible for maintaining a high rate of cell division in the progress zone. RA is known to stimulate proliferation in cultured distal mesodermal cells of the limb bud at concentrations that exist endogenously (Ide and Aono, 1988). So CRABP may mediate this function of RA by interacting with the retinoic acid receptors and ultimately the genes controlling proliferation.

Figs 10–18. Sections of chick embryos treated with affinity-purified rabbit anti-rat CRABP antibody (Figs 10–16) or rabbit anti-rat CRBP antibody (Figs 17–18) to reveal areas of specific immunoreactivity which are shown by the brown HRP reaction product. 10, section through the trunk at the forelimb level of a stage 16 embryo showing CRABP labelled cells in the mantle layer of the neural tube (arrows). Bar = 50 μm. 11, higher power view of Fig. 10 showing a string of cells (arrowheads) in the sclerotome which are CRABP immunoreactive. Bar = 25 μm. 12, section through the trunk at the forelimb level of a stage 22 embryo to reveal intense CRABP labelling on the periphery of the neural tube as well as in the nerves (n) and dorsal root ganglia (drg). Bar = 100 μm. 13, higher power view of Fig. 12 showing that only the sensory axons are immunoreactive (arrowheads) whereas the adjacent motor axons are unlabelled (arrows). Bar = 50 μm. 14, higher

power view of Fig. 12, to show the labelling of individual cell bodies in the dorsal root ganglion (arrow). Bar = 50 μm. 15, section through the developing gut of a stage 22 embryo showing individual CRABP-positive cells in the thick gut wall (arrows). The secretory lining (sl) does not label in contrast to Fig. 17. Bar = 50 μm. 16, section through the neural tube of a stage 24 embryo which reveals intense CRABP reactivity in the dorsal roof plate (arrow). Bar = 25 μm. 17, CRBP immunoreactivity in a stage 24 embryo showing that only three areas label. One is the ventral floor plate (vfp), another is the secretory lining of the gut (sl) and the other is the myotome (m). Bar = 100 μm. 18, higher power view of Fig. 17 to show CRBP labelling in the cells of the ventral floor plate (arrow) rather than the fibres passing beneath which are CRABP positive (Figs 13 and 14). Bar = 50 μm.

In the anteroposterior axis, the role that CRABP might play seems different depending on whether we consider normal development or the results of experimental interference. In normal development, the gradients of RA and CRABP are of opposite polarity. This would result in a flat distribution of holo-CRABP thereby losing the positional differences that were generated in the first place. We have suggested (Maden *et al.* 1988) that the function of CRABP in the AP axis is to steepen the gradient of free RA. The 2.5-fold enrichment of endogenous RA in the posterior region would result in a change of only 15% in maximum binding across the limb which is rather small to specify the complexities of limb structure. A steeper gradient would increase this difference and may also lower the overall concentration of free RA (measured as 10^{-8}) so that it would be able to interact with the receptor (K_d 10^{-9}–10^{-10} M).

In the case of experimental interference, the gradient of CRABP with a high point at the anterior side conveniently explains why a ZPA graft or a RA implant only works to maximum effect when placed on the anterior side (Tickle *et al.* 1975, 1985). The concentration of holo-CRABP would be too low on the posterior side to cause a change in gene activity. When placed in the centre of the limb bud a ZPA graft or a RA implant is attenuated and this may be because the CRABP concentration is lower than at the anterior margin resulting in the transference of less RA to the nuclear receptors. In other situations this type of explanation is readily applicable. For example when fragments of the limb bud are cocultured, an anterior quarter with a posterior quarter results in far greater growth and cartilage differentiation than do two anterior quarters or two posterior quarters (Suzuki and Ide, 1987). The extra growth comes from the anterior fragment under the influence of the posterior one and these authors suggest that the lack of responsiveness of the posterior fragment itself may be due to the lack of a receptor. With a high CRABP concentration in the anterior fragments and a high RA concentration in the posterior fragments these results are readily explicable.

However, we are now left with two different mechanisms of action depending on whether we are considering the normal limb or the experimental limb, which is rather unsatisfying. Once again only with more information, particularly the involvement of the nuclear receptors, can we hope to unravel these complexities.

Finally, in the interests of universality it is worth mentioning that CRABP has been detected at high levels in the mouse limb bud (Kwarta *et al.* 1985). We have confirmed this result and the fact that CRBP is also present in mouse limb buds at about 1/10th the levels of CRABP (Table 1). So the same principles may apply throughout vertebrate limb development.

The developing spinal cord of the chick

CRABP

When the amount of CRABP in protein preparations from whole chick embryos is estimated by sucrose gradient analysis, high levels are observed (Fig. 9). In this preparation, as distinct from isolated limb buds (Fig. 1), nonspecific binding is seen at a higher molecular weight (approx. 66K) and is caused, at least in part, by [^{3}H]RA binding to albumin in the blood. The amount of CRABP in embryos is of the same order as that found in limb buds (Table 1).

Thus, with immunocytochemistry, we might expect to find extensive staining and that is indeed the case. Stage 16 to 24 embryos have been sectioned to look at the tissue distribution of CRABP. The myotome showed light staining at each stage and particularly at later stages the dermal and connective tissue cells showed immunoreactivity. But the most intensely stained cells were of neural or neural crest origin.

At stage 16 individual cells in the mantle layer of the neural tube particularly on the lateral and ventral sides had high levels of CRABP (Fig. 10). There appeared to be two populations of labelled cells, large cells that may be postmitotic early differentiating neurons and small, flattened cells particularly noticeable in the ventral floor plate region. These may form the pia on the outside of the neural tube. Certain neural crest cell populations were also heavily immunoreactive. There was a line of labelled cells stretching from the dorsal neural tube through the sclerotome to the lateral edge of the dorsal aorta (arrowheads in Fig. 11). These cells were present only in the anterior half of each sclerotome suggesting that they were neural crest cells in the process of migrating.

At stage 18, the mantle layer cells of the neural tube were again strongly immunoreactive as were individual cells between the neural tube and the myotome aggregating at the future site of the dorsal root ganglion. An additional site of localisation was a group of cells on each lateral edge of the dorsal aorta.

By stage 22, immunoreactivity in the neural tube had become much more extensive and intense (Figs 12–14). Cells of the mantle layer, dorsal roof plate and commissural axons which pass medial, lateral and through the motor horns and cross the ventral floor plate were labelled. Some of the dorsal root ganglion cells were labelled (Fig. 14) and particularly striking was immunoreactivity in axons passing out from the ganglion (arrowheads in Fig. 13). These axons maintained a dorsal position as they joined motor axons from the ventral horn and thus the two subpopulations of axons in the mixed nerve could clearly be seen. An additional site of immunoreactivity which first appeared at this stage was in individual cells of the walls of the developing gut (Fig. 15). It is likely that these are migrating neural crest cells which will form the enteric ganglia.

At stage 24, the distribution of immunoreactivity had not appreciably changed from stage 22. The dorsal roof plate labelling became more discrete (Fig. 16), a greater number of cells in the dorsal root ganglia were labelled and the selective staining of sensory axons in the brachial plexus was more apparent.

CRBP

Sucrose gradient assays revealed that the embryo had

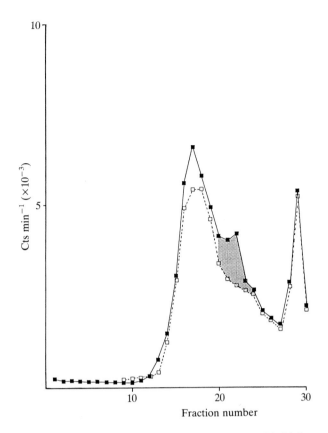

Fig. 19. Sucrose density gradient profile of stage 24 chick embryo cytosol to detect the presence of CRBP. μg protein was incubated with 66 nM-[³H]all-*trans*-retinol (Amersham, specific activity 60 Ci mmol⁻¹) alone (■——■) or in the presence of 500× M excess cold all-*trans*-retinol (□---□). As in Fig. 9 there are two peaks of radioactivity, one is non-specific (left) and one is specific for CRBP (right). Although equivalent amounts of protein were used, the level of CRBP (hatched area) is far less than the level of CRABP measured in Fig. 9.

low levels of CRBP (Fig. 19, Table 1). Like the limb bud there was about 1/10th of the amount of CRBP in the embryo as CRABP.

We did not therefore expect to see very much in our immunocytochemical analysis, which proved to be the case. However, the distribution of immunoreactivity was very surprising. At all stages examined, the secretory lining of the developing gut showed intense labelling (Fig. 17). This is in obvious contrast to CRABP immunoreactivity, which highlighted individual cells in the walls not the epithelium (Fig. 15).

The second area of immunoreactivity was the ventral floor plate cells (Fig. 18). Again, in contrast to CRABP where the commissural fibres passing *below* the floor plate labelled (see Figs 13 and 14), with CRBP it was the cells of the floor plate itself that were labelled. Also, in contrast was the labelling of the dorsal roof plate with CRABP (Fig. 16) and the ventral floor plate with CRBP.

The only other area of immunoreactivity was the myotome (Fig. 17).

Speculations

The patterns of CRABP and CRBP immunoreactivity in the trunk of the chick embryo show discrete and striking contrasts in three areas: the neural tube, the neurons and the gut.

In the neural tube, CRABP reactivity is found in cells in the mantle layer which become the commissural neurons and in the dorsal roof plate. CRBP is found only in the ventral floor plate. The ventral floor plate is an important decision-making region which first attracts commissural axons towards it and then causes these axons to make abrupt right-angled turns to project in the rostrocaudal axis along the lateral surface of the floor plate (Dodd and Jessell, 1988; Tessier-Lavigne *et al.* 1988). In the light of the observations reported here, it is possible that the ventral floor plate is rich in retinol, which it metabolises to RA and releases as a chemoattractant. Since commissural fibres have CRABP only, they are able to take up RA and respond accordingly by growing towards the source. This attractive theory can initially be tested by determining whether RA or perhaps retinol are indeed chemoattractants for neurons and specifically commissural neurons.

Sensory neurons are highly immunoreactive to CRABP whereas motor neurons are not. This suggests that RA may play a role in the decision-making process involved in the differentiation of sensory *vs* motor nerves. Alternatively RA may be involved in the guidance of axons into, for example, the limb in the same way that was proposed above for commissural axons. Again it would be a simple matter to test whether RA is a chemoattractant for nerves.

The secretory lining of the gut labels with CRBP whereas individual cells in the thick wall of the gut label with CRABP. These CRABP-positive cells are most likely to be neural crest cells migrating through the gut walls to form the enteric plexus (Maden *et al.* 1989). CRBP is present in the epithelium of the rat intestine (Ong *et al.* 1982) and we would therefore expect to find it in the chick embryo. However, in rats there is another distinct species of CRBP, CRBP(II) (Ong, 1984), which is present in the intestinal epithelium at 1000× the level of CRBP (Crow and Ong, 1985). It is possible that the immunoreactivity we have described here is detecting chick CRBP(II) which in the chick may be less immunologically distinct from CRBP than in the rat. In any case, the location of this CRBP immunoreactivity implies a role in the absorption of retinol from the gut.

Concluding remarks

The above data on the levels and localisation of CRABP and CRBP in the regenerating amphibian limb, the chick limb bud and the chick nervous system provide evidence to support the view that these binding proteins and their ligands, retinol and retinoic acid, are involved in the generation of pattern in these systems.

Interestingly, similar localisations have recently been reported, particularly in the limb, concerning homoeobox genes. In *Xenopus* and mouse the XLHbox 1 protein is localised in the forelimb bud in the form of a gradient with the high point on the anterior side (Oliver *et al.* 1988). It is also strongest in proximal regions of the limb and absent at the distal tip and absent from hindlimb buds. The Hox-7 transcript is present in the mouse initially throughout the limb bud, but later it localises to the distal and posterior periphery under the ectoderm and later still to interdigital mesenchyme (Robert *et al.* 1989; Hill *et al.* 1989). In the chick, Ghox 2.1 has been investigated with *in situ* hybridisation to reveal a patch of expression at the anterior margin of the chick limb bud in a proximal region (Wedden *et al.* 1989).

In addition, these genes are also expressed in the nervous system as are many other homoeobox genes (Holland and Hogan, 1988). Thus there is an association both in the limb and the nervous system between homoeobox genes, CRABP/CRBP and retinoids. Since RA is known to be able to activate the transcription of homoeobox genes (Mavilio *et al.* 1988) these three components may be intimately associated with the generation of pattern in the embryo.

References

BENBROOK, D., LERNHARDT, E. AND PFAHL, M. (1988). A new retinoic acid receptor identified from a hepatocellular carcinoma. *Nature, Lond.* **333**, 669–672.

BONELLI, F. C. AND DELUCA, L. M. (1985). A high-performance liquid chromatography technique that separates cellular retinol-binding protein from cellular retinoic acid-binding protein. *Analyt. Biochem.* **147**, 251–257.

BRAND, N., PETKOVICH, M., KRUST, A., CHAMBON, P., DE THE, H., MARCHIO, A., TIOLLAIS, P. AND DEJEAN, A. (1988). Identification of a second human retinoic acid receptor. *Nature, Lond.* **332**, 850–853.

CHYTIL, F. AND ONG, D. E. (1984). Cellular retinoid-binding proteins. In *The Retinoids*, vol. 2 (ed. M. B. Sporn, A. B. Roberts and D. S. Goodman), pp. 90–123. Orlando, Florida: Academic Press.

CROW, J. A. AND ONG, D. E. (1985). Cell-specific immunohistochemical localisation of a cellular retinol-binding protein (type two) in the small intestine of rat. *Proc. natn. Acad. Sci. U.S.A.* **82**, 4707–4711.

DALY, A. K. AND REDFERN, C. P. F. (1987). Characterisation of a retinoic-acid-binding component from F9 embryonal-carcinoma-cell nuclei. *Eur. J. Biochem.* **168**, 133–139.

DODD, J. AND JESSELL, T. M. (1988). Axon guidance and the patterning of neuronal projections in vertebrates. *Science* **242**, 692–699.

EICHELE, G., TICKLE, C. AND ALBERTS, B. M. (1985). Studies on the mechanism of retinoid-induced pattern duplications in the early chick limb bud: temporal and spatial aspects. *J. Cell Biol.* **101**, 1913–1920.

GIGUERE, V., ONG, E. S., SEGUI, P. AND EVANS, R. M. (1987). Identification of a receptor for the morphogen retinoic acid. *Nature, Lond.* **330**, 624–629.

HASSELL, J. R., PENNYPACKER, J. P., YAMADA, K. M. AND PRATT, R. M. (1978). Changes in cell surface proteins during normal and vitamin A-inhibited chondrogenesis *in vitro*. *Ann. N. Y. Acad. Sci.* **312**, 406–409.

HILL, R. E., JONES, P. F., REES, A. R., SIME, C. M., JUSTICE, M. J., COPELAND, N. G., JENKINS, N. A., GRAHAM, E. AND DAVIDSON, D. R. (1989). A new family of mouse homeo box-containing genes: molecular structure, chromosomal location, and developmental expression of Hox-7.1. *Genes and Development* **3**, 26–37.

HOLLAND, P. W. H. AND HOGAN, B. (1988). Expression of homeobox genes during mouse development: a review. *Genes and Development* **2**, 773–782.

IDE, H. AND AONO, H. (1988). Retinoic acid promotes proliferation and chondrogenesis in the distal mesodermal cells of chick limb bud. *Devl Biol.* **130**, 767–773.

KALTER, H. AND WARKANY, J. (1959). Experimental production of congenital malformations in mammals by metabolic procedure. *Physiol. Rev.* **39**, 69–115.

KEEBLE, S. AND MADEN, M. (1986). Retinoic acid-binding protein in the axolotl: distribution in mature tissues and time of appearance during limb regeneration. *Devl Biol.* **117**, 435–441.

KEEBLE, S. AND MADEN, M. (1989). The relationship among retinoid structure, affinity for retinoic acid-binding protein, and ability to respecify pattern in the regenerating limb. *Devl Biol.* **132**, 26–34.

KIM, W-S. AND STOCUM, D. L. (1986). Retinoic acid modifies positional memory in the anteroposterior axis of regenerating limbs. *Devl Biol.* **114**, 170–179.

KWARTA, R. F., KIMMEL, C. A., KIMMEL, G. L. AND SLIKKER, W. (1985). Identification of the cellular retinoic acid-binding protein (CRABP) within the embryonic mouse (CD-1) limb bud. *Teratology* **32**, 103–111.

MADEN, M. (1982). Vitamin A and pattern formation in the regenerating limb. *Nature, Lond.* **295**, 672–675.

MADEN, M. (1983a). The effect of vitamin A on the regenerating axolotl limb. *J. Embryol. exp. Morph.* **77**, 273–295.

MADEN, M. (1983b). The effect of vitamin A on limb regeneration in *Rana temporaria*. *Devl Biol.* **98**, 409–416.

MADEN, M., KEEBLE, S. AND COX, R. A. (1985). The characteristics of local application of retinoic acid to the regenerating axolotl limb. *Roux's Arch. devl. Biol.* **194**, 228–235.

MADEN, M., ONG, D. E., SUMMERBELL, D. AND CHYTIL, F. (1988). Spatial distribution of cellular protein binding to retinoic acid in the chick limb bud. *Nature, Lond.* **335**, 733–735.

MADEN, M., ONG, D. E., SUMMERBELL, D., CHYTIL, F. AND HIRST, E. A. (1989). Cellular retinoic-acid binding protein and the role of retinoic acid in the development of the chick embryo. *Devl Biol.* (submitted).

MADEN, M. AND SUMMERBELL, D. (1986). Retinoic acid-binding protein in the chick limb bud: identification at developmental stages and binding affinities of various retinoids. *J. Embryol. exp. Morph.* **97**, 239–250.

MAVILIO, F., SIMEONE, A., BONCINELLI, E. AND ANDREWS, P. W. (1988). Activation of four homoeobox gene clusters in human embryonal carcinoma cells induced to differentiate by retinoic acid. *Differentiation* **37**, 73–79.

McCORMICK, A., SHUBEITA, H. E. AND STOCUM, D. L. (1988). Cellular retinoic acid binding protein: detection and quantitation in regenerating axolotl limbs. *J. exp. Zool.* **245**, 270–276.

NAPOLI, J. L. AND RACE, K. R. (1987). The biosynthesis of retinoic acid from retinol by rat tissues *in vitro*. *Archs Biochem. biophys.* **255**, 95–101.

NIAZI, I. A., PESCITELLI, M. J. AND STOCUM, D. L. (1985). Stage-dependent effects of retinoic acid on regenerating urodele limbs. *Roux's Arch. devl Biol.* **194**, 355–363.

NIAZI, I. A. AND SAXENA, S. (1978). Abnormal hind limb regeneration in tadpoles of the toad, *Bufo andersoni*, exposed to excess vitamin A. *Folia Biol. (Krakow)* **26**, 3–8.

OLIVER, G., WRIGHT, C. V. E., HARDWICKE, J. AND DE ROBERTIS, E. M. (1988). A gradient of homeodomain protein in developing forlimbs of *Xenopus* and mouse embryos. *Cell* **55**, 1017–1024.

ONG, D. E. (1984). A novel retinol-binding protein from rat. *J. biol. Chem.* **259**, 1476–1482.

ONG, D. E. (1985). Vitamin A-binding proteins. *Nutr. Rev.* **43**, 225–232.

ONG, D. E. AND CHYTIL, F. (1978). Cellular retinoic acid-binding protein from rat testis. Purification and characterisation. *J. biol. Chem.* **253**, 4551–4554.

ONG, D. E., CROW, J. A. AND CHYTIL, F. (1982). Radioimmunochemical determination of cellular retinol- and cellular retinoic acid-binding proteins in cytosols of rat tissues. *J. biol. Chem.* **257**, 13 385–13 389.

OTONELLO, S., PETRUCCI, S. AND MARAINI, G. (1987). Vitamin A uptake from retinol-binding protein in a cell-free system from pigment epithelial cells of bovine retina. *J. biol. Chem.* **262**, 3975–3981.

PETKOVICH, M., BRAND, N. J., KRUST, A. AND CHAMBON, P. (1987). A human retinoic acid receptor which belongs to the family of nuclear receptors. *Nature, Lond.* **330**, 444–450.

ROBERT, B., SASSOON, D., LACQ, B., GEHRING, W. AND BUCKINGHAM, M. (1989). *Hox-7*, a mouse homeobox gene with a novel pattern of expression during embryogenesis. *EMBO J.* **8**, 91–100.

SAARI, J. C., BREDBERG, L. AND GARWIN, G. G. (1982). Identification of the endogenous retinoids associated with three cellular retinoid-binding proteins from bovine retina and retinal pigment epithelium. *J. biol. Chem.* **257**, 13 329–13 333.

SIEGENTHALER, G. AND SAURAT, J. H. (1985). Cellular retinoid-binding proteins in normal and diseased human skin. In *Retinoids: New Trends in Research and Therapy* (ed. J. H. Saurat), pp. 168–174. Basel: Karger.

SUMMERBELL, D. (1983). The effect of local application of retinoic acid to the anterior margin of the developing chick limb. *J. Embryol. exp. Morph.* **78**, 269–289.

SUZUKI, H. R. AND IDE, H. (1987). Positional heterogeneity of interaction between fragments of avian limb bud in organ culture. *Devl Biol.* **124**, 41–49.

TAKASE, S., ONG, D. E. AND CHYTIL, F. (1979). Cellular retinol-binding protein allows specific interaction of retinol with the nucleus *in vitro*. *Proc. natn. Acad. Sci. U.S.A.* **76**, 2204–2208.

TAKASE, S., ONG, D. E. AND CHYTIL, F. (1986). Transfer of retinoic acid from its complex with cellular retinoic acid-binding protein to the nucleus. *Archs Biochem. biophys.* **247**, 328–334.

TESSIER-LAVIGNE, M., PLACZEK, M., LUMSDEN, A. G. S., DODD, J. AND JESSELL, T. M. (1988). Chemotropic guidance of developing axons in the mammalian central nervous system. *Nature, Lond.* **336**, 775–778.

THALLER, C. AND EICHELE, G. (1987). Identification and spatial distribution of retinoids in the developing chick limb bud. *Nature, Lond.* **327**, 625–628.

THOMS, S. D. AND STOCUM, D. L. (1984). Retinoic acid-induced pattern duplication in regenerating urodele limb. *Devl Biol.* **103**, 319–328.

TICKLE, C., ALBERTS, B., WOLPERT, L. AND LEE, J. (1982). Local application of retinoic acid to the limb bond mimics the action of the polarizing region. *Nature, Lond.* **296**, 564–566.

TICKLE, C. AND CRAWLEY, A. (1988). The effects of local application of retinoids to different positions along the proximo-distal axis of embryonic chick wings. *Roux's Arch. devl Biol.* **197**, 27–36.

TICKLE, C., LEE, J. AND EICHELE, G. (1985). A quantitative analysis of the effect of all-*trans*-retinoic acid on the pattern of chick wing development. *Devl Biol.* **109**, 82–95.

TICKLE, C., SUMMERBELL, D. AND WOLPERT, L. (1975). Positional signalling and specification of digits in chick limb morphogenesis. *Nature, Lond.* **254**, 199–202.

WEDDEN, S. E., PANG, K. AND EICHELE, G. (1989). Expression pattern of homeobox-containing genes during chick embryogenesis. *Development* **105**, 639–650.

WOLPERT, L. (1969). Positional information and the spatial pattern of cellular differentiation. *J. theor. Biol.* **25**, 1–47.

WOLPERT, L., LEWIS, J. AND SUMMERBELL, D. (1975). Morphogenesis of the vertebrate limb. In *Cell Patterning* (Ciba Found. Symp. **29**), pp. 95–119. Associated Scientific: Amsterdam.

Development 1989 Supplement, 121–131
Printed in Great Britain © The Company of Biologists Limited 1989

Molecular approaches to vertebrate limb morphogenesis

SUSAN M. SMITH, KEVIN PANG, OLOF SUNDIN, SARAH E. WEDDEN, CHRISTINA THALLER and GREGOR EICHELE

Department of Cellular and Molecular Physiology, Harvard Medical School, 25 Shattuck Street, Boston, MA 02115, USA

Summary

It has long been proposed that concentration gradients of morphogens provide cues to specify cell fate in embryonic fields. Recent work in a variety of vertebrate systems give *bona fide* evidence that retinoic acid, the biologically active form of vitamin A, is a candidate for such a morphogen. In the developing chick wing, for example, locally applied retinoic acid triggers striking changes in the pattern along the anteroposterior axis. Instead of giving rise to a wing with the normal 234 digit pattern, wing buds treated with retinoic acid develop a 432234 mirror-image symmetrical digit pattern.

For this review, we focus on three aspects of limb morphogenesis. (1) We summarize the experimental evidence supporting the notion that retinoic acid is a candidate morphogen. (2) Limb buds contain high levels of cellular retinoic-acid-binding protein (CRABP). Using order of magnitude calculations, we evaluate how the concentration of CRABP might affect the occupancy state of the retinoic acid receptor. (3) We discuss the spatio-temporal expression pattern of homeobox-containing genes in the developing limb and speculate about the possibility that retinoic acid influences the pattern of expression of homeobox genes.

Key words: limb morphogenesis, molecular approach, retinoic acid, homeobox-containing genes, retinoic acid receptor, morphogen gradient, retinoic-acid-binding protein.

1. Retinoic acid, a candidate morphogen in the developing vertebrate limb

A dominant force in embryonic development is the coordinate expression of the genetic program (Davidson, 1986). For example, early insect pattern formation is orchestrated at least in part by a network of transcriptional regulators, i.e. nuclear proteins that act in a cell-autonomous fashion (Akam *et al.* 1988; Ingham, 1988). However, cells in an embryo do not necessarily behave autonomously but are influenced by a variety of extracellular signals, some of which act over short distances (cell–matrix interactions) while others are long-range signals acting over many cell diameters. One can guess that long-range signals are especially helpful if embryos consist of a large number of cells that have to develop in a coordinate fashion (Wolpert, 1969; Crick, 1970; Meinhardt, 1982). Well-known examples of extracellular signals that can influence cell fate and cell differentiation are growth factors that interact with cell surface receptors (e.g. Smith, 1989), and small molecule hormones (e.g. steroids, thyroid hormones) that bind to specific nuclear receptor proteins (e.g. Evans, 1988; Beato, 1989).

Is there any evidence that small molecule substances take part in pattern formation? Saunders and Gasseling (1968) discovered that transplanting posterior chick wing bud mesenchyme to the anterior margin of a host

wing bud results in a mirror-image symmetrical duplication of the host's hand plate. Instead of the normal pattern with digits **2**, **3**, and **4**, a **432234** pattern will frequently develop (Fig. 1). The tissue capable of inducing duplications is known as zone of polarizing activity (ZPA) or polarizing region. ZPA activity is not species specific as it is found in all amniotes so far examined (reviewed in Tickle, 1980). Moreover, selected other embryonic tissues such as ventral (but not dorsal) tail bud mesenchyme (Saunders and Gasseling, 1983) and Hensen's node (Hornbruch and Wolpert, 1986) induce duplications when grafted into the chick wing or leg bud. One interpretation of the fact that other tissues are biologically active in the duplication assay is that the ZPA is a non-specific inducer (see e.g. Saunders and Gasseling, 1983). However, an equally valid argument is that at a molecular and cellular level, the mechanism of pattern formation in different parts of the embryo are related.

Wolpert and colleagues (e.g. Tickle *et al.* 1975) have suggested that the ZPA releases a diffusible, labile morphogen that spreads across the limb bud and thereby forms a concentration gradient. The character of each digit would be specified by the concentration of the morphogen. The model of a diffusible small molecule signalling compound has been contested. Iten and colleagues, for example, have proposed that the limb pattern is formed as a consequence of local interactions between cells (see e.g. Javois, 1984; Bryant and Muneoka, 1986). Oster *et al.* (1985) put forward a model of limb morphogenesis that is based on a combination of matrix deswelling and mechanical forces between cells. However, when these models were proposed little was known about their cellular and molecular basis. Therefore, it is essential to find the ZPA morphogen or to identify the specific molecules that can account for the postulated pattern generating cell–cell interactions.

Is there a rationale to identify a morphogen molecule? The ZPA has a volume $\leqslant 0.1\,\mu l$. Assuming a morphogen concentration of $20\,nM$ and a molecular weight of the morphogen of 300, then 1000 ZPAs would contain less than one nanogram of morphogen. Without prior knowledge of its chemical properties the morphogen would be extremely difficult to identify. Not discouraged by these considerations, Alberts and Tickle as early as 1976 began to search for the putative ZPA morphogen (Bruce M. Alberts, personal communication). They believed it to be a hydrophobic substance because a hydrophobic molecule could readily diffuse laterally in the plasma membrane and thus move from one cell to the next without having to transverse the voluminous, hydrophilic extracellular matrix and also to risk entering a capillary and be removed from the limb bud. Alberts and Tickle prepared organic solvent extracts of ZPA tissue. The extracts were absorbed onto small inert beads that were then implanted like ZPA to the anterior wing bud margin (Bruce M. Alberts, personal communication). In addition, Alberts and Tickle impregnated beads with various 'off the shelf' compounds such as dibutyryl cyclic AMP or thalidomide and implanted the beads into buds. None of these efforts led to altered limb patterns, yet as we

will see below the reasoning and strategy were basically correct.

In the early eighties, Tickle and colleagues (1982) and also Summerbell (1983) discovered that retinoic-acid-impregnated pieces of DEAE paper, newsprint or ion exchange beads induce pattern duplications when implanted at the anterior wing bud margin (Fig. 1). Subsequent work showed that in addition to inducing morphologically identical duplications, ZPA grafts and retinoic acid treatment display a very similar dose-, time- and position-dependence (Table 1). This similarity led to the obvious question of whether retinoic acid is the morphogen proposed by the above gradient model. Alternatively, might retinoic acid simply convert cells surrounding the implant into ZPA, which in turn provides the actual signal? There is in fact some support for this suggestion, because tissue next to the retinoic-acid-releasing implant can give rise to duplications when grafted into a host bud (Summerbell and Harvey, 1983). As pointed out by Tickle *et al.* (1985), the two possibilities are not necessarily mutually exclusive. It could be that retinoic acid released from the implant indeed generates ZPA but that at the same time this induced ZPA also synthesizes and releases retinoic acid. To resolve these issues it is important to determine whether ZPA cells can synthesize retinoic acid. A first step in this direction has been the demonstration that limb buds can synthesize retinoic acid *in situ* from its biosynthetic precursor retinol (Thaller and Eichele, 1988). To demonstrate *in situ* metabolism, beads impregnated with [³H]retinol were implanted at the posterior wing bud margin next to the ZPA. A number of metabolites were generated in this assay, including retinal (the intermediate between retinol and retinoic acid) and retinoic acid. It will now be important to

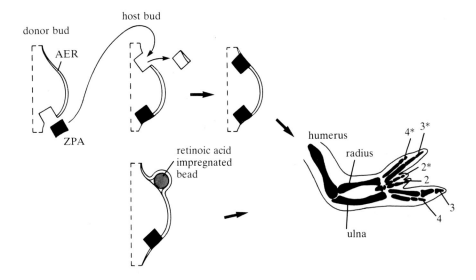

Fig. 1. Grafting posterior mesenchyme – the ZPA – from a donor chick limb bud to the anterior margin of a host wing bud results in the formation of additional digits. The digit pattern shown here is a **432234** pattern with additional digits **2**, **3**, and **4** (marked with an asterisk). It must be realized that the ZPA is defined only by this grafting assay and is histologically indistinguishable from the surrounding mesenchymal tissue. Morphologically identical duplications are obtained by locally releasing retinoic acid from an anteriorly implanted bead. The bead is tucked underneath the apical ectodermal ridge (AER) opposite the ZPA.

Table 1. *Comparison between ZPA and retinoic acid releasing beads*

Observation	ZPA implants	retinoic acid application
pattern duplication is dose dependent	additional **2** requires 30 cells[a] additional **3** requires 70 cells additional **4** requires ⩾130 cells	additional **2** requires ⩽5 nM[b] additional **3** requires 10 nM additional **4** requires 25 nM
position dependence	anterior: mirror-image duplications from either treatment posterior: normal pattern from either treatment[b,c] tip of wing bud: additional digits, no mirror symmetry from either treatment[c,d]	
induction of additional digits requires prolonged treatment	graft removed after[e] 13 h: normal pattern 15 h: additional **2** 17 h: additional **3**	bead removed after[f] 10 h: normal pattern 13 h: additional **2** 15 h: additional **3** 17 h: additional **4**

[a] Tickle, 1981.
[b] Tickle *et al.* 1985 and unpublished data by C. Thaller and G. Eichele.
[c] for ZPA see e.g. Tickle *et al.* 1975.
[d] the observations with retinoic acid are work in progress by G. Eichele.
[e] Smith, 1980.
[f] Eichele *et al.* 1985.

compare the rate of conversion of retinol to retinoic acid in ZPA and non-ZPA tissue to find out whether the ZPA is special with regard to retinoic acid production.

A question of considerable interest is whether applied retinoic acid forms a concentration gradient across the limb bud or whether the blood circulating in the vascularized limb bud would prevent the establishment of a stable gradient. Initial studies performed with retinoic acid showed that retinoids can generate a concentration gradient in the limb bud (Tickle *et al.* 1985). Detailed analyses by Eichele and Thaller (1987) using the morphogenetically active synthetic retinoid TTNPB (E-4-[2-(5,6,7, 8-tetrahydro-5,5,8,8-tetramethyl-2-naphthalenyl)-1-propenyl]benzoic acid) showed that the distribution of applied retinoids along the anteroposterior axis was exponential, and that stable gradients can be set up (Fig. 2). However, if the bead was removed, the gradient collapsed within a few hours (Eichele *et al.* 1985). This observation implies that the gradient of applied retinoid (TTNPB or retinoic acid) is a steady-state gradient, i.e. its maintenance requires the continuous presence of a source that is balanced by a 'sink' in the form of clearance by blood circulation and by enzymatic degradation of the retinoid.

The diffusion coefficient (D) of TTNPB in the limb bud is about 10^{-7} cm^2 s^{-1} (Eichele and Thaller, 1987). This value for D suggests that retinoids are not freely diffusible, but interact with cellular retinoic-acid-binding protein that is found in the limb bud (Kwarta *et al.* 1985; Maden and Summerbell, 1986). Knowing D affords an estimate of the time required to establish a diffusion gradient as 3 to 4 hours. This time span is in a range compatible with the time scale of pattern specification in developing vertebrate limbs. The main conclusion is that retinoids provided from a local source such as a bead or the ZPA can readily set up a diffusion gradient in the limb bud, but that it is necessary to maintain the source, otherwise the gradient will dissipate. In a broader sense, these studies demonstrate that

diffusion gradients of hydrophobic substances are feasible in tissues.

The seminal discovery of the effect of retinoic acid on limb morphogenesis prompted the obvious question of whether limb buds contain endogenous retinoic acid. To find out, Thaller and Eichele (1987) extracted homogenates of large numbers of limb buds with organic solvent mixtures. The extracts were analyzed by high-performance liquid chromatography (HPLC). These analyses clearly demonstrated the presence of all-*trans*-retinol, all-*trans*-retinoic acid, and all-*trans*-retinal, as well as approximately 6 additional retinoids whose identities are currently being determined (Thaller and Eichele, unpublished observations). A limb bud at Hamburger–Hamilton stage 21, a stage when applied retinoic acid induces extra digits, contains about 6.5 pg of endogenous retinoic acid, corresponding to a mean tissue concentration of 25 nM. This is close to the concentration needed in the bud tissue to induce a full set of additional digits (20–30 nM). Hence physiological doses of applied retinoic acid induce duplications. The tissue level of all-*trans*-retinol at stage 21 is approximately 600 nM and that of all-*trans*-retinal about 10 nM. It is important to realize that the concentrations given here are total retinoid concentrations. A substantial fraction of each retinoid is probably specifically bound to protein (see below), but extraction with organic solvents will denature these proteins and release the bound ligand.

To examine whether retinoic acid is enriched in the posterior region, as one would expect if retinoic acid is the morphogen released by the ZPA, limb buds were dissected into a smaller posterior portion containing the ZPA and a larger ZPA-free anterior piece (see Fig. 3, insert). The concentration of retinoic acid in each of the two pieces was determined by HPLC and is shown in Fig. 3. It amounts to 50 nM posteriorly and 20 nM anteriorly. Hence there is 2.5 times more RA in the ZPA than in non-ZPA tissue. By contrast, retinol is almost uniformly partitioned at a concentration of

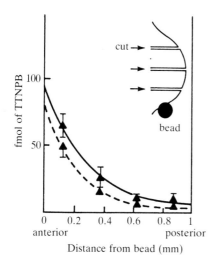

Fig. 2. Spatial distribution of ^{3}H-TTNPB (a synthetic retinoic acid analog) in the chick wing bud that is found following treatment for 9 h (solid line) or 15 h (broken line). The TTNPB-releasing bead was implanted at the anterior wing bud margin. The dose used in this experiment would generate a full set of additional digits. After 9 and 15 h of incubation *in ovo*, the bead was removed and the bud was dissected into four blocks of roughly equal size (see insert). Blocks of about 20 treated buds were pooled and the amount of TTNPB was determined by HPLC and scintillation counting. Note, cells localized anteriorly are exposed to a 5- to 10-fold higher concentration of TTNPB than cells located posteriorly.

approximately 600 nm. It goes without saying that retinoic acid will not be distributed in a step-wise fashion (Fig. 3), but since retinoic acid is a small molecule, it will spread across the limb bud in the form of a smooth gradient. We assume that this gradient resembles that of TTNPB shown in Fig. 2. If we accept this line of reasoning, it becomes clear that the gradient of endogenous retinoic acid would span a concentration range of about half an order of magnitude. This implies that cells in the limb bud would have to sense relatively small concentration differences. That they are capable of doing this can be deduced from the dose–response analyses: it was found that to generate a pattern with an additional digit **4** requires about 5 to 10 times more retinoic acid or TTNPB than is required to form a pattern with an extra digit **2** (Tickle *et al.* 1985; Eichele and Thaller, 1987). Possibly, sensing a shallow gradient requires some form of an amplification mechanism (de The *et al.* 1989). However, while important for the detailed mechanism of action, such a mechanistic issue should not detract from the main point that cells are able to interpret small changes in retinoic acid concentration.

How do cells 'measure' retinoic acid? This question touches upon a central yet poorly understood aspect of gradient models, that of thresholds (Slack, 1987). The idea is that a particular threshold concentration of a morphogen specifies a certain structure such as a digit **4** (high concentration) or a digit **2** (low concentration). If the concentration difference between the high and the

low end of a gradient were 10000 fold, it would be easy to establish distinct threshold levels. However, the laws of diffusion preclude gradients of small molecules to be so steep, at least over the dimension of a limb bud. One is faced then with the problem of how a shallow gradient can be read and interpreted in such a way as to specify a sequence of digits. The burden of this task is most likely put on the 'recording mechanism', much in the same way as the measurement of weak signals, e.g. light from a distant star, depends on a sophisticated recording device.

A critical element of this recording mechanism almost certainly is the retinoic acid receptor which has molecular properties suitable for the measurement and interpretation of a gradient. So far, three distinct receptors for retinoic acid (RAR) have been reported. They are known as α retinoic acid receptor (αRAR), β retinoic acid receptor (βRAR) (Guiguère *et al.* 1987; Petkovich *et al.* 1987; Benbrook *et al.* 1988; Brand *et al.* 1988) and γ retinoic acid receptor (γRAR) (Krust *et al.* 1989; Zelent *et al.* 1989). The three RARs are encoded on separate genes, but their sequences reveal that they are highly homologous and that they belong to a multigene family that includes the receptors for steroid hormones, thyroid hormones and vitamin D_3. It is well established that these receptors are transcription factors that upon ligand binding are targeted to specific regulatory sequences in the 5′ region of ligand-controlled genes (e.g. Evans, 1988; Beato, 1989). As a consequence of receptor binding, the target gene is activated. Hence αRAR, βRAR and γRAR provide a direct link between the small molecule ligand and the expression of yet to be identified target genes (see also below). It is worth noting that hormone receptors can be very diverse, as best exemplified by the thyroid hormone receptor family (Sap *et al.* 1986; Weinberger *et al.* 1986), which displays alternative splicing (Izumo and Mahdavi, 1988; Hodin *et al.* 1989), opposite-strand transcription (Lazar *et al.* 1989; Miyajiama *et al.* 1989) and negative transcriptional regulation (Damm *et al.* 1989). It is possible that the receptors for retinoic acid exhibit a similar diversity. This would be valuable for a fine tuning of transcriptional regulation.

2. The effect of cellular retinoic-acid-binding protein on the concentration of free retinoic acid and on the occupancy of retinoic acid receptor

A major unresolved question is how the shallow gradient of retinoic acid (see Figs 2 and 3) can account for the formation of several distinct digits. The problem is particularly intriguing because the experimentally determined mean concentration of endogenous retinoic acid in the limb bud is about 20–30 nm, while the K_d for the steroid hormone receptor family (to which the receptor for retinoic acid belongs) typically ranges between 0.05 and 0.6 nm (Green *et al.* 1986; Weinberger *et al.* 1986; Sap *et al.* 1986; Benbrook and Pfahl, 1987; Dobson *et al.* 1989). The dilemma is that at such a high ligand concentration, all RAR molecules would be

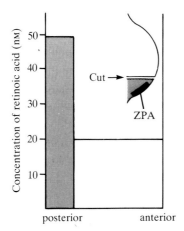

Fig. 3. Concentration of retinoic acid in the anterior and posterior region of a stage 21 limb buds (for stages of chick development see Hamburger and Hamilton, 1951). Approximately 1000 wing and leg buds were dissected into a posterior block (shaded area, 0.2 μl volume), which includes the ZPA, and a larger anterior block (open area, 0.6 μl volume). The amount of retinoic acid in each block was quantified by HPLC. The width of each rectangle is proportional to the volume of the posterior and anterior tissue block. The height of the rectangles represents the concentration of retinoic acid.

saturated with ligand, which precludes any form of regulation. If retinoic acid and its gradient have any role in pattern specification, then the concentration of free retinoic acid in the limb bud cells must somehow be lowered to a value in the range of the dissociation constant of RAR. The way to resolve this issue is to realize that limb buds contain much more cellular retinoic-acid-binding protein (CRABP) than RAR. Hence, most retinoic acid is actually bound to CRABP, resulting in a free retinoic acid concentration within the range of a K_d typical for a nuclear receptor. In what follows we will calculate the concentration of free retinoic acid in the cell under the assumption that the system is in equilibrium.

As can be seen in Fig. 3, the total retinoic acid concentration in the posterior quarter of the limb bud is 50 nM, and 20 nM in the anterior three quarters. Fig. 2 shows that a retinoid locally applied from a bead will spread across the limb bud in the form of an exponential (see also Eichele and Thaller, 1987). It is reasonable to assume that endogenous retinoic acid distributes in a similar fashion and not stepwise as the experimentally determined distribution of Fig. 3 seems to suggest. The question is what concentration range the endogenous retinoic acid gradient spans. For the following order of magnitude calculations, we will use a gradient of 70 nM (posterior) to 15 nM (anterior). Comparison of Figs 2 and 3 suggests that these values are reasonable, although they are of course *not* experimentally determined.

How much of the total retinoic acid is inside cells? It is not known how retinoic acid is partitioned between the cell and the extracellular matrix. However, CRABP is abundant in cells, while no retinoid-binding proteins

have been detected in the extracellular matrix. Hence, we will assume that most retinoic acid is cellular. CRABP and RAR are the two known cellular proteins that tightly bind retinoic acid (there are certainly metabolic enzymes that interact with retinoic acid, but they remain unidentified and probably are not abundant). Limb bud CRABP has been characterized, and has an apparent K_d of 2.0–2.2 nM (Kwarta *et al.* 1985), similar to the K_d of CRABP that was isolated from testis (4 nM; Ong and Chytil, 1978). An unusually high apparent K_d of 140–280 nM was reported for chick limb bud CRABP by Maden and Summerbell (1986); the reason for this discrepancy is unclear. We will use a K_d of 2 nM. Both papers are in agreement on the CRABP content in limb bud: 25 pmol mg^{-1} cytosolic protein (Kwarta *et al.* 1985) and 14–28 pmol mg^{-1} cytosolic protein (Maden and Summberell, 1986). Given that a stage 21 limb bud has a volume of 0.75 μl (Eichele and Thaller, 1987), a cytosolic protein content of about 15 μg per bud (C. Thaller, unpublished observation), and an average CRABP content of 20 pmol mg^{-1}, the estimated concentration of CRABP amounts to about 400 nM. CRABP is not uniformly distributed across the chick limb bud (Maden *et al.* 1988). False color-image analysis of immunohistochemically stained CRABP in limb bud sections reveals that the CRABP gradient is about 3-fold, and in opposite direction to the gradient of ligand. These authors make the point that a CRABP gradient opposing that of retinoic acid steepens the gradient of free retinoic acid.

We can estimate the amount of bound and free retinoic acid, in the presence of CRABP and RAR as follows:

$$[RA_{total}] = [RA_{free}] + [RA \cdot CRABP] + [RA \cdot RAR] \tag{1a}$$

It seems reasonable to assume that the cellular concentration of RAR is similar to that of other nuclear receptors (3 to 7 nM; Koblinsky *et al.* 1972; Katzenellenbogen *et al.* 1983). Because $[CRABP_{total}] \gg [RAR_{tot}]$ equation (1a) can be simplified to

$$[RA_{total}] = [RA_{free}] + [RA \cdot CRABP] \tag{1b}$$

where $[RA_{total}]$ is the experimentally determined concentration of retinoic acid depicted in Fig. 3. Moreover

$$[CRABP_{total}] = [CRABP_{free}] + [RA \cdot CRABP] \tag{2}$$

Substituting equations (1b) and (2) in terms of $[RA_{free}]$ yields

$$[RA \cdot CRABP] = [RA_{total}] - [RA_{free}] \tag{3}$$

$$[CRABP_{free}] = [CRABP_{total}] - \{[RA_{total}] - [RA_{free}]\} \tag{4}$$

since

$$K_d = [RA_{free}][CRABP_{free}]/[RA \cdot CRABP] \tag{5}$$

substituting (3) and (4) into (5) yields

$$K_d = \frac{[RA_{free}]([CRABP_{total}] - [RA_{total}] + [RA_{free}])}{[RA_{total}] - [RA_{free}]} \tag{6}$$

Table 2. *Theoretical concentration of free retinoic acid as a function of the concentration of CRABP and total retinoic acid*

	[CRABP$_{total}$]	[RA$_{total}$]	[RA$_{free}$]	p/a ratio of [RA$_{free}$]
anterior	400 nM	20 nM	0.105 nM	1
posterior	400 nM	20 nM	0.105 nM	
anterior	400 nM	70 nM	0.420 nM	5.4
posterior	400 nM	15 nM	0.078 nM	
anterior	200 nM	70 nM	1.052 nM	20.6
posterior	600 nM	15 nM	0.051 nM	
posterior	10 nM	70 nM	60.32 nM	1600
anterior	800 nM	15 nM	0.038 nM	

Equation (6) can be rearranged to calculate [RA$_{free}$], the unbound retinoic acid available for binding to RAR. Table 2 shows the results of such calculations for four scenarios: (1) no gradients (lines 1 and 2), (2) a 4.6-fold retinoic acid gradient (lines 3 and 4), (3) a 4.6-fold retinoic acid gradient and an opposite 3-fold CRABP gradient (lines 5 and 6), (4) a 4.6-fold retinoic acid gradient and a very steep CRABP gradient (lines 7 and 8). Two interesting conclusions can be drawn from Table 2:

(1) A comparison of [RA$_{total}$] with [RA$_{free}$] clearly shows that, except for the scenario of line 7, most retinoic acid will be bound to CRABP. Hence, as qualitatively predicted above, the concentration of free retinoic acid is indeed in the range of the K_d of a nuclear receptor.

(2) If CRABP is uniformly distributed, the gradient of free and total retinoic acid are similar (5.4- vs. 4.6-fold) and shallow. However, a merely 3-fold CRABP gradient in the opposite direction will give rise to a 20-fold gradient of free retinoic acid. The striking conclusion from these first approximations is that the combination of ligand and binding protein puts the free retinoic acid concentration into such a range where moderate changes in ligand concentration that occur in space (Fig. 3) and time (Thaller and Eichele, in preparation) could result in substantial changes of receptor occupancy and a concomitant change of receptor-mediated transactivation.

These approximate calculations invite speculation on the role of CRABP in development. For example, a cell could regulate its retinoic acid sensitivity simply by altering CRABP expression, in addition to directly regulating retinoic acid concentrations. Thus, local domains of varying retinoid sensitivity can be created without having to alter the entire organism's circulating retinoid levels. To think along these lines is especially attractive in view of the observations that retinoic acid seems to regulate cellular retinol-binding protein and perhaps CRABP expression as well (Kato *et al.* 1985). Thus a modest retinoic acid gradient can be converted to a potent signal, by interactions with CRABP and RAR.

3. Differential expression of homeobox-containing genes in the developing limb

An important advance in understanding the mechanisms of pattern formation was made possible by the discovery of the homeobox, a 180 bp motif that encodes the DNA-binding domain of a multigene family of transcriptional regulators (see Gehring, 1987; Herr *et al.* 1989 and references therein). Genes containing a homeobox were first discovered in the genome of *Drosophila melanogaster* (McGinnis *et al.* 1984a; Scott and Weiner, 1984). A combination of genetic studies with analyses of the spatiotemporal expression pattern in wild-type and mutant embryos has demonstrated that the orchestrated expression of this class of genes contributes in an important way to the specification of the body pattern in insects (reviewed e.g. in Akam *et al.* 1988; Ingham, 1988). McGinnis *et al.* (1984b) were the first to show that the homeobox is also present in the genomes of vertebrates. This raised the question of whether the high degree of conservation of gene structure implies conservation of corresponding functions in such disparate organisms as insects and mammals. The answer to this question is not easily forthcoming. In *Drosophila*, the spatial expression pattern of homeobox genes can be correlated with subsequently formed structures, e.g. *Ubx* and *Antp* expression specifies metameric identities (e.g. Scott *et al.* 1983; Peifer *et al.* 1987). In vertebrates such correlations are not as straightforward to establish. Moreover, the most valuable insights in the case of *Drosophila* have come from comparisons of the expression patterns in wild-type embryos and in loss-of-function or null mutants, a route that is presently not accessible for vertebrate systems.

In the past four years, a number of laboratories have embarked on the strategy of spatially and temporally mapping the expression of various homeobox genes during embryonic development of several vertebrate organisms, most notably the mouse (reviewed e.g. by Dressler and Gruss, 1988 and Wright *et al.* 1989). These studies demonstrate that most homeobox genes are clustered in the genome, that they are regionally expressed and that their spatiotemporal expression pattern is developmentally regulated. Similar to the situation in *Drosophila*, the expression pattern along the anteroposterior axis reflects the position of the genes in the cluster (e.g. Duboule and Dollé, 1989; Graham *et al.* 1989). While it is attractive to think that homeobox genes define the organization of the vertebrate embryo in a similar way as they do in the fly, that is, by combinatorial patterns of expression, such a view needs much more experimental substantiation than is currently available. A potentially fruitful avenue towards understanding the role of homeobox genes in vertebrate pattern formation are interspecies comparisons of homolog expression patterns. Classical embryology has gained much from comparative studies and such an approach might also be fruitful at a molecular level. While this strategy is still relatively new, a few interesting observations and insights have emerged. In keeping with the general theme of this review, the data discussed below pertain mainly to the developing limb.

Development of the limb can be divided into two phases. During the first phase the limb bud forms by a bulging out of the embryonic flank. At this stage the bud consists of apparently uniform mesenchyme encased in a jacket of ectoderm. During the second phase the mesenchyme terminally differentiates into an intricate pattern of tissues such as cartilate, bone, muscle, dermis etc. In the chick, the first phase encompasses Hamburger–Hamilton stages 16 to 22/23, while the second phase goes from stage 23 onward. The corresponding stages in mouse are day 8.75 to day 10.75, and day 10.75 onward. Experimental manipulations in the chick that result in a change of pattern must be performed during the first phase to be effective. For example, the local application of retinoic acid yields digit duplications only if performed prior to Hamburger–Hamilton stage 22 (Summerbell, 1983). Thus it makes sense to assume that the global pattern of the limb is specified primarily during the first phase of development; hence gene expression studies aimed at pattern formation ought to focus on phase 1. In what follows we will briefly discuss recent studies that have revealed regionalized (i.e. non-uniform) expression of homeobox genes in limb buds of mouse, *Xenopus* and chicken.

Among the first studies to demonstrate regionalized expression of homeobox genes was that of Oliver *et al.* (1988; for a schematic illustration of the spatial expression pattern of this and the other homeoboxes, see Fig. 4). Using an antibody, they observed that in *Xenopus* embryos, XlHbox 1 protein is expressed in both ectoderm and mesenchyme in the forelimb, but in the hind limb is expressed only in the ectodermal layer. They further observed that XlHbox 1 protein forms a gradient that runs from anterior to posterior, and proximal to distal. Staining of forelimbs of mouse and chick with the same antibody reiterates this pattern of expression (Oliver *et al.* 1988, 1989). Examination of older mouse embryos shows that expression is transient, because by day 13 (approximately stage 27 in chick), staining is extremely weak and limited to the distal ectoderm (Oliver *et al.* 1988). The authors suggest that XlHbox 1 may play a morphogenetic role in the limb, and is perhaps repressed by retinoic acid, whose concentration gradient runs counter to that of XlHbox 1 protein. This hypothesis is provocative in light of recent studies which have examined the newt homolog of XlHbox 1 (NvHbox 1 or FH-2) as a gene possibly playing a role in limb regeneration (Savard *et al.* 1988; Tabin, 1989). Expression of NvHbox 1 is clearly higher in proximal than distal blastema. It is well established that application of retinoic acid to regenerating urodele limbs proximalizes the regenerate (Maden, 1982; Thoms and Stocum, 1984). If distal blastema are first generated by amputation, and the animals are then treated with retinoic acid, one might expect that the proximalizing effect of retinoic acid increases the level of NvHbox 1 transcripts. Neither study found such an increase. Savard *et al.* (1988) as well as Tabin (1989)

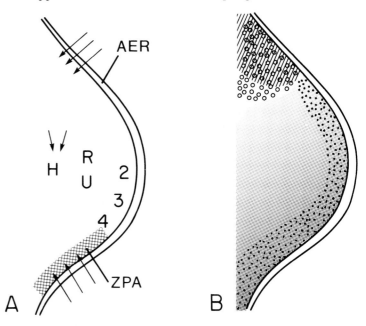

Fig. 4. Idealized scheme of a limb bud of a stage 20 embryo indicating various domains of known fate or function (A) and the expression pattern of homeobox genes in the limb mesenchyme (B). A shows a fate map (Stark and Searls, 1973; Hinchliffe *et al.* 1981) of the chicken wing to indicate the location of the cells that will form humerus (H), radius, (R), ulna (U) and the three digits (**2,3,4**). The shaded area demarcates the zone of polarizing activity (ZPA). The apical ectodermal ridge (AER) reaches around the buds periphery. Arrows are directed where in subsequent stages programmed cell death will take place (for details see e.g. Hinchliffe and Ede, 1973). B displays a schematic representation of the domains of expression of Xlbox 1 (open circles), Ghox 2.1 (stippled), Hox 5.2 (solid, shaded gradient) and Hox 7.1 (dots along periphery). For details see Text. Note that the expression patterns are *idealized* and that the actual stages of limb development examined in the various studies may be slightly different. In addition, the data shown are compiled from several different species.

suggests that NvHbox 1 may either not be involved in the specification of the proximodistal axis or that retinoic acid interferes at a level that does not involve the regulation of NvHbox 1 expression.

Using another antibody probe, Oliver *et al.* (1989) have recently characterized the expression pattern of Hox 5.2 in early mouse, frog and chick limb buds. They found that Hox 5.2 expression is complementary to that seen with XlHbox 1. Moreover, Hox 5.2 is predominantly expressed in the distally located progress zone, a region harboring the pool of undifferentiated cells that are responsible for limb outgrowth (Summerbell *et al.* 1973). Hence, Hox 5.2 could be involved in regulation of limb outgrowth. Dollé and Duboule (1989) have independently isolated Hox 5.2 and their *in situ* hybridization studies reveal a pattern identical to that reported by Oliver and colleagues. Oliver *et al.* suggest that one of the reasons for XlHbox 1 and Hox 5.2 being expressed in two non-overlapping sets of cells could be mutual repression. Homeobox cross-regulation is not unprecedented, e.g. in *Drosophila Ubx* represses *Antp*

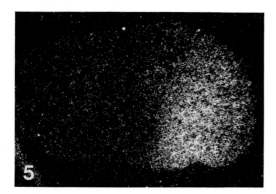

Fig. 5. Spatial distribution of Ghox 2.1 transcripts in a forelimb bud of a stage 22 chick embryo revealed by *in situ* hybridization. The section passes through the proximal region of the bud. Posterior is to the left and dorsal to the top. The highest density of grains is found in the anteroproximal region of the bud.

transcription by direct binding of *Ubx* proteins to DNA sequences near the *Antp* P1 promoter (Hafen *et al.* 1984; Carroll *et al.* 1986; Beachy *et al.* 1988).

A third example of a homeobox gene that is non-uniformly expressed in the limb bud is Hox 7.1. *In situ* hybridization showed that in early mouse limb buds of 9.5 days (forelimb is equivalent to stage 20/21 chick) Hox 7.1 is expressed distally, in the progress zone (Robert *et al.* 1989; Hill *et al.* 1989). The authors raise the possibility that Hox 7.1 is associated with mesenchymal–ectodermal interactions since it is expressed in the progress zone that lies directly underneath the apical ectodermal ridge (AER). In the chick limb bud, the AER is necessary for normal development of the underlying mesenchyme and *vice versa* (Kieny, 1960, 1968). For example, if the ridge is removed, the resulting limb is truncated (Saunders, 1948; Summerbell, 1974). Moreover, grafting of a piece of flank ectoderm onto the dorsal face of the limb bud leads to a second AER and subsequently to a super-numerary limb (Carrington and Fallon, 1986). Hill *et al.* (1989), who have also studied Hox 7.1 expression in mouse embryos, make the additional point that in early limb buds (9.5 days), Hox 7.1 is expressed at high levels along the posterior margin (see their Fig. 7F). This region coincides with the ZPA. In later limb buds (13.5 days), maximal expression of Hox 7.1 is found in the tissue of the interdigital spaces; that is, in those cells that are destined to die (Saunders and Gasseling, 1962). Thus the initial pattern of expression seen may not only pertain to mesenchymal–ectodermal interactions, but may also be a preparatory stage for later, more focused expression in the interdigital spaces.

An *in situ* hybridization study showed that the chicken homeobox gene Ghox 2.1 is expressed in the proximoanterior portion of the bud (Fig. 5). The domain of expression does not correlate with subsequent cytodifferentiation patterns. Wedden *et al.* (1989) have pointed out that part of the region of Ghox 2.1 expression later undergoes programmed cell death (Fig. 4A). However, they emphasize that Ghox 2.1 is

unlikely to act as a global signal for inducing cell death in the limb, because no similar zone of expression is seen along the posterior margin that also undergoes programmed cell death (see Fig. 4A).

Northern analysis of RNA shows that the following homeobox genes are also expressed in the developing or regenerating limb: in chicken homeobox genes, Ghox 1.6, 2.2, 2.3 (Sundin, Pang and Eichele, unpublished data; Wedden *et al.* 1989), in newt, FH-1 (Tabin, 1989), in humans homeobox gene c1 (Simeone *et al.* 1987) and, in the mouse, the *En-1* (Joyner and Martin, 1987; Davis and Joyner, 1988) genes. It will be important to see whether some of these transcripts are non-uniformly expressed in the limb bud. What is also needed is a systematic examination of the expression pattern of all known homeobox genes at the critical stages of limb formation. The description of the normal expression pattern will have to be complemented by analyses of limb buds of mutant embryos or of embryos whose limb buds are experimentally manipulated.

In sum: it is clear from this synopsis that the early limb rudiment, despite being a rather simple tissue, undergoes complex changes in gene expression that precede terminal differentiation. The homeobox genes mentioned here are expressed in a very distinct spatio-temporal pattern in the limb bud. Their pattern of expression does not simply anticipate or reflect the arrangement of subsequently generated terminally differentiated tissues, but forms a prepattern that perhaps subdivides the limb into regions of specific morphogenetic fate.

4. Retinoic acid and regulation of gene expression

Since the receptors of RA are transcriptional regulators, it is likely that retinoic acid affects pattern formation through the regulation of one or more key genes early during development of the limb bud. At present it is not known which genes are directly regulated by retinoic acid, but there are some promising candidates. For example, it has been found that retinoic acid treatment will induce the expression of several homeobox genes, either in differentiating teratocarcinoma cells (e.g. Colberg-Poley *et al.* 1985; Deschamps *et al.* 1987; Schulze *et al.* 1987; Mavilio *et al.* 1988; Dony and Gruss, 1988; La Rosa and Gudas, 1988*b*) or in primary cultures of embryonic brain (Deschamps *et al.* 1987). The most comprehensive analysis of a homeobox gene induced by RA treatment of teratocarcinoma cells has been performed by La Rosa and Gudas (1988*a,b*). They carried out a differential screen to identify any mRNA species that selectively increase early upon retinoic-acid-induced differentiation of mouse F9 teratocarcinoma cells and obtained a cDNA clone of homeobox gene Hox 1.6. Both induction and maintenance of Hox 1.6 expression required the continuous presence of retinoic acid. Experiments with inhibitors of RNA and protein synthesis suggested but did not prove transcriptional regulation, as data from *in vitro* nuclear run-off transcription were not reported. Hence, a second possibility is that retinoic acid stabilizes Hox 1.6 mRNA. Finally, induction of Hox 1.6 might also be a secondary effect, due to other changes in the F9 cells that accompany the early commitment to differentiation. Strong evidence for the regulation of transcription could be obtained by fusing the upstream region of a retinoic-acid-induced gene to a reporter gene, and then showing that this reporter gene is also induced by retinoic acid. This approach allows one to dissect the regulatory region into DNA sequence elements responsible for regulation by retinoic acid. Should these sequence elements also be sites that bind RAR, this would provide strong evidence that RAR directly regulates the gene.

A particularly illuminating example of the gene fusion approach is provided by a recent study of growth hormone (GH) transcription. Bedo *et al.* (1989) have found that retinoic acid treatment of human GH1 pituitary cells leads to a dramatic increase in GH expression especially when retinoic acid is applied in conjunction with either glucocorticoids or thyroid hormone. This same synergism is observed when one measures the expression of a CAT reporter gene fused to the growth hormone 5′ regulatory region, supporting the view that, in this case, regulation by retinoic acid is at the level of transcription. Umesono *et al.* (1988) have also shown that a short DNA sequence, the thyroid hormone response element, can confer retinoic acid inducibility upon a neutral reporter gene. This is an intriguing observation in view of the 62 % protein sequence homology between the DNA recognition domains of human RAR and human β thyroid hormone receptor, and suggests the possibility of competition or synergism between the two receptors for cognate regulatory sites. Finally, there might exist morphogenetically active compounds other than retinoic acid. If other morphogens are present in the limb bud, it is possible that their receptors interact with RAR to specify cell fate and pattern formation. This mode of action is reminiscent of the intricate regulatory network through which the bithorax complex, for example, assigns segment identities to the *Drosophila* embryo (Peifer *et al.* 1987).

In conclusion, the establishment of the anteroposterior limb pattern can now be rephrased in terms of a signal transduction mechanism consisting of (1) the enzyme(s) that synthesize retinoic acid, (2) the signal in the form of retinoic acid, (3) receptors that function as retinoic-acid-dependent transcription factors, and (4) target genes that are responsible for generating the actual pattern. The question posed at the beginning of this review was whether there is any evidence for the old idea that small molecules are involved in pattern formation. It seems to us that a broad variety of experiments, in part reviewed here, qualify retinoic acid as such a molecule.

We wish to thank Drs George Flentke and Jack Kirsch for helpful discussion. Work from the authors' laboratory is supported by grants HD 20209 from the National Institutes of Health and NP 630 from the American Cancer Society. S.M.S. and S.E.W. were supported by a fellowship from MDA and NATO, respectively.

References

AKAM, M. E., DAWSON, I. AND TEAR, G. (1988). Homeotic genes and the control of segment diversity. *Development* **104 (Suppl.),** 123–133.

BEACHY, P. A., KRASNOW, M. A., GRAVIS, E. R. AND HOGNESS, D. S. (1988). An *Ultrabithorax* protein binds sequences near its own and the *Antennapedia* P1 promoters. *Cell* **55,** 1069–1081.

BEATO, M. (1989). Gene regulation by steroid hormones. *Cell* **56,** 335–344.

BEDO, G., SANTISTEBAN, P. AND ARANDA, A. (1989). Retinoic acid regulates growth hormone gene expression. *Nature* **339,** 231–234.

BENBROOK, D. AND PFAHL, M. (1987). A novel thyroid hormone receptor encoded by a cDNA clone from a human testis library. *Science* **238,** 788–791.

BENBROOK, D., LERNHARDT, E. AND PFAHL, M. (1988). A new retinoic acid receptor identified from rat hepatocellular carcinoma. *Nature* **333,** 669–672.

BRAND, N. J., PETKOVICH, M., KRUST, A., CHAMBON, P., DE THÉ, H., MARCHIO, A., TIOLLAIS, P. AND DEJEAN, A. (1988). Identification of a second human retinoic acid receptor. *Nature* **332,** 850–853.

BRYANT, S. V. AND MUNEOKA, K. (1986). Views of limb development and regeneration. *Trends in Genetics* **2,** 153–156.

CARRINGTON, J. L. AND FALLON, J. F. (1986). Experimental manipulation leading to induction of dorsal ectodermal ridges on normal limb buds result in a phenocopy of the Eudiplopodia chick mutant. *Devl Biol.* **116,** 130–137.

CARROLL, S. B., LAYMON, R. A., MCCUTCHEON, M. A., RILEY, P. D. AND SCOTT, M. P. (1986). The localization and regulation of *Antennapedia* protein expression in Drosophila embryos. *Cell* **47,** 113–122.

COLBERG-POLEY, A. M., VOSS, S. D., CHOWDHURY, K. AND GRUSS, P. (1985). Structural analysis of murine genes containing homeobox sequences and their expression in embryonal carcinoma cells. *Nature* **314,** 731–738.

CRICK, F. H. C. (1970). Diffusion in embryogenesis. *Nature* **225,** 420–422.

DAMM, K., THOMPSON, C. C. AND EVANS, R. M. (1989). Protein encoded by v-*erbA* functions as a thyroid hormone receptor antagonist. *Nature* **339,** 593–597.

DAVIDSON, E. H. (1986). *Gene Activity in Early Development.* Orlando, Florida: Academic Press.

DAVIS, C. A. AND JOYNER, A. L. (1988). Expression patterns of the homeo box-containing genes *En-1* and *En-2* and the proto-oncogene *int-1* diverge during mouse development. *Genes and Dev.* **2,** 1736–1744.

DESCHAMPS, J., DE LAAF, R., VERRIJZER, P., DE GOUW, M., DESTREE, O. F. AND MEIJLINK, F. (1987). The mouse Hox 2.3 homeobox-containing gene: regulation in differentiating pluripotent stem cells and expression pattern in embryos. *Differentiation* **35,** 21–30.

DE THÉ, H., MARCHIO, A., TIOLLAIS, P. AND DEJEAN, A. (1989). Differential expression and ligand regulation of the retinoic acid receptor alpha and beta genes. *EMBO J.* **8,** 429–433.

DOBSON, A. D. W., CONNEELY, O. M., BEATTIE, W., MAXWELL, B. L., MAK, P., TSAI, M.-J., SCHRADER, W. T. AND O'MALLEY, B. W. (1989). Mutational analysis of the chicken progesterone receptor. *J. biol. Chem.* **264,** 4207–4211.

DOLLÉ, P. AND DUBOULE, D. (1989). Two gene members of the murine HOX-5 complex show regional and cell-type specific expression in developing limbs and gonads. *EMBO J.* **8,** 1507–1515.

DONY, C. AND GRUSS, P. (1988). Expression of a murine homeobox gene precedes the induction of c-fos during mesodermal differentiation of P19 teratocarcinoma cells. *Differentiation* **37,** 115–122.

DRESSLER, G. R. AND GRUSS, P. (1988). Do multigene families regulate vertebrate development? *Trends in Genetics* **4,** 214–219.

DUBOULE, D. AND DOLLÉ, P. (1989). The structural and functional organization of the murine Hox gene family resembles that of Drosophila homeotic genes. *EMBO J.* **8**, 1497–1505.

EICHELE, G., TICKLE, C. AND ALBERTS, B. M. (1985). Studies on the mechanism of retinoid-induced pattern duplications in the early chick limb bud: temporal and spatial aspects. *J. Cell Biol.* **101**, 1913–1920.

EICHELE, G. AND THALLER, C. (1987). Characterization of concentration gradients of a morphogenetically active retinoid in the chick limb bud. *J. Cell Biol.* **105**, 1917–1923.

EVANS, R. M. (1988). The steroid and thyroid hormone receptor super-family. *Science* **240**, 889–895.

GEHRING, W. J. (1987). Homeo boxes in the study of development. *Science* **236**, 1245–1252.

GRAHAM, A., PAPALOPULU, N. AND KRUMLAUF, R. (1989). Murine and Drosophila homeobox gene complexes have common features of organization and expression. *Cell* **57**, 367–378.

GREEN, S., WALTER, P., KUMAN, V., KRUST, A., BORNERT, J.-M., ARGOS, P. AND CHAMBON, P. (1986). Human oestrogen receptor cDNA: sequence, expression and homology to v-erb-A. *Nature, Lond.* **320**, 134–139.

GUIGUERE, V., ONG, E. S., SEGUI, P. AND EVANS, R. M. (1987). Identification of a receptor for the morphogen retinoic acid. *Nature, Lond.* **330**, 624–629.

HAFEN, E., LEVINE, M. AND GEHRING, W. J. (1984). Regulation of Antennapedia transcript distribution by the bithorax complex in Drosophila. *Nature* **307**, 287–289.

HAMBURGER, V. AND HAMILTON, H. (1951). A series of normal stages in the development of the chick embryo. *J. Morph.* **88**, 49–92.

HERR, W., STURM, R. A., CLERC, R. G., CORCORAN, L. M., BALTIMORE, D., AHARP, P. A., INGRAHAM, H. A., ROSENFELD, M. G., FINNEY, M., RUVKUN, G. AND HORVITZ, H. R. (1989). The POU domain: a large conserved region in the mammalian *pit-1*, *oct-1*, *oct-2*, and *Caenorhabditis elegans unc-86* gene products. *Genes Dev.* **2**, 1513–1516.

HILL, R. E., JONES, P. F., REES, A. R., SIME, C. M., JUSTICE, M. J., COPELAND, N. G., JENKINS, N. A., GRAHAM, E. AND DAVIDSON, D. R. (1989). A family of mouse homeo box-containing genes: molecular structure, chromosomal location, and developmental expression of Hox 7.1. *Genes and Dev.* **3**, 26–37.

HINCHLIFFE, J. R. AND EDE, D. A. (1973). Cell death and the development of limb form and skeletal pattern in normal and *wingless* (*ws*) chick embryos. *J. Embryol. exp. Morph.* **30**, 753–772.

HINCHLIFFE, J. R., GARCIA-PORRERO, J. A. AND GUMPEL-PINOT, M. (1981). The role of the zone of polarizing activity in controlling the differentiation of the apical mesenchyme of the chick wing-bud: histochemical techniques in the analysis of a developmental problem. *Histochem. J.* **13**, 643–658.

HODIN, R. A., LAZAR, M. A., WINTMAN, B. I., DARLING, D. S., KOENIG, R. J., LARSEN, P. R., MOORE, D. D. AND CHIN, W. W. (1989). Identification of a thyroid hormone receptor that is pituitary-specific. *Science* **244**, 76–79.

HORNBRUCH, A. AND WOLPERT, L. (1986). Positional signalling by Hensen's node when grafted to the chick limb bud. *J. Embryol. exp. Morph.* **94**, 257–265.

INGHAM, P. W. (1988). The molecular genetics of embryonic pattern formation in Drosophila. *Nature* **335**, 25–34.

IZUMO, S. AND MAHDAVI, V. (1988). Thyroid hormone receptor α isoforms generated by alternative splicing differentially activate myosin HC gene transcription. *Nature* **334**, 539–000.

JAVOIS, L. C. (1984). Pattern specification in the developing limb. In *Pattern Formation: a Primer in Developmental Biology* (ed. G. M. Malacinski and S. V. Bryant), pp. 557–589. New York: Macmillan Publishing.

JOYNER, A. L. AND MARTIN, G. R. (1987). *En-1* and *En-2*, two mouse genes with sequence homology to the *Drosophila engrailed* gene: expression during embryogenesis. *Genes Dev.* **1**, 29–38.

KATO, M., BLANER, W. S., MERTZ, J. R., DAS, K., KATO, K. AND GOODMAN, D. S. (1985). Influence of retinoid nutritional status on cellular retinol- and cellular retinoic acid-binding protein concentrations in various rat tissues. *J. biol. Chem.* **260**, 4832–4838.

KATZENELLENBOGEN, J. A., CARLSON, K. E., HEIMAN, D. F., ROBERTSON, D. F., WEI, L. L. AND KATZENELLENBOGEN, B. S. (1983). Efficient and highly selective covalent labeling of the estrogen receptor with [³H]-tamoxifen aziridine. *J. biol. Chem.* **258**, 3487–3495.

KIENY, M. (1960). Rôle inducteur du mésoderme dans la différenciation précoce du bourgeon de membre chez l'embryon de poulet. *J. Embryol. exp. Morph.* **8**, 457–467.

KIENY, M. (1968). Variation de la capacité inductrice du mésoderme et de la competence de l'ectoderme au cours de l'induction primaire du burgeon de membre, chez l'embryon de poulet. *Archs Anat. microsc. Morph. exp.* **57**, 401–418.

KOBLINSKY, M., BEATO, M., KALIMI, M. AND FEIGELSON, P. (1972). Glucocorticoid-binding proteins of rat liver cytosol. II. Physical characterization and properties of the binding proteins. *J. biol. Chem.* **247**, 7897–7904.

KRUST, A., KASTNER, H., PETKOVICH, M., ZELENT, A. AND CHAMBON, P. (1989). A third human retinoic acid receptor, H RARγ. *Proc. natn. Acad. Sci. U.S.A.* **86**, 5310–5314.

KWARTA, R. F., JR, KIMMEL, C. A., KIMMEL, G. L. AND SLIKKER, W., JR (1985). Identification of the cellular retinoic acid binding protein (cRABP) within the embryonic mouse (CD-1) limb bud. *Teratology* **32**, 103–111.

LA ROSA, G. J. AND GUDAS, L. J. (1988*a*). An early effect of retinoic acid: cloning of an mRNA (ERA-1) exhibiting rapid and protein synthesis-independent induction during teratocarcinoma stem cell differentiation. *Proc. natn. Acad. Sci. U.S.A.* **85**, 329–333.

LA ROSA, G. J. AND GUDAS, L. J. (1988*b*). Early retinoic acid-induced F9 teratocarcinoma stem cell gene ERA-1: Alternate splicing creates transcripts for a homeobox-containing protein and one lacking a homeobox. *Mol. cell. Biol.* **8**, 3906–3917.

LAZAR, M. A., HODIN, R. A., DARLING, D. S. AND CHIN, W. W. (1989). A novel member of the thyroid/steroid hormone receptor family is encoded by the opposite strand of the rat c-erbAα transcriptional unit. *Mol. cell. Biol.* **9**, 1128–1136.

MADEN, M., ONG, D. E., SUMMERBELL, D. AND CHYTIL, F. (1988). Spatial distribution of cellular protein binding to retinoic acid in the chick limb bud. *Nature, Lond.* **335**, 733–735.

MADEN, M. AND SUMMERBELL, D. (1986). Retinoic acid-binding protein in the chick limb bud: identification at developmental stages and binding affinities of various retinoids. *J. Embryol. exp. Morph.* **97**, 239–250.

MADEN, M. (1982). Vitamin A and pattern formation in the regenerating limb. *Nature, Lond.* **295**, 672–675.

MAVILIO, F., SIMEONE, A., BONCINELLI, E. AND ANDREWS, P. W. (1988). Activation of four homeobox gene clusters in human embryonal carcinoma cells induced to differentiate by retinoic acid. *Differentiation* **37**, 73–91.

McGINNIS, W., LEVINE, M., HAFEN, E., KUROIWA, A., GEHRING, W. J. (1984*a*). A conserved DNA sequence found in homeotic genes of the *Drosophila* Antennapedia and bithorax complexes. *Nature* **308**, 428–433.

McGINNIS, W., GARBER, R. L., WIRZ, J., KUROIWA, A. AND GEHRING, W. J. (1984*b*). A homologous protein coding sequence in *Drosophila* homeotic genes and its conservation in other metazoans. *Cell* **37**, 403–408.

MEINHARDT, H. (1982). *Models of Biological Pattern Formation.* New York: Academic Press.

MIYAJIMA, N., HORIUCHI, R., SHIBUYA, Y., FUKUSHIGE, S., MATSUBARA, K., TOYOSHIMA, K. AND YAMAMOTO, T. (1989). Two erbA homologs encoding proteins with different T₃ binding capacities are transcribed from opposite DNA strands of the same genetic locus. *Cell* **57**, 31–39.

OLIVER, G., WRIGHT, C. V. E., HARDWICKE, J. AND DEROBERTIS, E. M. (1988). A gradient of homeodomain protein in developing forelimbs of *Xenopus* and mouse embryos. *Cell* **55**, 1017–1024.

OLIVER, G., SIDELL, N., FISKE, W., HEINZMANN, C., MOHANDAS, T., SPARKES, R. S. AND DE ROBERTIS, E. M. (1989). Complementary homeo protein gradients in the developing limb. *Genes Dev.* **3**, 641–650.

ONG, D. E. AND CHYTIL, F. (1978). Cellular retinoic acid-binding protein from rat testis. Purification and characterization. *J. biol. Chem.* **253**, 4551–4554.

OSTER, G. F., MURRAY, J. D. AND MAINI, P. K. (1985). A model for chondrogenic condensations in the developing limb: the role of extracellular matrix and cell tractions. *J. Embryol. exp. Morph.* **89**, 93–112.

PEIFER, M., KRACH, F. AND BENDER, W. (1987). The bithorax complex: control and segmental identity. *Genes Dev.* **1**, 891–898.

PETKOVICH, M., BRAND, N. J., KRUST, A. AND CHAMBON, P. (1987). A human retinoic acid receptor which belongs to the family of nuclear receptors. *Nature, Lond.* **330**, 444–450.

ROBERT, B., SASSOON, D., JACQ, B., GEHRING, W. AND BUCKINGHAM, M. (1989). Hox-7, a mouse homeobox gene with a novel pattern of expression during embryogenesis. *EMBO J.* **8**, 91–100.

SAP, J., MUNOZ, A., DAMM, K., GOLDBERG, Y., GHYSDAEL, J., LEUTZ, A., BEUG, H. AND VENNSTROM, B. (1986). The c-erb-A protein is a high-affinity receptor for thyroid hormone. *Nature, Lond.* **324**, 635–640.

SAVARD, P., GATES, P. B. AND BROCKES, J. P. (1988). Position dependent expression of a homeobox gene transcription in relation to amphibian limb regeneration. *EMBO J.* **7**, 4275–4282.

SAUNDERS, J. W. JR (1948). The proximo-distal sequence of origin of parts of the chick wing and the role of the ectoderm. *J. exp. Zool.* **108**, 363–403.

SAUNDERS, J. W., GASSELING, M. T. AND SAUNDERS, L. C. (1962). Cellular death in morphogenesis of the avian wing. *Devl Biol.* **5**, 147–178.

SAUNDERS, J. W. AND GASSELING, M. T. (1968). Ectodermal-mesenchymal interactions in the origin of wing symmetry. In *Epithelial–mesenchymal Interactions* (ed. R. Fleischmajer and R. E. Billingham), pp. 78–97. Baltimore: Williams and Wilkins.

SAUNDERS, J. W. JR AND GASSELING, M. T. (1983). New insights into the problem of pattern regulation in the limb bud of the chick embryo. In *Limb Development and Regeneration* (ed. J. F. Fallon and A. I. Caplan), pp. 67–76. New York: A. Liss.

SCHULZE, F., CHOWDHURY, K., ZIMMER, A., DRESCHER, U. AND GRUSS, P. (1987). The murine homeo box gene product, Hox 1.1 protein, is growth-controlled and associated with chromatin. *Differentiation* **36**, 130–137.

SCOTT, M. P., WEINER, A. J., POLISKY, B. A., HAZELRIGG, T. I., PIROTTA, V., SCALENGHE, F. AND KAUFMAN, T. C. (1983). The molecular organization of the *Antennapedia* complex of *Drosophila*. *Cell* **35**, 763–776.

SCOTT, M. P. AND WEINER, A. J. (1984). Structural relationships among genes that control development: Sequence homology between the Antennapedia, ultrabithorax and fushi tarazu loci of *Drosophila*. *Proc. natn. Acad. Sci. U.S.A.* **81**, 4115–4119.

SIMIONE, A., MAVILLIO, F., ACAMPORA, D., GIAMPAOLA, A., FAIELLA, A., ZAPPAVIGNA, V., D'ESPOSITA, M., RUSSO, G., BONCINELLI, E. AND PESCHLE, C. (1987). Two human homeo box genes, c1 and c8: structure analysis and expression in embryonic development. *Proc. natn. Acad. Sci. U.S.A.* **84**, 4914–4918.

SLACK, J. M. W. (1987). Morphogenetic gradients – past and present. *Trends Biochem. Sci.* **12**, 200–204.

SMITH, J. C. (1980). The time required for positional signalling in the chick wing bud. *J. Embryol. exp. Morph.* **60**, 321–328.

SMITH, J. C. (1989). Mesoderm induction and mesoderm-inducing factors in early amphibian development. *Development* **105**, 665–677.

STARK, R. J. AND SEARLS, R. L. (1973). A description of chick wing development and a model of limb morphogenesis. *Devl Biol.* **33**, 317–333.

SUMMERBELL, D. (1974). A quantitative analysis of the excision of the AER from the chick limb bud. *J. Embryol. exp. Morph.* **32**, 651–660.

SUMMERBELL, D. (1983). The effects of local application of retinoic acid to the anterior margin of the developing chick limb. *J. Embryol. exp. Morph.* **78**, 269–289.

SUMMERBELL, D. AND HARVEY, F. (1983). Vitamin A and the control of pattern in developing limbs. In *Limb Development and Regeneration* (ed. J. F. Fallon and A. I. Caplan), pp. 109–118. New York: A. Liss.

SUMMERBELL, D., LEWIS, J. AND WOLPERT, L. (1973). Positional information in chick limb morphogenesis. *Nature, Lond.* **244**, 492–496.

TABIN, C. (1989). Isolation of potential vertebrate limb-identity genes. *Development* **105**, 813–820.

THALLER, C. AND EICHELE, G. (1987). Identification and spatial distribution of retinoids in the developing chick limb bud. *Nature, Lond.* **327**, 625–628.

THALLER, C. AND EICHELE, G. (1988). Characterization of retinoid metabolism in the developing chick limb bud. *Development* **103**, 473–483.

THOMS, S. D. AND STOCUM, D. L. (1984). Retinoic acid-induced pattern duplications in regenerating urodele limbs. *Devl Biol.* **103**, 319–328.

TICKLE, C. (1980). The polarizing region and limb development. In *Development in Mammals*, vol. 4 (ed. M. H. Johnson), pp. 101–136. Amsterdam: Elsevier/North-Holland Biomedical Press.

TICKLE, C. (1981). The number of polarizing region cells required to specify additional digits in the developing chick wing. *Nature, Lond.* **289**, 295–298.

TICKLE, C., SUMMERBELL, D. AND WOLPERT, L. (1975). Positional signalling and specification of digits in chick limb morphogenesis. *Nature, Lond.* **254**, 199–202.

TICKLE, C., ALBERTS, B. M., WOLPERT, L. AND LEE, J. (1982). Local application of retinoic acid to the limb bud mimics the action of the polarizing region. *Nature, Lond.* **296**, 564–565.

TICKLE, C., LEE, J. AND EICHELE, G. (1985). A quantitative analysis of the effect of all-trans-retinoic acid on the pattern of chick wing development. *Devl Biol.* **109**, 82–95.

UMESONO, K., GIGUERE, V., GLASS, C. K., ROSENFELD, M. G. AND EVANS, R. M. (1988). Retinoic acid and thyroid hormone induce gene expression through a common responsive element. *Nature, Lond.* **336**, 262–265.

WEDDEN, S., PANG, K. AND EICHELE, G. (1989). Expression pattern of homeobox-containing genes during chick embryogenesis. *Development* **105**, 639–650.

WEINBERGER, C., THOMPSON, C. C., ONG, E. S., LEBO, R., GRUOL, D. J. AND EVANS, R. M. (1986). The c-erb-A gene encodes a thyroid hormone receptor. *Nature, Lond.* **324**, 641–646.

WOLPERT, L. (1969). Positional information and the spatial pattern of cellular differentiation. *J. theor. Biol.* **25**, 1–47.

WRIGHT, C. V. E., CHO, K. W. Y., OLIVER, G. AND DEROBERTIS, E. M. (1989). Vertebrate homeodomain proteins: families of region-specific transcription factors. *Trends Biochem. Sci.* **14**, 52–56.

ZELENT, A., KRUST, A., PETKOVICH, M., KASTNER, P. AND CHAMBON, P. (1989). Cloning of murine α and β retinoic acid receptors and a novel receptor γ predominantly expressed in skin. *Nature* **339**, 714–717.

Development 1989 Supplement, 133–140 (1989)
Printed in Great Britain © The Company of Biologists Limited 1989

Steroid hormone receptor homologs in development

ANTHONY E. ORO[1,2], KAZUHIKO UMESONO[1] and RONALD M. EVANS[1]

[1] *Howard Hughes Medical Institute, Salk Institute for Biological Sciences, La Jolla, California 92138-9216, USA*
[2] *Department of Biological Sciences, University of California, San Diego, La Jolla, California 92093, USA*

Summary

The steroid/thyroid receptor superfamily are ligand-dependent transcription factors which consist of distinct functional domains required for transcriptional control of a network of genes. Members of this superfamily are beginning to be studied for their contribution to embryogenesis. Two human receptors for the vertebrate morphogen retinoic acid have been isolated and further characterized on model promoters. Moreover, the presence of homologs of these receptors in *Drosophila* reveals that members of this superfamily predate the divergence of the vertebrates and invertebrates. One locus is *knirps-related* (*knrl*), whose product is closely related to that of the gap segmentation gene *knirps* (*kni*). *knrl* is one of the most diverged steroid receptor-like molecules and displays a spatially restricted blastoderm pattern.

Key words: steroid hormone, thyroid receptor, transcriptional control, *Drosophila*, *knirps*.

I. Development as a problem of differential gene regulation

In the 1930s T. H. Morgan theorized that the process of development occurred by the differential expression of small invisible entities called genes and that expression of different sets of these genes gives rise to differences in the adult organism (Morgan, 1934). Indeed differential gene expression does appear to play an important part in normal development as many classes of transcriptional regulators have been recently isolated and shown to play important roles in embryogenesis (Dressler and Gruss, 1988). One of them is the steroid/thyroid receptor superfamily of proteins. These proteins are receptors for small hydrophobic molecules which as nuclear hormone–receptor complexes mediate their effects. The biologically active ligands play roles in both homeostasis in the adult and development, as illustrated in Table 1. For example, the adrenal steroids widely influence energy metabolism, controlling glycogen, muscle, and mineral metabolism as well as mediating behavioral responses to perceived stress. They have widespread effects on the immune and nervous systems and influence the determination of neural crest fate. The sex steroids provoke the development and determination of body sexual dimorphisms including the reproductive organs embryonically, the central nervous system perinatally, and reproductive behavior in the adult. Aberrant production of these hormones have been associated with a broad spectrum of clinical disease. Further, both thyroid and steroid hormones appear to be important in metamorphosis. Thyroidectomy inhibits tadpole maturation to a frog, but addition of thyroxine to its drinking water induces all of the changes into a terrestrial adult (Schwind, 1933).

Similarly, ecdysteroids are required for insect metamorphosis, allowing the various molts into adulthood (Ashburner, 1971).

An initial insight into how small, relatively simple molecules elicit such a diversity of complex responses was provided by the identification of steroid and thyroid hormone receptors with radiolabeled ligands in the early 1970s (Jensen and DeSombre, 1972). After the addition of hormone, the receptor apparently underwent a conformational change such that it associated with high affinity binding sites in chromatin and induced or repressed a limited number of genes (Ivaric and O'Farrell, 1978). This type of experiment led to the idea that these receptors controlled a specific network of genes in order to facilitate homeostasis. Purification and biochemical characterization of the glucocorticoid receptor was accompanied by the identification of a variety of glucocorticoid responsive genes (Yamamoto, 1985; Ringold, 1985). Each gene contained a short *cis*-acting sequence (about 20 bp) in the promoter region which was required for hormone-dependent activation of transcription (called a hormone responsive element or HRE, Scheidereit *et al.* 1983; Chandler *et al.* 1983; Karin *et al.* 1984). Selectivity of gene expression is achieved by synthesis of the cognate ligand, restricted expression of a receptor in specific cells and tissues, the presence of an HRE in the promoter of a particular gene, and the presence of other transcription factors required for that promoter to function at normal levels.

II. Functional domains

The cloning of the human glucocorticoid receptor

Table 1. *Major biologically active small hydrophobic molecules*

Hormone	Cellular source	Principal adult action	Known developmental action
Glucocorticoid[a,b]	Adrenal	Carbohydrate synthesis Stress behaviour	Influence neural crest fate
Mineralocorticoid[a]	Adrenal	Salt and water balance	?
Estrogens[a] Androgens Progesterone	Gonads, Adrenal	Sexual reproduction Behaviour and physiology	Reproductive organ development and neural development
Thyroxine[a,c]	Thyroid gland	Basal metabolic rate	Neural development Amphibian metamorphosis
$1,25(OH)_2$ Cholecaliferol[a]	Kidney	Calcium, phosphate balance	Bone development
Retinoids[c]	Liver, Intestine	Structural elements of vision	Positional information
Ecdysone[d]	Prothoracic gland Ovary	Oogenesis	Insect molting and metamorphosis
Juvenile hormone[d]	Corpus Allatum	Oogenesis	Inhibition of insect maturation

Known biological actions of some hydrophobic, small molecules in different species. Selected references: a: Felig *et al.* 1981; b: Anderson and Axel, 1986; c: Ham and Veomott, 1980; d: Steel and Davey, 1985.

(hGR) provided the first completed structure of a steroid receptor and permitted the molecular dissection of the receptor as a transcription factor (Hollenberg *et al.* 1985). An understanding of the action of steroids requires a mechanistic explanation for how a single transcription factor, when bound to its ligand, acts as a sequence-specific, positive and negative regulatory factor and a delineation of the unique domains in the receptor dedicated to each phenomenon. Through cotransfection studies using the 'cis–trans vector assay', the hGR can be studied as a model hormone–hormone receptor system. Activation of transcription can be analyzed through a *cis*-vector employing the mammary tumor virus (MTV) promoter (Giguere *et al.* 1986), while repression of transcription can be studied on the α-glycoprotein hormone promoter (Oro *et al.* 1988b). Effects of mutations can be rapidly assayed for their transcriptional effects in the presence or absence of hormone (Figure 1).

Both activation and repression by hGR share some common features. First, both processes demonstrate a requirement for the DNA-binding domain and reflect the fact that positive and negative regulation are DNA sequence-specific. Deletions in this cysteine-rich, zinc finger region destroy all function. Second, the carboxyl terminal deletions show that activation and repression require an intact ligand binding domain and the presence of hormone. Consistent with previous results for activation (Godowski *et al.* 1987), removal or replacement of this region by heterologous sequences leads to hormone independence for both processes.

In contrast, several experiments provide criteria that distinguish positive and negative regulatory effects of the hGR. First, the amino terminal domain that contains a potent activator sequence (Tau 1) is not necessary for *trans*-repression. The Tau domain can be placed on heterologous DNA-binding domains such as Gal4 or moved to other parts of the receptor and still maintain function (Hollenberg and Evans, 1988). These facts substantiate the duality of receptor function and high-

light the observation that deletion of Tau 1 engenders a more potent repressor. Second, heterologous proteins such as β-galactosidase can functionally replace the hGR carboxyl terminus only in repression. Removal of the carboxyl terminus results in a receptor variant with greatly reduced repression and activation activity (Figure 1). The addition of a β-galactosidase moiety selectively increases repression and not activation activity, while addition of a mineralocorticoid receptor carboxyl terminus increases both activities (Oro *et al.* 1988b). Given the lack of amino acid identity or similar charge distribution between the hGR, hMR and β-gal, one plausible model is that hGR represses through its carboxyl terminus simply by steric hindrance but requires specific sequences for activation activity.

III. A superfamily of proteins

Analysis of the amino acid sequence of the hGR revealed a segment with striking relatedness to the viral oncogene erbA (Weinberger *et al.* 1985). Two groups initiated the characterization of the erbA proto-oncogene product which led to its identification as the thyroid hormone receptor (Weinberger *et al.* 1986; Sap *et al.* 1986). Although steroid and thyroid hormones are not structurally or biosynthetically related, the existence of a common structure for their receptors supports the proposal that there is a large superfamily of genes whose products are ligand-responsive transcription factors. Apparently it is the analogous action of the hormones that is reflected in the homologous structure of their receptors. An extension of this proposal predicts that other small, hydrophobic molecules may interact with structurally related intracellular receptors in order to modulate the expression of specific networks of genes. Molecular cloning studies support this proposal as the receptors for many of the molecules listed in Table 1 including estrogen, progesterone, aldosterone, and vitamin D have been isolated (For review see Evans, 1988).

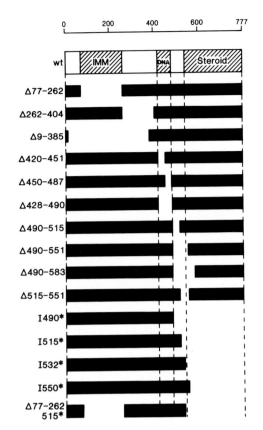

	α168 CAT REPRESSION		MTV ACTIVATION	
	−DEX	+DEX	−DEX	+DEX
wt	*	100	**	100
Δ77–262	*	140±10	**	10
Δ262–404	*	195±95	**	85
Δ9–385	*	160±18	**	10
Δ420–451	*	*	**	**
Δ450–487	*	*	**	**
Δ428–490	*	*	**	**
Δ490–515	*	74±11	**	95
Δ490–551	*	*	**	**
Δ490–583	*	*	**	**
Δ515–551	*	*	**	**
I490*	*	*	**	**
I515*	22±8	22±8	10	10
I532*	11±2	11±2	10	10
I550*	31±6	31±6	40	40
Δ77–262 515*	24±6	24±6	1	1

Fig. 1. Structure-and-function analysis reveals functional domains required for activation and repression. Deletion mutants previously characterized for activation, DNA binding and steroid binding were assayed on the alpha promoter. The wild-type receptor consists of IMM, immunogenic region which coincides with the Tau 1 region: DNA, DNA-binding domain, Steroid, ligand-binding domain. Scale above refers to amino acid number. Numbers on the left indicate deleted amino acids while asterisks next to the number indicate the amino acid linker insertion mutant at which the receptor is truncated. % of wild-type activity was determined by assigning RSV control plasmid as zero activity and the wild-type hGR as 100% in each experiment plus or minus the standard error of the mean. The mutants were previously assayed for activation in (Hollenberg *et al.* 1987). * indicates activity is less than 10% of wild-type repression activity on the alpha168 promoter, ** indicates less than 1% of activation activity on the MTV promoter.

Three generalizations can be made from these studies. First, the core DNA-binding domain sequence is highly conserved with nine cysteines forming the two metal-binding finger structures. The sequence conservation ranges from 42 to 94% and reflects the diversity of HREs that the receptors recognize. Second, the homology in the ligand-binding domain is more graded and generally parallels the structural relatedness of the hormones themselves. Although the overall homology of the carboxyl terminal region is less than 15%, each receptor still maintains two clusters of amino acid identities between receptors as distinct as the human receptors and the *Drosophila* receptor-like molecule E75 (Segraves, 1988). The exact functional contributions these conserved regions make is unclear, with functions conserved between receptors as possible candidates: hormone binding, dimerization, transactivation or transrepression. Lastly, although the amino terminus is not conserved, it may contribute to important functional differences between receptors. Deletions in this region of the glucocorticoid receptor reduce activity by 10- to 20-fold (Hollenberg *et al.* 1987; Danielsen *et al.* 1987), whereas the A and B forms of the progesterone receptor, which differ by 128 amino acids at the amino terminus, have strikingly different capacities to regulate gene expression (Tora *et al.* 1988).

IV. Steroid hormone receptor homologs in development

Although it is widely believed that differential regulation of gene expression is the critical level at which development is controlled, this does not provide a conceptual framework for how specific processes like spatial organization or pattern formation are achieved. Many mechanisms have been proposed to explain patterning in different organisms, but one long-standing theory is that certain patterns are formed through the establishment of a gradient of a diffusible substance or morphogen (Crick, 1975). One example of a morphogen is the *Drosophila bicoid* protein, which acts in a diffusible concentration gradient to establish anterior polarity of the embryo (Driever and Nusslein-Volhard, 1988). Another example is the vitamin A-related metabolite, retinoic acid (RA). Work by numerous laboratories over the last several years has indicated that the RA manifests morphogenic properties in vertebrates (Maden, 1982). Evidence from work on the developing chick limb bud suggested that RA was produced in a gradient with its highest concentration posteriorly at the zone of polarizing activity. Recently, RA was directly shown to be present in the chick limb bud in a 2·5-fold concentration gradient across the limb (Thaller and Eichele, 1987), supporting its morphogenic role. Moreover, reversal of the gradient by the addition of exogenous RA resulted in duplication of limb structures such as the digits (Tickle *et al.* 1975). One important question to be answered is how a shallow RA gradient can be transmitted into different cell fates.

Two retinoic acid receptors have been identified that are members of the steroid hormone receptor superfamily. The identification of the retinoic acid receptor α

A.

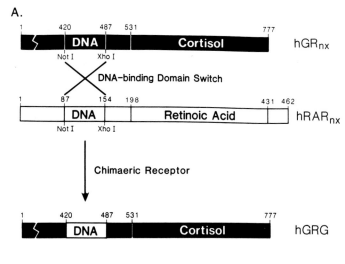

B.

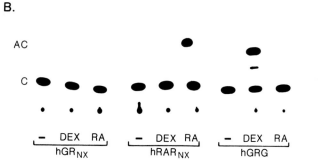

Fig. 2. The human retinoic acid receptor activates through
a thyroid hormone response element. (A) Construction of
the chimaeric receptor hGRG. The hGRnx and hRARnx
are mutated hGR and hRARa, respectively, with common
*Not*I and *Xho*I sites in the cDNAs. The amino acid
numbers represent the possible domain boundaries in the
receptor proteins. The ligand binding domains are indicated
by their cognate hormones, DNA-binding domains by
'DNA'. The chimaeric receptors were created by
exchanging the DNA-binding domains at the *Not*I/*Xho*I
sites. (B) Transactivation of a T3 responsive reporter by the
hybrid receptors. Expression plasmids encoding mutant
receptors were cotransfected into CV-1 cells together with
the ΔMTV-TREp linked to the chloramphenicol
acetyltransferase gene reporter (CAT) in the presence or
absence of 100 nm inducer and assayed 36 h later for CAT
activity. No effect on CAT activity was observed using the
parent vector pRShGRnx. When pRShRARnx was
cotransfected, retinoic acid mediated a 10-fold induction.
AC and C are the acetylated (AC) and unacetylated (C)
forms of [^{14}C]chloramphenicol.

(Giguere *et al.* 1987; Petkovich *et al.* 1987) was facili-
tated by the modular nature of these proteins. Exchanging the DNA-binding domain of the retinoic acid
receptor for the homologous region from the hGR, a
hybrid molecule was generated that activates GRE
responsive promoters (such as the MTV-LTR) in response to retinoic acid (See Figure 2A, Giguere *et al.*
1987). RAR *β* had been discovered by examination of
integration sites of the hepatitis B virus into hepatocellular carcinomas (Dejean *et al.* 1986; deThe *et al.*
1987). Subsequently, using a similar domain-swap ap-

proach, the receptor was shown to bind retinoic acid
with high affinity (Brand *et al.* 1988; Benbrook *et al.*
1988). The structure of the two receptors are very
similar (90 % in the ligand-binding domain), but the *β*
form of the receptor transactivates at a slightly lower
concentration of RA (Brand *et al.* 1988). Moreover,
RNA from the two receptor genes have different tissue
distributions. RNA from the *α* form is expressed in
hematopoietic cell lines while RNA from the *β* receptor
has a more complex distribution, being highest in the
brain, kidney and prostate (deThe *et al.* 1989).

By analogy with steroid receptors, a potential model
for transmission of positional information *via* the
morphogen retinoic acid is through the two retinoic
acid receptors. Upon ligand binding, the receptors
would trigger the activation or repression of specific
networks of genes. Key to this model is that the
RAR is a sequence-specific transcriptional activator.
Interestingly, the RAR*α* was found to activate at high
levels through a previously isolated HRE for the
thyroid hormone receptor (Umesono *et al.* 1988). This
result was predicted based upon the structural relatedness of the DNA-binding domains between the RAR
and the thyroid hormone receptor. Although the biological significance has not yet been established, the two
distinct receptor systems may indeed regulate an overlapping set of genes. While an authentic RAR response
element has not been characterized, another apparent
target of regulation for the retinoic acid receptors is the
β receptor gene itself. From RNA analysis of hepatoma
cells, the expression of the *β* receptor appears to
increase in a cycloheximide-independent manner while
the expression of the *α* receptor remains constant in
response to RA (deThe *et al.* 1989). One interpretation
of these data is that the *β* receptor is autoregulated,
perhaps to amplify the expression of the set of genes it
regulates. How this amplification plays a role in the
establishment of positional information and to which
genes the receptor transmits the information are questions being actively pursued.

Retinoic acid has a clear role within the developing
organism in the establishment of positional information. However, other small molecule ligands might
exist that act in distinct developmental paradigms to
establish positional information or determine cell fate,
and which might act *via* a steroid hormone receptor-like
molecule. Moreover, the need for a well-characterized
embryological and genetic system with which to analyze
the function of these molecules pointed to the *Drosophila melanogaster* system for study.

To identify homologs of the vertebrate steroid receptors, a Southern blot of *Drosophila* genomic DNA was
probed with a cDNA fragment encoding the hRAR*α*
DNA-binding domain (Giguere *et al.* 1987; Petkovich *et
al.* 1987) Under conditions of reduced hybridization
stringency, six distinct *Eco*RI bands ranging in size from
2 kb to greater than 12 kb were detected. Screening of a
Drosophila genomic library using the same probe and
hybridization conditions resulted in the isolation of
three distinct single copy gene loci (Oro *et al.* 1988a).

One class of inserts mapped on the third chromosome

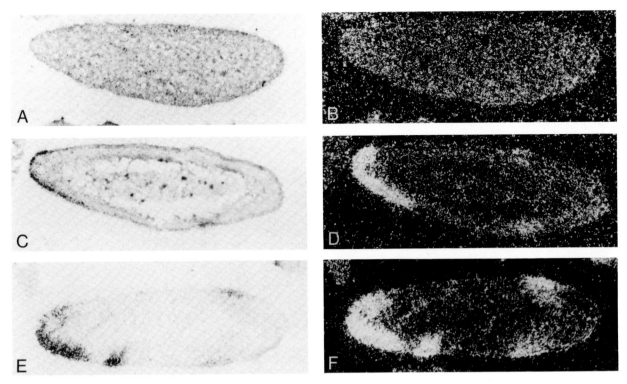

Fig. 3. Spatial localization of *knrl* transcripts in early embryos. Visualization of *knrl* transcripts by *in situ* hybridization to sections of wild-type *Drosophila melanogaster* embryos reveals both maternal and zygotic expression. Embryos are oriented with anterior to the left and dorsal at the top. Staging followed Campos-Ortega and Hartenstein, 1985 (A (brightfield) and B (darkfield)). Cleavage-stage embryo showing the spatially uniform distribution of apparent maternal *knrl* transcripts. (C and D) Embryo at syncytial blastoderm showing apparent early zygotic *knrl* expression in an anteroventral domain extending from 80–100 % of egg length along the ventral side of the embryo. Also apparent is the first appearance of the most posterior of the three cellular blastoderm expression domains (see below). (E and F) Cellular blastoderm pattern of *knrl* expression. Slightly oblique section showing intense anteroventral transcript accumulation (domain I), as well as the two more posterior transcript stripes at approximately 70 % (domain II) and 25 % (domain III) of egg length ventrally. Transcript accumulation in domain II is always observed to be at a significantly higher level ventrally than dorsally.

at cytologic position 77E, the same location as the previously identified gap segmentation gene *kni* (Nusslein-Volhard and Wieschaus, 1980). *kni* mutants had been previously isolated in a genetic screen for zygotic mutants affecting embryonic pattern formation and falls into a small set of genes required for abdominal segmentation (Nusslein-Volhard *et al.* 1987). Mutational analysis indicates that *kni*[+] activity apparently interacts with maternally derived information (Lehmann and Nusslein-Volhard, 1986).

The genomic and corresponding cDNA clones for the RAR homolog were sequenced and predicted amino acid sequence was found to have a striking similarity to the predicted amino acid sequence of the *kni* product (Nauber *et al.* 1988) and thus called *knirps-related* (*knrl*) (Oro *et al.* 1988*a*). Southern blots of *kni* mutant and wild-type genomic DNA revealed mutant DNAs XT1 and XT106 removed both *kni* and *knrl* loci localizing both genes to cytological positions 77E3–5. Further, *kni* mutant FC[13] contained a two kb deletion in the *kni* transcription unit while leaving *knrl* apparently intact (Oro, unpublished). No phenotypic differences in the abdominal region are seen between the *kni* mutants (R. Lehmann, personal communication), indicating that

the *kni* function is epistatic to the putative *knrl* function. Loss-of-function alleles for *knrl* are required before the developmental role of the *knrl* product can be addressed.

The *knrl* gene is expressed early in development. Northern blot of stage-specific RNA showed a single RNA species of approximately 3·8 kb expressed at low levels between 0 and 3 h after egg-laying (AEL) and at significantly higher levels in later embryos, larvae and adults. The spatial location of *knrl* transcripts was assayed by *in situ* hybridization on sections of 0–2 and 2–4 hour embryos (Figure 3). After egg deposition and until approximately the 8th nuclear division, a weak, spatially uniform distribution of apparently maternal transcript was detected (Figures 3A and 3B). The first apparently zygotic expression is detected at nuclear division 12, when the *knrl* transcript is localized to a small anteroventral region of the embryo (Figures 3C and 3D), at approximately 80–100 % of egg length (EL) on the ventral side (domain I). Expression in this domain intensifies through the cellular blastoderm stage, and two additional circumferential bands of transcript become detectable, centered at approximately 70 % EL ventrally (domain II) and 25 % EL

A.   Amino Acid Alignment of DNA-binding Domains

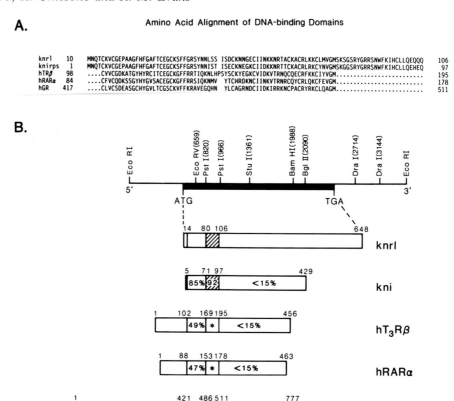

Fig. 4. Comparison of the predicted *knrl* product to vertebrate steroid/thyroid hormone receptors. (A) Alignment of the DNA-binding domains of representative members of the superfamily, showing the conserved amino acids and the extensive structural similarity between *knrl* and *kni*. Note that the identity of *knrl and kni* extends past the conserved Gly and Met residues of the DNA-binding domain. (B) Overall structural comparison of the predicted protein sequence of *knrl* to other members of the steroid/thyroid hormone receptor superfamily. Comparisons of the region marked DNA are to the 66–68 amino acid DNA-binding domains and the region marked Ligand Binding is compared with the amino acids starting at a point 25 amino acids past the conserved Gly and Met residues of the DNA binding domain. The intervening 25 amino acids are highly related between *knrl* and *kni*, but not significantly related to the other vertebrate receptors (indicated by an asterisk). As there is no significant similarity of *knrl* to the other receptors in the carboxyterminal region, no specific alignment of these regions is shown. The programs of Devereux *et al.* 1984 were used for comparison. Numbers indicate amino acids as detailed in Oro *et al.* 1988; Nauber *et al.* 1988 Weinberger *et al.* 1986; Giguere *et al.* 1987 and Hollenberg *et al.* 1985 for *knrl, kni, hTRβ, hRAR,* and *hGR,* respectively.

ventrally (domain III) (Figures 3E and 3F). It is noteworthy that expression in domain II appears significantly more intense ventrally than dorsally.

A comparison of the predicted *knrl* protein with other members of the steroid/thyroid receptor superfamily is shown in Figure 4. First, sequence alignment demonstrates greatest similarity with the other receptors in the 67 amino acids of the putative *knrl* DNA-binding domain (Figure 4A). Between amino acids 14 and 80 of *knrl* there is 85 % amino acid identity with the *kni* product, 49 % with the human thyroid receptor, 47 % with the human retinoic acid receptor and 43 % with the human glucocorticoid receptor. Interestingly, the *knrl* and *kni* DNA-binding domains both contain a glycine in the region linking the two zinc fingers (residues 39 and 30 in *knrl* and *kni*, respectively), at a position which in all other receptors is either an arginine or lysine. This further suggests a common origin for these two genes. Second, amino acid sequence analysis

reveals a highly conserved stretch of 30 amino acids immediately following the DNA-binding domain. Between other steroid receptors little or no homology exists (Figure 4), while this region in *knrl* or *kni* is more conserved than the DNA-binding domain. Other transcription factors also contain regions of high conservation outside of the DNA-binding domain, such as the POU domain in homeoproteins (Herr *et al.* 1988). Perhaps this region plays a novel role in receptor function.

Further, the homology of the predicted *knrl* gene product to vertebrate steroid receptors suggests that its function is ligand-dependent. If this is the case, such a ligand might constitute a previously unrecognized small-molecule morphogen, and some of the genes involved in regulating *knrl* function might affect the synthesis of the ligand or storage of a ligand precursor, rather than regulating *knrl* expression. However, the unrelatedness of the *knrl* carboxy terminus to that of the other receptors makes it difficult to predict a potential ligand. As mentioned above, even distant receptors have particular structural similarities in the carboxyl terminus. Perhaps the *knrl* product is a constitutive transcriptional regulator, and functions entirely without a ligand. Finger swap experiments similar to those used to identify the retinoic acid receptor may illuminate these differences.

Conclusion

Development of an organism is a complex biochemical process. Part of the understanding of the mechanisms has come about from the study of classes of transcription factors such as the steroid/thyroid hormone receptors whose ligands share common biophysical properties and a common mechanism of action in environmentally modulating gene expression and triggering specific networks of genes. The identification of the retinoic acid receptor has allowed the proposal that the morphogenic properties this ligand exerts are mediated through a hormone–hormone receptor complex which regulates a network of genes. Elucidation of proteins that interact with the receptors and their ligand as well as the receptor target genes, their spatial pattern of expression and function will allow new insight into further mechanisms of vertebrate development. Analysis of related receptor systems will identify new paradigms of receptor action. Characterization of one class of *Drosophila* retinoic acid receptor homologs identified a locus highly related in amino acid sequence to the gap segmentation gene *kni* with a spatially restricted expression pattern. These two receptors are the most highly diverged members of the gene superfamily; functional analysis may reveal a new class of transcriptional activators. Finally, the characterization of *Drosophila* steroid receptor homologs may reveal receptor systems common to both invertebrates and vertebrates. Although the gross structural features of developing embryos are distinct, common mechanisms using common or related molecules may be uncovered.

The authors would like to acknowledge Mike McKeown, Jon Margolis, Jim Posakony and Charles Zuker for help with the *Drosophila* work and Chris Glass, Vincent Giguere and M. G. Rosenfeld for work on retinoic acid receptor activation. R.M.E. is an investigator for the Howard Hughes Medical Institute and also acknowledges NIH support. A.E.O. is supported by the Medical Scientist Training Program, General Medical Grant PSH GM07198.

References

AKERBLOM, I., SLATER, E. P., BEATO, M., BAXTER, J. D. & MELLON, P. L. (1988). Negative regulation by glucocorticoids through interference with a cAMP responsive enhancer. *Science* **241**, 350–353.

ANDERSON, D. J. & AXEL, R. (1986). A bipotential neuroendocrine precursor whose choice of cell fate is determined by NGF and glucocorticoids. *Cell* **47**, 1079–1090.

ASHBURNER, M. (1971). Induction of puffs in polytene chromosomes of in vitro cultured salivary glands of *Drosophila melanogaster* by ecdysone and ecdysone analogues. *Nature, Lond.* **230**, 222–224.

BENBROOK, D., LERNHARDT, E. & PFAHL, M. (1988). A new retinoic acid receptor identified from a hepatocellular carcinoma. *Nature, Lond.* **333**, 669–672.

BRAND, N., PETKOVICH, M., KRUST, A., CHAMBON, P., DETHE, H., MARCHIO, A., TIOLLAIS, P. & DEJEAN, A. (1988). Identification of a second human retinoic acid receptor *Nature* **332**, 850–853.

CAMPOS-ORTEGA, J. & HARTENSTEIN, V. (1986). *The Embryonic Development of Drosophila melanogaster*, New York, USA; Springer-Verlag. pp. 9–84.

CHANDLER, V. L., MALER, B. A. & YAMAMOTO, K. R. (1983). DNA sequences bound specifically by glucocorticoid receptor in vitro render a heterologous promoter hormone responsive in vivo. *Cell* **33**, 489–499.

CRICK, F. (1975). Diffusion in morphogenesis *Nature* **225**, 420–422.

DANIELSON, M., NORTHROP, J. P., JONKLAAS, J. & RINGOLD, G. M. (1987). Domains of the glucocorticoid receptor involved in specific and nonspecific deoxyribonucleic acid binding, hormone activation, and transcriptional enhancement. *Mol. Endo.* **1**, 816–822.

DEJEAN, A., BOUGUELERET, L., GRZESCHIK, K. & TIOLLAIS, P. (1986). Hepatitis B virus DNA integration in a sequence homologous to v-erbA and steroid receptor genes in a hepatocellular carcinoma. *Nature, Lond.* **322**, 70.

DETHE, H., MARCHIO, A., TIOLLAIS, P. & DEJEAN, A. (1987). A novel steroid thyroid hormone receptor-related gene inappropriately expressed in human hepatocellular carcinoma. *Nature, Lond.* **330**, 667.

DETHE, H., MARCHIO, A., TIOLLAIS, P. & DEJEAN, A. (1989). Differential expression and regulation of the retinoic acid receptor α and β genes. *EMBO J.* **8**, 429–433.

DEVEREUX, J., HAEBERLI, P. & SMITHIES, O. (1984). A comprehensive set of seqeuence analysis programs for the VAX. *Nucleic Acids Res.* **12**, 387–395.

DRESSLER, G. R. & GRUSS, P. (1988). Do multigene families regulate vertebrate development? *Trends in Genetics* **4**, 214–219.

DRIEVER, W. & NUSSLEIN-VOLHARD, C. (1988). The *bicoid* protein determines position in the *Drosophila* embryo in a concentration-dependent manner. *Cell* **54**, 95–104.

EVANS, R. M. (1988). The steroid and thyroid hormone receptor superfamily. *Science* **240**, 889–895.

FELIG, P., BAXTER, J. D., BROADUS, A. E. & FROHMAN, L. A. (1981). *Endocrinology and Metabolism*. New York: McGraw-Hill.

GIGUERE, V., HOLLENBERG, S. M., ROSENFELD, M. G. & EVANS, R. M. (1986). Functional domains of the human glucocorticoid receptor. *Cell* **46**, 645–652.

GIGUERE, V., ONG, E. S., SEGUI, P. & EVANS, R. M. (1987). Identification of a receptor for the morphogen retinoic acid. *Nature, Lond.* **330**, 624–629.

GODOWSKI, P. J., RUSCONI, S., MIESFELD, R. & YAMAMOTO, K. R. (1987). Glucocorticoid receptor mutants that are constitutive activators of transcriptional enhancement. *Nature* **325**, 365–368.

HAM, R. G. & VEOMETT, M. J. (1980). *Mechanisms of Development*, St. Louis, Mosby Co., p. 428–470 and 643–658.

HERR, W., STURM, R. A., CLERC., R. G., CORCORAN, L. M., BALTIMORE, D., SHARP, P. A., INGRAHAM, H. A., ROSENFELD, M. G., FINNEY, M., RUVKUN, G. & HORVITZ, H. R. (1988). The POU Domain: A large conserved region in the mammalian Pit-1, Oct-1, Oct-2, and *Caenorhabditis elegans unc-86* gene products. *Genes and Dev.* **2**, 1513–1516.

HOLLENBERG, S. M., WEINBERGER, C., ONG, E. S., CERELLI, G., ORO, A., LEBO, R., THOMPSON, E. B., ROSENFELD, M. G. & EVANS, R. M. (1985). Primary structure and expression of a functional human Glucocorticoid receptor cDNA. *Nature* **318**, 635–641.

HOLLENBERG, S. M. & EVANS, R. M. (1988). Multiple and cooperative transactivation domains of the human glucocorticoid receptor. *Cell* **55**, 899–906.

HOLLENBERG, S. M., GIGUERE, V., SEGUI, P. & EVANS, R. M. (1987). Colocalization of DNA-binding and transcriptional activation functions in the human glucocorticoid receptor. *Cell* **49**, 39–46.

IVARIE, R. D. & O'FARRELL, P. H. (1978). The glucocorticoid domain: steroid-mediated changes in the rate of synthesis of rat hepatoma proteins, *Cell* **13**, 41–55.

JENSEN, E. V. & DeSOMBRE, E. R. (1972). Mechanism of action of the female sex hormones. *Annual Rev. Biochem* **41**, 203.

KARIN, M., HASLINGER, A., HOLTGREVE, A., RICHARDS, R. I., KRAUTER, P., WESTPHAL, H. M. & BEATO, M. (1984). Characterization of DNA sequences through which cadmium and glucocorticoid hormones induce human metallothionein-IIa, *Nature* **308**, 513.

LEHMANN, R. & NUSSLEIN-VOLHARD, C. (1986). Abdominal segmentation, pole cell formation, and embryonic polarity require the localized activity of oskar, a maternal gene in *Drosophila. Cell* **47**, 141–152.

MADEN, M. (1982). Vitamin A and pattern formation in the regenerating limb *Nature* **295**, 672–675.

MORGAN, T. H. (1934). *Embryology and Genetics.* New York, USA: Columbia University Press p.11–17.

NAUBER, U., PANKRATZ, M. J., LEHMANN, R., KIENLIN, A., SEIFERT, E., KLEMM, U. & JACKLE, H. (1988). Abdominal segmentation of the *Drosophila* embryo requires a hormone receptor-like protein encoded by the Gap gene *knirps. Nature, Lond.* **336**, 489–492.

NUSSLEIN-VOLHARD, C., FROHNHOFER, H. G. & LEHMANN, R. (1987). Determination of anteroposterior polarity in *Drosophila. Science* **238**, 1675–1681.

NUSSLEIN-VOLHARD, C. & WIESCHAUS, E. (1980). Mutations affecting segment number and polarity in *Drosophila. Nature, Lond.* **287**, 795–801.

ORO, A. E., HOLLENBERG, S. M. & EVANS, R. M. (1988*b*). Transcriptional inhibition by a glucocorticoid receptor-β-galactosidase fusion protein *Cell* **55**, 1109–1114.

ORO, A. E., ONG, E. S., MARGOLIS, J. S., POSAKONY, J. W., MCKEOWN, M. & EVANS, R. M. (1988*a*). The *Drosophila* gene *knirps-related* is a member of the steroid-receptor gene superfamily *Nature, Lond.* **336**, 493–496.

PETKOVICH, M., BRAND, N. J., KRUST, A. & CHAMBON, P. (1987). A human retinoic acid receptor which belongs to the family of nuclear receptors. *Nature, Lond.* **330**, 444–450.

RINGOLD, G. M. (1985). Steroid hormone regulation of gene expression. *Ann. Rev. Pharmacol. Toxicol.* **25**, 529–566.

SAP, J., MUNOZ, A., DAMM, K., GOLDBERG, Y., GHYSDAEL, J., LEUTZ, A., BEUG, H. & VENNSTROM, B. (1986). The c-erbA protein is a high-affinity receptor for thyroid hormone. *Nature, Lond.* **324**, 635.

SCHEIDEREIT, C., GEISSE, S., WESTPHAL, H. M. & BEATO, M. (1983). The Glucocorticoid receptor binds to defined nucleotide sequences near the promoter of Mouse Mammary Tumour Virus. *Nature, Lond.* **30**, 749–752.

SCHWIND, J. L. (1933). Tissue Specificity at the time of metamorphosis in Frog larvae. *J. exp Zool.* **66**, 12.

SEGRAVES, W. (1988). Molecular and genetic analysis of the E75 ecdysone-responsive gene of *Drosophila melanogaster,* Ph.D. Thesis, Stanford University.

STEEL, C. G. H. & DAVEY, K. G. (1985). Integration of the insect endocrine system, in Kerkut, G.A. & Gilbert, L.I., eds, *Comprehensive Insect Physiology Biochemistry and Pharmacology,* Oxford, Pergamon, Vol **8**, p.1–35.

THALLER, C. & EICHELE, G. (1987). Identification and spatial distribution of retinoids in the developing chick limb bud. *Nature, Lond.* **327**, 625–628.

TICKLE, C., SUMMERBELL, D. & WOLPERT, L. (1975). Positional signalling and specification of digits in chick limb morphogenesis *Nature* **254**, 199–202.

TORA, L., GRONEMEYER, H. J., TURCOTTE, B., GAUB, M. P. & CHAMBON, P. (1988). The N-terminal region of the chicken progesterone receptor specifes target gene activation. *Nature, Lond.* **333**, 185–188.

UMESONO, K., GIGUERE, V., GLASS, C. K., ROSENFELD, M. G. & EVANS, R. M. (1988). Retinoic acid and thyroid hormone induce gene expression through a common responsive element. *Nature, Lond.* **334**, 262–265.

WEINBERGER, C., HOLLENBERG, S. M., ROSENFELD, M. G. & EVANS, R. M. (1985). Domain structure of human glucocorticoid receptor and its relationship to the v-erbA oncogene product. *Nature, Lond.* **318**, 670–672.

WEINBERGER, C., THOMPSON, C. C., ONG, E. S., LEBO, R., GRUOL, D. J. & EVANS, R. M. (1986). The c-erbA gene encodes a thyroid hormone receptor *Nature, Lond.* **324**, 641.

YAMAMOTO, K. R. (1985). Steroid receptor regulated transcription of specific genes and gene networks. *A. Rev. Genet.* **19**, 209–252.

Development 1989 Supplement, 141–148 (1989)
Printed in Great Britain © The Company of Biologists Limited 1989

The role of fibroblast growth factor in early *Xenopus* development

J. M. W. SLACK, B. G. DARLINGTON, L. L. GILLESPIE, S. F. GODSAVE, H. V. ISAACS
and G. D. PATERNO

Imperial Cancer Research Fund, Developmental Biology Unit, Department of Zoology, South Parks Road, Oxford OX1 3PS

Summary

In early amphibian development, the mesoderm is formed around the equator of the blastula in response to an inductive signal from the endoderm. A screen of candidate substances showed that a small group of heparin-binding growth factors (HBGFs) were active as mesoderm-inducing agents *in vitro*. The factors aFGF, bFGF, kFGF and ECDGF all show similar potency and can produce inductions at concentrations above about 100 pM. The product of the murine *int-2* gene is also active, but with a lower specific activity. Above the induction threshold there is a progressive increase of muscle formation with dose. Single blastula ectoderm cells can be induced and will differentiate in a defined medium to form mesodermal tissues. All inner blastula cells are competent to respond to the factors but outer cells, bearing oocyte-derived membrane, are not.

Inducing activity can be extracted from *Xenopus* blastulae and binds to heparin like the previously described HBGFs. Antibody neutralization and Western blotting experiments identify this activity as bFGF. The amounts present are small but would be sufficient to evoke inductions *in vivo*. It is not yet known whether the bFGF is localized to the endoderm, although it is known that inducing activity secreted by endodermal cells can be neutralized by heparin.

The competence of ectoderm to respond to HBGFs rises from about the 128-cell stage and falls again by the onset of gastrulation. This change is paralleled by a rise and fall of binding of ^{125}I-aFGF. Chemical cross-linking reveals that this binding is attributable to a receptor of relative molecular mass about 130×10^3. The receptor is present both in the marginal zone, which responds to the signal *in vivo*, and in the animal pole region, which is not induced *in vivo* but which will respond to HBGFs *in vitro*.

In the embryo, the induction in the vicinity of the dorsal meridian is much more potent than that around the remainder of the marginal zone circumference. Dorsal inductions contain notochord and will dorsalize ventral mesoderm with which they are later placed in contact. This effect might be due to a local high bFGF concentration or, more likely, to the secretion in the dorsal region of an additional, synergistic factor. It is known that TGF-β-1 and -2 can greatly increase the effect of low doses of bFGF, although it has not yet been demonstrated that they are present in the embryo. Lithium salts have a dorsalizing effect on whole embryos or on explants from the ventral marginal zone, and also show potent synergism when applied together with HBGFs.

Key words: *Xenopus laevis*, mesoderm induction, mesoderm-inducing factors, fibroblast growth factor, fibroblast growth factor receptor, transforming growth factor beta, competence, morphogens.

Introduction

Work in experimental embryology has given us a fairly detailed picture of the processes of regional specification occurring in the *Xenopus* embryo prior to gastrulation. These processes are collectively called 'mesoderm induction' because they lead to the formation of a ring of mesodermal tissue around the equator of the blastula (Nieuwkoop, 1969; Dale *et al.* 1985; Gurdon *et al.* 1985; Jones and Woodland, 1987). This knowledge has made it possible to ask meaningful biochemical questions about the nature of the signals and the responses and about how they can lead to the

formation of a spatial pattern of specified regions in two or three dimensions.

Briefly, we believe that the egg is divided into three cytoplasmic zones by the onset of the first cleavage: animal, ventrovegetal and dorsovegetal. The animal hemisphere will form epidermis in the absence of inductive signals, but also has the competence to form mesodermal and probably endodermal tissues in response to such signals. The vegetal hemisphere consists of a large 'ventral inducing' zone and a small 'dorsal inducing' zone comprising less than 90° of latitude around the dorsal meridian (Dale and Slack, 1987b). During the blastula stages, these two regions emit signals which induce, respectively, an extended region of ventral mesoderm around most of the equator, and a small organizer region on the dorsal side. The signals are quite short range, their influence extending only a few cell diameters (Gurdon, 1989), but, because of simultaneous migration of cells down into the equatorial zone, about 40 % of the animal hemisphere eventually becomes recruited into the mesoderm (Dale and Slack, 1987*a*). These signals are the first two of the 'three-signal model' which our group has advanced to explain mesodermal patterning, the third being a dorsalization of the mesoderm as a function of distance from the organizer (Slack and Forman, 1980; Smith and Slack, 1983; Dale and Slack, 1987*b*). This model may need to be revised as new data come in but at present we believe that it still provides the best unified account of the known facts.

This understanding naturally leads us to ask three questions: (1) What is the molecular nature of the inducing substances? (2) Are dorsal and ventral signals qualitatively or quantitatively different? (3) What is the molecular nature of the competence of the animal hemisphere cells? Two critically important clues were provided by recent experiments on signal transmission. Grunz and Tacke (1986) showed that the signals could pass through a nucleopore filter in the absense of cell processes, and Warner and Gurdon (1987) showed that the signals could pass from vegetal to animal cells even when gap junction communication had been blocked. These biological experiments greatly narrowed the possible range of mechanisms and firmly pointed towards signals that consisted of *secreted extracellular substances*. In this paper, we describe our recent work on the role of fibroblast growth factor in mesoderm induction. Work on TGFβ-like factors is described in the accompanying paper by Smith and his colleagues.

Which factors are active?

Although sources of mesoderm-inducing factors (MIFs) were discovered many years ago, they tended to excite little interest. This was for three reasons: they came from heterologous sources; they were assayed as grafted pellets, a method that precludes quantitative biochemistry; and most were very crude extracts. The best characterized was the 'vegetalizing factor' of Tiedemann (1982) isolated from late chick embryos, but even this did not inspire confidence in the wider scientific community. We started work on the subject in 1984, following our reinvestigation of the basic mesoderm induction phenomenon, and commenced by establishing an assay procedure for MIFs which was quantitative and which worked in solution. Briefly, this consists of treating animal pole explants with serial dilutions of the test substance and defining the minimum concentration required to provoke an induction as 1 unit ml^{-1}. The full procedure is described in Godsave *et al.* (1988; see also Cooke *et al.* 1987). We then attempted to extend Tiedemann's work on the chick embryo factor using our improved assay, but, following

the report by Smith (1987) of inducing activity secreted by a *Xenopus* cell line, we turned our attention to an investigation of known growth factors. In our initial screen, we tested a wide range of factors and found only three that were active. These were basic fibroblast growth factor (bFGF), embryonal carcinoma derived growth factor (ECDGF) and acidic fibroblast growth factor (aFGF), all of which belonged to a small group of heparin-binding growth factors (Slack *et al.* 1987). More recently, we have examined some of the FGF-like oncogenes that have recently been discovered (Paterno *et al.* 1989). We have done this by *in vitro* transcription of cDNAs from plasmids containing SP6/T7 bacteriophage promoters followed by translation in a rabbit reticulocyte lysate. The lysate can then be assayed directly by treating ectoderm explants with a series of dilutions, and the specific activity determined by measurement of the concentration of the translated protein. So far, we have examined kFGF, which is the product of the human *ks* and *hst* oncogenes (Delli-Bovi *et al.* 1987; Taira *et al.* 1987), and INT-2, the product of the murine *int-2* oncogene (R. Smith *et al.* 1988). Both are active as mesoderm-inducing factors. The specific activity of the kFGF is very similar to that of the a and bFGF, while the specific activity of INT-2 is very much lower. Considering the factors as a group, there is a good correlation between their mesoderm-inducing activity and their mitogenic activity when tested on mammalian fibroblasts. This suggests that similar signal transduction machinery is being used for the two processes. It should be emphasized that MIFs do not have any *mitogenic* effect on *Xenopus* blastula ectoderm cells, which are already cleaving every 30 min in the absence of growth factors and are probably incapable of further stimulation.

Meanwhile, work in other laboratories has shown that some factors belonging to the TGFβ family are also active. These are TGFβ-2 (Rosa *et al.* 1988) and the XTC-MIF of Smith (Smith, 1987; J. C. Smith *et al.* 1988) and so at the time of writing we have a total of seven active factors.

Which factors are present in the embryo?

Obviously the minimum requirement for identification of an endogenous morphogen is that the substance should be present in the embryo at the developmental stage when the relevant events are happening, and in amounts that are capable of exhibiting the observed degree of biological activity. We have approached this problem directly by asking whether a MIF can be obtained from the *Xenopus* blastula, and which of the seven or more candidates it is. Our results show that it is possible to purify a MIF from *Xenopus* blastulae using heparin-affinity chromatography and that it consists of two proteins of M_r 19 and 14×10^3 which react with antibodies against bFGF (Slack and Isaacs, 1989). The quantity in blastulae is about 10 ng ml^{-1} which is sufficient to account for the ventral but not the dorsal induction. The biological properties and specific activity of the *Xenopus* bFGF seem similar to the bovine bFGF which has been used for most of our experiments on the responses of animal cells. All the MIF activity in a crude embryo or ovary extract can be inhibited by a neutralizing antibody to bFGF, but not by antibodies to a or k FGF or TGFβ-2. Parallel work by Kimelman *et al.* (1988) has also shown the presence of bFGF mRNA and protein in *Xenopus* blastulae. Their estimate of quantity is much greater than ours but, unlike ours, it is not based on the use of quantitative biological assay methods.

We would obviously predict that the bFGF would be secreted by the cells of the vegetal hemisphere. So far, immunolocalization on embryo sections has not proved successful, probably because of the small quantities present. We have shown that the MIF released by vegetal cells in transfilter experiments can be neutralized by heparin, as can both *Xenopus* and bovine bFGF, but not by anti-bFGF antibodies. This may mean that the bFGF is secreted as part of some complex not recognised by our neutralizing antibody, but further work is necessary to prove beyond doubt that the vegetal cells really secrete bFGF. One problem in this regard is the well-known fact that bFGF lacks a classical signal sequence for secretion (Abraham *et al.* 1986), and so there remains some uncertainty about its mechanism of release from cells.

Effects of FGF on ectoderm explants

In this work, it has been found that the properties of a and bFGF in their capacity as MIFs are very similar indeed. In what follows, 'FGF' will be used to refer to either form indifferently.

Untreated explants from around the animal pole of *Xenopus* blastulae develop into solid masses of epidermal cells. It can be shown by using antibodies to epidermal markers that 100% of cells become epidermal (Fig. 1A–D). Mesoderm inductions can be provoked by FGF concentrations in excess of about 100 pM (Fig. 2A). After explants are exposed to FGF nothing much appears to happen for the first few hours, the explants round up with their blastocoelic surface inside and the cells continue to cleave just like untreated explants. However, it is the first 90 min or so of exposure that are critical. After this time, the FGF can be withdrawn without affecting the course of subsequent events. Then, while control embryos are undergoing gastrulation, the explants elongate with the original closure point at one end and the original animal pole at the other (Fig. 1E). Within a batch, the degree of elongation depends on the applied dose, but between batches there is considerable variation. After 24–36 h of culture, the induced explants start to swell and soon become transparent (Fig. 1F). These vesicles invariably contain mesodermal tissues although the quantity and type depends on the applied dose (Godsave *et al.* 1988; Slack *et al.* 1988). At low doses inductions consist of small amounts of mesenchyme and mesothelium with the occasional wisp of muscle while at higher doses we see increasing amounts of mesenchyme and increasing amounts of muscle (Fig. 1G,H; Fig. 2B). Notochord is sometimes observed following the higher dose treatments, particularly when *in vitro* translated bFGF is used, but its formation is not very predictable. This dose–response curve is significantly different from that obtained with XTC-MIF, which will induce notochord reliably at a low multiple of the minimum inducing concentration (J. C. Smith *et al.* 1988), however, it is probably rather similar to that of *Xenopus* bFGF (Fig. 3).

We have examined the location of ^{125}I-labelled FGF in explants and find that it binds mainly to those plasma membranes that are exposed at the blastocoelic surface. There is little binding to the plasma membrane of the external surface (oocyte-derived or O-membrane) and little penetration into the cell mass (Darlington, 1989). The maximal response to the high doses consists of about 20% muscle by cell composition with an additional 10–20% of mesenchyme and this probably represents all the cells that were exposed on the blastocoelic surface of the explant at the time of treatment. The fact that many cells in induced explants are still epidermal may be entirely due to the limited penetration of the FGF since our studies of single cells leads us to believe that all cells without O-membrane are potentially inducible (see below).

Competence of the ectoderm

Using animal–vegetal combinations from different stages, it has been shown that the competence of the ectoderm to respond to the natural signal(s) extends from about stage 6 (64 cells) to about stage $10\frac{1}{2}$ (Jones and Woodland, 1987). We have studied the *onset* of competence to FGF in the ectoderm by exposing for a period of 90 min explants taken from different stages and this shows that competence begins at about stage 7. We have studied the *loss* of competence by permanent exposure of ectoderm explants taken from different stages and this shows that competence is lost between stages 9 and 10 (Slack *et al.* 1988). Furthermore, the *degree* of competence can be assessed by measurement of the amount of muscle formed by explants from different stages in response to a standard dose, and this shows a rise and fall with the peak at stage 8 (Darlington, 1989). So the competence for FGF seems to rise at about the same time as competence for the natural MIF(s) but falls rather earlier, since there are about 3 h between stage 9 and $10\frac{1}{2}$ at 22–24°C. Competence to respond to XTC-MIF seems to persist into gastrulation, until stage $10\frac{1}{2}$–11 according to our measurements (Darlington, 1989).

Since inductions arise in response to FGF concentrations in the pM range we expected that an essential molecular component required for competence would be a specific receptor. We have probed for a receptor on explanted tissues using ^{125}I-aFGF and the cross-linking agent BS$_3$. This has shown that a receptor is present and appears as two gel bands of M_r about 130 and 140×10^3,

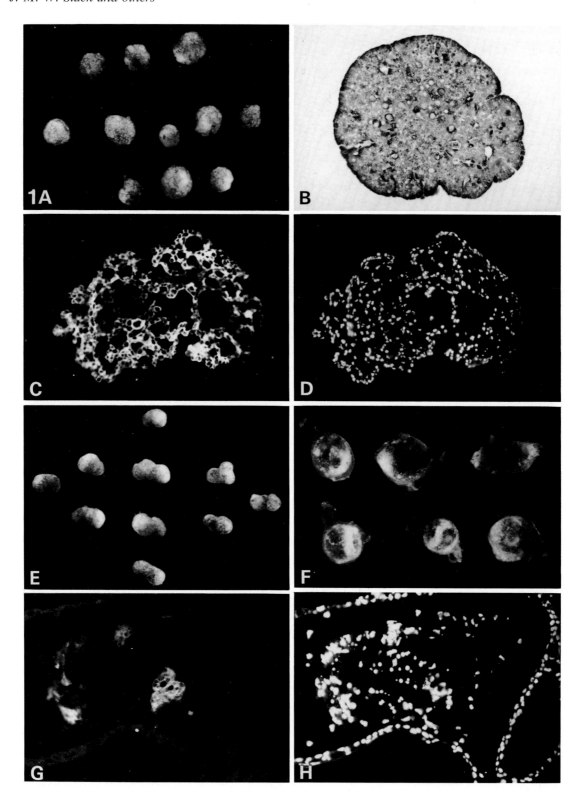

Fig. 1. Mesoderm induction by FGF. (A) Untreated ectoderm explants after 16 h. (B) Histological section of untreated ectoderm after 3 days. (C) Section stained with an antibody directed against cytokeratin XK70. All cells are stained. (D) Same section stained with DAPI to show cell nuclei. (E) FGF-treated explants after 16 h. (F) FGF-treated explants after 3 days ('vesicles'). (G) Section of induced explant stained with 12/101 anti-muscle antibody. (H) Same section stained with DAPI.

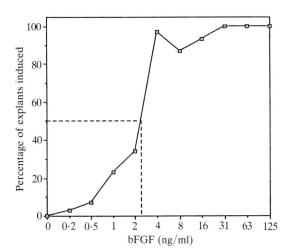

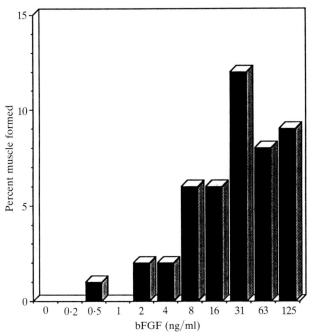

Fig. 2. FGF dose–response curves. (A) Percentage of explants induced by different concentrations of bovine bFGF. (B) Amount of muscle formed in ectoderm explants exposed to different concentrations of bFGF.

similar to the mammalian FGF receptor (Gillespie *et al.* 1989). Binding studies show that about 70–80 % of bound ^{125}I-FGF can be competed out by an excess of unlabelled FGF. Assuming that this represents binding to the specific receptor then the density is about 3×10^8 molecules mm^{-2} of cell surface which is within the range of values measured for mammalian cells. The binding curve shows a half-maximal value of about 3–4 nM and a plateau at about 10 nM, which is very similar to the dose–response curve for muscle formation. This suggests that the receptor binding is a *limiting step* in the response. If it were not, then a maximal response, in this case a maximal percentage of cells induced, would be obtained at an FGF concentration below that required to saturate the receptors.

The receptor density has been studied by binding of ^{125}I-aFGF to ectoderm explants taken from different embryonic stages. The competable binding rises by a factor of 10 between the early and middle blastula, and falls again to the starting level by the onset of gastrulation. This closely parallels the rise and fall of competence to respond to FGF and suggests that competence is indeed controlled by receptor density.

Competition experiments have shown that both a and bFGF bind to the same receptor but TGFβ-2 does not. This again resembles the situation in mammalian cells and makes it probable that the extended period of competence that ectoderm explants show when treated with XTC-MIF is due to the presence of separate TGFβ receptors.

We have measured the regional distribution of FGF receptors in stage 8 blastulae by binding studies on explants (Gillespie *et al.* 1989). This shows, as predicted, that FGF receptors are present both in the marginal zone region, which normally responds to the signal *in vivo*, and in the animal pole region, which can

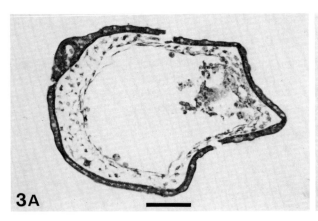

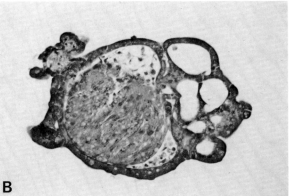

Fig. 3. Ectoderm explants induced by *Xenopus* bFGF and cultured for three days. (A) 4 units ml^{-1}. (B) 32 units ml^{-1}. Scale bar, 100 μm.

respond in experimental situations but would not normally do so *in vivo*. There is a slight excess of receptor density in the marginal zone but this is only 50 % more than the animal pole value, so it would seem that the normal extent of mesoderm induction is determined by the extent of the signal and not by the presence of a more highly competent tissue in the marginal zone. There is no difference in receptor density between dorsal and ventral regions of the animal hemisphere, so this cannot account for the difference between dorsal and ventral inductions. FGF receptor is also present in the vegetal region. We do not know whether these cells need FGF for their normal development since we cannot deprive them of it in the way that we can deprive the animal cells. However, since they do not normally turn into mesoderm, we can deduce that mesodermal competence consists of something more than the presence of FGF receptors on the cell surface.

Competence of individual ectoderm cells

Some other workers have noticed that isolated ectoderm cells will not differentiate into mesodermal cell types after induction, although their differentiation into epidermis may be suppressed (Symes *et al.* 1988). This phenomenon has been called the 'community effect' (Gurdon, 1988). We have found that this requirement can be met by a few simple macromolecular additives to the culture medium. Single internal blastula ectoderm cells can be induced if they are treated with FGF and then cultured in the presence of gamma-globulin on a surface coated with fibronectin and laminin. Usually they give rise to monotypic clones of muscle or an 'epithelium' which is a non-muscle, non-epidermal cell type, possibly a form of kidney. Sometimes mixed colonies are formed with more than one mesodermal cell type. When cells are treated for only 2 h with FGF, the colonies are always monotypic (Godsave and Slack, 1989). We are presently using this culture system to examine the specification of single cells isolated from different parts of the marginal zone of normal embryos, and have shown that mesodermal clones can be obtained from the marginal zone of midblastulae.

Further experiments involving the induction of single cells have shown that cells bearing the oocyte-derived membrane (O-membrane) are non-inducible (Darlington, 1989). The most informative protocol has involved (1) labelling of donor embryos by injection with the lineage label rhodamine-dextran-amine (RDA), (2) isolating single labelled cells in Ca^{2+}-free medium, (3) wrapping these in ectodermal jackets from unlabelled embryos, (4) inducing the whole sandwich with FGF or another MIF before it has sealed. When inner cells wholly surrounded by cleavage membrane (C-membrane) are used then many progeny of the labelled cell are found in the induction. However, when cells bearing O-membrane are used only a very few progeny are found to be induced. Close examination of these few shows that all of them are themselves wholly surrounded by C-membrane, and must therefore have

arisen from the original cell by tangential cleavage. So they do not represent exceptions but rather they are important positive controls, showing that the culture conditions do not militate against mesoderm differentiation. A further control in these experiments is provided by the fact that the cells that do not form mesoderm *do* form epidermis, showing that the failure to form mesoderm is not due to some damage inflicted on the cells in the course of the manipulations.

The nature of the dorsal induction

It is generally agreed that the signal near the dorsal meridian differs from that around the remainder of the blastula circumference. Some workers have tended to think that it is qualitatively similar but more intense while others have leaned towards the view that it is qualitatively different. If we accept that bFGF is *the* ventral morphogen, then the quantitative view seems unlikely since notochord inductions are not reliably produced even by very high concentrations of FGF, and the uniform distribution of FGF receptor shows that the dorsal and ventral ectoderm will respond alike to similar concentrations of FGF. However, it has been shown that the effect of FGF can be modified by other factors. There is strong synergism between FGF and TGFβ-1 (Kimelman and Kirschner, 1987) and between FGF and lithium ion (Slack *et al.* 1988). Neither TGFβ-1 nor Li are active as mesoderm-inducing factors on their own and the synergism is usually manifested as an excess formation of muscle rather than by induction of notochord. TGFβ-2 does have mesoderm-inducing activity on its own, and like FGF does not usually induce notochord. However, the synergism between FGF and TGFβ-2 is strong enough to give reliable induction of notochord (E. Amaya, pers. comm.). We have seen above that the receptors for FGF and TGFβ on *Xenopus* ectoderm are distinct but the synergistic effects suggest that there is a common intermediate at some level in the signal transduction pathway. This intermediate is presumably one whose level can be elevated by Li$^+$.

A reasonable working hypothesis based on these data might be that bFGF is the ventral morphogen and bFGF+TGFβ-2 the dorsal morphogen. We would further suppose that the FGF system is prelocalized in the vegetal hemisphere of the egg while the TGFβ system is activated on the dorsal side only as a result of the postfertilization cytoplasmic movements (see Fig. 4 and Gerhart *et al.* this volume). This would then explain the effects of UV radiation and Li$^+$ on whole embryos. If the vegetal hemisphere of the egg is irradiated with a sufficient dose of UV light then the cytoplasmic movements are inhibited and a radially symmetrical ventral embryo is formed (Grant and Wacaster, 1972; Cooke and Smith, 1987). The simplest interpretation of this is that the FGF system is normally present in the vegetal hemisphere all around the circumference and is unaffected by the treatment while the TGFβ system would depend on the postfertilization cytoplasmic movements

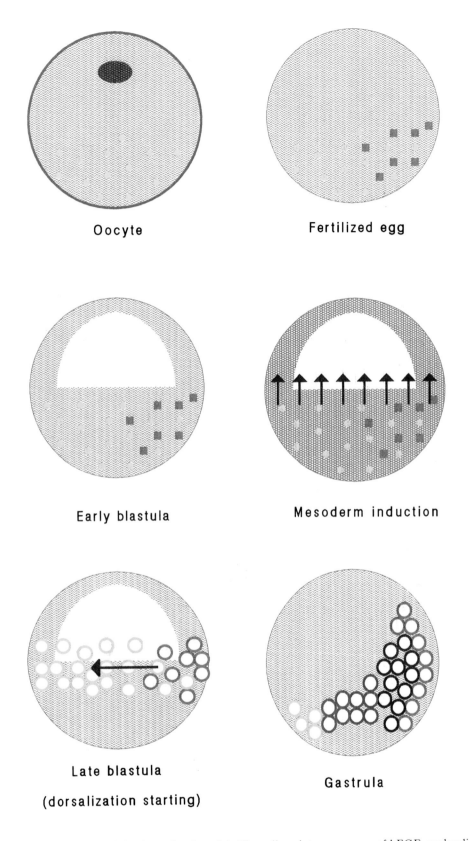

Oocyte

Fertilized egg

Early blastula

Mesoderm induction

Late blastula

(dorsalization starting)

Gastrula

Fig. 4. Diagram of current version of the three-signal model. The yellow dots are sources of bFGF, prelocalized in the oocyte. The red squares are sources of TGFβ-2 (or XTC-MIF) which become activated and localized on the dorsal side following fertilization. The green colour represents FGF receptors rising and falling during the blastula stages. The arrows represent short-range diffusion of the morphogens. The open circles represent cells: red for organizer type, yellow for ventral mesoderm type, other colours for intermediate mesodermal types formed by dorsalization.

which are blocked by the UV dose. Li$^+$ treatment of the early embryo produces a symmetrical dorsalization (Kao *et al.* 1986; Cooke and Smith, 1988). Here the postfertilization movements have already happened but we presume that the Li can elevate the concentration of a signal transduction intermediate and so mimic the effect of a uniform dorsal stimulus. It has been shown that lithium will dorsalize isolated ventral marginal explants to the level of large muscle masses (Slack *et al.* 1988; Kao and Elinson, 1988).

In fact, we have no evidence at present that the *Xenopus* homologue of TGFβ-2 is present in the early embryo and it may be that some other TGFβ-like molecule is doing the job. An obvious candidate is the XTC-MIF of Smith since this has chemical properties resembling TGFβ and is currently the most active of all the MIFs and the only one that will induce notochord on its own. Another possibility is the Vg1 product. Here we know that the mRNA is present in the embryo and localized in the vegetal hemisphere (Weeks and Melton, 1987; Yisrael *et al.*, this volume). However, there does not appear to be any preferential localization on the dorsal side, and perhaps more seriously there is as yet no indication of any biological activity shown by the protein. Clearly more data is needed in this area and in particular data on the presence, distribution and activity of TGFβ-like molecules in the early *Xenopus* embryo.

References

ABRAHAM, J. A., MERGIA, A., WHANG, J. L., TUMULO, A., FRIEDMAN, J., HJERRILD, K. A., GOSPODAROWICZ, D. & FIDDES, J. C. (1986). Nucleotide sequence of a bovine clone encoding the angiogenic protein, basic fibroblast growth factor. *Science* **233**, 545–548.

COOKE, J. & SMITH, E. J. (1988). The restrictive effect of early exposure to lithium upon body pattern in Xenopus development, studied by quantitative anatomy and immunofluorescence. *Development* **102**, 85–99.

COOKE, J. & SMITH, J. C. (1987). The midblastula cell cycle transition and the character of mesoderm in u.v.-induced non-axial *Xenopus* development. *Development* **99**, 197–210.

COOKE, J., SMITH, J. C., SMITH, E. J. & YAQOOB, M. (1987). The organization of mesodermal pattern in *Xenopus laevis*: experiments using a *Xenopus* mesoderm-inducing factor. *Development* **101**, 893–908.

DALE, L. & SLACK, J. M. W. (1987*a*). Fate map for the 32 cell stage of Xenopus laevis. *Development* **99**, 527–551.

DALE, L. & SLACK, J. M. W. (1987*b*). Regional specification within the mesoderm of early embryos of Xenopus laevis. *Development* **100**, 279–295.

DALE, L., SMITH, J. C. & SLACK, J. M. W. (1985). Mesoderm induction in Xenopus laevis. *J. Embryol. exp. Morph.* **89**, 289–313.

DARLINGTON, B. G. (1989). The responses of ectoderm to mesoderm induction in early embryos of Xenopus laevis. PhD thesis, University of Oxford.

DELLI-BOVI, P., CURATOLA, A. M., KERN, F. G., GRECO, A., ITTMANN, M. & BASILICO, C. (1987). An oncogene isolated by transfection of Kaposi's sarcoma DNA encodes a growth factor that is a member of the FGF family. *Cell* **50**, 729–737.

GILLESPIE, L. L., PATERNO, G. D. & SLACK, J. M. W. (1989). Analysis of competence: Receptors for fibroblast growth factor in early Xenopus embryos. *Development* **106**, 00–00.

GODSAVE, S. F., ISAACS, H. & SLACK, J. M. W. (1988). Mesoderm

inducing factors: a small class of molecules. *Development* **102**, 555–566.

GODSAVE, S. F. & SLACK, J. M. W. (1989). Clonal analysis of mesoderm induction. *Devl Biol.* (in press).

GRANT, P. & WACASTER, J. F. (1972). The amphibian gray crescent region – a site of developmental information? *Devl Biol.* **28**, 454–471.

GRUNZ, H. & TACKE, L. (1986). The inducing capacity of the presumptive endoderm of Xenopus laevis studied by transfilter experiments. *Wilhelm Roux' Arch. devl Biol.* **195**, 467–473.

GURDON, J. B. (1988). A community effect in animal development. *Nature, Lond.* **336**, 772–774.

GURDON, J. B. (1989). The localization of an inductive response. *Development* **105**, 27–33.

GURDON, J. B., FAIRMAN, S., MOHUN, T. J. & BRENNAN, S. (1985). The activation of muscle specific action genes in Xenopus development by an induction between animal and vegetal cells of a blastula. *Cell* **41**, 913–922.

JONES, E. A. AND WOODLAND, H. L. (1987). The development of animal cap cells in *Xenopus*: a measure of the start of animal cap competence to form mesoderm. *Development* **101**, 557–563.

KAO, K. R. & ELINSON, R. P. (1988). The entire mesodermal mantle behaves as Spemann's organizer in dorsoanterior enhanced Xenopus laevis embryos. *Devl Biol.* **127**, 64–77.

KAO, K. R., MASUI, Y. & ELINSON, R. P. (1986). Lithium induced respecification of pattern in Xenopus laevis embryos. *Nature, Lond.* **322**, 371–373.

KIMELMAN, D., ABRAHAM, J. A., HAAPARANTA, T., PALISI, T. M. & KIRSCHNER, M. W. (1988). The presence of fibroblast growth factor in the frog egg: its role as a natural mesoderm inducer. *Science* **242**, 1053–1056.

KIMELMAN, D. & KIRSCHNER, M. (1987). Synergistic induction of mesoderm by FGF and TGF-b and the identification of an mRNA coding for FGF in the early Xenopus embryo. *Cell* **51**, 869–877.

NIEUWKOOP, P. D. (1969). The formation of the mesoderm in urodelean amphibians I. Induction by the endoderm. *Wilhelm Roux' Arch. EntwMech. Org.* **162**, 341–373.

PATERNO, G. D., GILLESPIE, L. L., DIXON, M. S., SLACK, J. M. W. & HEATH, J. K. (1989). Mesoderm inducing properties of INT-2 and kFGF: two oncogene encoded growth factors related to FGF. *Development* **106**, 00–00.

ROSA, F., ROBERTS, A. B., DANIELPOUR, D., DART, L. L., SPORN, M. B. & DAWID, I. B. (1988). Mesoderm induction in amphibians: The role of TGFβ-2-like factors. *Science* **239**, 783–785.

SLACK, J. M. W., DARLINGTON, B. G., HEATH, J. K. & GODSAVE, S. F. (1987). Mesoderm induction in early Xenopus embryos by heparin-binding growth factors. *Nature, Lond.* **326**, 197–200.

SLACK, J. M. W. & FORMAN, D. (1980). An interaction between dorsal and ventral regions of the marginal zone in early amphibian embryos. *J. Embryol. exp. Morph.* **56**, 283–299.

SLACK, J. M. W. & ISAACS, H. V. (1989). Presence of basic fibroblast growth factor in the early Xenopus embryo. *Development* **105**, 147–154.

SLACK, J. M. W., ISAACS, H. V. & DARLINGTON, B. G. (1988). Inductive effects of fibroblast growth factor and lithium ion on Xenopus blastula ectoderm. *Development* **103**, 581–590.

SMITH, J. C. (1987). A mesoderm inducing factor is produced by a Xenopus cell line. *Development* **99**, 3–14.

SMITH, J. C. & SLACK, J. M. W. (1983). Dorsalization and neural induction: properties of the organizer in Xenopus laevis. *J. Embryol. exp. Morph.* **78**, 299–317.

SMITH, J. C., YAQOOB, M. & SYMES, K. (1988). Purification, partial characterisation and biological effects of the XTC mesoderm-inducing factor. *Development* **103**, 591–600.

SMITH, R., PETERS, G. & DICKSON, C. (1988). Multiple RNAs expressed from the int-2 gene in mouse embryonal carcinoma cell lines encode a protein with homology to fibroblast growth factor. *EMBO J.* **7**, 1013–1022.

SYMES, K., YAQOOB, M. & SMITH, J. C. (1988). Mesoderm induction in Xenopus laevis: responding cells must be in contact for mesoderm formation but suppression of epidermal differentiation can occur in single cells. *Development* **104**, 609–618.

TAIRA, M., YOSHIDA, T., MIYAGAWA, K., SAKAMOTO, H., TERADA, M. & SUGIMURA, T. (1987). cDNA sequence of human transforming gene hst and identification of the coding sequence required for transforming activity. *Proc. natn. Acad. Sci. U.S.A.* **84**, 2980–2984.

TIEDEMANN, H. (1982). Signals of cell determination in embryogenesis. pp. 275–287 in 33rd Colloguium Gesellschaft Biologische Chimie ed. Jaenicke L. Springer, Berlin.

WARNER, A. E. & GURDON, J. B. (1987). Functional gap junctions are not required for muscle gene activation by induction in Xenopus embryos. *J. Cell Biol.* **104**, 557–564.

WEEKS, D. L. & MELTON, D. A. (1987). A maternal messenger RNA localised to the vegetal hemisphere in Xenopus eggs codes for a growth factor related to TGFβ. *Cell* **51**, 861–867.

Development 1989 Supplement, 149–159
Printed in Great Britain © The Company of Biologists Limited 1989

Inducing factors and the control of mesodermal pattern in *Xenopus laevis*

J. C. SMITH, J. COOKE, J. B. A. GREEN, G. HOWES and K. SYMES*

Laboratory of Embryogenesis, National Institute for Medical Research, The Ridgeway, Mill Hill, London NW7 1AA, UK

* Present address: Department of Zoology, University of California, Berkeley, CA 94720, USA

Summary

The mesoderm of *Xenopus laevis* and other amphibia is formed through an inductive interaction during which cells of the vegetal hemisphere act on cells of the animal hemisphere. Two groups of factors mimic the effects of the vegetal hemisphere. One group consists of members of the fibroblast growth factor (FGF) family, while the other is related to transforming growth factor type *β* (TGF-*β*). In this paper we discuss the evidence that the FGF family represents 'ventral' mesoderm-inducing signals, and the TGF-*β* family 'dorsal' signals. The evidence includes a discussion of the cell types formed in response to each type of factor, the fact that only XTC-MIF (a member of the TGF-*β* family) and not bFGF can induce animal pole ectoderm to become Spemann's organizer, and an analysis of the timing of the gastrulation movements induced by the factors.

Key words: mesoderm induction, mesoderm-inducing factors, bFGF, XTC-MIF, thresholds, gastrulation, amphibian embryo, *Xenopus laevis*, developmental timers.

Introduction

The mesoderm of *Xenopus laevis*, and of other amphibian embryos, is formed through an inductive interaction in which cells of the vegetal hemisphere of the embryo act on blastomeres of the overlying marginal zone (Nieuwkoop, 1969, 1973; Sudarwati and Nieuwkoop, 1971; reviewed by Smith, 1989; Fig. 1A). This interaction is usually demonstrated by juxtaposing tissue from the animal cap and the vegetal pole (Fig. 1B). Normally, the animal cap material is too far from vegetal blastomeres to receive an inductive signal and when cultured alone it forms 'atypical epidermis' – cells that stain with antibodies to keratin but which do not adopt normal epidermal morphology (see Smith *et al.* 1985). However, when animal cap cells are placed in contact with vegetal cells a significant proportion (about 40 %) differentiate as mesodermal cell types, including notochord and muscle (Dale *et al.* 1985; Gurdon *et al.* 1985).

Recently, significant progress has been made towards identifying the 'mesoderm-inducing factors' (MIFs) produced by vegetal pole cells. The candidates fall into two classes. One consists of members of the TGF-*β* family and includes XTC-MIF (Smith, 1987; Smith *et al.* 1988; Rosa *et al.* 1988), TGF-*β*2 (Rosa *et al.* 1988) and perhaps the protein encoded by the localized mRNA Vg1 (Rebagliati *et al.* 1985; Weeks and Melton, 1987). TGF-*β*1 is unusual in that it has no mesoderm-inducing activity alone, but acts synergistically with members of the other class of MIFs, the FGF family (Kimelman and Kirschner, 1987). Active members of this family include aFGF, bFGF and embryonal carcinoma-derived growth factor (ECDGF) as well as the protein products of the *kFGF* and *INT-2* oncogenes (Slack *et al.* 1987; Kimelman and Kirschner, 1987; Paterno *et al.* 1989; see preceding paper by Slack and his colleagues).

In this paper, we compare the effects of the two classes of MIF and discuss how they might act together to establish the correct spatial pattern of cellular differentiation in the mesoderm of *Xenopus*. We then review what problems remain in coming to understand how combinations of inducing factors might set up the remarkably constant mesodermal pattern of *Xenopus* (Cooke and Smith, 1987).

The three-signal model

A series of experimental embryological experiments has led to the 'three-signal' model for the formation of mesoderm in the early amphibian embryo (see Smith *et al.* 1985). This model is explained in detail in the preceding paper in this volume by Slack *et al.* and will only be described briefly here (Fig. 2). Thus during oogenesis, which takes several months in *Xenopus*, the egg becomes polarized such that yolk, pigment and, most importantly, informational macromolecules, become localized to particular regions along the animal–vegetal axis (see Gerhart, 1980; Wylie *et al.* 1985; Melton, 1987; Yisraeli and Melton, 1988; Yisraeli *et al.* this volume). Until fertilization, however, the egg is radially symmetrical around the animal–vegetal axis: every meridian has the potential to form dorsal axial structures.

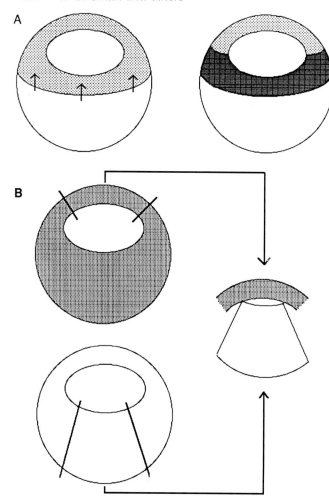

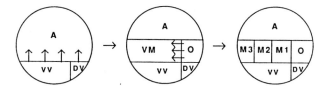

Fig. 2. The three-signal model. Two mesoderm induction signals are assumed to derive from the vegetal region of the early blastula. The dorsal–vegetal (DV) signal induces dorsal mesoderm, or 'organizer' tissue (O) while the ventral vegetal signal (VV) induces general ventral mesoderm (VM). The ventral mesoderm then receives a signal from the organizer, probably during gastrulation, which results in the formation of additional muscle (M1) and perhaps pronephros (M2); only the most remote tissue (M3) remains as ventral blood-forming mesoderm.

Fig. 1. Mesoderm induction. (A) At early blastula stages the *Xenopus* embryo can be considered to consist of two cell types: presumptive ectoderm in the animal hemisphere (light stippling) and presumptive endoderm in the vegetal hemisphere (no stippling) (Jones and Woodland, 1986). During mesoderm induction a signal from the vegetal hemisphere induces overlying equatorial cells to form mesoderm (heavy stippling). This view is somewhat simplified for it is not possible to draw an accurate line between vegetal inducing cells and animal pole responding cells. Indeed, it may be that some cells both produce and respond to the signal. (B) The classical demonstration of mesoderm induction. Blastomeres from the animal pole of a lineage-labelled blastula-staged embryo are placed in contact with cells from the vegetal pole of an unlabelled embryo.

This symmetry is broken at fertilization, when the sperm entry point defines the direction of rotation of the cortex of the egg with respect to the subcortical cytoplasm. The orientation of this rotation in turn accurately predicts the future dorsoventral axis of the embryo (see Gerhart *et al.* this volume). The mechanism by which this occurs is unknown, but it is clear that most of the dorsoventral patterning information thus created is in the vegetal region of the egg. This can be demonstrated using animal–vegetal combinations; when animal pole cells are combined with dorsal

vegetal blastomeres they form notochord, a dorsal mesodermal cell type, while ventral vegetal blastomeres induce blood, mesenchyme and mesothelium which are usually regarded as ventral mesodermal cell types (Boterenbrood and Nieuwkoop, 1973; Dale *et al.* 1985; Dale and Slack, 1987*b*; see Smith, 1989). An analogous experiment was performed by Gimlich and Gerhart (1984), who showed that embryos made radially symmetrical by UV irradiation of the vegetal hemisphere of the egg shortly after fertilization could be 'rescued' by dorsal vegetal, but not ventral vegetal, blastomeres.

It should be noted that the terms 'dorsal' and 'ventral' are somewhat misleading when applied to the preneurula-stage embryo. As a result of the earlier and more vigorous gastrulation movements on the 'dorsal' side of the embryo, these cells form most of the head and anterior of the larva, including structures which in the final morphology are 'ventral', as well as the notochord and some somitic tissue of the trunk. Consequently, blastomeres on the 'ventral' side tend to form ventral structures in the trunk region of the embryo, but axial structures more posteriorly (Cooke and Webber, 1985; Keller, 1975, 1976; Smith and Slack, 1983; Cleine and Slack, 1985; Dale and Slack, 1987*a*).

Thus, at the blastula stage one can distinguish, by operational criteria, at least two types of mesoderm induction signal. One of these induces predominantly dorsal cell types and one ventral. But two signals, or even three or four, from the vegetal hemisphere are unlikely to be sufficient to establish directly a complex and reproducible pattern of mesodermal cell types. One indication that more signalling subsequently takes place is that the fate map of *Xenopus* shows that at least half of the muscle of the embryo arises from the ventral side of the embryo (Cooke and Webber, 1985; Keller, 1976; Dale and Slack, 1987*a*), whereas the ventral vegetal blastomeres induce very little muscle from responding animal pole tissue (Dale *et al.* 1985; Dale and Slack, 1987*b*). This paradox can be resolved by the third signal of the model, which is produced by dorsal mesoderm cells and which acts on adjacent ventral mesoderm to cause it to form muscle instead of ventral tissues. This interaction can be demonstrated by juxtaposing dorsal and ventral marginal zones *in vitro*. Normally, in isolation, the ventral tissue forms blood, mesenchyme and mesothelium, but in response to the dorsal tissue it forms muscle instead. The dorsal tissue, meanwhile, forms notochord as usual (Slack and Forman, 1980; Smith *et al.* 1985; Dale and Slack, 1987*b*). An alternative demonstration of this phenomenon of dorsalization is to implant dorsal marginal zone tissue into the ventral marginal zone of a host early gastrula (Smith and Slack, 1983). This is the famous organizer graft of Spemann and Mangold (1924), and results in an embryo with mirror-image symmetry in the mesoderm which is also reflected in the induction of two neural tubes (Gimlich and Cooke, 1983; Smith and Slack, 1983; Jacobson, 1984).

The three-signal model is summarized in Fig. 2. It is important to note that the model does not address the acquisition of anteroposterior positional values. This is rather poorly understood although the current models are discussed in this volume by Gerhart and his colleagues. One suggestion these authors make, however, is that the completeness of the anteroposterior axis depends upon the size of the organizer, the region designated 'O' in Fig. 2. We present some results below which are consistent with this view.

Mesoderm-inducing factors

As outlined in the Introduction, mesoderm-inducing factors in *Xenopus* fall into two families: FGF and TGF-β. The members of these families are summarized in Table 1. At present, no member of either family satisfies all the criteria for being a true morphogen (see Slack and Isaacs, 1989; Wolpert, this volume). Thus for the TGF-β family the most active inducer is XTC-MIF (Smith *et al.* 1988; Green *et al.*, in preparation) but it is not yet known whether the molecule is present in the early embryo. One member of the TGF-β family which *is* present in the embryo is the Vg1 protein (Dale *et al.* 1989; Tannahill and Melton, 1989), but it is not yet known whether this has mesoderm-inducing activity.

The situation is slightly clearer with the FGF family, where it is known that bFGF is present in the embryo in sufficient quantity to act as a mesoderm inducer (Kimelman *et al.* 1988; Slack and Isaacs, 1989). It is not known, however, if the protein is localized to the vegetal region of the embryo, and indeed this seems unlikely because bFGF is synthesized throughout oogenesis and would be expected to be free to diffuse throughout the oocyte. In addition, *Xenopus* bFGF, like bovine bFGF, carries no secretion signal sequence (Abraham *et al.* 1986; Kimelman *et al.* 1988), so it is not clear how it might escape from vegetal blastomeres. To confirm that bFGF plays a role in mesoderm induction it is necessary, therefore, to ablate the protein from the embryo and show that mesoderm formation is disrupted.

Thus it is not clear whether the two *Xenopus*-derived inducing factors available in pure form – XTC-MIF and bFGF – play a role in normal development. Nevertheless, it has been possible to carry out important experiments with the molecules, and as we discuss below the

results are consistent with bFGF being the ventral vegetal inducing signal and XTC-MIF, or something like it, the dorsal signal.

XTC-MIF and bFGF: dorsal and ventral signals

We outline below three types of experiment that indicate that XTC-MIF and bFGF mimic, respectively, the dorsal and ventral mesoderm-inducing signals represented in Fig. 2. This conclusion is important in itself, but, as we show, the work should lead to improved understanding of thresholds in development, of Spemann's organizer, of the control of cell motility, and of timing in development.

Concentration-dependent effects of XTC-MIF and bFGF

The first series of experiments investigates the effects of exposing *Xenopus* animal pole regions to different concentrations of XTC-MIF or *Xenopus* bFGF (XbFGF). Animal caps were dissected from embryos at the midblastula stage and cultured in inducing factor until sibling embryos reached the swimming tadpole stage. In order that all the cell types present could be recognized, and to preserve the three-dimensional structure of the explants, the specimens were fixed, sectioned and stained by conventional histological procedures, before being examined under the microscope.

Two conclusions could be drawn from this experiment. First, only XTC-MIF, and not XbFGF, induced notochord from animal pole tissue (Smith *et al.* 1988; Green *et al.* in preparation; see Godsave *et al.* 1988 and Slack *et al.* 1988 for results with bovine bFGF). This strongly suggests that XTC-MIF more resembles the dorsal mesoderm-inducing signal and XbFGF the ventral. The second conclusion is that the type of induction observed depends upon the concentration of inducing factor. Thus for XbFGF, $1\,\mathrm{ng\,ml^{-1}}$ causes all explants to become induced, but the cell types formed only rarely include muscle; most of the induced tissue is best described as mesenchyme and mesothelium (Fig. 3E). These cell types are often regarded as 'ventral mesoderm' but it is worth emphasizing that without molecular markers this classification is tentative at best, and may result from a regrettable tendency to classify any tissue formed in response to a 'mesoderm-inducing factor' as 'mesoderm'. The best justification for the view is that the cells resemble mesoderm in their social behaviour and adhesive preferences (Cooke and Smith, 1989) and that they resemble the cell types formed by animal pole tissue after juxtaposition with ventral vegetal pole tissue (Dale *et al.* 1985; see Smith, 1989). Higher concentrations of XbFGF begin to induce muscle, but $25-50\,\mathrm{ng\,ml^{-1}}$ is required for the formation of significant amounts (Fig. 3F) (Green *et al.*, in preparation; see Godsave *et al.* 1988 and Slack *et al.* 1988 for results with bovine bFGF). As stated above, notochord is never observed.

A similar transformation in cell types is seen with XTC-MIF. Low concentrations (less than $1\,\mathrm{ng\,ml^{-1}}$)

tend to induce mesenchyme and mesothelium (Fig. 3B) while higher concentrations result in muscle formation (Fig. 3C). However, with XTC-MIF muscle formation is maximal at about 5 ng ml^{-1} and in some experiments muscle differentiation falls off beyond this point to be replaced by notochord and neural tissue (Fig. 3D) (Smith *et al.* 1988). The transformation from muscle differentiation to notochord formation is, however, somewhat variable (Green *et al.* in preparation) and this is currently under investigation.

Rather than considering XbFGF as a weaker meso-

derm inducer than XTC-MIF, it may be more accurate to regard the two factors as producing qualitatively different types of mesoderm rather than different 'grades' of the same type. Some cell-biological evidence for this point of view is provided by recent studies on MIF-induced gastrulation movements (below) but additional molecular evidence comes from recent work by Rosa (1989) which shows that the gene Mix.1 is strongly activated by XTC-MIF but not by XbFGF, at concentrations where both induce mesoderm.

The observation that different concentrations of

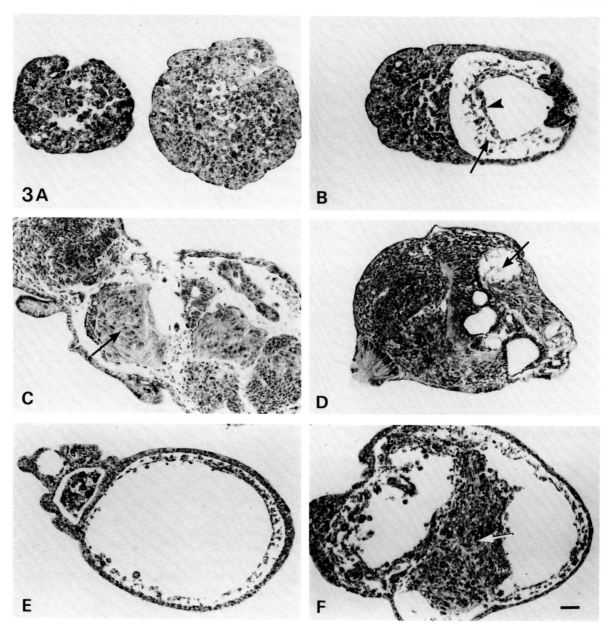

Fig. 3. Cell types formed in response to bFGF and XTC-MIF. (A) Animal pole regions cultured in the absence of mesoderm-inducing factors form 'atypical epidermis'. (B) 0.2 ng ml^{-1} XTC-MIF causes the formation of 'mesenchyme' (arrow) and 'mesothelium' (arrowhead). (C) 1–2 ng ml^{-1} XTC-MIF is sufficient to induce quite large amounts of muscle from animal pole regions (arrow). (D) In some experiments with high concentrations of XTC-MIF, notochord is formed (arrow). Notice the cement gland at the opposite side of the explant. (E) 1–10 ng ml^{-1} *Xenopus* bFGF causes the formation of mesenchyme and mesothelium. (F) Concentrations of approximately 50 ng ml^{-1} bFGF are required to induce muscle (arrow). Scale bar in (F) is 50 μm, and also applies to frames (A) to (E).

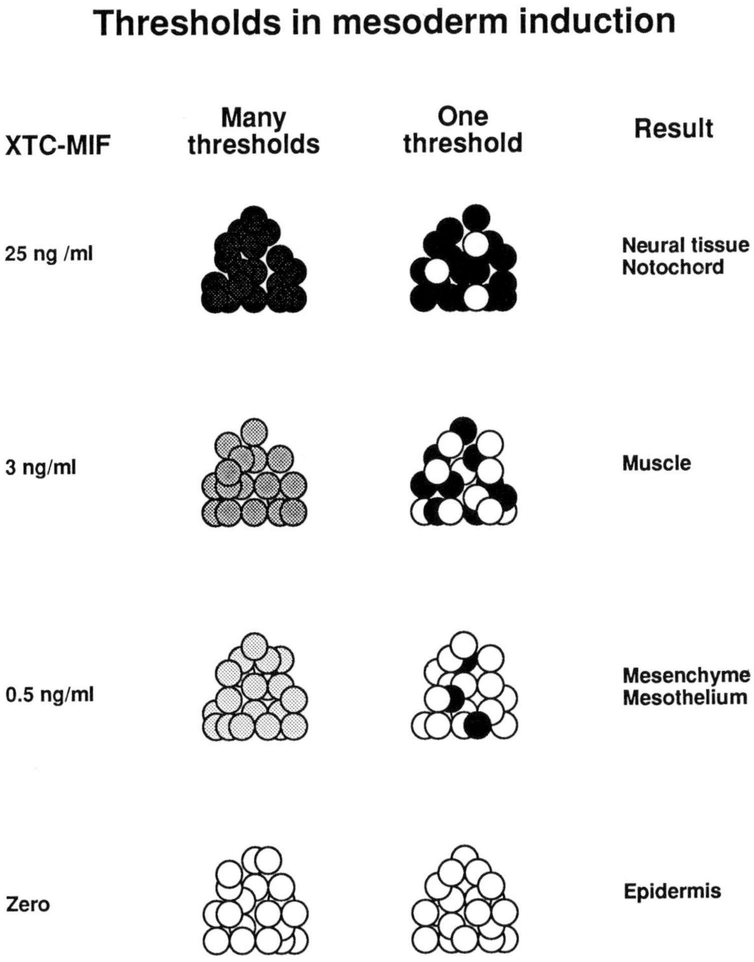

Thresholds in mesoderm induction

XTC-MIF	Many thresholds	One threshold	Result
25 ng /ml			Neural tissue Notochord
3 ng/ml			Muscle
0.5 ng/ml			Mesenchyme Mesothelium
Zero			Epidermis

Fig. 4. Two models for thresholds in mesoderm induction. In one model (left), each individual cell has a qualitatively different response to different concentrations of XTC-MIF; that is, each cell has many thresholds. The levels of response directly determines how the cell eventually differentiates. In the other model (right) each cell has only one threshold, and the cell types that eventually form depend on the proportion of cells that exceed that threshold. This model requires that there be communication between cells during, or shortly after induction by XTC-MIF.

XTC-MIF tend to cause the formation of different cell types raises the question of thresholds in development (Lewis *et al.* 1977). What form might these thresholds take? According to one view, each responding animal pole cell would have many thresholds, each activated at a certain concentration of XTC-MIF (Fig. 4; see Smith, 1989). Thus at $0.5 \, \text{ng ml}^{-1}$ XTC-MIF the first threshold would be exceeded and mesenchyme and mesothelium would form. Higher concentrations would cause further thresholds to be exceeded so that at, say, $25 \, \text{ng ml}^{-1}$ the cells would be programmed to form notochord and neural tissue. The following experiment, however, argues against such a model, and we go on to suggest an alternative view that the threshold phenomenon represents a cell population effect.

It is possible to disaggregate animal pole blastomeres by culturing animal caps in calcium- and magnesium-free medium. Such cells can be kept as a small heap or they can be dispersed over the culture dish, essentially as described by Sargent *et al.* (1986). If either heaped or dispersed cells are reaggregated at the early gastrula stage, by addition of divalent cations, they go on to form epidermis, their normal fate. If heaped cells are exposed to XTC-MIF, washed, and then reaggregated at the early gastrula stage, when mesodermal competence is almost over, they form muscle, epidermis, and sometimes notochord (Fig. 5; Symes, 1988). This

indicates that deprivation of divalent cations does not affect the primary response to XTC-MIF. By contrast, when cells are dispersed during exposure to XTC-MIF, muscle formation does not occur after reaggregation, although epidermal differentiation is supressed (Fig. 5; Symes, 1988). Several experiments, including measurements of rates of RNA and protein synthesis, indicate that this response is not due to toxicity of XTC-MIF (Symes *et al.* 1988).

These results suggest that mesoderm formation after exposure to XTC-MIF is not a direct response, but one which requires contact-dependent cell–cell interactions during induction. If this is so, the changes in patterns of cell differentiation with different concentrations of XTC-MIF might occur through these interactions, and it may only be necessary for blastomeres to have one threshold to XTC-MIF. Indirect evidence for a single threshold is that the time of onset of gastrulation movements in response to XTC-MIF, one of the earliest responses to induction yet observed (Symes and Smith, 1987; Cooke and Smith, 1989), and one that relates directly to mesodermal cell type, does not depend on the concentration of factor (Cooke and Smith, 1989; see below).

An alternative view of thresholds in mesoderm induction is that the phenomenon represents a cell population effect, with the proportion of cells responding to

XTC-MIF does not act on single cells to induce mesoderm

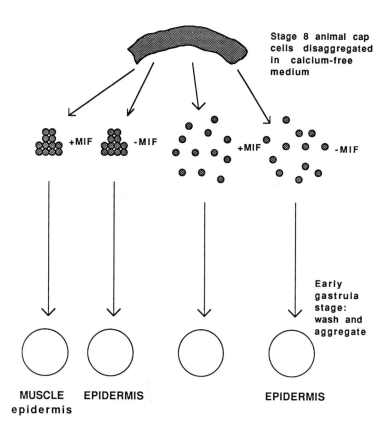

Stage 8 animal cap
cells disaggregated
In calcium-free
medium

+MIF   -MIF   +MIF   -MIF

Early
gastrula
stage:
wash and
aggregate

MUSCLE   EPIDERMIS   EPIDERMIS
epidermis

Fig. 5. Design of experiment to show that cell contact is required during treatment with XTC-MIF if muscle (and probably other mesodermal cell types) is to form. Animal caps are dissociated at the early blastula stage and cultured as indicated, either in a small heap or dispersed over the surface of an agar-coated Petri dish. Some cultures contain XTC-MIF. At the beginning of gastrulation, near the end of the period of competence to respond to XTC-MIF, the cultured blastomeres are thoroughly washed, reaggregated, and cultured until sibling embryos reached stage 40. The results were obtained by immunofluorescence analysis of specimens. Note that in the absence of XTC-MIF both 'heaped' and 'dispersed' cultures form epidermis and no muscle. When 'heaped' cells are exposed to XTC-MIF they eventually form epidermis and muscle, but neither cell type is detected if blastomeres are exposed to XTC-MIF while dispersed.

induction determining which cell types eventually form. Each cell, for example, could have a single binary on/off switch which is tripped by the primary inducing factor. Secondary signals, whose local strength would depend on the proportion of nearby 'switched on' cells, would then determine cell fate. Thus if 10 % of the cells respond to the primary signal, the population as a whole might form mesenchyme and mesothelium; if 50 % respond, muscle might arise; and, if 90 %, the cells might form notochord and neural tissue (Fig. 4). In future work, we hope to test this idea by mixing induced and uninduced cells in different proportions.

One way in which the proportion of cells responding to induction might influence cell differentiation could involve a timing mechanism. The sequence of cell differentiation in the mesoderm of *Xenopus* seems to follow the dorsoventral axis. Thus the notochord, the most dorsal mesodermal cell type, becomes visible as a separate group of cells at the late gastrula stage (Keller *et al.* 1985), and presumably this is preceded by transcription-dependent changes in the cell surfaces of these cells. Activation of muscle-specific actin genes occurs at the late gastrula stage (Gurdon *et al.* 1985), while transcription of globin genes, which characterize the most ventral cell type, blood, does not start until the tailbud stage (Banville and Williams, 1985). According to one model, similar to Cooke's (1983) 'serial diversion theory', cells induced by XTC-MIF or FGF might pass through phases of development during which they are

capable of differentiating first as notochord, then as muscle, and then as successively more ventral cell types. For differentiation to occur there must be a threshold level of a second signal, whose concentration depends upon the proportion of cells that are induced. If a small number of cells initially responded to induction, the concentration of second signal would be slow to build up, so that the phases during which notochord or muscle pathways can be entered will have passed, and their only option is to form ventral cell types. If many cells responded to induction, the second signal would accumulate rapidly, so that notochord could be formed. One reason why XTC-MIF but not bFGF can induce notochord might be that they produce different second signals which build up at different rates or have different specific activities. Alternatively, the accumulation of second signal in response to FGF may start later in development. Recent results on the timing of gastrulation movements induced by XTC-MIF and bFGF, described below, may support the latter idea (Cooke and Smith, 1989).

The requirement for cell contact between animal pole blastomeres during induction by XTC-MIF, if mesoderm is to form, bears upon some recent results of Gurdon (1988). Gurdon finds that the ability of an animal pole cell to form muscle in response to vegetal pole cells is dependent on the presence of other, similarly induced, animal pole cells. He calls this phenomenon the 'community effect'. It is possible that the effect is merely permissive; that is, that cells specified as muscle simply cannot express their appropriate phenotype as isolated individuals. Alternatively, cell contact could be instructive in the sense that the disposition and abundance of induced cells could decide which and how much of several fates eventually appear.

XTC-MIF-treated animal cap cells behave as Spemann's organizer

The above results suggest that animal pole cells exposed to XTC-MIF should be regarded as dorsal mesoderm, because they form notochord. A further property of dorsal mesoderm, however, is that it should also produce the dorsalizing signal mentioned above (see Fig. 2). We have tested this prediction by microinjecting XTC-MIF, bFGF or a control solution into the blastocoels of *Xenopus* embryos at the early blastula stage. Two hours later, small pieces of animal pole tissue are removed from these embryos, washed carefully, and grafted to the ventral marginal zones of host embryos (Fig. 6). The results show that ectoderm treated with XTC-MIF, but not with bFGF or a control solution, does indeed behave as Spemann's organizer and therefore produces a dorsalization signal (Cooke *et al.* 1987; Cooke, 1989). Experiments using lineage-labelled grafts confirm that the secondary axes in the

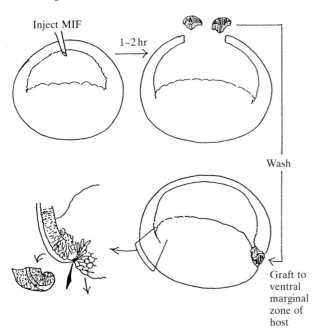

Fig. 6. Experiment to show that XTC-MIF-treated animal caps behave like Spemann's organizer. XTC-MIF, bFGF, or a control solution are injected into the blastocoel of a *Xenopus* embryo at the mid-blastula stage. 1–2 h later small pieces of animal cap tissue are dissected from the treated embryo, washed, and grafted to the ventral side of a host embryo.

The drawing at bottom left illustrates the architecture of the dorsal lip of the blastopore, the natural organizer. Only tissue above the bottle cells, consisting of dorsal mesoderm and suprablastoporal endoderm, has organizer activity; more vegetal endoderm lacks activity. Presumably XTC-MIF induces tissue of the former type.

double-dorsal embryos do consist largely of host tissue and have not arisen through self-differentiation of the graft (Cooke, 1989).

Interestingly, as would be predicted by the work of Gerhart *et al.* (this volume), the more 'powerful' the organizer (whether in terms of the concentration of XTC-MIF injected into the blastocoel or in terms of the size of the graft), the more complete the secondary axis formed, provided the cells having organizer activity are adequately localized within the tissue. Thus, presumptive ectoderm that has been exposed to a high concentration of XTC-MIF induces head, trunk and tail structures, while that exposed to lower concentrations might only induce trunk and tail. Finally, at the lowest concentrations of factor only tail is formed (Cooke, 1989). As with the concentration 'threshold' effects for XTC-MIF-induced cell differentiation, we do not yet know whether this gradation is mediated by a series of distinct organizer states in the cells, or through variation in the total number of cells in the graft that have been induced into an organizer 'state'.

These observations are of interest for three reasons. First, they confirm that XTC-MIF-treated ectoderm does indeed resemble dorsoanterior mesoderm, while bFGF-treated tissue is more similar to ventroposterior mesoderm, which lacks organizer activity (Smith and Slack, 1983). Second, the results offer an opportunity to screen for factors that represent the elusive organizer substance. It should be possible to conduct a differential screen to identify secreted molecules that are produced in response to XTC-MIF but not to bFGF. And finally, it may be possible to design experiments to explain how positional values are established along the anteroposterior axis of the embryo.

Inducing factors, gastrulation and the developmental timer

The first visible manifestation of mesoderm induction is gastrulation. In *Xenopus*, as in other Amphibia, gastrulation is under precise temporal and spatial control. This control is exerted through the cells of the mesoderm, which provide the motive force for gastrulation (Keller, 1986). Mesoderm-inducing factors, such as XTC-MIF and bFGF, induce gastrulation-like movements in animal pole tissue (Fig. 7) (Symes and Smith, 1987; Cooke *et al.* 1987; Rosa *et al.* 1988; Cooke and Smith, 1989), and this provides a new approach to the study of gastrulation (Smith, Symes, Hynes and DeSimone, in preparation).

One particularly interesting aspect of MIF-induced gastrulation movements concerns their timing. In a preliminary study Symes and Smith (1987) estimated the time of onset of gastrulation movements in isolated animal pole regions exposed to XTC-MIF. Within the limits of observation, the explants started to elongate at the equivalent of the early gastrula stage, irrespective of the stage at which they were exposed to the factor. This suggested that cells of the animal hemisphere contain a gastrulation 'timer', which is running even in those cells that would not normally need to refer to it.

Gastrulation movements induced by bFGF are less

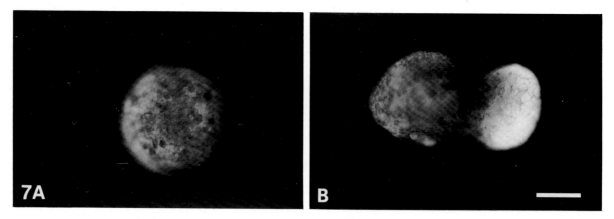

Fig. 7. XTC-MIF induces gastrulation-like movements in animal pole explants. (A) A control explant. (B) An induced explant 15 h after treatment with XTC-MIF. Scale bar in (B) is 200 μm, and also applies to (A).

dramatic (Slack *et al.* 1987), making it harder to estimate their time of onset. However, Cooke *et al.* (1987) and Cooke and Smith (1989) have introduced a technique to overcome this problem. This involves microinjecting MIFs into the blastocoels of *Xenopus* embryos so that the entire blastocoel roof becomes converted to mesoderm. As a result the whole of this tissue undergoes changes in cell shape and adhesion that mimic those occurring in the marginal zone of the embryo. The timing of these events can be estimated very precisely, by dissection of living and fixed embryos, and the first results confirmed those of Symes and Smith (1987) in showing that the time of onset of gastrulation-like movements is independent of the time of receipt of inducing factor. The data showed, however, that the time of onset was also independent of the concentration of factor and that the response could be very rapid. Thus if microinjection of the factor was delayed until just before the onset of gastrulation in the host embryo, the minimum possible interval between microinjection and onset of gastrulation movements in the ectopically induced mesoderm was at most 30 min (Cooke and Smith, 1989).

Microinjection of bFGF into the blastocoels of *Xenopus* embryos confirmed that the time of onset of the resulting ectopic gastrulation movements is, similarly, independent both of time of injection and of concentration of factor. However, the time at which bFGF-induced movements commence is significantly later, within the progress of the embryos 'own' gastrulation movements, than the time at which XTC-MIF-induced movements start. The interval, about 60 min, resembles the difference in time of gastrulation of dorsal and ventral mesoderm (Gerhart and Keller, 1986).

Here, then, is the third piece of evidence that XTC-MIF induces dorsal mesoderm and bFGF ventral; the gastrulation movements induced by the two factors differ in timing in a way that corresponds to the dorsal and ventral mesoderm of the early gastrula. But these results are also of great interest in the more general question of 'developmental timers'. Gurdon (1987) has emphasized that a significant difference between embryonic induction and other cellular interactions is indeed that in induction the time of response depends upon the responding tissue and not on the time of receipt of the signal. The example used by Gurdon was actin gene activation; Gurdon *et al.* (1985) showed that in animal–vegetal combinations this always occurs at the midgastrula stage, irrespective of the stage at which the combination was made. Thus, if the tissues were apposed at the early blastula stage, transcription occurred some 9.5 h later, but, if they were placed in contact at the early gastrula stage, the interval was only 5–7 h. In the molecular analysis of developmental time measurement, it may be more profitable to study the control of gastrulation than that of actin synthesis, because this is a much earlier response and there are likely to be fewer intervening steps between signal and response. In particular, it is noteworthy that one gastrulation-specific response, the ability to spread on a fibronectin-coated substrate, can occur in single cells (Smith, Symes, Hynes and DeSimone, in preparation), whereas muscle formation may require interactions between groups of cells (Gurdon, 1988; Symes *et al.* 1988). In the analysis of induction, it is a great advantage to be able to study single cells (Gurdon, 1987).

Conclusions

The work described in this paper summarizes the evidence that, of the two classes of mesoderm-inducing factor that have been discovered, members of the FGF family are likely to constitute the ventral vegetal signal, and members of the TGF-β family the dorsal vegetal signal. We think this is an important conclusion which should assist the design of future experiments aimed at understanding pattern formation in the mesoderm of *Xenopus* and perhaps other organisms.

Much, however, remains to be done. First, and seemingly most straightforward, it is necessary to establish just which of the inducing factors listed in Table 1 are present and active in the *Xenopus* embryo. It is then necessary to discover which of these are *required* for mesoderm formation, by inactivating the endogenous factors. At present it is not completely clear how this

Table 1. *Mesoderm-inducing factors in* Xenopus

| | | | Present in early embryo? | | |
Factor	Family	Active?	RNA	Protein	Localized?
Vg1[1]	TGF-β	Unknown	Yes	Yes	Yes
XTC-MIF[2]	TGF-β	Yes	Unknown	Unknown	Unknown
TGF-β1[3]	TGF-β	With FGF	Unknown	Unknown	Unknown
TGF-β2[4]	TGF-β	Yes	Unknown	Unknown	Unknown
aFGF[5]	FGF	Yes	Unknown	No	Unknown
bFGF[6]	FGF	Yes	Yes	Yes	Unknown
ECDGF[7]	FGF	Yes	Unknown	Unknown	Unknown
INT-2[8]	FGF	Yes	Unknown	Unknown	Unknown
kFGF[8]	FGF	Yes	Unknown	Unknown	Unknown

[1] Rebagliati *et al.* (1985); Weeks and Melton (1987); Melton (1987); Yisraeli and Melton (1988); Yisraeli *et al.* (this volume); Dale *et al.* (1989); Tannahill and Melton (1989).
[2] Smith (1987); Rosa *et al.* (1988); Smith *et al.* (1988).
[3] Kimelman and Kirschner (1987).
[4] Rosa *et al.* (1988).
[5] Slack *et al.* (1987); Slack *et al.* (1988); Slack and Isaacs (1989).
[6] Slack *et al.* (1987); Kimelman and Kirschner (1987); Kimelman *et al.* (1988); Slack and Isaacs (1989).
[7] Slack *et al.* (1987).
[8] Paterno *et al.* (1989).

might best be done. The most obvious approach is to microinject antisense oligonucleotides into the mature oocyte to destroy endogenous inducing factor mRNA (Shuttleworth and Colman, 1988), followed by maturing the oocyte by passage through a female frog and then fertilizing it (Holwill *et al.* 1987). However, this may not be effective because most Vg1 and bFGF protein seems to be synthesized during earlier oogenesis (Kimelman *et al.* 1988; Dale *et al.* 1989; Slack and Isaacs, 1989; Tannahill and Melton, 1989). An alternative approach might involve microinjection of antibodies against inducing factors into the fertilized egg. However, experiments such as these are difficult to control, and must be interpreted with care. When it is established which factors are involved in mesoderm induction it will be important to discover whether, like Vg1 (see Yisraeli *et al.* this volume), they are localized to the vegetal hemisphere, how that localization occurs, and, most importantly, how at least one of the factors becomes differentially activated on the dorsal side of the embryo in response to the postfertilization cortical rotation (see Gerhart *et al.* this volume).

It is also important to understand how factors like XTC-MIF and *Xenopus* bFGF exert different embryological, cellular and molecular effects, as outlined in this paper and elsewhere (Rosa, 1989; Green *et al.* in preparation). One possibility is that these differences are caused by the two factors activating different second messenger pathways, although the fact that the activity of both XTC-MIF and bFGF is enhanced by treatment of responding animal cap tissue with LiCl (Slack *et al.* 1988; Cooke *et al.* 1989) might be thought to argue that some of the signal transduction pathways are shared: one effect of lithium is to inhibit inositol monophosphatase (Hallcher and Sherman, 1980), thus blocking the recycling of InsP$_3$ to inositol and perhaps modulating the effects of any factor acting through inositol lipid-linked signalling systems (Drummond, 1987). This view of the effects of lithium is strengthened by the obser-

vation that the 'dorsalizing' effect of lithium, when microinjected into ventral blastomeres of the 32-cell stage embryo, is prevented by coinjection of equimolar *myo*-inositol (Busa and Gimlich, 1989). However, although these results are consistent with the suggestion that XTC-MIF and bFGF act through a similar second messenger pathway, lithium has so many other effects on cells that other interpretations are possible (see Slack *et al.* 1988).

A second aspect of the early response to inducing factors is that, as we discussed above, this is unlikely to specify cell differentiation directly; communication between the cells of an induced population seems to be required to define particular cell types (Symes *et al.* 1988). A signalling process of this sort seems to occur during gastrulation, and to be involved in establishing positional values along the anteroposterior axis of the embryo (see Gerhart *et al.* this volume). The nature of the molecules involved in this interaction is unknown at present, but it is possible that one of the early genes activated by XTC-MIF (Rosa, 1989) encodes a further signalling molecule.

Gastrulation itself may be controlled through a post-transcriptional response to mesoderm-inducing factors (Smith, Symes, Hynes and DeSimone, in preparation); animal pole cells can commence gastrulation-like movements in response to XTC-MIF within 30 min (Cooke and Smith, 1989), during which time even the early gene Mix.1 is only weakly activated (Rosa, 1989). Post-transcriptional events following treatment with XTC-MIF and bFGF are currently under investigation in this laboratory.

It is clear that mesoderm induction and mesodermal patterning in Amphibia are complicated processes that must involve sequential inductive interactions, different patterns of cell movement, post-transcriptional and post-translational controls, and the activation of many genes. At present our understanding is limited, but the identification of mesoderm-inducing factors, and the suggestion that the two groups of factors are active in different regions of the embryo, should allow us to improve our understanding quite rapidly.

References

ABRAHAM, J. A., MERGIA, A., WHANG, J. L., TUMOLO, A., FRIEDMAN, J., HJERRILD, K. A., GOSPODAROWICZ, D. AND FIDDES, J. C. (1986). Nucleotide sequence of a bovine clone encoding the angiogenic protein, basic fibroblast growth factor. *Science* **233**, 545–548.

BANVILLE, D. AND WILLIAMS, J. G. (1985). Developmental changes in the pattern of larval β-globin mRNA sequences, *J. mol. Biol.* **184**, 611–620.

BOTERENBROOD, E. C. AND NIEUWKOOP, P. D. (1973). The formation of the mesoderm in urodelean amphibians. V. Its regional induction by the endoderm. *Wilhelm Roux' Arch. devl Biol.* **173**, 319–332.

BUSA, W. B. AND GIMLICH, R. L. (1989). Lithium-induced teratogenesis in frog embryos prevented by a polyphosphoinositide cycle intermediate or a diacylglycerol analog. *Devl Biol.* **132**, 315–324.

CLEINE, J. H. AND SLACK, J. M. W. (1985). Normal fates and states of specification of different regions of the axolotl gastrula. *J. Embryol. exp. Morph.* **86**, 247–269.

COOKE, J. (1983). Evidence for specific feedback signals underlying pattern control during vertebrate embryogenesis. *J. Embryol. exp. Morph.* **76**, 95–114.

COOKE, J. (1989). Inducing factors, the body pattern and Spemann's organiser in amphibian development. *Development* **107**, 229–241.

COOKE, J. AND SMITH, J. C. (1987). The midblastula cell cycle transition and the character of mesoderm in u.v.-induced non-axial *Xenopus* development. *Development* **99**, 197–210.

COOKE, J. AND SMITH, J. C. (1989). Gastrulation and larval pattern in *Xenopus* after blastocoelic injection of a *Xenopus* inducing factor: experiments testing models for the normal organization of mesoderm, *Devl Biol.* **131**, 383–400.

COOKE, J., SMITH, J. C., SMITH, E. J. AND YAQOOB, M. (1987). The organization of mesodermal pattern in *Xenopus laevis*: experiments using a *Xenopus* mesoderm-inducing factor. *Development* **101**, 893–908.

COOKE, J., SYMES, K. AND SMITH, E. J. (1989). Potentiation by the lithium ion of morphogenetic responses to a *Xenopus* inducing factor. *Development* **105**, 549–558.

COOKE, J. AND WEBBER, J. A. (1985). Dynamics of the control of body pattern in the development of *Xenopus laevis*. I. Timing and pattern in the development of dorso-anterior and of posterior blastomere pairs isolated at the 4-cell stage. *J. Embryol. exp. Morph.* **88**, 85–112.

DALE, L., MATTHEWS, G., TABE, L. AND COLMAN, A. (1989). Developmental expression of the protein product of Vg1, a localized maternal mRNA in the frog *Xenopus laevis*. *EMBO J.* **8**, 1057–1065.

DALE, L. AND SLACK, J. M. W. (1987a). Fate map for the 32-cell stage of *Xenopus laevis*. *Development* **99**, 527–551.

DALE, L. AND SLACK, J. M. W. (1987b). Regional specification within the mesoderm of early embryos of *Xenopus laevis*. *Development* **100**, 279–295.

DALE, L., SMITH, J. C. AND SLACK, J. M. W. (1985). Mesoderm induction in *Xenopus laevis*: a quantitative study using a cell lineage label and tissue-specific antibodies. *J. Embryol. exp. Morph.* **89**, 289–312.

DRUMMOND, A. H. (1987). Lithium and inositol lipid-linked signalling mechanisms. *Trends in Pharmacological Sciences* **8**, 129–133.

GERHART, J. C. (1980). Mechanisms regulating pattern formation in the amphibian egg and early embryo. In *Biological Regulation and Development* (ed. R. Goldberger), pp. 133–316. New York: Plenum Press.

GERHART, J. C. AND KELLER, R. E. (1986). Region-specific cell activities in amphibian gastrulation. *A. Rev. Cell Biol.* **2**, 201–229.

GIMLICH, R. L. AND COOKE, J. (1983). Cell lineage and the induction of second nervous systems in amphibian development. *Nature, Lond.* **306**, 471–473.

GIMLICH, R. L. AND GERHART, J. C. (1984). Early cellular interactions promote embryonic axis formation in *Xenopus laevis*. *Devl Biol.* **104**, 117–130.

GODSAVE, S. F., ISAACS, H. V. AND SLACK, J. M. W. (1988). Mesoderm inducing factors: a small class of molecules. *Development* **102**, 555–566.

GURDON, J. B. (1987). Embryonic induction – molecular prospects. *Development* **99**, 285–306.

GURDON, J. B. (1988). Cell movements and a community effect in tissue morphogenesis. *Nature* **336**, 772–774.

GURDON, J. B., FAIRMAN, S., MOHUN, T. J. AND BRENNAN, S. (1985). The activation of muscle-specific actin genes in *Xenopus* development by an induction between animal and vegetal cells of a blastula. *Cell* **41**, 913–922.

HALLCHER, L. M. AND SHERMAN, W. R. (1980). The effects of lithium ion and other agents on the activity of *myo*-Inositol-1-phosphatase from bovine brain. *J. biol Chem.* **255**, 10 896–10 901.

HOLWILL, S., HEASMAN, J., CRAWLEY, C. R. AND WYLIE, C. C. (1987). Axis and germ line deficiencies caused by u.v. irradiation of *Xenopus* oocytes cultured *in vitro*. *Development* **100**, 735–743.

JACOBSON, M. (1984). Cell lineage analysis of neural induction: origins of cells forming the induced nervous system. *Devl Biol.* **102**, 122–129.

JONES, E. A. AND WOODLAND, H. R. (1986). Development of the ectoderm in *Xenopus laevis*: the definition of a monoclonal antibody to an epidermal marker. *Cell* **44**, 345–355.

KELLER, R. E. (1975). Vital dye mapping of the gastrula and neurula of *Xenopus laevis*. I. Prospective areas and morphogenetic movements of the superficial layer. *Devl Biol.* **42**, 222–241.

KELLER, R. E. (1976). Vital dye mapping of the gastrula and neurula of *Xenopus laevis*. II. Prospective areas and morphogenetic movements of the deep layer. *Devl Biol.* **51**, 118–137.

KELLER, R. E. (1986). The Cellular Basis of Amphibian Gastrulation. In *Developmental Biology: A Comprehensive Synthesis*, vol. **2**, *The Cellular Basis of Morphogenesis*. (ed. L. Browder), pp. 241–327. New York: Plenum Press.

KELLER, R. E., DANILCHIK, M., GIMLICH, R. AND SHIH, J. (1985). The function and mechanism of convergent extension during gastrulation of *Xenopus laevis*. *J. Embryol. exp. Morph.* **89**, Suppl. 185–209.

KIMELMAN, D., ABRAHAM, J. A., HAAPARANTA, T., PALISI, T. M. AND KIRSCHNER, M. (1988). The presence of FGF in the frog egg: its role as a natural mesoderm inducer. *Science* **242**, 1053–1056.

KIMELMAN, D. AND KIRSCHNER, M. (1987). Synergistic induction of mesoderm by FGF and TGFβ and the identification of an mRNA coding for FGF in the early *Xenopus* embryo. *Cell* **51**, 369–377.

LEWIS, J., SLACK, J. M. W. AND WOLPERT, L. (1977). Thresholds in development. *J. theor. Biol.* **65**, 579–590.

MELTON, D. A. (1987). Translocation of a localized maternal mRNA to the vegetal pole of *Xenopus* oocytes. *Nature, Lond.* **328**, 80–82.

NIEUWKOOP, P. D. (1969). The formation of mesoderm in Urodelean amphibians. I. Induction by the endoderm. *Wilhelm Roux' Arch. EntwMech. Org.* **162**, 341–373.

NIEUWKOOP, P. D. (1973). The "organization centre" of the amphibian embryo, its origin, spatial organization and morphogenetic action. *Adv. Morph.* **10**, 1–39.

NIEUWKOOP, P. D. AND FABER, J. (eds) (1967). *Normal Table of Xenopus laevis (Daudin)*, 2nd ed. Amsterdam: North-Holland.

PATERNO, G. D., GILLESPIE, L. L., DIXON, M. S., SLACK, J. M. W. AND HEATH, J. K. (1989). Mesoderm-inducing properties of INT-2 and kFGF: two oncogene-encoded growth factors related to FGF. *Development* **106**, 79–83.

REBAGLIATI, M. R., WEEKS, D. L., HARVEY, R. P. AND MELTON, D. A. (1985). Identification and cloning of localized maternal RNAs from *Xenopus* eggs. *Cell* **42**, 769–777.

ROSA, F. (1989). Mix.1, a homeobox mRNA inducible by mesoderm inducers, is expressed mostly in the presumptive endodermal cells of *Xenopus* embryos. *Cell* **57**, 965–974.

ROSA, F., ROBERTS, A. B., DANIELPOUR, D., DART, L. L., SPORN, M. B. AND DAWID, I. B. (1988). Mesoderm induction in amphibians: the role of TGF-β2-like factors. *Science* **329**, 783–785.

SARGENT, T. D., JAMRICH, M. AND DAWID, I. B. (1986). Cell interactions and the control of gene activity during early development of *Xenopus laevis*. *Devl Biol.* **114**, 238–246.

SHUTTLEWORTH, J. AND COLMAN, A. (1988). Antisense oligonucleotide-directed cleavage of mRNA in *Xenopus* oocytes and eggs. *EMBO J.* **7**, 427–434.

SLACK, J. M. W., DARLINGTON, B. G., HEATH, J. K. AND GODSAVE, S. F. (1987). Mesoderm induction in early *Xenopus* embryos by heparin-binding growth factors. *Nature, Lond.* **326**, 197–200.

SLACK, J. M. W. AND FORMAN, D. (1980). An interaction between dorsal and ventral regions of the marginal zone in early amphibian embryos. *J. Embryol exp. Morph.* **56**, 283–299.

SLACK, J. M. W. AND ISAACS, H. (1989). Presence of basic fibroblast growth factor in the early *Xenopus* embryo. *Development* **105**, 147–154.

SLACK, J. M. W., ISAACS, H. V. AND DARLINGTON, B. G. (1988). Inductive effects of fibroblast growth factor and lithium ion on *Xenopus* blastula ectoderm. *Development* **103**, 581–590.

SMITH, J. C. (1987). A mesoderm-inducing factor is produced by a *Xenopus* cell line. *Development* **99**, 3–14.

SMITH, J. C. (1989). Mesoderm induction and mesoderm-inducing factors in early amphibian development. *Development* **105**, 665–677.

SMITH, J. C., DALE, L. AND SLACK, J. M. W. (1985). Cell lineage labels and region-specific markers in the analysis of inductive interactions. *J. Embryol. exp. Morph.* **89 Supplement** 317–331.

SMITH, J. C. AND SLACK, J. M. W. (1983). Dorsalization and neural induction: properties of the organizer in *Xenopus laevis*. *J. Embryol. exp. Morph.* **78**, 299–317.

SMITH, J. C., YAQOOB, M. AND SYMES, K. (1988). Purification, partial characterization and biological properties of the XTC mesoderm-inducing factor. *Development* **103**, 591–600.

SPEMANN, H. AND MANGOLD, H. (1924). Uber Induktion von Embryonenanlagen durch Implantation artfremder Organisatoren. *Wilhelm Roux' Arch. EntwMech. Org.* **100**, 599–638.

SUDARWATI, S. AND NIEUWKOOP, P. D. (1971). Mesoderm formation in the Anuran *Xenopus laevis* (Daudin). *Wilhelm Roux' Arch. EntwMech. Org.* **166**, 189–204.

SYMES, K. (1988). Effects of a mesoderm-inducing factor on embryos and single cells of *Xenopus laevis*. PhD thesis, Council for National Academic Awards, UK.

SYMES, K. AND SMITH, J. C. (1987). Gastrulation movements provide an early marker of mesoderm induction in *Xenopus laevis*. *Development* **101**, 339–349.

SYMES, K., YAQOOB, M. AND SMITH, J. C. (1988). Mesoderm induction in *Xenopus laevis*: responding cells must be in contact for mesoderm formation but suppression of epidermal differentiation can occur in single cells. *Development* **104**, 609–618.

TANNAHILL, D. AND MELTON, D. A. (1989). Localised synthesis of the Vg1 protein during early *Xenopus* development. *Development* **106**, 775–786.

WEEKS, D. L. AND MELTON, D. A. (1987). A maternal mRNA localized to the vegetal hemisphere in *Xenopus* eggs codes for a growth factor related to TGFβ. *Cell* **51**, 861–867.

WYLIE, C. C., BROWN, D., GODSAVE, S. F., QUARMBY, J. AND HEASMAN, J. (1985). The cytoskeleton of *Xenopus* oocytes and its role in development. *J. Embryol. exp. Morph.* **89** (suppl.) 1–15.

YISRAELI, J. K. AND MELTON, D. A. (1988). The maternal mRNA Vg1 is correctly localized following injection into *Xenopus* oocytes. *Nature, Lond.* **336**, 592–595.

Development 1989 Supplement, 161–167 (1989)
Printed in Great Britain © The Company of Biologists Limited 1989

int-1 – a proto-oncogene involved in cell signalling

ANDREW P. McMAHON[1] and RANDALL T. MOON[2]

[1]*Department of Cell and Developmental Biology, Roche Institute of Molecular Biology, Nutley, NJ 07110, USA*
[2]*Department of Pharmacology SJ30, School of Medicine, University of Washington, Seattle, Washington 98195, USA*

Summary

The *int*-1 gene was originally identified as a locus activated by mouse mammary tumor virus insertion. Cloning and sequencing of the mouse gene indicates that *int*-1 encodes a 41K, 370 amino acid, cysteine-rich protein with a potential hydrophobic signal peptide sequence. Expression studies clearly indicate that *int*-1 enters the secretory pathway and is probably secreted, although definitive evidence is lacking.

Drosophila int-1 encodes the *wingless* gene. *wingless*, a segment-polarity gene, is required for the establishment of normal pattern in each segment. Genetic studies indicate that the *wingless* protein is probably secreted since it is required for the maintenance of stable gene expression in neighboring cells.

int-1 is also expressed during early neural stages of frog and mouse development. In the mouse, where expression is well characterized, *int*-1 RNA is restricted to the dorsal midline of the neural tube. By analogy with *Drosophila*, *int*-1 may operate to specify position within this structure. To test this idea, we have interfered with normal *int*-1 expression by injection of *int*-1 RNA into frog embryos. This results in a striking and specific aberration, bifurcation of the anterior neural tube. Thus, it seems possible that in vertebrates *int*-1 is able to influence patterning events.

Key words: *int*-1, proto-oncogene, *wingless*, positional signalling, neural expression, ectopic expression, neural tube bifurcation.

Introduction

In vertebrates, successful development of the primary germ layers and the various organs to which they give rise is critically dependent on cell signalling (see papers in this volume). However, until quite recently, the molecular nature of signalling processes has been a matter for conjecture. In view of the sophisticated molecular and genetic description of *Drosophila*, it is tempting to draw parallels between *Drosophila* and vertebrate development. In this paper, we review the evidence that implicates the *int*-1 gene in cell signalling in both *Drosophila* and vertebrates.

int-1 in mammary tumorigenesis

The *int*-1 gene was first identified following an analysis of mouse mammary tumour virus (MMTV) induced tumours, which occur quite frequently in certain strains of mice (for review, see Nusse, 1986, 1988). Reasoning that some of these tumours may result from proviral activation of cellular proto-oncognes, Nusse and Varmus (1982) analyzed sites of MMTV integration. The first locus isolated using this approach was termed *int*-1 (*int*=*int*egration). Since their initial report, several unrelated genes with similar modes of activation have been described (*int*-2, Peters *et al.* 1983; *int*-3 and *int*-4, Nusse, 1988). From analysis of many independent integrations, a clear picture of the role of MMTV has emerged. Proviral integration sites are clustered 5' and 3' of the *int*-1 gene with viral transcription in the opposite orientation to that of the *int*-1 gene (Nusse *et al.* 1984). Thus, MMTV activation of *int*-1 (and other genes of this class) presumably results from juxtaposition of MMTV enhancer sequences in close proximity to the *int*-1 locus. This arrangement leads to expression of *int*-1 in the mammary gland where, in normal circumstances, *int*-1 is apparently not expressed (Nusse and Varmus, 1982; Nusse *et al.* 1984). Importantly, MMTV integration always leaves the normal *int*-1 coding sequences intact. Therefore, inappropriate expression of the normal *int*-1 protein is implicated in cellular transformation (van Ooyen and Nusse, 1984). An *in vivo* role for MMTV directed *int*-1 expression in mammary tumorigenesis has been directly demonstrated in transgenic mice (Tsukamoto *et al.* 1988). However, it is clear that *int*-1 will not transform a broad range of cell types in culture, but only certain mammary epithelial cell lines (Brown *et al.* 1986; Rijsewijk *et al.* 1987*a*). Thus, abnormal expression of *int*-1 can have profound consequences for the phenotype of a cell, but the outcome depends on the cellular context in which *int*-1 is expressed.

162   *A. P. McMahon and R. T. Moon*

The *int*-1 protein

Analysis of genomic (van Ooyen and Nusse, 1984) and cDNA (Fung *et al.* 1985) sequences have established that mouse *int*-1 encodes a 370 amino acid, 41K polypeptide. There are several interesting features of this sequence. The amino terminal 48 amino acids are extremely hydrophobic and probably encode a signal peptide sequence which is cleaved at a potential signal peptidase cleavage site after amino acid 27 (Brown *et al.* 1987, Fig. 1). The remainder of the protein is highly cysteine rich (6 %), with over 50 % of these residues in the carboxyl-terminal 20 % of the protein (Fig. 1). There are four potential *N*-linked glycosylation sites, all of which are probably used (Fig. 1, Brown *et al.* 1987; Papkoff *et al.* 1987).

Papkoff *et al.* (1987) have used antisera against *int*-1 protein to demonstrate by crude cellular fractionation that *int*-1 protein is sequestered in membrane vesicles, but not detectably secreted. Using another approach,

we have examined expression of *int*-1 in *cos* cells. We inserted a small oligonucleotide encoding a ten amino acid residue of human *c-myc* in frame in the *int*-1 coding sequence (Fig. 2). The *int*-1 *myc* protein is specifically recognized by a monoclonal antibody 9E10 (Evan *et al.* 1985; Munro and Pelham, 1987). Immunohistochemical localization detects *int*-1 *myc* protein throughout the endoplasmic reticulum (McMahon, unpublished observations, Fig. 3). A control construct in which chick lysozyme is tagged with *myc* and the recently identified endoplasmic reticulum retention signals shows a similar localization (Munro and Pelham, 1987, Fig. 3). Similar results are obtained with untagged *int*-1 protein using anti *int*-1 antibodies (McMahon, unpublished observations). However, as in the studies of Papkoff *et al.* (1987), we failed to detect *int*-1 secreted into the

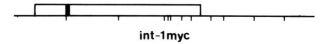

int-1myc

Fig. 2. Schematic representation of *int*-1 *myc* construct. The *int*-1 mRNA is drawn, with the coding sequence indicated by the open box. An oligonucleotide encoding 10 amino acids of human *c-myc* is inserted in frame (closed box) at a unique *Bam*HI site. The resultant *int*-1 *myc* RNA encodes a protein 381 amino acids in length which is specifically recognized by a monoclonal antibody, 9E10, directed against the *myc* epitope (Evan *et al.* 1985).

Fig. 1. Schematic representation of the *int*-1 protein sequence. Positions of cysteine residues are indicated by extended vertical lines, potential *N*-linked glycosylation sites by arrowheads and the potential signal peptide sequence by hatching.

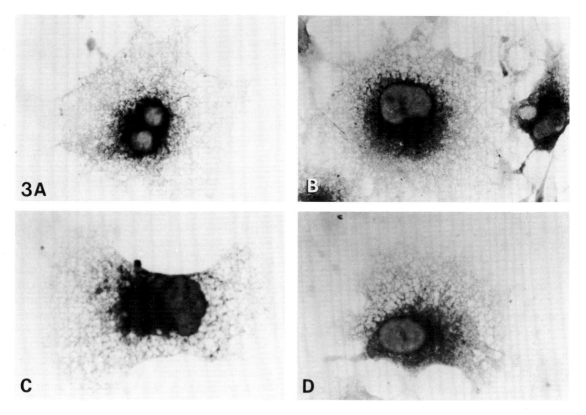

Fig. 3. Expression of the *int*-1 *myc* protein in *cos* cells. DNA constructs expressing either an e.r. resident protein tagged with the *myc* sequence (A,C) or *int*-1 *myc* (B,D) were introduced into *cos* cells. After 48 h, cells were fixed and the presence of the *myc* epitope in each of the fusion constructs visualized immunohistochemically, using an immunoperoxidase detection system. In both control and *int*-1 *myc* transfected cells, fusion proteins are detected throughout the endoplasmic reticulum of the cell.

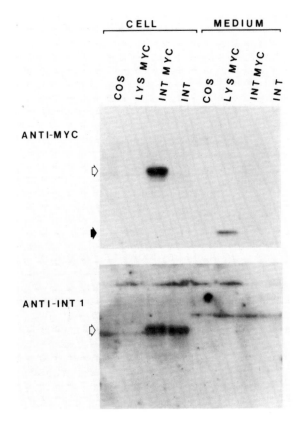

Fig. 4. Western blot analysis of *int*-1 and *int*-1 *myc* expression in *cos* cells. *cos* cells were transfected with DNA constructs expressing a lysozyme myc fusion construct *lys myc* containing the previously identified endoplasmic reticulum retention signal sequence (KDEL, Munro & Pelham, 1987), *int*-1 *myc* and *int*-1 untagged. Cells and media were analyzed for the presence of proteins using either a monoclonal antibody, *9E10*, which specifically recognizes the *myc* epitope (top panel) or mouse polyclonal antiserum directed against an *int*-1 peptide sequence (lower panel). *9E10* detects large quantities of the *int*-1 *myc* protein specifically in cells, but not in the medium (open arrow, top panel). In contrast, only low levels of *lys-myc* are present in cells, whereas *lys-myc* is readily detected in the medium (closed arrow). Thus, *int*-1 *myc* is not secreted, even under conditions in which a protein normally resident in the endoplasmic reticulum is secreted in large quantities. A similar result is obtained using antisera directed against the *int*-1 protein (lower panel). Neither *int*-1 nor *int*-1 *myc* are detected in the medium (open arrow, lower panel), indicating that insertion of the *myc* epitope is not responsible for the cellular restriction of the *int*-1 protein.

medium (Fig. 4), even under conditions in which significant amounts of the lysozyme-*myc* protein are inappropriately secreted (Fig. 4). Indirect evidence suggests that this is because *int*-1 or *int*-1 *myc* protein, when expressed at high levels, forms in insoluble precipitates in the endoplasmic reticulum (McMahon, unpublished observation). Taken together, these results suggest that *int*-1 enters the secretory pathway, is glycosylated, and may, under normal circumstances, be secreted.

The human (van Ooyen *et al.* 1985), frog (Noordermeer *et al.* 1989) and *Drosophila* (Baker, 1987; Rijsewijk *et al.* 1987*b*; Cabrera *et al.* 1987) *int*-1 genes have

been cloned and sequenced. Analysis of the predicted protein sequence indicates that even in distantly related species, *int*-1 is highly conserved. Mouse and human *int*-1 have 99 % amino acid similarity, mouse and frog 68 %, and mouse and *Drosophila* 54 %. While human, frog and mouse genes encode similar-sized proteins, *Drosophila int*-1 contains an additional 85 amino acids (Rijsewijk *et al.* 1987*a*). All proteins have a hydrophobic leader sequence that conforms to a consensus signal peptide sequence, and all 23 cysteine residues in the mouse sequence are conserved in human, frog and *Drosophila int*-1. Thus it is tempting to speculate that the high degree of sequence homology may reflect functional conservation in the normal role of *int*-1 protein in invertebrate and vertebrate species.

int-1 in *Drosophila*

int-1 in *Drosophila* is encoded by the gene *wingless* (Rijsewijk *et al.* 1987*b*). Viable flies carrying *wg* mutations were originally identified (Sharma, 1973) by a recessive mutation that causes a homeotic transformation of wing structures into a mirror-image duplication of the notum, another thoracic structure (Sharma and Chopra, 1976; Morata and Lawrence, 1977). Analysis of mosaic clones of *wg* mutant cells in a wild-type background indicates that *wg* is non-cell autonomous (Morata and Lawrence, 1977; Wieschaus and Riggleman, 1987), since small mutant clones appear normal. This suggests that a small patch of *wg* cells in a wild-type background is rescued by the normal product produced in neighboring cells. With the identification of additional lethal alleles of *wg* (Babu, 1977; Baker, 1987), it became apparent that *wg* was involved in the establishment of segmentation early in development. Specifically, *wg* is a member of the segment-polarity class of genes which are required for normal pattern in each segment (Nüsslein-Volhard and Wieschaus, 1980). Loss of *wg* and other segment-polarity genes results in deletion of a part of the normal pattern, and its replacement by a mirror-image duplication of anterior denticle bands (Nüsslein-Volhard and Wieschaus, 1980; Wieschaus and Riggleman, 1987). Thus, naked cuticle is replaced by additional denticles.

The cloning of *wg* (Baker, 1987; Rijsewijk *et al.* 1987*b*) has provided clues as to how the gene is regulated and to its role in segmentation. By the early gastrula stages, *wg* RNA expression is detected in a series of approximately 14 stripes in the embryonic epidermis (Fig. 5, Baker, 1987; Rijsewijk *et al.* 1987*b*). With the establishment of parasegmental grooves at the extended germ band stage, it is apparent that stripes of *wg* expression are located in the posterior one quarter of each parasegment, in what will become the posterior region of the compartment which consists of each anterior half-segment (Fig. 5, Baker, 1987). Thus, although *wg* RNA is located in only a small region of the presumptive segmental unit, loss of *wg* expression affects large areas of the segment. Taken together with the non-cell autonomy of *wg* clones in mosaics, these

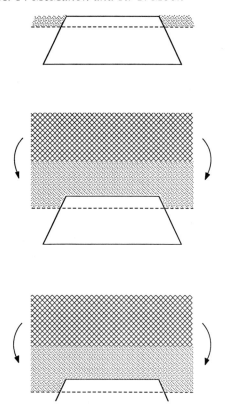

Fig. 5. *wg* expression in *Drosophila* segments. A cartoon of two normal *Drosophila* segments is presented; scale in the figure is approximate. In each segment (area between broken lines), *wg* (hatched) is expressed immediately anterior of the *en* (stippled) expressing cells and is required for continued expression of *en* (indicated by arrow in figure). In the absence of *wg* expression, the denticles that normally only occupy anterior regions of the segment (trapezoid box in figure) are duplicated in mirror-image symmetry and occupy most of the area of naked cuticle.

data strongly suggest that the *wg* protein product is involved in signalling between cells that establishes normal segmental pattern. This conjecture is supported by the analysis of the role of *wg* in regulating another segmentation gene, *engrailed* (*en*).

en is required for specification of posterior developmental compartments (Kornberg *et al.* 1985). Examination of the expression of *wg* and *en* indicates that they have similar but non-overlapping expression in each parasegment. *wg* is located immediately anterior to the parasegmental groove at extended germ band stages, whereas *en* is expressed in the adjacent cells that lie posterior to the groove (Baker, 1987). In *wg* null mutants, normal expression of *en* is established. However, in the absence of *wg*, *en* expression decays prematurely shortly after germ band elongation (Fig. 5, DiNardo *et al.* 1988), indicating that *wg* is required for the maintenance or the reinitiation of *en* expression in adjacent cells (DiNardo *et al.* 1988). Recently, secretion of *int*-1 protein and its uptake by *en* expressing cells has been directly observed in *Drosophila* embryos (Nusse, personal communication). Thus, the evidence suggests that *wg* is a secreted protein able to influence the

establishment of segmental pattern, at least in part by regulation of *en* expression.

int-1 in vertebrates

Normal *int*-1 expression has been best characterized in the mouse but, to date, observations have been confined to RNA expression. *Int*-1 is not expressed in detectable amounts in any adult tissue examined except the testis (Jakobovits *et al.* 1986; Shackleford and Varmus, 1987). Here expression is localized in postmeiotic, round spermatids (Shackleford and Varmus, 1987). During development, *int*-1 expression is restricted to the developing neural plate and neural tube (Wilkinson *et al.* 1987; Shackleford and Varmus, 1987). An extensive series of *in situ* hybridization experiments has provided a detailed picture of *int*-1 expression during mouse development (Wilkinson *et al.* 1987). At midgastrulation stages, prior to neural plate formation, *int*-1 RNA is not detected. One day later the fetus (~4–5 somites) has elevating head folds and a neural plate extending caudally. In the presumptive brain regions, *int*-1 expression is widespread over the anterior neural folds, but becomes localized to the tips of the neural folds more posteriorly. More caudal regions of the neural plate do not express *int*-1 at this time. Following neural tube closure, *int*-1 is localized at the dorsal midline of the neural tube, in presumptive mid-brain and along the developing spinal cord (Fig. 6). In the hind brain, *int*-1 is expressed at the edge of the rhombic lips at the junction of the pseudostratified neuroepithelium and the thin roof of ependymal cells that cover the hind brain. Thus, the expression of *int*-1 in the hind brain may represent the equivalent cells that express

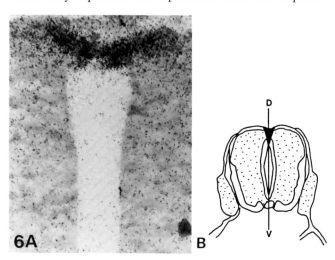

Fig. 6. *int*-1 expression in the mouse spinal cord. (A) *In situ* hybridization showing *int*-1 expression in a transverse section through a 10·5 day mouse presumptive spinal cord. *int*-1 is expressed at the dorsal midline (dorsal top in figure), in the glial roof plate cells and not in areas destined to form neurons. (B) Diagrammatic representation of *int*-1 expression about the doral–ventral (D–V) axis of symmetry, which separates the spinal cord into left and right halves.

int-1 in other regions that are not covered by this ependymal layer. Several small patches of *int*-1 RNA are detected in more rostral regions, but the predominant site of expression is at the dorsal midline. Expression is still detected at the dorsal midline of the developing spinal cord at 16·5 days (Wilkinson & McMahon, unpublished observation), and may be expressed beyond this time. However, the cells expressing *int*-1 are a non-mitotic population and, as the neural tube expands during development, elongation and flattening of these cells make it difficult to detect low levels of RNA. Essentially, the pattern of *int*-1 expression established by 10·5 days is maintained for several more days of fetal development.

Expression of *int*-1 during frog development has been examined by Northern blot analysis (Nordermeer *et al.* 1989). Expression was first detected at the neurula stage, consistent with a role for *int*-1 in frog neural tube development. However, *in situ* hybridization will be required to provide a more detailed analysis of RNA localization.

Expression of *int*-1 in the mouse at the dorsal midline correlates with several aspects of neural tube development. The dorsal midline is generated by the fusion of the neural folds, and it is from this region that the neural crest is derived. However, it seems unlikely that *int*-1 is involved in either of these events. Neural tube closure occurs at caudal positions in the 9·5 day embryo, preceding the rostral caudal extension of *int*-1 expression into this region (Wilkinson and McMahon, unpublished observation). Further, neural crest cells arise from the dorsal midline between 8·5 and 10·5 days of development (Tan and Morriss-Kay, 1985), whereas *int*-1 expression continues in this region several days after their migration. *int-1* is not detectably expressed in migrating neural crest cells (Wilkinson *et al.* 1987; Wilkinson and McMahon, unpublished observation).

A role for *int*-1 in neuronal migration seems plausible as the evidence presented so far indicates that *int*-1 is probably secreted and may alter gene expression in responsive cells. In this respect, it is noteworthy that substrate pathways for neuronal migration have been proposed to guide axonal migration in the dorsal columns that flank the areas of *int*-1 expression (Katz *et al.* 1980; Katz and Lasek, 1981; Willis and Coggeshall, 1978).

An alternative view of the role of *int*-1 in vertebrates, analogous to its role in *Drosophila*, is to suggest that *int*-1 is involved in specifying position about the midline. As illustrated in Fig. 6, *int*-1 expression occurs symmetrically around the dorsal–ventral axis of symmetry. Thus, cells left or right of the axis of symmetry would see equivalent levels of secreted *int*-1 protein and presumably respond in the same fashion. In an attempt to address the role of *int*-1 in vertebrate development, we have recently begun to manipulate expression *in vivo*. These initial experiments clearly indicate that inappropriate expression of *int*-1 has a dramatic and rather unexpected effect on the normal axial specification of *Xenopus* embryos (McMahon and Moon, in preparation).

Fig. 7. Development of *Xenopus* neurulae following injection of mouse *int*-1 mRNA into the fertilized egg. Fertilized *Xenopus* eggs were injected with synthetically derived, defective (upper) or normal (lower) *int-1 RNA*. Injection with defective mRNA has no effect on *Xenopus* development, whereas injection with normal *int*-1 mRNA causes embryos to duplicate their embryonic axis (arrow). Anterior is to left in Figure.

We have used the approach described by Harvey and Melton (1988) to express mouse *int*-1 in *Xenopus* embryos ectopically (McMahon and Moon, 1989). Fertilized eggs were injected with *int*-1 RNA and their subsequent development was monitored. Almost all embryos injected with *int*-1 RNA, but none injected with a variety of control RNAs, developed with a specific phenotype. At early neurula stages, embryos show a bifurcation of their anterior neural tube as a result of the duplication of the embryonic axis (Fig. 7). Therefore, ectopic expression of *int*-1 seems to interfere with the machinery for axial specification, which normally produces only one embryonic axis. This result is surprising, as it implies that *int*-1 is influencing processes operating during early gastrulation, which precedes normal *int*-1 expression in both the mouse and frog (Wilkinson *et al.* 1987; Noordermeer *et al.* 1989). However, it strongly suggests that inappropriate expression of *int*-1 can interfere with positional signalling in vertebrate development and suggests that *int*-1 normally operates in some aspect of this.

An *int-1* receptor

If *int*-1 is secreted and acts to regulate gene expression in responsive cells, what is the pathway of *int*-1 action? By analogy with growth factors, *int*-1 might be expected to operate through a receptor-mediated pathway. At present, there is no conclusive evidence for an *int*-1 receptor but, from the action of *wg* in *Drosophila*, a clear prediction can be made. Null mutants in an *int*-1 receptor should have a similar phenotype to segment-polarity mutants. However, unlike *wg* mutants which are non-cell autonomous, receptor mutants should exhibit cell autonomy. Several mutations have been described that resemble *wg* (Wieschaus and Riggleman, 1987; Perrimon and Mahowald, 1987), some of which are cell autonomous (Wieschaus and Riggleman, 1987). Clearly, this aspect of the action of *int*-1 will be under intense scrutiny in the future.

Concluding remarks

A major goal for developmental biologists is to elucidate those mechanisms that are shared by organisms separated by millions of years of evolution. We have attempted to draw parallels between the role of *int*-1 in positional signalling in *Drosophila* and its role in vertebrate development. Although at present we have little more than a rudimentary understanding of *int*-1 function in vertebrates, the future looks promising. The ability to manipulate *int*-1 expression in the frog provides a rapid and simple means by which ideas regarding the function and properties of *int*-1 protein may be tested. Similar experiments are also possible in transgenic mice and some are under way. However, perhaps the single most exciting possibility is the generation of homozygous mouse embryos which lack *int*-1 function (Thomas and Cappechi, 1987; Mansour *et al.* 1988). These experimental approaches together should provide conclusive evidence for or against a conserved role for *int*-1 in positional signalling.

We would like to thank Janet Champion for the *int*-1 *myc* expression studies, Roel Nusse and Olivier Destrée for communication of data prior to publication, Hugh Pelham for the gift of the *lys–myc* construct, Gerald Evan for the antibody *9E10*, Jeff Mann for critical reading of the manuscript, and Sharon Perry for the preparation of this manuscript.

References

BABU, P. (1977). Early developmental subdivisions of the wing disk in *Drosophila*. *Molec. gen. Genet.* **151**, 289–294.

BAKER, N. E. (1987). Molecular cloning of sequences from *wingless*, a segment polarity gene in *Drosophila*; the spatial distribution of a transcript in embryos. *EMBO J.* **6**, 1765–1770.

BROWN, A. M. C., WILDIN, R. S., PRENDERGAST, T. J. & VARMUS, H. E. (1986). A retrovirus expression vector expressing the putative mammary oncogene *int*-1 causes partial transformation of a mammary epithelial cell line. *Cell* **46**, 1001–1009.

BROWN, A. M. C., PAPKOFF, J., FUNG, Y.-K. T., SHACKLEFORD, G. M. & VARMUS, H. E. (1987). Identification of protein products encoded by the proto-oncogene *int*-1. *Mol. cell. Biol.* **7**, 3971–3977.

CABRERA, C. V., ALONSO, M. C., JOHNSTON, P., PHILLIPS, R. G. & LAWRENCE, P. A. (1987). Phenocopies induced with antisense RNA identify the *wingless* gene. *Cell* **50**, 658–663.

DINARDO, S., SHER, E., HEEMSKERK-JONGENS, J., KASSIS, J. A. & O'FARRELL, P. H. (1988). Two-tiered regulation of spatially patterned *engrailed* gene expression during *Drosophila* embryogenesis. *Nature* **332**, 604–609.

EVAN, G. I., LEWIS, G. K., RAMSAY, G. & BISHOP, J. M. (1985). Isolation of monoclonal antibodies specific for human *c-myc* proto-oncogene product. *Mol. cell. Biol.* **5**, 3610–3616.

FUNG, Y.-K. T., SHACKLEFORD, G. M., BROWN, A. M. C., SANDERS, G. S. & VARMUS, H. E. (1985). Nucleotide sequence and expression *in vitro* of cDNA-derived from mRNA of *int*-1, a provirally activated mouse mammary oncogene. *Mol. cell. Biol.* **5**, 3337–3344.

HARVEY, R. P. & MELTON, D. A. (1988). Microinjection of synthetic Xhox-1A homeobox mRNA disrupts somite formation in developing Xenopus embryos. *Cell* **53**, 687–697.

JAKOBIVITS, A., SHACKLEFORD, G. M., VARMUS, H. E. & MARTIN, G. R. (1986). Two proto-oncogenes implicated in mammary carcinogenesis, *int*-1 and *int*-2, are independently regulated during mouse development. *Proc. natn. Acad. Sci. U.S.A.* **83**, 7806–7810.

KATZ, M. J., LASEK, R. J. & NAUTA, H. J. W. (1980). Ontogeny of substrate pathways and the origin of the neural circuit pattern. *Neuroscience* **5**, 821–833.

KATZ, M. J. & LASEK, R. J. (1981). Substrate pathways demonstrated by transplanted Mauthner axons. *J. comp. Neurol.* **195**, 627–641.

KORNBERG, T., SIDEN, I., O'FARRELL, P. & SIMON, M. (1985). The *engrailed* locus of *Drosophila melanogaster*. In-situ localization of the transcripts reveals compartment specific expression. *Cell* **40**, 45–53.

MANSOUR, S. L., THOMAS, K. R. & CAPECCHI, M. R. (1988). Disruption of the proto-oncogene *int*-2 in mouse embryo-derived stem cells: a general strategy for targeting mutations to non selectable genes. *Nature* **336**, 348–352.

MCMAHON, A. P. & MOON, R. T. (1989). Expression of the proto-oncogene *int*-1 in *Xenopus* embryos leads to duplication of the embryonic axis. *Cell* (In press).

MORATA, G. & LAWRENCE, P. A. (1977). The development of *wingless*, a homeotic mutation of *Drosophila*. *Devl Biol.* **56**, 227–240.

MUNRO, S. & PELHAM, H. R. B. (1987). A C-terminal signal prevents secretion of hormonal *er* proteins. *Cell* **48**, 899–907.

NOORDERMEER, J., MEIJLINK, F., VERRIJZER, P., RIJSEWIJK, F. & DESTRÉE, O. (1989). Isolation of the *Xenopus* homologue of *int*-1 *wingless* and expression during neurula stages of early development. *Nucl. Acid. Res.* (In press).

NUSSE, R. & VARMUS, H. E. (1982). Many tumours induced by the mouse mammary tumour virus contain a provirus integrated in the same region of the host chromosome. *Cell* **31**, 99–109.

NUSSE, R., VAN OOYEN, A., COX, D., FUNG, Y.-K. T. & VARMUS, H. E. (1984). Mode of proviral activation of a putative mammary oncogene (*int*-1) on mouse chromosome 15. *Nature* **307**, 131–136.

NUSSE, R. (1986). The activation of cellular oncogenes by retroviral insertion. *Trends in Genetics* **2**, 244–247.

NUSSE, R. (1988). The *int* genes in mammary tumorigenesis and in normal development. *Trends in Genetics* **4**, 291–295.

NÜSSLEIN-VOLHARD, C. & WIESCHAUS, E. (1980). Mutations affecting segment number and polarity in *Drosophila*. *Nature* **287**, 795–801.

PAPKOFF, J., BROWN, A. M. C. & VARMUS, H. E. (1987). The *int*-1 proto-oncogene products are glycoproteins that appear to enter the secretory pathway. *Mol. cell. Biol.* **7**, 3978–3984.

PERRIMON, N. & MAHOWALD, A. P. (1987). Multiple functions of the segment polarity genes in *Drosophila*. *Devl Biol.* **119**, 587–600.

PETERS, G., BROOKES, S., SMITH, R. & DICKSON, C. (1983). Tumorigenesis by mouse mammary tumour virus; evidence for a common region for provirus integration in mammary tumours. *Cell* **33**, 369–377.

RIJSEWIJK, F., VAN DEEMTER, L., WAGENAAR, E., SONNENBERG, A. & NUSSE, R. (1987*a*). Transfection of the *int*-1 mammary oncogene in cuboidal RAC mammary cell line results in morphological transformation and tumorigenicity. *EMBO J.* **6**, 127–131.

RIJSEWIJK, F., SCHUERMANN, M., WAGENAAR, E., PARREN, P., WEIGEL, D. & NUSSE, R. (1987*b*). The *Drosophila* homolog of the mouse mammary oncogene *int*-1 is identical to the segment polarity gene *wingless*. *Cell* **50**, 649–657.

SHACKLEFORD, G. M. & VARMUS, H. E. (1987). Expression of the proto-oncogene, *int*-1, is restricted to postmeiotic male germ cells and the neural tube of midgestational embryos. *Cell* **50**, 89–95.

SHARMA, R. P. (1973). *Wingless*, a new mutant in *D. melanogaster*. *Dros. Inf. Ser.* **50**, 134.

SHARMA, R. P. & CHOPRA, V. L. (1976). Effect of *wingless* (*wg*) mutation on wing and haltere development in *Drosophila melanogaster*. *Devl Biol.* **48**, 461–465.

TAN, S. S. & MORRISS-KAY, G. (1985). The development and distribution of the cranial ceural crest in the rat embryo. *Cell Tissue Res.* **240**, 403–416.

THOMAS, K. R. & CAPECCHI, M. R. (1987). Site directed mutagenesis by gene targeting in mouse embryo-derived stem cells. *Cell* **5**, 503–512.

TSUKAMOTO, A. S., GROSSCHEDL, R., GUZMAN, R. C., PARSLOW, T. & VARMUS, H. E. (1988). Expression of the *int*-1 gene in transgenic mice is associated with mammary gland hyperplasia and adenocarcinomas in male and female mice. *Cell* **55**, 619–625.

VAN OOYEN, A. & NUSSE, R. (1984). Structure and nucleotide sequence of the putative mammary oncogene *int*-1, proviral insertions leave the protein coding domain intact. *Cell* **39**, 233–240.

VAN OOYEN, A., KWEE, V. & NUSSE, R. (1985). The nucleotide sequence of the human *int*-1 mammary oncogene; evolutionary conservation of coding and non-coding sequences. *EMBO J.* **4**, 2905–2909.

WIESCHAUS, E. & RIGGLEMAN, R. (1987). Autonomous requirements for the segment polarity gene *armadillo* during *Drosophila* embryogenesis. *Cell* **49**, 177–184.

WILKINSON, D. G., BAILES, J. A. & MCMAHON, A. P. (1987). Expression of the proto-oncogene *int*-1 is restricted to specific neural cells in the developing mouse embryo. *Cell* **50**, 79–88.

WILLIS, W. D. & COGGESHALL, R. E. (1978). *Sensory Mechanism of the Spinal Cord*. (John Wiley & Sons), pp. 197–259. London, England.

Development 1989 Supplement, 169–180 (1989)
Printed in Great Britain © The Company of Biologists Limited 1989

Models for positional signalling with application to the dorsoventral patterning of insects and segregation into different cell types

HANS MEINHARDT

Max-Planck-Institut für Entwicklungsbiologie, Spemannstraße 35/IV, 7400 TÜBINGEN FRG

Summary

Models of pattern formation and possible molecular realizations are discussed and compared with recent experimental observations. In application to the dorsoventral patterning of insects, it is shown that a superposition of two pattern-forming reactions is required. The first system generates the overall dorsoventral polarity of the oocyte, the second generates the positional information proper with a stripe-like region of high concentration along the ventral side of the embryo. A single reaction would be insufficient since the two reactions require different parameters. The model accounts for the orientation of the *DV* axes of the oocytes in the ovary of *Musca domestica* and *Sarcophaga*, independent of the *DV* axis of the mother, for the formation of several ventral furrows in the absence of the primary *gurken/ torpedo* system in *Drosophila*, as well as for the good size regulation of the dorsoventral axis as observed in some insect species.

Segregation of a homogeneous cell population into different cell types requires autocatalytic processes that saturate at relatively low concentrations and nondiffusible substances responsible for the autocatalytic feedback loops. Thus, these loops can be realized directly on the gene level *via* their gene products, for instance, by the mutual repression of two genes. A balance of the two cell types is achieved by a long-ranging substance interfering with the self-enhancing process. This substance is expected to have a more or less homogeneous distribution. This model accounts for the reestablishment of the correct proportion after an experimental interference and the change of determination after transplantation. Applications to the segregation of prestalk and prespore cells in *Dictyostelium* and of neuroblast cells from the ventral ectoderm in *Drosophila* are provided.

Key words: models, pattern formation, morphogenetic gradients, cell determination, *Drosophila*, segregation.

Introduction

Pattern formation during development of higher organisms requires communication among the cells. We have proposed several models for pattern formation for different developmental situations. They are based on molecularly feasible interactions. Using the new tools of molecular biology, several molecules have been identified that play a decisive role in the control of pattern formation. In this article, I provide a comparison between these models and recent experimental observations.

The models proposed can be summarized as follows:

(i) Primary gradients as well as periodic structure can be generated by local selfenhancement and long-range inhibition (Gierer and Meinhardt, 1972).

(ii) Stable cell states result from genes that feed back directly or indirectly on their own activation (e.g. transcription) but which compete with alternative genes for activation. Positive feedback and competition has the consequence that only one of the alternative genes remains active within one cell. By appropriate coupling with gradients generated by mechanism i or iii a position-dependent gene activation results (Meinhardt, 1978).

(iii) Borders between regions in which different genes are active act as organizing regions for the determination of substructures. Pairwise substructures, such as legs and wings, are initiated at the intersections of two borders, one resulting from a patterning in the anteroposterior, the other from a patterning in the dorsoventral dimension (Meinhardt, 1980, 1983a,b).

(iv) Ordered sequences of cell states result from a mutual long-range activation of cell states that locally exclude each other. This allows a controlled neighbourhood of cell states. Missing elements can be intercalated (Meinhardt and Gierer, 1980).

Pattern formation by local autocatalysis and long-range inhibition

The complexity of a higher organism cannot be present already within the egg in a hidden form since in many systems an early separation into two fragments leads to two complete embryos. If the egg contains prelocalized

170   *H. Meinhardt*

determinants, the question remains how this prelocalization has been achieved. We have proposed that primary pattern formation proceeds *via* local autocatalysis and long-range inhibition (Gierer and Meinhardt, 1972; Gierer, 1981; Meinhardt, 1982). This does not require a molecule with direct autocatalytic regulation, but autocatalysis can be a property of the system as a whole. For instance, if two substances, *A* and *B*, exist and *A* inhibits *B* and *vice versa*, a small increase of *A* above an equilibrium leads to a stronger repression of the *B* production and thus to a further increase of *A*, and so on in the same way as if *A* were be autocatalytic. The same holds for *B*. *A* and *B* together form a switching system in which either *A* or *B* is high. (The switch of the lambda phage between the lytic and the lysogenic phase is based on such a mutual repression; see Ptashne *et al.* 1980). To allow pattern formation, a long-ranging signal is required which interferes with the mutual competition of the two substances. For instance, if *A* has won the *A*–*B* competition in a particular region, *B* must win in the surroundings. A possible realization would be that the *A* molecules control the production of a substance *C* which, in turn, either inhibits the *A* or promotes *B* production. These modes are equivalent since, in competing systems, a selflimitation is equivalent to the support of the competitor. A more symmetrical pattern arises if the long-ranging help is reciprocal. In Eq. 1a–c, an interaction is described in which the diffusible antagonistic substance *C* is produced under control of the *A* molecules. It undermines the repression of *B* production by the *A* molecules. No direct autocatalytic interaction is assumed.

$$\frac{\partial a}{\partial t} = \frac{\rho}{\kappa + b^2} - \mu_a + D_a \frac{\partial^2 a}{\partial x^2} + \rho_0 . \quad \text{(Eq. 1a)}$$

$$\frac{\partial b}{\partial t} = \frac{\rho}{\kappa + a^2/c^2} - \mu_b + D_b \frac{\partial^2 b}{\partial x^2} + \rho_0 . \quad \text{(Eq. 1b)}$$

$$\frac{\partial c}{\partial t} = \gamma a - \mu_c c + D_c \frac{\partial^2 c}{\partial x^2} . \quad \text{(Eq. 1c)}$$

Fig. 1 shows the formation of graded distributions by such interaction. A high *A* concentration is formed at one side, a high *B* concentration at the other with countergradients in-between. If one of the components is missing due to a mutation, the remaining one will have a high concentration everywhere. Modifications of this mechanism that account for the formation of stripes or for segregating cell populations will be discussed further below.

Pattern formation by autocatalysis and long-range inhibition has many regulatory properties known to exist in real systems. In fragments, the pattern can regenerate. Small external asymmetries can be amplified and therefore used to orient the emerging pattern. The pattern itself, however, is, except for the orientation, to a large degree independent of the triggering asymmetry.

However, the actual mechanism found in a developing system can be more complicated. The equations contain, for instance, simple diffusion terms. However, the passage of larger molecules from one cell to the

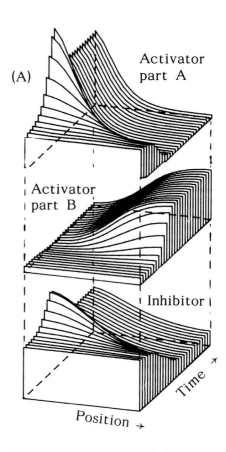

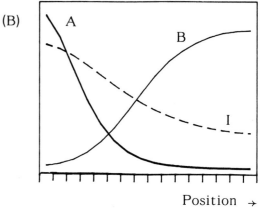

Fig. 1. Realization of autocatalysis by an inhibition of an inhibition. If two substances, *A* and *B*, inhibit each other's production in a nonlinear way (Eq. 1), a small increase of one of the substances above the steady state leads to its further increase. Both substances together have the property of 'selfenhancement', such as required for pattern formation (part *A* and part *B* of the activator). The long-ranging inhibitor (*c* in Eq.1) is assumed to antagonize the repression of *B*-production by the *A*-molecules. Thus, only inhibitory interactions are involved in this scheme. (A) Generation of graded distributions in a linear array of cells as function of time. The pattern is initiated by random fluctuations. (B) Concentrations at the final stable steady state. *A* and *B* are distributed in countergradients, the inhibitor distribution has the same polarity as the *A* distribution but is shallower due to the higher diffusion rate.

other can be a complex process, requiring active transport mechanisms through the membrane, not just leakage. Further, a particular developmental step involving pattern formation is embedded in a series of events and this requires a coupling with other pattern-forming systems. For instance, the organization of a particular embryonic axis requires a precise orientation in relation to the other axes. Or, size-regulation becomes much improved by a superposition of two such reactions, one determining the position, the other the size of the structures. Other examples will be discussed below in more detail.

Stabilization of apical dominance by a feedback on the source density

Usually the size of morphogenetic fields increases during the growth of the embryo. A graded concentration profile can be maintained only over a range of about a factor two. Growth to larger extensions bears the danger that the pattern flips over into symmetric or periodic distributions (Fig. 2A). A possible solution would be a conversion of the dynamically regulated pattern into a more stable pattern at an early stage, for

instance, by position-dependent gene activation. The initial patterning mechanism would subsequently become suppressed. However, such a mechanism is inappropriate for systems that show regulation over a large range of sizes. For instance, a hydra maintains its polar structure over substantial growth but, nevertheless, a fragment of 1/10 of the normal body size is still able to regenerate.

The range of dominance of the activated region, the apical dominance, can be increased by an order of magnitude if a feedback of the activator on the source density exists (Meinhardt and Gierer, 1974). Usually the sources of the activator and inhibitor synthesis are assumed to be homogeneously distributed, except for small random fluctuations. If, however, an increased activator concentration leads to an increase of the source density, it becomes unlikely that, in a region at a distance from the activated region, i.e. in a region of lower source density, the inhibition can be overcome and a secondary maximum appears. Thus, the apical dominance is stabilized (Fig. 2B). In addition, the graded source density distribution provides information about the polarity of the tissue. Small fragments will regenerate an activator maximum in the region of relatively highest source density, i.e. according to the

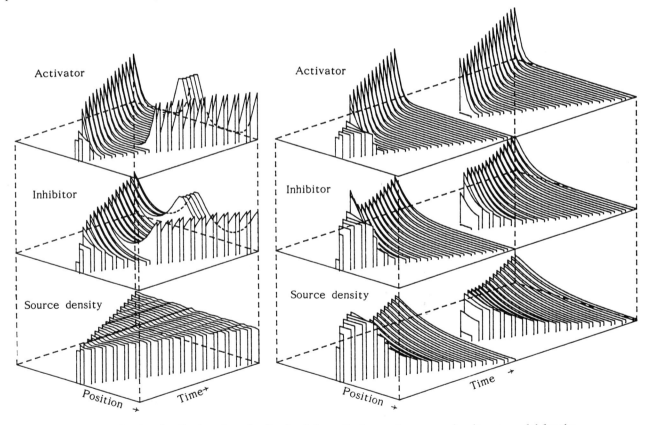

Fig. 2. Stabilization of polar distributions by a feedback of the activator on the source density – a model for the maintenance of apical dominance in Hydra. In a growing field, a system based on autocatalysis and long-range inhibition forms a pattern if a critical size is exceeded. However, with further growth, a tendency exists to switch into a symmetrical and later into a periodic pattern, a pattern which is inappropriate to supply unique positional information. (B) If the activator (or the inhibitor) has a feedback on the source density, the source density becomes graded. The graded source density stabilizes the polar distribution since at a region of low source density, the initiation of secondary maxima is unlikely. The graded source density provides the long-lasting information about the polarity of the system. A small fragment regenerates a pattern according to the original polarity.

original polarity. This requires that the source density has a longer time constant in comparison with the activator. The simulation in Fig. 2B shows the maintenance of polarity during a period of substantial growth as well as the regeneration of a small fragment.

The source density can be, for instance, the density of a certain cell type to which the activator and inhibitor synthesis is restricted. An increased activator concentration could lead to an increased proliferation or differentiation, such that more cells of this type are formed. The head activator isolated from hydra and other tissues (see Schaller, this volume) may be a factor involved in the generation of a graded source density. Addition of head activator leads to the differentiation of more nerve cells from stem cells while, in turn, under normal conditions, the head activator is mostly produced by the nerve cells. The source gradient would be a morphogenetic gradient in the terms of Morgan (1904), a gradient in the tendency to form a particular structure. The tissue in the field that bears the highest tendency will form the structure.

A model for the dorsoventral organization of insects

In *Drosophila*, the dorsoventral (DV) axis is organized by at least two pattern-forming systems. One, the *torpedo/gurken* system, acts during early oogenesis and requires an interaction between genes expressed in the soma and in the germline (Schüpbach, 1987). A second one, the *dorsal/Toll* system, provides the proper positional information and acts during early embryogenesis (Anderson and Nüsslein-Volhard, 1984*a,b*; Anderson, 1987). According to the model outlined below, the first system generates an orienting asymmetry for the second. The model provides an explanation why such a superposition of two systems is required, how the region of high concentration of the dorsoventral gradient achieves a stripe-like shape along the whole anteroposterior extension, how the DV axis becomes oriented in the ovary and why in many systems this axis shows a good size regulation.

Generation of dorsoventral polarity requires selforganizing mechanisms

In *Musca domestica* and *Sarcophaga*, the orientations of the DV axes of the developing oocytes in the ovary provide a strong indication that a mechanism with selforganizing capabilities is at work. These orientations can be detected by the eccentric position of the germinal vesicle. In *Musca domestica* (Kleine-Schonnefeld and Engels, 1981) and in *Sarcophaga* (Geysen *et al.* 1988), the dorsal sides are oriented towards a point within the ovary (Fig. 3A,B). Thus, the DV polarity of an oocyte can have any orientation indicating that the DV axes are not under the control of the DV axis of the mother.

As mentioned above, pattern formation and especially the generation of polar patterns within a cell or a field of cells can be accomplished by local autocatal-

ysis and long-range inhibition. If the inhibitory molecule (or one of several inhibitory molecule species) diffuses in a restricted manner from one oocyte or follicle to a neighbour, a mutual orientation results. Let us assume, for reasons that will become clearer below, that the dorsal side is the activated region of this primary system. If in one oocyte an activator maximum has been formed, the dorsal side is fixed. In a neighbouring cell, due to the restricted diffusion of the inhibitor, the dorsal side will be formed at the largest possible distance from the first. Thus, its dorsal side will point in the same direction. Fig. 3C shows a simulation of this process. In performing such computer simulations, it is very difficult to avoid influences of the boundary. For instance, if inhibitor penetrates the envelope of the ovary less easily than the oocytes or follicles themselves, those sides that point towards the boundary of the ovary will become the nonactivated or ventral sides. The orientation of the outermost layer of oocytes directs the orientation of the next inner layer and so on. In agreement with this model is the finding by Geysen *et al.* (1988) that the regularity of the outside–inside orientation is much higher in oocytes close to the outer boundary. This effect is reproduced in the simulation. According to the model, the regularity at more central positions is diminished by two facts. First, random fluctuations can lead to a random selection of an orientation before that oocyte is reached by the orienting wave. Second, a spot at which many dorsal sides point towards each other leads to a less stable situation due to the local accumulation of the inhibitor. In contrast, a misalignment of some oocytes leads to a more stable situation.

In summary, these experiments and their simulations indicate that the dorsoventral polarity is initially a labile system and minor influences either from the outer margin of the ovary or from nearby oocytes or follicles are sufficient for an orientation. The irregularities indicate that a slavish transmission of a strong polarizing signal is not involved but that an oocyte is capable of generating a DV polarity on its own.

Orientation of the dorsoventral axis perpendicular to the anterior–posterior axis

The formation of a local high concentration creating dorsoventral polarity must be restricted to an equatorial zone in relation to the anterior and posterior pole. The latter poles appear to be predetermined by the position of the follicle within the ovary. The following model is able to produce such pattern. The anterior and the posterior pole of an oocyte is marked by a maximum of either the same or two different activator–inhibitor systems (Fig. 4). If the inhibitor of the DV system has some cross-reaction with that of the AP-system, the high point of the former system will appear at a maximum distance from the terminal poles, i.e. at an equatorial position, as it is required.

The use of the same signal at the anterior and the posterior pole has the advantage that the pattern is necessarily symmetrical, providing more safely the prerequisites to localize the future dorsal side. Exper-

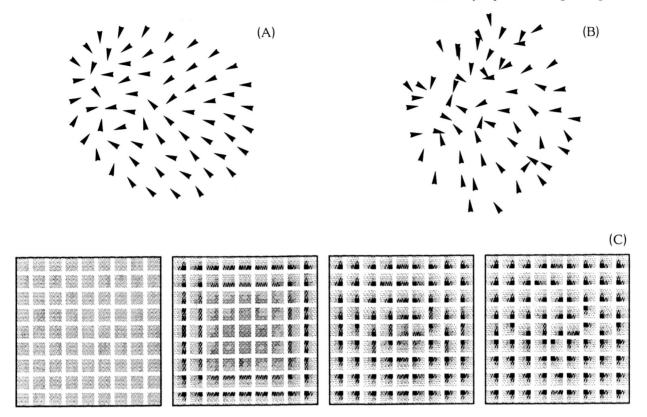

Fig. 3. Alignment of the dorsoventral (*DV*) axes of developing oocytes in the ovary. (A) Observations of Kleine-Schonnefeld and Engels (1981) in *Musca domestica* and (B) of Geysen *et al.* (1988) in *Sarcophaga*: Shown is a cross-section through an ovary. Each arrowhead indicates an oocyte with its *DV*-polarity. The tips of the arrowheads indicate the dorsal sides. They are oriented towards a point within the ovary but not aligned with the *DV*-axis of the mother. (C) Model: It is assumed that the *DV*-polarity of the oocytes or follicles is generated by an activator–inhibitor system, that the inhibitor can diffuse in a restricted manner from one oocyte or follicle (small square) to the neighbouring oocytes and that the outer envelope is impermeable. The position of the activated region is assumed to determine the future dorsal side. Shown are stages in the generation of the *DV*-pattern. The activator concentration is indicated by the density of dots. The oocytes close to the outer envelope become polarized first due to their asymmetric environment. The activated regions point away from the outer envelope due to the accumulation of the inhibitor there. The *DV*-polarity of the remaining oocytes become aligned due to the restricted diffusion of the inhibitor. Each dorsal side tends to keep distance from other dorsal sides. The model reproduces the preferential orientation of the dorsal sides towards the center as well as the higher degree of misalignment at more central positions. (Fig. A redrawn from Kleine-Schonnefeld, 1981; Fig. B from Geysen *et al.* 1988).

imentally it has been shown by *P*-element insertions and β-galactosidase staining that the follicle cells surrounding the anterior and the posterior pole are marked very early during oocyte development (Fasano and Kerridge, 1988). Some of these insertions mark the anterior, some the posterior and some mark both poles simultaneously. Similarly, a staining of a pair of cells at both poles with the same antibody has been described by Brower, Smith and Wilcox (1980). Therefore, a symmetrical pattern as expected by the model seems to be available.

The model requires that the range of the inhibitor covers the whole field in order to obtain a single activator maximum. Diffusion of the activator facilitates the localization of the maximum between the two terminal poles at an optimum position. The resulting maximum is expected to have a patch-like shape with similar extensions in the *AP* as well as in the *DV* axis. It is assumed that this pattern formation occurs early in oocyte development, in *Drosophila* under control of

genes such as *K10*, *gurken* and *torpedo* (Schüpbach, 1987). Due to its patch-like shape, it is inadequate to supply positional information for the *DV* axis, but, as shown below, it can orient a second pattern-forming system which generates an activator maximum with a stripe-like extension.

Generation of positional information for the dorsoventral *axis*

In *Drosophila*, the positional information for the *DV*-axis is generated by a different system in which about 11 genes are involved (Anderson and Nüsslein-Volhard, 1984*a,b*; Anderson, 1987). The proper signal is provided by the *dorsal* protein which has, in the early embryo, a graded distribution (Steward *et al.* 1988; Nüsslein-Volhard and Roth, 1989). In agreement with the prediction of genetic observations (Nüsslein-Volhard, 1979) the ventral side carries the high *dorsal* concentration. In contrast, the distribution of the *dorsal* mRNA is nearly homogeneous. Two proteins involved in the generation of the dorsal gradient, *snake* (DeLotto and Spierer, 1986) and *easter* (Chasan and Anderson, 1989), have homologies to serine proteases. (Such enzymatic activities play a decisive role in cascade-like amplification processes in the blood coagulation, see Furie and Furie, 1988). Another key gene is *Toll*. Injection of wild-type cytoplasm into *Toll*-mutants can initiate the formation of a new ventral region at the point of injection independent of the original DV polarity of the egg (Anderson, Bokla and Nüsslein-Volhard, 1985).

Formation of stripe-like distributions requires saturation of selfenhancement and activator diffusion

To provide positional information for the *DV*-axis, a region of high concentration must be generated which has different extensions along the main body axes. It must extend over the whole anteroposterior axis but must have a short extension along the dorsoventral axis. According to the model, such a stripe-like distribution requires a limitation in the mutual competition between neighbouring cells (Meinhardt, 1988). If activator autocatalysis saturates at relatively low activator concentration, more cells remain activated although at a lower level. Stripe formation requires, in addition, a modest diffusion of the activator. Due to this diffusion, activated regions tend to occur in large coherent patches since, if a cell is activated, the probability is high that the neighbouring cell becomes activated too. On the other hand, it is necessary that activated cells are close to nonactivated cells into which the inhibitor can diffuse, otherwise no activation above average would be possible. The two seemingly contradictory requirements, coherent patches and proximity of nonactivated cells are satisfied if a stripe-like pattern is formed

(Fig. 5). Each activated cell is bordered by other activated cells but nonactivated cells are not too far away.

Fig. 6 shows a simulation of the emergence of the *dorsal* pattern as function of time under the orienting influence of the primary *DV*-system mentioned above. The stripe-like extension from pole to pole is clearly visible. Due to the saturation, neighbouring elements can remain activated without downregulating competition. The activator–inhibitor mechanism used for this simulation is, of course, only an example. An inhibition of an inhibition mechanism may be involved as well (see Figs 1, 7E).

Without activator diffusion, the decision to become activated would be a cell-autonomous process and a sprinkled pattern of activated cells would result (Fig. 6D, see also Fig. 7). The requirement of activator diffusion is compatible with experimental observations. The *Toll* gene product appears to be a transmembrane protein (Hashimoto, Hudson and Anderson, 1988). The *snake* protein is presumably an extracellular serine protease (DeLotto and Spierer, 1986). Thus, a substantial part of the molecular interactions leading to the *dorsal* gradient presumably takes place outside of the cells or can pass from one cell to the next.

Saturation of autocatalysis leads, in addition to stripe formation, to a good size regulation (Gierer and Meinhardt, 1972). The number of activated cells becomes a certain proportion of the nonactivated cells as long as the range of the inhibitor is comparable with the size of the morphogenetic field. This accounts for the fact that some insect species show complete pattern regulation after a longitudinal ligation (Sander, 1971). A complete embryo is formed in each fragment, of course with an even shorter dorsoventral extension.

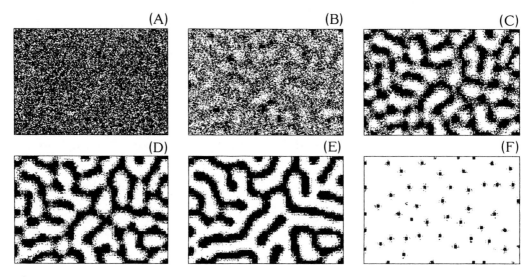

(A)   (B)   (C)

(D)   (E)   (F)

Fig. 5. (A–E) Stages in the formation of a stripe-like pattern. Assumed is an activator–inhibitor system and a saturation of autocatalysis at low activator concentration which limits the competition among neighbouring cells. More cells remain activated, although at a lower level. Small diffusion of the activator leads to the tendency to form coherent activated regions. Stripes are the most stable pattern since activated cells have activated cells in the neighbourhood but, nevertheless, nonactivated cells are nearby into which the inhibitor can escape. (F) For comparison, without saturation but otherwise the same parameters and initial conditions, a bristle-like pattern results. The maximum concentration is about ten times higher than in Fig. E.

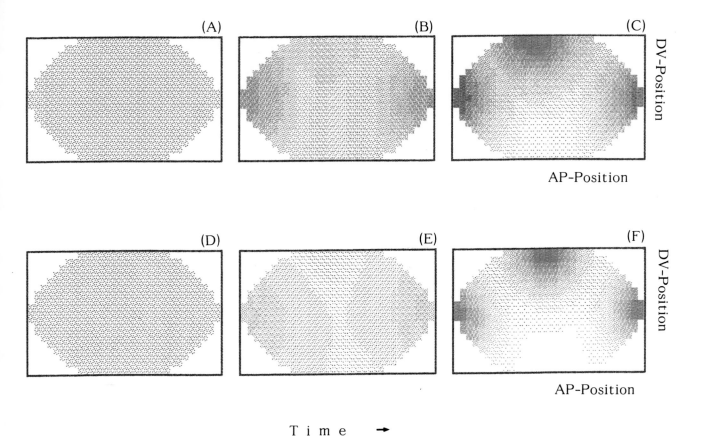

$$\text{Time} \longrightarrow$$

Fig. 4. Formation of orthogonal coordinate systems. (A) Generation of an anterior, a posterior and a dorsal pole by three activator–inhibitor systems coupled by a cross-reaction of the inhibitors. Due to the cross-reaction, the high activator concentrations determining the anterior (blue) and posterior pole (red) appear at opposite ends of the field. Due to a longer time constant, the high concentration determining the dorsal side (green) develops with some delay. It keeps maximum distance from the anterior as well as from the posterior pole because its activator is also inhibited by the inhibitor of the anterior and posterior system. The calculation is made with a two-dimensional array of cells which represents a cross-section through an oocyte or follicle. (B) A system of two pattern-forming reactions is sufficient if the dorsoventral pattern is oriented by a symmetrical pattern with a high concentration of the same activator (red) at both the anterior and the posterior pole. (For the generation of a symmetrical pattern, see Fig. 2A). Again, the high activation determining the dorsal side (green) appears at maximum distance from both poles. Shown is the initial, an intermediate and the final stable pattern. The density of dots is a measure for the concentration. The high concentration at the dorsal side is assumed to orient a second pattern-forming reaction that provides the proper positional information for the dorsoventral axis (see Fig. 6).

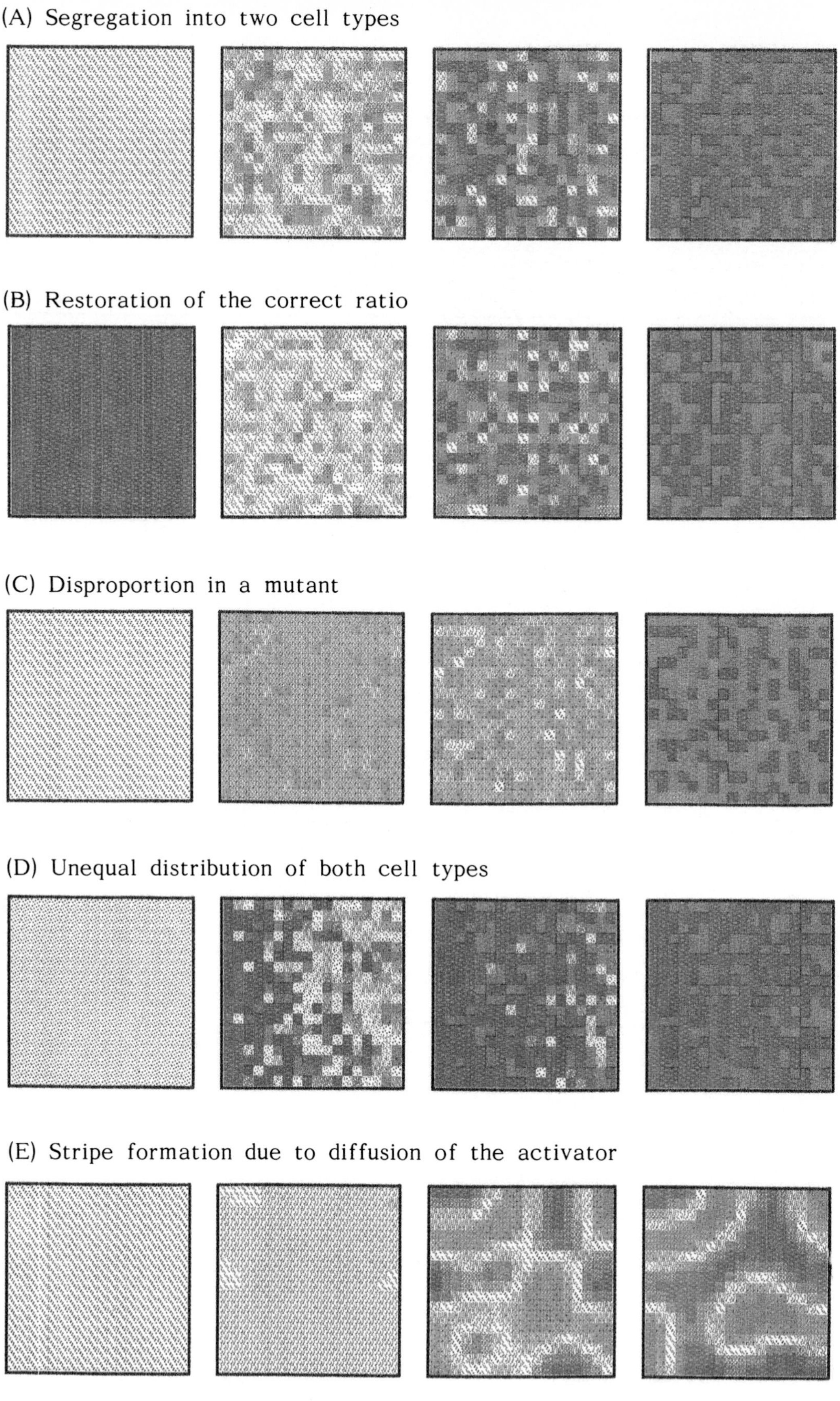

(A) Segregation into two cell types

(B) Restoration of the correct ratio

(C) Disproportion in a mutant

(D) Unequal distribution of both cell types

(E) Stripe formation due to diffusion of the activator

Fig. 7. Model for the segregation of a homogeneous cell population into two cell types. Assumed are two genes, *A* and *B*, which repress each other in a nonlinear way (Eq. 1). This creates an instable situation in which either *A* (red) or *B* (blue) becomes activated. *Via* a long-ranging substance, a balanced ratio of both cell types is achieved (see also Fig. 1). Since the gene products are assumed to be nondiffusible, the choice of a particular pathway in a particular cell is largely independent of the choice in a neighbouring cell. No tendency exists to form coherent patches. Due to a saturation of the selfenhancement in the *A–B* system (high κ in Eq.1), no zone of inhibition is formed around a cell with a particular differentiation. (A) Stages in the segregation. (B) Determination is reversible. For instance, a homogeneous population of *B*-cells is unstable. The cells return first to the semistable steady state followed by a repetition of the patterning process, restoring in this way the correct ratio. (C) Change of the ratio due to a mutation. In this example, a reduced production of the substance *C* leads to an overproduction of *A*-cells. (D) Superposition of a graded pattern can lead to a preferential appearance of one cell type at a particular position. (E) For comparison, with diffusion of the *A* and *B* products, a stripe-like pattern would be formed.

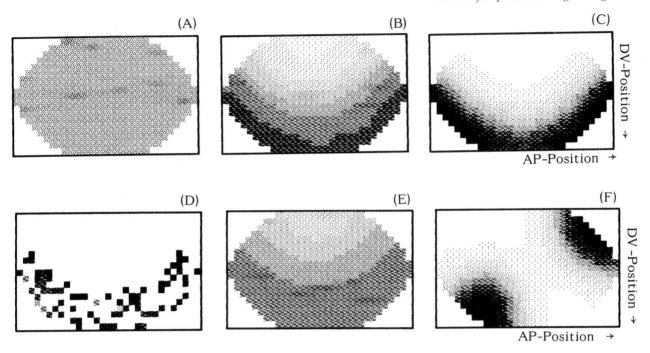

Fig. 6. Model for the generation of positional information for the dorsoventral axis. Assumed is an activator–inhibitor system with stripe-forming capabilities (Fig. 5; a system based on an inhibition of an inhibition, such as shown in Fig. 1 and 7E, would work as well). (A–C) Stages in the generation of a stripe-like high concentration along the ventral side connecting the anterior and posterior pole. (D) Without diffusion of the activator, the high ventral stripe would disintegrate into separated spots. (E,F) For reproducible pattern formation an orienting influence is required. Due to an inhibitory interference from the primary *DV*-system (Fig. 4) the effective source density (E) is reduced at the dorsal side. The outcoming pattern is, due to the selforganizing properties, to a large degree independent of the orienting pattern. However, without this orienting influence several high points can appear at arbitrary positions, in agreement with the observation that often several ventral furrows are formed in the case of a nonfunctional *gurken/torpedo* system (Schüpbach, 1987).

Coupling with the primary DV-system

In the absence of additional cues, the high *dorsal* stripe could have any orientation within the embryo. Even the formation of several high points or stripes would be possible (Fig. 6F). As mentioned, this cue is assumed to be provided by the primary *DV*-system (green in Fig. 4). The lowest concentration of this pattern has a stripe-like extension in the egg which connects the two poles. Thus, it is conceivable that the primary *DV*-pattern has an inhibitory influence on the second *DV*-pattern.

If the *torpedo/gurken* system, the assumed primary system, is nonfunctional, a general ventralization takes place (Schüpbach, 1987). This is compatible with the view that it exerts an inhibitory influence spreading out from the dorsal side on the *dorsal/Toll* system. It could be that such negative influence is responsible for the remaining polarity in dominant *Toll*-alleles. In embryos developing from eggs laid by mothers without a functional *gurken/torpedo* system, very often two sites of invagination are formed (Schüpbach, 1987). In the model, in the absence of the orienting influence of the primary system, several high ventral points can emerge (Fig. 6F). If this interpretation turns out to be correct, this would be strong support for the suggestion that *dorsal/Toll* system on its own is able to generate a pattern and that the primary system provides the

information only where the high *dorsal* concentration should appear.

The question may arise whether the *dorsal/Toll* system is a pattern-forming system at all. According to the model, the region with the least repression of the primary system would have a shape quite close to the high *dorsal* distribution. The advantage of having a pattern-forming system would be its capacity for self-regulation. For instance, the precise shape of the high *dorsal* stripe would be independent of the contour lines of the inhibition exerted by the primary system and, thus, it would be independent of the egg shape. The possibility that a new ventral side can be induced in a *Toll* mutant at a dorsal position of the egg, despite the fact that a functional primary system was present, is a further indication that the primary system provides only an asymmetry and does not dictate the fate.

Segregation of cell populations

A very common patterning process is the segregation of an originally homogeneous cell population into two different cell types. The segregation of neuroectodermal cells into neuroblasts and in ventral ectodermal cells in *Drosophila* (see Campos-Ortega, 1988; Artavanis-Tsakonas, 1988; Hartley, this volume) or the formation of prestalk and prespore cells in *Dictyostelium* (see Williams, this volume) may serve as examples. Common to both systems is a very good regulation of the proportion of the two cell types. Removal of either prespore or prestalk cells leads to the restoration of the correct ratio due to reprogramming. In the insect system, ablation of neuroblast cells causes ectodermal cells to take over the fate of the deleted cell (Doe and Goodman, 1985). Transplantation of marked ectodermal cells from the neuroectodermal region into a younger host can cause a switch into the neuronal pathway (Technau and Campos-Ortega, 1985).

Molecules have been identified that play a decisive role in the formation of these patterns. In the slime mould, a molecule called DIF is required for prestalk formation (see Kay, this volume). In the insect system, about six genes are required for the formation of ectodermal cells (see Campos-Ortega, 1988; Artavanis-Tsakonas, 1988), among them the genes *Notch* and *Delta*.

It has been regarded as a surprise, and counterintuitive for a morphogenetically active substance, that both molecules, DIF and the *Notch* product, appear to be almost homogeneously distributed. However, according to the model discussed below substances with such distribution are a necessary component.

A model for segregation must have the following features: (i) In a certain proportion of the cells, a particular gene becomes activated. The remaining cells remain either in a ground state or activate an alternative gene. (ii) The proportion of the two cell types is regulated. Removal of one cell type leads to a reprogramming of some of the remaining cells, such that the correct ratio becomes restored. (iii) The two cell types appear more or less at intermingled positions.

With the appropriate parameters, the activator-inhibitor mechanism can reproduce these features and the known experimental and genetic data are compatible with such an interpretation. As already discussed above, if the activator autocatalysis saturates at low activator concentrations, the number of activated cells reaches a certain proportion of the nonactivated cells. Since the local activator increase is limited due to the saturation, the degree of competition between neighbouring cells is limited too. Thus, neighbouring cells can remain activated independent of the range of the inhibitor. The system is able to regulate: For instance, if relatively too few cells are activated, the level of the inhibitor is lower than that required for an equilibrium. More and more cells switch from the nonactivated into the activated state. This leads to an increase of the inhibitor concentration until no further switching is possible. At this stage, the correct ratio is obtained. The reverse argument is valid if too many cells are activated.

If the activator is nondiffusible, the decision whether a cell will become activated is to a large extent independent of the decision made by a neighbouring cell. Only on average, the correct ratio must be maintained. The chance to become activated is not increased by an activated neighbour. As long as no other constraints are superimposed, random fluctuations are decisive. Acti-

vated and nonactivated cells emerge at intermingled positions.

A possible realization of the selfenhancement, which is especially appropriate for the segregation into two different cell types, is a mutual repression of two genes, *A* and *B*. Such a system has been already introduced in connection with the generation of graded distributions (Fig. 1). Two genes that mutually repress each other in a nonlinear way resemble an unstable system. In a particular cell, one gene will remain active and the alternative gene suppressed. Again, a long-ranging substance is required to achieve a balanced ratio of the two cell types. The essential differences to the version used for Fig. 1 are (i) the molecules involved in the selfenhancement are nondiffusible and (ii) the selfenhancement saturates.

The simulation Fig. 7, performed with Eq. 1 under these conditions, shows the segregation into two types, the restoration of the correct ratio and the over-representation of one cell type in a mutant (caused at this example by a lower production rate of *C*, Eq. 1c). The latter simulation shows also that the ratio of cells at which either *A* or *B* becomes activated can be easily adapted to the needs of the organism by the change of a parameter such as production (or decay) rates, parameters that can be easily encoded in the genetic network.

The model predicts that the mutual repression must be nonlinear, a requirement that is satisfied if the active agents are dimers of the gene products. The importance of the saturation has been mentioned. In Eq.1 the degree of saturation is given by the Michaelis–Menten constants κ since they determine the maximum production rate if the alternative gene is completely repressed, i.e. if the concentration of their gene product would be zero.

In *Drosophila* embryos, the density of neuroblasts is higher at more ventral positions. In *Dictyostelium*, more *prestalk* cells are formed initially at the top of the aggregates. According to the model, small spatial inhomogeneities can change the local cell density while the overall ratio is maintained (Fig. 7D).

Alternative molecular realization and comparison with available experiments

The reaction schemes outlined above are only examples to illustrate the general principle envisaged. Alternative molecular realizations are conceivable. For instance, if all the cells produce a substrate *S* and the activated cells remove that substrate, the resulting *S*-concentration depends on the ratio of the activated cells, the consumers, to the total number of cells, the producers. Such a model has been proposed for the regulation of prestalk–prespore cells in *Dictyostelium* (Fig. 8; Meinhardt 1983*c*).

The gene *Notch* is transcribed in many cell types including neuroblasts and ectodermal cells (Hartley *et al.* 1987). This is compatible with the substrate-depletion scheme if ventral ectodermal cells remove the

(A)

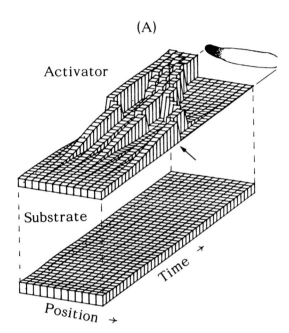

(B)

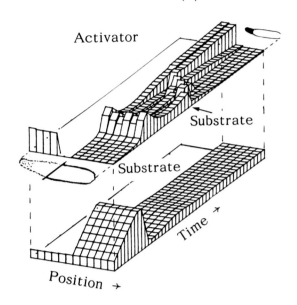

(C)

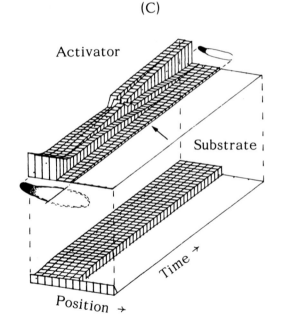

Fig. 8. Role of homogeneously distributed substances in balancing the ratio of two cell types, exemplified by a model for prestalk/prespore cell differentiation in the slime mould *Dictyostelium discoideum*. Assumed is a pattern-forming system consisting of an autocatalytic activator and a substrate (possibly DIF, see Kay, this volume) which is removed in the process of autocatalysis. (A) Activated cells appear at intermingled positions (see Williams, this volume). They are assumed to sort out by an independent process (Meinhardt, 1983c). The substrate concentration does not change during this process since substrate removal by all cells at the steady state is the same as that by the fewer, but fully activated, cells. Due to the assumed high diffusion rate, the substrate has a near-homogeneous distribution. (B) Removal of the activated cells (the prestalk cells, the substrate-consumer) leads to a dramatic increase of the substrate. A new activation occurs in the remaining cell population and the patterning process is repeated. Eventually, the correct ratio of activated *versus* nonactivated cells becomes restored. (C) Removal of nonactivated (prespore) cells leads to a reduction of substrate concentration which causes the activator concentration to decrease below the saturation level and the competition to start again. Some of the previously activated (prestalk) cells switch to nonactivated cells. Although the substrate concentration appears to have no pattern of interest and although concentration changes take place only under certain experimental conditions, the substrate (or more general, the antagonist of selfenhancement) plays the decisive role in the balancing of cell types (other modes of action of the DIF-molecule are conceivable as well. For instance, it can be an inhibitor for prespore development, especially if ammonia acts as inhibitor for prestalk development, see Meinhardt, 1983c).

Notch product, an EGF-like factor. The *Notch* concentration would provide a measure for the ratio of ventral ectodermal cells, the consumer, to the total number of *Notch*-producing cells. Thus, the function of *Notch* could be to accomplish a precise regulation of this ratio.

The product of the gene *Delta* has been interpreted as a diffusible inhibitor of the neuronal pathway (Vässin *et al.* 1987). It is produced by the neuroblasts. If *Delta* is such an inhibitor, why is this pathway not blocked in

those cells exposed to the highest *Delta* concentration, i.e. in the neuroblasts that produce *Delta*? The answer in terms of the model is that the local selfenhancement is so strong that it overcomes the selfproduced antagonistic effect due to the diffusion of the latter into the surroundings. In addition, as mentioned, this inhibition may be indirect and may result from an activation of genes required for the ectodermal pathway that locally exclude the activation of neuroblast-specific genes.

Hartley *et al.* (1988) have reported that the gene *Enhancer of split, E(spl)* is transcribed in cells of the neurogenic pathway (N), is cell-autonomous and thus does not code for a diffusible factor, such as *Notch* or *Delta*, but nevertheless is required for the ectodermal pathway (E). If this observation is correct, according to the model, *E(spl)* could be involved in the reaction chain active in the N-cells leading to a diffusible molecule (*Delta?*) which inhibits the N-pathway, thus providing the E-pathway with a chance to win the competition in a certain fraction of cells. If *E(spl)* were involved in receiving such a signal, the expression of *E(spl)* would be also expected in the E-cells since the N-pathway must be suppressed in these cells. On the other hand, from the models, genes are expected that are active in cells of the E-pathway only. If mutant, the E-genes are incapable to compete with the N-genes and all cells would follow the N-pathway.

The role of homogeneously distributed substances in the segregation of cell populations

As mentioned, the *Notch* product in *Drosophila* and the differentiation-inducing-factor DIF in slime moulds are more or less homogeneously distributed. This may be in contrast to the expectation that morphogenetic substances must have position-dependent, for instance, graded or spike-like distributions to allow region-specific gene activation. According to the model, homogeneously distributed substances play a decisive role for segregating cell populations since they provide a measure of how many cells of a particular type are present. The system does not require that a separate prepattern provides the signal for one or the other gene to be activated. The regulation of the ratio of cell types proceeds *via* diffusible and thus more or less homogeneously distributed substance(s). This is illustrated in the simulation of the *prestalk/prespore* regulation in *Dictyostelium* (Fig. 8). The distribution of the substrate (e.g. DIF) remains almost homogeneous and constant during the segregation process. However, after removal of the prestalk cells (the substrate consumer), a dramatic increase of the substrate (Fig. 8B) takes place until a new activation is fired, enabling a repetition of the segregation process.

In the slime moulds, a high diffusion rate of the proportion-controlling substance is especially important since the prestalk cells sort out at the tip of the slug. Thus, distances between the different cell types that should obtain a balanced ratio can be very high, but nevertheless, removal of prespore cells at the rear end of the slug should lead to a reprogramming of prestalk cells at the tip (see Fig. 8C). In contrast, if the differentiated cell types remain in intermingled positions, as long as regulation is required, the range of the diffusible substance can be small to maintain everywhere a locally balanced ratio of both cell types.

Since, in such systems, the cell states are stable only if the correct ratio is given, an isolated cell will lose its commitment and return to the semistable steady state.

In the example given above, in an isolated cell, both gene *A* and gene *B* will become moderately activated, independent of whether originally *A* or *B* was active since otherwise too much or too little of the antagonist would be present (see also Fig. 7B). Therefore, it is not surprising that transplantation of a single cell can cause a change of its commitment (Technau, Becker and Campos-Ortega, 1988; Campos-Ortega, 1988) since it was isolated for a certain time during the experiment.

Conclusion: Expected function of molecules involved in positional signalling

From the point of view of the models proposed for positional signalling, molecules with specific roles and properties are expected. In the following, their expected general purpose as well as more specific properties, such as required for particular developmental situations, are summarized.

Substances or systems of substances with selfenhancing properties, called activators, are required if *de novo* patterns are to be generated. Preexisting asymmetries can be used to orient the pattern. The range of the activator determines the size of coherent patches. If this range is of the order of the field size, polar distributions emerge (Fig. 1). If the autocatalysis saturates, a certain proportion of the total number of cells will become activated independent of the total number of cells. If in such a case the activator is nondiffusible, a homogeneous cell population segregates into different cell types (Fig. 7). They appear at intermingled positions. In contrast, if the activator is diffusible, stripes are preferentially formed (Fig. 5). The precise localization requires an orienting influence by other pattern-forming systems (Fig. 6).

Antagonistic substances limit the spread of the autocatalytic reaction. They can work by a direct inhibitory effect (Fig. 2), by depletion of a substrate required for autocatalysis or by the long-range activation of a feedback loop which locally excludes the first. The range of the antagonist determines the distance at which secondary maxima can be formed. If the size of the field is larger than this range, periodic pattern will emerge (Fig. 2A). In the systems with saturating autocatalysis mentioned above, the antagonist has a more homogeneous distribution and controls the ratio of the activated *versus* nonactivated cells. The range of the antagonist can determine the range over which size regulation is effective.

For the generation of patterns that are stable in time, the antagonist must have a shorter time constant, otherwise oscillations will occur (Meinhardt and Gierer, 1974). An example of the latter case is the periodic secretion of cAMP by aggregating amoeba of *Dictyostelium discoideum*, a system in which the molecular mechanism of selfenhancement and the antagonistic reaction is fully understood (see Devreotes, this volume).

According to the model, long-range activation of alternative feedback loops which exclude each other locally plays an important role in systems in which the neighbourhood of structures is controlled. An example is the intrasegmental pattern of insects or insect appendages. Such a mechanism is able to generate an ordered sequence of structures in space without global control by a morphogen gradient (Meinhardt and Gierer, 1980). This mechanism allows the repair of discontinuities by intercalation, if necessary with polarity reversal. This mutual-activation mechanism has obtained strong support by a recent observation of Martinez-Arias, Baker and Ingham (1988). They found that the product of the *wingless*-gene is required for normal expression of the *engrailed* gene, although *engrailed* is expressed in a neighbouring region (Baker, 1988).

In the models, communication between cells has been regarded as a simple diffusion, as a leakage. The actual mechanism can be more complicated, involving transmembrane proteins, cleavage of molecules that stick out of the cells, as well as receptors on the cell surface that receive the signal. For instance, the product of the *wingless*-gene mentioned appears to be a transmembrane protein. If such more complicated mechanisms are involved in the exchange of molecules between the cells, a pattern-forming system can appear to be more complex.

The feedback loops required for segregation into different cell types can be realized directly on the gene level since the corresponding substances should not diffuse. Such loops can consist, for instance, of a mutual repression of genes. If, on the other hand, a graded distribution of molecules is generated and used as positional information (Wolpert, 1969, and this volume), an interpretation by a concentration-dependent gene activation is required. This is possible if the decisive genes have properties formally similar to the pattern-forming reactions mentioned above, in that the genes have a direct or indirect feedback on their own activation but compete with each other. Sharp borders between regions of different gene activities are formed due to this autoregulation and competition. The autoregulation leads to a permanent activation of the genes, independent whether the positional signal is present or not. Meanwhile, positive autoregulation has been demonstrated for many genes (see, for instance, Kuziora and McGinnis, 1988; Bienz and Tremml, 1988; Hiromi and Gehring, 1987).

The term 'morphogenetic gradient' is used in the literature for two very different concepts. (i) Morphogenetic gradients as a graded ability of a tissue to form a particular structure upon regeneration (Morgan, 1904). The tissue with the relatively highest ability will form that structure. This concept has been introduced to account for the regeneration of fragments of tubularia with predictable polarity. In the models proposed, this graded ability corresponds to the graded source density (Fig. 2B). (ii) Morphogenetic gradients as substances that provide positional information (see Wolpert, this volume) by their absolute concentration *via* a concentration-dependent gene activation. In terms of the model, the activator, the inhibitor or any substance

under their control or which spreads from a localized source can act as such a gradient. A clear distinction should be made between these two concepts.

For the generation of subfields such as limb fields, positional information can be created at the borders between regions of different determinations (Meinhardt, 1980; 1983a,b). According to this model, it is not that first a limb field is formed which later becomes subdivided into anterior and posterior as well as into dorsal and ventral parts; to the contrary, it is assumed that the structures are formed around borders generated in a preceding step. This model has found strong support, for instance by the finding that the gene responsible for the posterior compartment in *Drosophila, engrailed*, is expressed at the correct positions and with sharp borders already at the blastoderm stage (Kuner *et al.* 1985), long before any imaginal disk could be formed. The proximodistal dimension is assumed to be organized by a gradient generated by a cooperation of the anterior and posterior, as well as the dorsal and ventral compartment. The result would be a cone-shaped distribution, centered over the intersection of the two compartment borders. The gene *decapentaplegic* is presumably involved in this process (see Gelbart, this volume). A cone-shaped pattern is appropriate to organize, for instance, a leg disc with the concentrically arranged primordia of the leg segments as well as for the separation of the cells forming the imaginal disc from the cells forming the surrounding larval ectoderm.

According to this model, genes such as *engrailed* or *wingless* have two functions. Primarily, they are involved in the generation of a cell state (or in the mutual stabilization of two cell states) forming one element in a sequence of cell states which constitute together a segment with a defined polarity. In a second step, the juxtaposition of two such cell states provides a prerequisite to form a substructure such as a leg or a wing. The confrontation of other pairs of cell states provides the signal to form a segment border (Meinhardt, 1984; 1986).

The borders generating positional information for vertebrate limb development are less clear. Oliver *et al.* (1988a,b) found a large region of XIHbox1 expression in *Xenopus* and mouse with a posterior border within the forelimb, close to the predicted position of a border (Meinhardt, 1983a). An indication for the second predicted border coincident with the apical ectodermal ridge has not yet been obtained.

The models mentioned above have been proposed on the basis of regulatory properties of developing systems. The new tools of molecular biology provide an opportunity to isolate the molecules involved in the patterning process. I hope that both approaches provide a fertile interaction.

References

ANDERSON, K. V. (1987). Dorsal-ventral embryonic pattern genes of *Drosophila*. *Trends Genetics* **3**, 91–97.
ANDERSON, K. V., BOKLA, L. & NÜSSLEIN-VOLHARD, C. (1985). Establishment of dorsal-ventral polarity in the *Drosophila*

embryo: The induction of polarity by the *Toll* gene product. *Cell* **42**, 791–798.

ANDERSON, K. V. & NÜSSLEIN-VOLHARD, C. (1984a). Genetic analysis of dorsal-ventral embryonic pattern in *Drosophila*. In *Pattern Formation. A Primer in Developmental Biology* (G.M. Malacinski & S.V. Bryant, ed.), pp. 269–289, Macmillan.

ANDERSON, K. V. & NÜSSLEIN-VOLHARD, C. (1984b). Information for the dorsal-ventral pattern of the *Drosophila* embryo is stored as maternal mRNA. *Nature, Lond.* **311**, 223–227.

ARTAVANIS-TSAKONAS, S. (1988). The molecular biology of the *Notch* locus and the fine tuning of differentiation in *Drosophila*. *Trends Genetics* **4**, 95–100.

BAKER, N. E. (1988). Localization of transcripts from the *wingless* gene in whole *Drosophila* embryos. *Development* **103**, 289–298.

BIENZ, M. & TREMML, G. (1988). Domain of *Ultrabithorax* expression in *Drosophila* visceral mesoderm from autoregulation and exclusion. *Nature, Lond.* **333**, 576–578.

BROWER, D. L., SMITH, R. J. & WILCOX, M. (1980). A monoclonal antibody specific for diploid epithelial cells in *Drosophila*. *Nature, Lond.* **285**, 403–405.

CAMPOS-ORTEGA, J. (1988). Cellular interactions during early neurogenesis of *Drosophila* melanogaster. *Trend Neurosc.* **11**, 400–405.

CHASAN, R. & ANDERSON, K. V. (1989). The role of *easter*, an apparent serine protease, in organizing the dorsal-ventral pattern of the *Drosophila* embryo. *Cell* **56**, 391–400.

DELOTTO, R. & SPIERER, P. (1986). A gene required for the specification of dorsal-ventral pattern in *Drosophila* appears to encode a serine protease. *Nature, Lond.* **323**, 688–692.

DOE, C. Q. & GOODMAN, C. S. (1985). Early events in insect neurogenesis. I. Developmental and segmental differences in the pattern of neuronal precursor cells. *Devl Biol.* **111**, 193–205.

FASANO, L. & KERRIDGE, S. (1988). Monitoring positional information during oogenesis in adult *Drosophila*. *Development* **104**, 245–253.

FURIE, B. & FURIE, B. C. (1988). The molecular basis of blood coagulation. *Cell* **53**, 505–518.

GEYSEN, J., CARDOEN, J., VANEYNDE, S., GREENS, C. & DELOOF, A. (1988). Cellular and molecular markers of anteroposterior and dorsoventral organisation in the vitellogenic follicles of adult *Sarcophaga bullata* (Diptera) and dorsoventral orientation of follicles in the ovary. *Wilhelm Roux' Arch. devl Biol.* **197**, 101–109.

GIERER, A. (1981). Generation of biological patterns and form: Some physical, mathematical, and logical aspects. *Prog. Biophys. molec. Biol.* **37**, 1–47.

GIERER, A. & MEINHARDT, H. (1972). A theory of biological pattern formation. *Kybernetik* **12**, 30–39.

HARTLEY, D. A., PREISS, A. & ARTAVANIS-TSAKONAS, S. (1988). A deduced gene product from the *Drosophila* neurogenic locus, *Enhancer of split*, shows homology to mammalian G-protein beta subunit. *Cell* **55**, 785–795.

HARTLEY, D. A., XU, T. & ARTAVANIS-TSAKONAS, S. (1987). The embryonic expression of the *Notch* locus of *Drosophila melanogaster* and the implications of point mutations in the extracellular EGF-like domain of the predicted protein. *EMBO J.* **6**, 3407–3417.

HASHIMOTO, C., HUDSON, K. L. & ANDERSON, K. V. (1988). The *Toll* gene of *Drosophila*, required for dorsal-ventral embryonic polarity, appears to encode a transmembrane protein. *Cell* **52**, 269–279.

HIROMI, Y. & GEHRING, W. J. (1987). Regulation and function of the *Drosophila* segmentation gene *fushi tarazu*. *Cell* **50**, 963–974.

KLEINE-SCHONNEFELD, H. & ENGELS, W. (1981). Symmetrical pattern of follicle arrangement in the ovary of *Musca domestica* (insecta, Diptera). *Zoomorphology* **98**, 185–190.

KUNER, J. M., NAKANISHI, M., ALI, Z., DREES, B., GUSTAVSON, E., THEIS, J., KAUVAR, L., KORNBERG, T. & O'FARRELL, P. H. (1985). Molecular cloning of *engrailed*: A gene involved in the development of pattern in *Drosophila melanogaster*. *Cell* **42**, 309–316.

KUZIORA, M. A. & MCGINNIS, W. (1988). Autoregulation of a *Drosophila* homeotic selector gene. *Cell* **55**, 477–485.

MARTINEZ-ARIAS, A., BAKER, N. E. & INGHAM, P. W. (1988). Role of segment polarity genes in the definition and maintenance of cell states in the *Drosophila* embryo. *Development* **103**, 151–170.

MEINHARDT, H. (1978). Space-dependent cell determination under the control of a morphogen gradient. *J. theor. Biol.* **74**, 307–321.

MEINHARDT, H. (1980). Cooperation of compartments for the generation of positional information. *Z. Naturforsch.* **35c**, 1086–1091.

MEINHARDT, H. (1982). *Models of Biological Pattern Formation.* Academic Press, London.

MEINHARDT, H. (1983a). A boundary model for pattern formation in vertebrate limbs. *J. Embryol. exp. Morph.* **76**, 115–137.

MEINHARDT, H. (1983b). Cell determination boundaries as organizing regions for secondary embryonic fields. *Devl Biol.* **96**, 375–385.

MEINHARDT, H. (1983c). A model for the prestalk/prespore patterning in the slug of the slime mold *Dictyostelium discoideum*. *Differentiation* **24**, 191–202.

MEINHARDT, H. (1984). Models for positional signalling, the threefold subdivision of segments and the pigmentation pattern of molluscs. *J. Embryol. exp. Morph.* **83**, (Supplement) 289–311.

MEINHARDT, H. (1986). Hierarchical inductions of cell states: A model for segmentation in *Drosophila*. *J. Cell Sci. Suppl.* **4**, 357–381.

MEINHARDT, H. (1988). Models for maternally supplied positional information and the activation of segmentation genes in *Drosophila* embryogenesis. In *Development* **104 Supplement**, 95–110.

MEINHARDT, H. & GIERER, A. (1974). Applications of a theory of biological pattern formation based on lateral inhibition. *J. Cell Sci.* **15**, 321–346.

MEINHARDT, H. & GIERER, A. (1980). Generation and regeneration of sequences of structures during morphogenesis. *J. theor. Biol.* **85**, 429–450.

MORGAN, T. H. (1904). An attempt to analyse the phenomena of polarity in tubularia. *J. exp. Zool.* **1**, 587–591.

NÜSSLEIN-VOLHARD, C. (1979). Maternal effect mutations that alter the spatial coordinates of the embryo of *Drosophila melanogaster*. In *Determination of Spatial Organization* (ed. S. Subtelney and I. R. Konigsberg), pp. 185–211. New York: Academic Press.

NÜSSLEIN-VOLHARD, C. & ROTH, S. (1989). Axis determination in insect embryos. *Ciba Foundation Symp.* (in press).

OLIVER, G., WRIGHT, C. V. E., HARDWICKE, J. & DEROBERTIS, E. M. (1988a). A gradient of homeodomain protein in developing forelimbs of *Xenopus* and mouse embryos. *Cell* **55**, 1017–1024.

OLIVER, G., WRIGHT, C. V. E., HARDWICKE, J. & DEROBERTIS, E. M. (1988b). Differential antero-posterior expression of two proteins encoded by a homeobox gene in *Xenopus* and mouse embryos. *EMBO J.* **7**, 3199–3209.

PTASHNE, M., JEFFREY, A., JOHNSON, A. D., MAURER, R., MEYER, B. J., PABO, C. O., ROBERTS, T. M. & SAUER, R. T. (1980). How the lambda repressor and Cro work. *Cell* **19**, 1–11.

SANDER, K. (1971). Pattern formation in longitudinal halves of leaf hopper eggs (Homoptera) and some remarks on the definition of "Embryonic regulation". *Wilhelm Roux' Archiv EntwMech. Org.* **167**, 336–352.

SCHÜPBACH, T. (1987). Germ line and soma cooperate during oogenesis to establish the dorsoventral pattern of egg shell and embryo in *Drosophila* melanogaster. *Cell* **49**, 699–707.

STEWARD, R., ZUSMAN, S. B., HUANG, L. H. & SCHEDL, P. (1988). The dorsal protein is distributed in a gradient in early *Drosophila* embryos. *Cell* **55**, 487–495.

TECHNAU, G. M., BECKER, T. & CAMPOS-ORTEGA, J. A. (1988). Reversible commitment of neural and epidermal progenitor cells during embryogenesis of *Drosophila melanogaster*. *Wilhelm Roux' Arch. devl Biol.* **197**, 413–418.

TECHNAU, G. M. & CAMPOS-ORTEGA, J. A. (1985). Fate-mapping in wild-type *Drosophila melanogaster*. II. Injections of horseradish peroxidase in cells of the early gastrula stage. *Wilhelm Roux' Arch. devl Biol.* **194**, 196–212.

VÄSSIN, H., BREMER, K. A., KNUST, E. & CAMPOS-ORTEGA, J. A. (1987). The neurogenic gene Delta of *Drosophila melanogaster* is expressed in neurogenic territories and encodes a putative transmembrane protein with EGF-like repeats. *EMBO J.* **6**, 3431–3440.

WOLPERT, L. (1969). Positional information and the spatial pattern of cellular differentiation. *J. theor. Biol.* **193**, 296–307.

Index of Authors and Titles

Subject Index